Negotiating the Nuclear Non-Proliferation Treaty

This volume offers a critical historical assessment of the negotiation of the Treaty on the Non-Proliferation of Nuclear Weapons (NPT) and of the origins of the nonproliferation regime.

The NPT has been signed by 190 states and was indefinitely extended in 1995, rendering it the most successful arms control treaty in history. Nevertheless, little is known about the motivations and strategic calculi of the various middle and small powers in regard to their ultimate decision to join the treaty despite its discriminatory nature. While the NPT continues to be central to current nonproliferation efforts, its underlying mechanisms remain under-researched. Based on newly declassified archival sources and using previously inaccessible evidence, the contributions in this volume examine the underlying rationales of the specific positions taken by various states during the NPT negotiations. Starting from a critical appraisal of our current knowledge of the genesis of the nonproliferation regime, contributors from diverse national and disciplinary backgrounds focus on both European and non-European states in order to enrich our understanding of how the global nuclear order came into being.

This book will be of much interest to students of nuclear proliferation, Cold War history, security studies, and IR.

Roland Popp is a Senior Researcher at the Center for Security Studies, ETH Zurich, Switzerland.

Liviu Horovitz is a PhD Candidate at the Center for Security Studies, ETH Zurich, Switzerland.

Andreas Wenger is Director of the Center for Security Studies, ETH Zurich, Switzerland.

CSS Studies in Security and International Relations

Series Editor: Andreas Wenger

Center for Security Studies, Swiss Federal Institute of Technology (ETH), Zurich

The *CSS Studies in Security and International Relations* series examines historical and contemporary aspects of security and conflict. The series provides a forum for new research based upon an expanded conception of security and will include monographs by the Center's research staff and associated academic partners.

Origins of the European Security System
The Helsinki Process revisited
Edited by Andreas Wenger,
Vojtech Mastny and Christian Nuenlist

Russian Energy Power and Foreign Relations
Edited by Jeronim Perovic,
Robert W. Orttung and
Andreas Wenger

European–American Relations and the Middle East
From Suez to Iraq
Edited by Daniel Möckli and
Victor Mauer

EU Foreign Policymaking and the Middle East Conflict
The Europeanization of national foreign policy
Patrick Müller

The Politics of Nuclear Non-Proliferation
A pragmatist framework for analysis
Ursula Jasper

Regional Organisations and Security
Conceptions and practices
Edited by Stephen Aris and
Andreas Wenger

Peacekeeping in Africa
The evolving security architecture
Edited by Thierry Tardy and
Marco Wyss

Russia's Security Policy under Putin
A critical perspective
Aglaya Snetkov

Strategic Culture, Securitisation and the Use of Force
Post-9/11 security practices of liberal democracies
Wilhelm Mirow

Negotiating the Nuclear Non-Proliferation Treaty
Origins of the nuclear order
Edited by Roland Popp, Liviu Horovitz
and Andreas Wenger

Negotiating the Nuclear Non-Proliferation Treaty

Origins of the nuclear order

Edited by Roland Popp, Liviu Horovitz and Andreas Wenger

LONDON AND NEW YORK

First published 2017
by Routledge
2 Park Square, Milton Park, Abingdon, Oxon OX14 4RN

and by Routledge
711 Third Avenue, New York, NY 10017

Routledge is an imprint of the Taylor & Francis Group, an informa business

© 2017 selection and editorial matter, Roland Popp, Liviu Horovitz and
Andreas Wenger; individual chapters, the contributors

The right of the editors to be identified as the authors of the editorial
matter, and of the authors for their individual chapters, has been asserted
in accordance with sections 77 and 78 of the Copyright, Designs and
Patents Act 1988.

All rights reserved. No part of this book may be reprinted or reproduced or
utilized in any form or by any electronic, mechanical, or other means, now
known or hereafter invented, including photocopying and recording, or in
any information storage or retrieval system, without permission in writing
from the publishers.

Trademark notice: Product or corporate names may be trademarks or
registered trademarks, and are used only for identification and explanation
without intent to infringe.

British Library Cataloguing-in-Publication Data
A catalogue record for this book is available from the British Library

Library of Congress Cataloging-in-Publication Data
Names: Popp, Roland, 1970– editor. | Horovitz, Liviu, editor. | Wenger,
Andreas, editor.
Title: Negotiating the Nuclear Non-proliferation Treaty : origins of the
nuclear order / edited by Roland Popp, Liviu Horovitz and Andreas
Wenger.
Description: Abingdon, Oxon ; New York, NY : Routledge, 2017. | Series:
CSS studies in security and international relations | Includes
bibliographical references and index.
Identifiers: LCCN 2016017191| ISBN 9781138690172 (hardback) |
ISBN 9781315536576 (ebook)
Subjects: LCSH: Treaty on the Non-proliferation of Nuclear Weapons
(1968 June 12) | Nuclear nonproliferation.
Classification: LCC KZ5670 .N44 2017 | DDC 341.7/34–dc23
LC record available at https://lccn.loc.gov/2016017191

ISBN: 978-1-138-69017-2 (hbk)
ISBN: 978-1-315-53657-6 (ebk)

Typeset in Times New Roman
by Wearset Ltd, Boldon, Tyne and Wear

Contents

Notes on contributors   vii

1   **Introduction: small and middle powers in the emergence of a discriminatory regime**   1
ROLAND POPP

PART I
Nuclear nonproliferation and alliance cohesion   7

2   **The long road to the NPT: from superpower collusion to global compromise**   9
ROLAND POPP

3   **In favor of "effective" and "non-discriminatory" non-dissemination policy: the FRG and the NPT negotiation process (1962–1966)**   36
ANDREAS LUTSCH

4   **The birth of a nuclear non-proliferation policy: the Netherlands and the NPT negotiations, 1965–1966**   58
ELMAR HELLENDOORN

5   **"A turning point in postwar foreign policy": Italy and the NPT negotiations, 1967–1969**   77
LEOPOLDO NUTI

6   **Nonproliferation under pressure: the nuclear debate within the Warsaw Pact, 1965–1968**   97
LAURIEN CRUMP-GABREËLS

vi *Contents*

PART II
Global and regional dynamics in negotiating the NPT   117

7   **Unusual suspects down under: Australia's choice for the nonproliferation treaty**   119
CHRISTINE M. LEAH

8   **Between idealism, activism, and the bomb: why did India reject the NPT?**   137
A. VINOD KUMAR

9   **Non-nuclear Japan? Satō, the NPT, and the US nuclear umbrella**   161
FINTAN HOEY

10   **Mexican nuclear diplomacy, the Latin American nuclear-weapon-free zone, and the NPT grand bargain, 1962–1968**   178
JONATHAN HUNT

11   **"A glaring defect in the system": nuclear safeguards and the invisibility of technology**   203
JACOB DARWIN HAMBLIN

PART III
Conclusion   221

12   **Nuclear technology and political power in the making of the nuclear order**   223
ANDREAS WENGER AND LIVIU HOROVITZ

Index   240

Contributors

Editors

Liviu Horovitz is a PhD candidate at the ETH Zurich. His dissertation focuses on the utility of predominant force within international relations. Prior to his doctoral studies, he held a research position within the nuclear-policy working group at the CSS, worked for the Preparatory Commission for the Comprehensive Nuclear-Test-Ban Treaty Organization in Vienna, and was a research associate at the James Martin Center for Nonproliferation Studies in Monterey. His work has been printed, for instance, in *Journal of Strategic Studies, European Security, Nonproliferation Review, Bulletin of the Atomic Scientists*, and *Washington Quarterly*.

Roland Popp is Senior Researcher and the Team Head of the nuclear-policy working group at the Center for Security Studies (CSS) at ETH Zurich. His historical research focuses on Cold War history, the politics of nuclear proliferation, and the international history of the Middle East. In 2014, he was a Visiting Scholar at the Robert S. Strauss Center at the University of Texas at Austin. His academic publications include articles in *The International History Review, Middle East Journal*, and *Cold War History*.

Andreas Wenger is Professor of International and Swiss Security Policy at the ETH Zurich and has been the Director of the Center for Security Studies (CSS) since 2002. His doctoral dissertation analyzed the role of nuclear weapons in the Cold War international system. The focus of his main ongoing research interests lies in security and strategic studies and the history of international relations. He has published, inter alia, in the *Journal of Cold War Studies, Cold War History, Presidential Studies Quarterly*, and *Vierteljahrshefte für Zeitgeschichte*.

Authors

Laurien Crump-Gabreëls is an Assistant Professor at the University of Utrecht in the Netherlands, where she obtained her doctorate *cum laude* in January 2014. Before that she worked in secondary education for ten years. She is the viii *Contributors*

author of *The Warsaw Pact Reconsidered: International Relations in Eastern Europe, 1955–69*, which was published by Routledge in 2015. She has also published numerous articles on the Warsaw Pact, using newly available sources from various archives in Eastern Europe. In 2012 she was attached as a Senior Associate Member to the Russian and Eurasian Studies Centre at St. Antony's College, Oxford.

Jacob Darwin Hamblin is a Professor of History at Oregon State University. He received the 2014 Paul Birdsall Prize from the American Historical Association for his book, *Arming Mother Nature: The Birth of Catastrophic Environmentalism* (2013). His other books include *Poison in the Well: Radioactive Waste in the Oceans at the Dawn of the Nuclear Age* (2008), and *Oceanographers and the Cold War* (2005).

Elmar Hellendoorn is a PhD Candidate at Utrecht University. His dissertation, to be defended in early 2016, is about the early history of the Netherlands' nuclear policy (1954–1966). This work traces the interaction between enrichment technology, NATO nuclear strategy, and Euro-American order. Before starting with his PhD, he worked as a strategist at the Netherlands' Ministry of Foreign Affairs. He holds MA degrees from the College of Europe, Bruges, and Utrecht University. He also comments in the media and provides geopolitical consultancy services on an independent basis.

Fintan Hoey is an Assistant Professor of History at Franklin University Switzerland, was previously a Government of Ireland Doctoral Scholar at the Humanities Institute, University College Dublin, Ireland, and held a Japan Foundation Japanese Studies Fellowship at Rikkyo University, Tokyo. He has previously published on Japan's defense policy and his monograph, *Satō, America and the Cold War: U.S.–Japanese Relations, 1964–72*, was published by Palgrave Macmillan in 2015.

Jonathan Hunt is a Lecturer in Modern Global History at the University of Southampton and received his doctorate in United States and International History from the University of Texas at Austin in 2013. He has been a fellow of the Woodrow Wilson Center, the Eisenhower Institute, the Center for International Security and Cooperation at Stanford University, RAND Corporation, and the Fox Center for Humanistic Inquiry at Emory University. Jonathan is also the author of articles and book chapters on the negotiation of the NPT and US–Soviet summitry under Ronald Reagan and Mikhail Gorbachev.

A. Vinod Kumar is an Associate Fellow at the Institute for Defence Studies and Analyses (IDSA), New Delhi and a Visiting Faculty at the Institute of Foreign Policy Studies (IFPS), University of Calcutta. His areas of expertise include nuclear issues, missile defense, and foreign policy. Kumar's first book titled *India and the Nuclear Non-Proliferation Regime: The Perennial Outlier* was published by Cambridge University Press in 2014.

Contributors ix

Christine M. Leah is a Postdoctoral Fellow with the Grand Strategy Program at Yale University. Previously, she was a Stanton Postdoctoral Fellow in Nuclear Security at MIT, a visiting fellow at the Rajaratnam School of International Studies, a summer research fellow at RAND, and a research intern at IISS-Asia, the Australian Strategic Policy Institute, IISS-London, the French Ministry of Defense, and the UMP office of Mr. Nicolas Sarkozy. She authored *Australia and the Bomb*, and has published in *Comparative Strategy*, *The Journal of Strategic Studies*, *Asian Security*, *The Australian Journal of International Affairs*, *The National Interest*, *The Diplomat*, and with *RSIS* and *RAND*.

Andreas Lutsch is a Stanton Nuclear Security Postdoctoral Fellow at the Center for International Security and Cooperation, Stanford University, and Assistant Professor at the Julius-Maximilians-University Würzburg, Germany. Previously, he worked as a research fellow at the Johannes Gutenberg University Mainz, Germany. He wrote a PhD dissertation entitled *Westbindung oder Gleichgewicht? Die nukleare Sicherheitspolitik der Bundesrepublik Deutschland zwischen Atomwaffensperrvertrag und NATO-Doppelbeschluss (1961–1979)*, Mainz 2014 (accepted for publication in cooperation with ZMSBw, Potsdam).

Leopoldo Nuti is Professor of History of International Relations at Roma Tre University, Co-Director of the Nuclear Proliferation International History Project, and President of the Italian Society of International History. He has published extensively in Italian, English, and French on US-Italian relations and Italian foreign and security policy. His latest books are *La sfida nucleare. La politica estera italiana e le armi nucleari, 1945–1991* (Bologna: Il Mulino, 2008) [The Nuclear Challenge: Italian Foreign Policy and Atomic Weapons, 1945–1991] and, as a co-editor, *The Euromissiles Crisis and the End of the Cold War* (Stanford: Stanford University Press, 2015).

1 Introduction[1]

Small and middle powers in the emergence of a discriminatory regime

Roland Popp

The 1968 Treaty on the Non-Proliferation of Nuclear Weapons (NPT) is widely regarded as the cornerstone of the broader nonproliferation regime that aims to forestall the further spread of nuclear weapons and related technologies. The NPT has been signed by 190 states and was indefinitely extended in 1995, making it the most successful arms control treaty in history. While it is central to current global nonproliferation efforts and routinely cited as a successful compromise ("a grand bargain") between the competing priorities of nonproliferation, disarmament and access to peaceful nuclear technologies, the treaty's underlying mechanisms are less widely understood.

The main theoretical conundrum of the NPT is its apparent success in spite of the fact that it is openly discriminatory in defining two different classes of parties to the treaty, nuclear (NWS) and non-nuclear-weapon states (NNWS). While the reason for its acceptance by NWS is easy to understand, since the treaty legitimizes their possession of nuclear weapons, the decisions by NNWS to accede are much harder to grasp. First and foremost, the regime established by the NPT was deeply asymmetrical, since it openly violated the fundamental principle of the modern international state system: the norm of sovereign equality. This formal inequality established in the NPT is the root cause of the ongoing dispute over the real purpose behind the treaty and what is often called the need for a balanced implementation of its three "pillars" of nonproliferation, disarmament, and peaceful uses of nuclear technology.[2]

Given the NPT's present-day centrality, the shortage of accounts examining the historical circumstances of its creation is surprising. In fact, this also holds true for the emergence of the wider nonproliferation regime, which has been neglected by historians in favor of other aspects of nuclear policy during the Cold War. Earlier research dealing with the NPT primarily covered the negotiations between the superpowers in the 1960s and the role of nonproliferation in the wider politics of détente, usually with a special focus on Western alliance dynamics and on the future nuclear status of the Federal Republic of Germany (FRG). As a consequence, there has been very little investigation of the motivations and strategic calculi of the various middle and small powers that joined the treaty.[3] The recent "renaissance" (Scott Sagan) in nuclear studies promises to make up for this negligence. The present volume is part of

2   R. Popp

these ongoing efforts to widen our knowledge and understanding of the nuclear realm.[4]

The contributions in this volume investigate various aspects of the NPT negotiations which so far have not received much attention. Above all, the main focus of this volume is the attitudes and positions adopted by a selection of NNWS up to 1968, when the treaty was opened for signature. The chapters included in the volume focus on both European and non-European states. The positions of the latter have so far been largely ignored by scholars, despite their significant role in the maintenance of the regime in the present. Based on newly declassified archival and previously inaccessible other evidence, these country studies give an impression of how governments other than the superpowers perceived the global proliferation threat and how they reacted to efforts at the creation of a global agreement to forestall such proliferation. Quite a number of the cases covered in the volume deal with states which seriously considered, if only temporarily, acquiring an independent nuclear deterrent. Indeed, one of the cases studied here, India, ultimately abstained from joining the NPT and instead manufactured her own nuclear weapons.

Those states which decided to accede to the NPT faced the challenge of protecting their own interests of various kinds, such as preventing nuclear acquisition by neighboring states, receiving defense commitments from their allies, developing their civilian nuclear capabilities and protecting their commercial competitiveness. As the various chapters demonstrate, there is no single answer as to why NNWS ultimately acceded to the NPT – the decisions were filtered through a multitude of often conflicting factors and influences, juxtaposing domestic politics, considerations of prestige, bureaucratic infighting, technological competence, personal rivalries, regional confrontations, patron-client relationships, and scientific ambitions based on "developmentalist" identities, to name but a few.

Part I: nuclear nonproliferation and alliance cohesion

The contributions to this volume examine the disposition of NNWS towards the general idea of a global nonproliferation agreement as well as the various attempts of middle and small powers to wield their influence on the drafting process of the NPT. Mirroring the historical sequence of events leading to the NPT, Part I of the volume starts by focusing on the setting in a divided Europe during the Cold War and by weighing the interdependent issues of extended deterrence, alliance cohesion and proliferation concerns.

Roland Popp's contribution traces the structural conditions of the time and the specific actions by the superpowers as they prepared the stage for serious negotiations on nonproliferation in the early 1960s, leading to the agreement between Moscow and Washington on the basic provisions of the NPT in late 1966 and the subsequent cooperation between the two in finalizing the treaty after shepherding it through international institutions. Popp identifies three distinctive time periods on the way towards the conclusion of the NPT, and he

Introduction 3

synthesizes existing interpretations with archival source material from US archives in order to identify openings for questioning or revising the prevalent master narrative on the emergence of the NPT. Besides the US, Soviet and British perspectives, another state on which a considerable amount of new scholarship is available is the FRG.

Andreas Lutsch offers a reinterpretation of the West German position on non-proliferation based on a broad empirical foundation. Dissenting from the prevalent view in the literature regarding the FRG's genuine ambitions for national control over nuclear weapons, Lutsch instead interprets Bonn's policies as being inspired by a "limited nuclear revisionism" which had as its objective to strengthen and enhance its own position inside the Western alliance. Following this interpretative line, the emergence of the NPT had an only limited effect on the FRG and, according to Lutsch, none at all with a view to nonproliferation, given the non-existence of actual intentions with regard to nuclear acquisition.

In line with the recent trend towards investigating the nuclear convictions of specific leaders and individuals in IR literature on proliferation, *Elmar Hellendoorn* traces the development of Dutch nonproliferation policies, based on documents which had been unavailable until recently. Providing an interesting example of a non-great power faced with the dangers and opportunities that, for a middle power like the Netherlands, emanated from the appearance of a new instrument of international politics such as the NPT, Hellendoorn stresses the pivotal role of Max van der Stoel inside the Ministry of Foreign Affairs. According to Hellendoorn, van der Stoel used the NPT negotiations to abandon the inherited position on a future European nuclear option in order to strengthen the Atlanticist orientation in Dutch foreign policy. Hellendoorn's argument, however, transcends the dimension of simple bureaucratic politics, as he stresses the intentional leveraging of internationalist ideas by van der Stoel and his supporters, demonstrating how difficult it is in practice to distinguish between utilitarian and idealistic motives.

Leopoldo Nuti offers new information on the Italian case which resembles the West German one in many respects. He portrays Rome's initial reaction to early NPT drafts as even more hostile than Bonn's, mostly due to a strong desire for status parity vis-à-vis other European powers of similar size. In an interesting exposition of states' multifaceted reactions to the emerging nonproliferation regime, Nuti analyzes the parallel Italian efforts to influence the final treaty text while simultaneously expanding its own nuclear capabilities in the fields of nuclear naval propulsion and uranium enrichment as well as intensifying nuclear collaboration with the French.

In her original contribution, *Laurien Crump-Gabreëls* highlights an aspect of nonproliferation diplomacy which often goes unmentioned. Based on a wide array of source materials from Eastern European archives, she examines the nuclear debate amongst the members of the Warsaw Pact. Confirming many accounts in the past two decades, Crump-Gabreëls provides ample evidence for the limitations of Soviet hegemony inside the Eastern Bloc and the unexpected freedom of maneuver of smaller states vis-à-vis Moscow. Her special focus is on

4   *R. Popp*

the unique position, in this context, of Romania, which used the NPT consultations to underline and strengthen its ambitions towards a more independent position, de facto blocking any Warsaw Pact decision-making on the treaty for a considerable time. Hers is a good example of the opportunities provided to small and middle powers during the NPT negotiation phase. At the same time, she demonstrates how the disunity of NNWS played into the hands of the superpowers, since Romanian objections absolved Moscow from serious consultations, resulting in a *fait accompli* which in the end Bucharest itself was forced to accept.

Part II: global and regional dynamics in negotiating the NPT

Part II of the book moves away from the European theater and analyzes the global dimensions of the fledging regime. The main factors impinging upon the negotiations substantially differ from the European setting. Ideas of nuclear sharing play only a peripheral role, if any, while questions of the credibility of extended deterrence are still relevant. A reoccurring issue in many chapters is the 1964 nuclearization of the People's Republic of China (PRC), the formative event for the appraisal of the nonproliferation idea in most of East Asia, South Asia, and Oceania. Another discernible aspect is the basic mistrust and skepticism vis-à-vis the intentions of the superpowers that was prevalent in the capitals of those states which regarded themselves as part of the Global South.

In her examination of the Australian case, *Christine Leah* identifies various objectives and purposes behind Canberra's nuclear policy, some of which, however, proved to be irreconcilable. Leah diverts from the majority view in the existing literature, and downgrades the contribution of reaffirmed US security guarantees for Australia's ultimate decision to join the treaty. She outlines the strong sense of abandonment and a perceived threat from China, Indonesia, and Japan amongst the ruling elite and the remarkable determination to pursue a nuclear option, if only a latent one, through heavy investment in a civilian nuclear infrastructure. These concerns shaped the contentious internal debates on the NPT. According to Leah, apart from accomplishing the technological status of nuclear latency, it took a general calming of the security situation in East Asia in the early 1970s and a change in government before the country could accede to the NPT.

Vinod Kumar focuses on India's diplomatic activism during the NPT negotiations against the backdrop of a changing security setting in South Asia in the aftermath of the 1964 PRC nuclear test. The emergence of the NPT forced Delhi to decide between Nehruvian internationalism and non-aligned leadership on one hand and the strategic need to counter the Chinese challenge on the other. While much more limited than the other contributors by official secrecy and the unavailability of pivotal evidence, Kumar examines in detail the volatile Indian diplomatic record during the negotiations in UN committees and the desperate attempts to reconcile the conflicting determinants of Indian policy. He

Introduction 5

demonstrates the interplay between strategic pressures and growing resentment against what Indians perceived as an asymmetrical and even discriminatory treaty. These factors ultimately persuaded one of the global pioneers of disarmament and arms control to reject the NPT.

Similar threat perceptions deriving from the PRC test were detectable in Japan. As *Fintan Hoey* demonstrates in his chapter, based on Japanese source material, the country shared with India a strong aversion to all things nuclear, having been the only country in history to have suffered an attack by atomic weapons. Hoey confirms recent findings by other scholars regarding the ambivalence of Japanese nuclear abstinence as codified in the famous "Three Non-Nuclear Principles" of 1967. While the public affirmation seemed to turn Japanese accession to the NPT into a foregone conclusion, Hoey portrays the somewhat confusing route taken by Tokyo as resulting from several and often contradictory sources such as public opinion, a substantial lobby inside the strategic elite favoring an independent deterrent, the need to recalibrate the alliance relationship with Washington, and the desire for the reversion of Okinawa.

Jonathan Hunt's contribution deals with the successful efforts by Latin American and Caribbean states, parallel to the ongoing NPT negotiations, to establish a nuclear-weapon-free zone (NWFZ) in their world region, thereby offering an alternative route towards nonproliferation. Based on impressive multi-archival research, Hunt's contribution focuses on the interplay between the two negotiation processes. His chapter is at the same time a country case study on the specific role played by Mexico in that respect. His examination of the way in which Mexican nonproliferation diplomacy succeeded in leveraging its prominent role regarding regional denuclearization into the position of an influential participant in the wider NPT negotiations provides an outstanding example of the opportunities offered to small and middle powers during that period.

Departing from national perspectives and instead investigating interactions inside international institutions in order to highlight heretofore underappreciated aspects of nonproliferation diplomacy, *Jacob Darwin Hamblin* analyzes the implementation of the safeguards regime at the International Atomic Energy Agency (IAEA) against the backdrop of ongoing NPT negotiations. Departing from conventional wisdom, Hamblin identifies European suppliers as the main proponents of laxness and flexibility with respect to nuclear technology transfers, ultimately rendering many of those transactions "invisible" to safeguards. Contradicting the general trend towards more robust nonproliferation obligations as set by the movement towards the NPT, his chapter demonstrates how delicate the nonproliferation regime in fact was in its early years.

Taking stock of the emerging regime

Taken together, the chapters in this volume offer a comprehensive, if not complete, and critical historical assessment of the negotiation of the NPT during the middle Cold War and of the beginnings of the global nuclear order. In the final chapter, *Andreas Wenger* and *Liviu Horovitz* reflect and synthesize the main

6 *R. Popp*

findings of the various chapters. Their answer as to why an overwhelming majority of states joined the regime in the end, despite its discriminatory aspects, builds upon the fundamental but also ambivalent relationship between nuclear technology and political power that informs the nuclear choices of small and medium powers.

Notes

1 The contributions in this volume are based on papers first presented at the conference "The Making of a Nuclear Order: Negotiating the Nuclear Non-Proliferation Treaty" in Ittingen, Switzerland, March 1–2, 2014, convened by the Center for Security Studies (CSS) at ETH Zurich in collaboration with the Nuclear Proliferation International History Project (NPIHP) funded by the Carnegie Corporation of New York.
2 See Steven E. Miller, *Nuclear Collisions: Discord, Reform and the Nuclear Nonproliferation Regime* (Cambridge, MA: American Academy of Arts and Sciences, 2012).
3 Two exceptions are the older works, albeit on a very limited empirical basis: Onkar S. Marwah and Ann Schulz, ed., *Nuclear Proliferation and the Near-Nuclear Countries* (Cambridge, MA: Ballinger Pub. Co, 1975); Johan Jørgen Holst, ed., *Security, Order and the Bomb: Nuclear Weapons in the Politics and Defence Planning of Non-Nuclear Weapon States* (Oslo: Universitetsforlaget, 1972). On the wider regime, see the contributions in Roland Popp and Andreas Wenger, ed., "Special Issue: The Origins of the Nuclear Nonproliferation Regime," *The International History Review* 36, no. 2 (2014): 195–323.
4 Scott Sagan, "Two Renaissances in Nuclear Security Studies," in H-Diplo/ISSF Forum on "What We Talk about When We Talk about Nuclear Weapons," June 15, 2014, at http://issforum.org/ISSF/PDF/ISSF-Forum-2.pdf (last accessed March 20, 2016).

Part I

Nuclear nonproliferation and alliance cohesion

2 The long road to the NPT

From superpower collusion to global compromise

Roland Popp[1]

Any attempt at historical contextualization of the origins of and progress towards the Treaty on the Non-Proliferation of Nuclear Weapons (NPT), commonly referred to as the Nonproliferation Treaty, has to contend with an idealized ex post facto view of a global bargain between nuclear "haves" and "have-nots" – the view that it was an epochal step in taming the nuclear dynamics that were endangering the world order, and in regulating and stabilizing the Cold War system, as well as the system which followed. Examined in its actual historical context, however, the NPT does not look much like an early cornerstone of an emerging global security governance system. On the contrary, it leaves a much more parochial impression. This is because it was a process driven and dominated by the two superpowers, and tied – at least until late in the negotiations – to more narrow Cold War imperatives, i.e., the perceived need to freeze the status quo in Europe, rather than global concerns regarding looming proliferation cascades. At the same time, instability and nuclear crises and confrontations on the global level were having an effect on Europe as well, since these developments affected perceptions of balance and threat along the Iron Curtain. It was this interdependence between the regional nuclear dimension in Europe and the global nuclear dimension which convinced the superpowers of the need to find a universal solution to the proliferation problem.

This volume deals with the perspectives, motivations, and actions of the actual "targets" of the NPT, the non-nuclear-weapon states (NNWS), during the time of the negotiations. To aid understanding, and to allow the reader to contextualize the many references to details of the ongoing negotiations between Moscow and Washington and, later on, between the superpowers and the other UN members, this chapter will provide a critical historical overview of the negotiations. Given the NPT's salience, it is surprising that no multi-archival examination of its origins has been written, and that there is no single account of the superpower negotiations which led to the treaty's conclusion.[2] Our current knowledge of the circumstances and forces that created the present nuclear order comes mostly from the writings of former officials involved in the NPT negotiations.[3] In view of this gap, this chapter will provide an overview of the negotiations, divided into three specific time periods in the trajectory that led to the point at which the NPT was opened for signature in July 1968. Each section will

10   R. Popp

identify and discuss the basic developments and events that took place during the specific period, then conclude with an analysis of the main dynamics that drove progress towards a global nonproliferation agreement and offer some alternatives to established interpretations.

Disarmament diplomacy and nuclear sharing: origins of the idea of a general non-dissemination agreement before 1961

The "Nth country" problem, as the issue of nuclear proliferation was often referred to during this period, received only secondary attention during the early Cold War years, since officials and strategists were primarily focused on deterrence and the nuclear balance. Half-hearted attempts to establish international control of the atom during the 1940s mostly served propagandistic purposes. US President Eisenhower's *Atoms for Peace* program promised nuclear assistance for peaceful purposes and also created the institutional outlines of a future regime that would see the creation of the International Atomic Energy Agency (IAEA) in 1957 and its system of international safeguards. The entry into the "missile age" after the "Sputnik Shock" irrevocably changed the structural conditions of the struggle between the superpowers, while at the same time unleashing centrifugal forces inside their alliance systems. In this context, the first formal nonproliferation proposal based on a cut-off agreement, albeit vague and conditional, was put forward during international arms control negotiations as part of a Western "package" disarmament plan in August 1957. The Soviets, providing the blueprint for the basic divide in approaches to nonproliferation for years to come, then responded with a proposal of their own. The Soviet proposal committed nuclear powers "not to place these weapons at the disposal of any other States or commands of military blocs," thus obviously targeting NATO (North Atlantic Treaty Organization) plans for allied sharing of nuclear weapons. The prospect of future nuclear parity led to a shift away from treating arms control negotiations mainly as tools for ideological competition. This opened the door to an incrementalist approach to arms control and the pursuit of a separate agreement to slow down or even inhibit the move towards further nuclear dissemination.[4] Internally, concerns regarding the spread of nuclear weaponry grew:

> if we sit idly by and allow a situation to develop in which other nations enter the atomic competition, we may find that we have failed to do the things that would have made the difference between mutual destruction and survival,

an alarmed President Eisenhower commented.[5] US Secretary of State John Foster Dulles familiarized a wider audience with the looming prospect of a world of "nuclear plenty," when "the pettiest and most irresponsible dictator could get hold of weapons with which to threaten immense harm" and called for immediate action to "prevent a promiscuous spread of nuclear weapons throughout the world."[6] Eisenhower informed Soviet leader Khrushchev in the spring of

1960 that it was US policy "to avoid the widening of the circle of nuclear powers" and invited the Soviet Union to cooperate on this matter.[7] Rapid technological progress, such as the development of the hydrogen bomb, with its far greater destructive potential, by the United States (1952), the Soviet Union (1953/1955) and Britain (1957), and the deployment of new delivery systems such as intercontinental ballistic missiles (ICBMs) raised the awareness of an emerging nuclear stalemate, based on mutual assured destruction, and advanced nuclear deterrence into the organizing principle of both superpowers' national security policies. This led a growing number of officials in Washington and Moscow to believe that some form of superpower collusion on the nonproliferation issue might indeed have a stabilizing effect on the global situation. Indeed, at this point the world seemed to be moving slowly towards embracing the idea of nuclear non-dissemination. However, a number of factors rendered actual progress difficult.

The international atmosphere of the early Cold War, illustrated by propaganda wars, subversionary activities, espionage and a general lack of trust, was hardly conducive to serious negotiations on a global nonproliferation agreement. While both superpowers went to great lengths to guard their own nuclear secrets, they nonetheless assigned low priority to the general idea of nonproliferation. On the contrary, both Moscow and Washington were supportive, or at least tolerant, of the nuclear ambitions of their close allies. The US initiated a nuclear rapprochement with the United Kingdom, culminating in a close Anglo-American nuclear alliance, and seriously considered for a time a similar arrangement with the French. Given that further proliferation seemed inevitable, some US officials argued in favor of assisting selected allies "to achieve nuclear capabilities as efficiently and expeditiously as possible in order to increase alliance cohesion and best maintain a U.S. influence over the design, production and use of their nuclear weapons."[8] For their part, the Soviets actively supported the nuclear ambitions of their Chinese Communist allies, an effort only abandoned in July 1960 when Khrushchev ordered the departure of all Soviet advisers from the People's Republic.

While the new awareness of vulnerability strengthened to some extent the arguments made by arms control supporters, it also had the effect of casting doubt on extended nuclear deterrence and the security guarantees provided by the US to its allies. The Eisenhower administration reacted to the dwindling credibility of US defense commitments by emphasizing the policy of nuclear sharing with allies – de facto, if not de jure, transferring physical control over US tactical and strategic nuclear weapons deployed in Europe to its allies. This even involved pre-delegating authority for the use of nuclear weapons to senior military commanders on the ground.[9] Although this later appeared a rather nonchalant, even careless, approach to proliferation, it had its own logic at the time. Nuclear sharing arrangements as established during the 1950s and as envisaged in the collective NATO force, designated the Multilateral Nuclear Force (MLF), had several aims. They aimed, first, to give West Europeans a greater say in nuclear war planning and decision-making, second, to mollify fears of US abandonment in case of an outbreak of war and, third, to strengthen the cohesion within NATO. Finally, it was hoped that the MLF, by creating the impression of direct participation in nuclear decision-making, would also quench the desires of the West Germans, Italians and others to follow the British and French examples and build their own independent nuclear deterrent. The Soviets, however, never bought into this depiction of the MLF as a nonproliferation device first and foremost, and they vigorously opposed the creation of such a force throughout that period.[10] In a formal sense, the MLF issue would remain the main stumbling block for the negotiation of a nonproliferation agreement until late 1966.

As attempts by the superpowers to negotiate on the non-dissemination of nuclear weapons seemed unlikely to succeed during the "crisis years" of the Cold War, other international actors filled the void. These transnational societal actors such as peace movements, arms control activists and anti-nuclear groups emerged in reaction to global tensions and the growing danger of nuclear war. Their main activities in the nuclear sphere, however, were mostly directed against existing nuclear arsenals and the environmental consequences of continued nuclear testing, and only to a lesser extent against the rather more theoretical threat of further horizontal proliferation.[11] Instead, building upon the anti-nuclear sentiment which had been present inside UN disarmament institutions from the beginning, neutral and non-aligned countries took the lead with respect to nonproliferation. Beginning in 1958, Ireland sponsored a number of UN General Assembly (UNGA) resolutions directed at preventing a future "atomic *sauve-qui-peut.*" However, the initiative quickly became entangled in US–Soviet controversies over nuclear sharing within the Western alliance. The United States supported the next Irish resolution on the matter one year later, whereas the Soviet Bloc abstained, but subsequently opposed the 1960 resolution.[12] It was not until 1961 that the actors involved finally agreed on the text of a resolution which then was accepted unanimously by the UNGA. Sketching out the central provisions of the future NPT, the "Irish Resolution" of December 1961 called upon all states to negotiate an agreement

> under which the nuclear States would undertake to refrain from relinquishing control of nuclear weapons and from transmitting the information necessary for their manufacture to States not possessing such weapons, and provisions under which States not possessing nuclear weapons would undertake not to manufacture or otherwise acquire control of such weapons [...].[13]

Often praised in later accounts as an example of the important role played by the Neutral and Non-aligned, the Irish resolution was in fact the outcome of long exchanges between Dublin and Washington. The phrase "relinquishing control" originated from the latter, and was regarded as implicitly compatible with existing NATO nuclear sharing arrangements and with the planned MLF. The final adoption of the 1961 resolution was preceded by weeks of consultations between the US and its NATO partners on the exact formulations that would make it possible for the Western Bloc to support the initiative.[14] Ireland's "dogged determination" to achieve progress in the nonproliferation sphere therefore appears much less independent-minded than later observers have chosen to portray it.[15]

Unsurprisingly, the Soviets interpreted the Irish resolution as stipulating the conclusion of a nonproliferation agreement that actually banned any kind of nuclear sharing altogether. Given the long-term importance of the Irish initiative, historical nonproliferation research has downplayed a parallel Swedish initiative which resulted in another UNGA resolution, adopted on the same day as the Irish one. The Undén Plan, named after Swedish Foreign Minister Östen Undén, took a different approach to preventing the further spread of nuclear weapons. Instead of assigning the existing nuclear powers with the role of negotiating an international regime to which all other states would adhere, the Swedish resolution viewed the proliferation problem through the lens of regional security and shifted the emphasis entirely to non-nuclear powers by encouraging them to organize themselves voluntarily in nuclear-free clubs, i.e., regional nuclear weapon free zones (NWFZ). Club members would also refuse to host nuclear weapons on their territories on behalf of any other country, thereby ruling out present and prospective nuclear arrangements within NATO.[16] Given the incompatibility of the Swedish plan with deterrence necessities and the intentional denigration of any role for the great powers – "the Swedes were wicked to do it without consultation with us," US Secretary of State Rusk complained internally – most Western Bloc countries followed Washington's advice and voted against the Undén plan.[17] The Soviet Bloc voted in favor – Moscow had previously supported nuclear free zones in Central Europe (the 1957 Rapacki Plan) and in the Far East, the Baltic Sea, and the Balkan–Adriatic Region (1959).[18]

For an accurate portrayal of nonproliferation history, it is therefore important to note that NWFZs presented an alternative route to inhibiting the further spread of nuclear weapons. Nowadays often treated as complementary and secondary initiatives, NWFZs in fact posed a threat to the preferred US approach to nonproliferation through the creation of an international regime. The concept of a NWFZ, however, was incompatible with extended nuclear deterrence, seen by Washington as indispensable to credible defense in Europe and Northeast Asia. In addition, the Undén Plan would have in practice banned defense alliances with nuclear powers, thereby prohibiting global power projection as such. Following the Swedish route instead of the Irish one in the pursuit of nonproliferation might have indeed led to a less lopsided bargain than the final compromise of 1968, which forced the NNWS to shoulder all the burden. While the general idea of the NWFZ approach remained vivid during the 1960s, the superpowers managed to take control of the negotiations on the general objectives and main provisions of a nonproliferation agreement following the 1961 resolutions.

Finding a formula: alliance politics and the path towards US–Soviet agreement on the main NPT provisions, 1962–1966

During the early 1960s, nonproliferation slowly moved into the limelight through public references by politicians and strategists and the efforts of peace activists – although for the latter, the ongoing nuclear arms race and the test ban debate were always of much greater importance. Simultaneously, rapid scientific progress amongst a second tier of nuclear-capable states raised concerns, as did the growing awareness of impending scientific breakthroughs in uranium enrichment using gas centrifuge technology, subverting the assumption of impassable technological barriers to the acquisition of atomic weaponry by states beyond the industrial elite.[19] To give one example, a study by the US Department of Defense in July 1962 estimated that over the next ten years sixteen states would be added to the four which now had a nuclear capability.[20]

Following the Irish Resolution, US Secretary of State Dean Rusk and Soviet Foreign Minister Andrei Gromyko initiated the first discussions on a separate nonproliferation agreement in March 1962 in Geneva. Progress was limited, besides Soviet support for the objective of establishing a nonproliferation agreement "on a global scale." Moscow insisted at this point on wording which would explicitly refer to the denuclearization of the two Germanys, pinpointing this as the major item of Soviet concern. In order to assuage Soviet fears, the US side followed up the early discussions with a general outline of a two-part non-dissemination agreement and some clarification of the meaning of "indirect transfer" of nuclear weapons in planned multilateral sharing arrangements. The Soviets' counter-proposal, submitted the same month, while signifying "a potentially important shift" according to Rusk, still contained the main sticking point of prohibiting "transfer of nuclear weapons through military alliances." US–Soviet talks resumed in early 1963, but quickly got bogged down again over the issue of transfer, against the background of the ongoing talks over the MLF concept inside the Western alliance. At one point the Soviets even threatened that if the MLF was implemented, they would be compelled to "respond in kind, by seeing to it that the appropriate countries friendly toward the USSR receive nuclear weapons."[21]

Although they had as yet led nowhere, these were the first serious exchanges on nuclear nonproliferation between the Cold War antagonists. Emblematic of the changed international setting after the Cuban crisis was the fact that diplomats could even mock their opposites for past transgressions in the nuclear field. Hinting at past Soviet support for the Chinese program, Rusk taunted the Soviet ambassador in May 1963 that "you have already lost your virginity on this point and we are still trying to preserve ours".[22] The improved atmosphere did not facilitate the finding of agreement, however. Moscow's position hardened during the course of 1963, and it now demanded a clause which would not only have prohibited the MLF but also the NATO stockpile agreements that were already in place. For its part, Washington's persisting hopes of following through with

Long road to the NPT   15

the MLF project in effect thwarted parallel nonproliferation talks with the Soviets. The US tried in vain to convince the Soviets that the MLF would be the most preferable means "for binding the Germans safely in this fashion, instead of leaving them a prey to dangerous Gaullist fancies or other adventurous notions," in the hope that the Soviets would later on accept the force as a *fait accompli* that did not stand in the way of a non-dissemination agreement in the future.[23] By 1964, the MLF concept had developed into a projected fleet of about 25 surface ships armed with 200 Polaris missiles, multilaterally owned, controlled and (mixed-)manned by participating NATO members. Nonetheless, European allies remained divided, with the two nuclear powers of the United Kingdom and France now both vehemently opposed to the idea.[24] The Johnson administration publicly reaffirmed the US commitment to the MLF once again in April 1964 in response to the FRG's increasing pressure for some visible progress. However, general doubts about the feasibility of the MLF persisted, leading the Johnson administration to (unofficially) withdraw US support for the project by the end of the year, while theoretically leaving the door open for a European initiative.[25]

In retrospect, from the perspective of the advocates of a global nonproliferation regime, the failed attempts to forge agreement on nonproliferation during those years must go down as a missed opportunity. Both Moscow and Washington shared a congruence of interests in preventing both the FRG and the People's Republic of China (PRC) from acquiring an independent nuclear deterrent, and a global regime seemed to be a promising way of achieving such an outcome, at least with respect to the former. Regarding the latter, the US and the USSR at times even flirted with the idea of colluding with each other with the aim of arresting the PRC's nuclear military progress through the use of force.[26] The apogee of this short-lived opportunity for a comprehensive "package deal" linking contested Cold War questions such as the status of West Berlin, confirmation of the FRG's non-nuclear status, and the arrest of the PRC's nuclear ambitions was the dispatch of veteran US diplomat Averell Harriman to Moscow in July 1963 for negotiations on a test ban agreement. During preparatory talks for the Harriman mission, there were serious internal discussions on the advantages of prioritizing a global nonproliferation agreement, at one point prompting President Kennedy to raise the possibility of "giving up the MLF concept" in return.[27] But the Soviets shied away from openly confronting Beijing, while the majority view within the Kennedy administration deemed Western alliance cohesion to be of far greater importance than progress on non-diffusion at the time.[28] The opportunity, if there ever was one, quickly passed. Instead, the US, the Soviet Union and the United Kingdom settled for the conclusion of a Limited Test-Ban Treaty (LTBT), signed on August 5, 1963, banning nuclear testing in the atmosphere, under water and in space.[29]

While important in addressing the environmental aspects of nuclear testing, the LTBT's significance with respect to nonproliferation has often been exaggerated. It might have been "a good start toward the goal of a global nonproliferation regime" (Francis Gavin) in the sense of it being the first serious

16   *R. Popp*

arms control agreement to be successfully negotiated between the superpowers, and in that it established an important precedent with its claim to universality and the subsequent accession of most states including many suspected of military nuclear ambitions, foremost the FRG.[30] However, while the President seemed to have believed that even a limited ban would inhibit nuclear diffusion, US security experts predicted that not much of a slowing down effect would result from the LTBT.[31] Also, the available evidence does not suggest that Moscow expected to see the LTBT result in a strong nonproliferation impulse.[32] A 1964 US study was unable to identify serious obstacles to underground testing by would-be-proliferators in the future, given recent scientific and technological advances.[33] Furthermore, the fact that testing continued underground – both superpowers would indeed accelerate their test activities in comparison to the pre-1963 period – arguably led to an acceleration of the arms race.[34] By impeding the ambitions of would-be-proliferators through the ban on atmospheric testing while allowing existing nuclear powers to enlarge and improve their existing arsenals, the LTBT also set the precedent of dividing the world into nuclear "haves" and "have-nots", a division which would later turn into the main organizing principle of the NPT.[35]

The "success" of achieving a test ban accord with Moscow also created for the first time the impression of a superpower condominium that excluded most middle powers from discussions of salient global security issues. Both the US and the USSR therefore had to reassure their European allies in response to the LTBT. Criticism of the LTBT as "another Versailles," originating in Bonn, was mollified through reaffirmation of the MLF idea by Washington. Unbeknownst to the West, this coincided with a Soviet actions in late 1963 to show more flexibility in order to make a nonproliferation agreement acceptable to the US. Khrushchev argued that the conclusion of a NPT would present an obstacle to West German nuclear ambitions to acquire nuclear arms, and would also help prevent the creation of a MLF later on. Strident opposition from Poland and the German Democratic Republic forced Khrushchev to abandon the idea.[36] With superpowers' stances on nonproliferation implacable for the time being, the issue returned to international forums. The US and the USSR had agreed in September 1961 on general principles for continued disarmament talks, leading, inter alia, to the creation of a new multilateral negotiating body. Mirroring the increasing number of UN member states as a consequence of the accelerating process of decolonization, the decrepit Geneva Committee on Disarmament had now expanded due to the inclusion of eight new members from non-aligned states, turning it into the Eighteen-Nation Disarmament Committee (ENDC). In subsequent years, the ENDC would turn into the most visible international forum for nonproliferation negotiations.[37] Non-aligned powers kept the nonproliferation momentum alive through their own initiatives, such as the initiative by five Latin American countries in April 1963 calling for the creation of a regional NWFZ and the similar resolution by the Organization of African Unity in July 1964. The Second Non-Aligned Summit Conference followed suit in October 1964. While direct negotiations between the superpowers still remained the focal

Long road to the NPT 17

point, NNWS succeeded in having their demands for a NPT heard, and they emphasized the need for universal adherence to a treaty, reciprocal concessions by existing nuclear powers such as a comprehensive test ban, and parallel or even antecedent measures towards the goal of general and complete disarmament. These were visible signs of another major hurdle to be faced in the future once Moscow and Washington agreed on the basic provisions of an agreement.[38]

Superpower talks on nonproliferation continued during 1964 and 1965 along lines that were by now established, with little apparent room for compromise given the continued official support for the MLF by the US and vehement opposition to any form of nuclear sharing by the Soviets. US–Soviet disagreement on the effect of the MLF on nonproliferation continued within the ENDC, with the Soviet representative accusing the US of intending to "giv[e] the West German revenge-seekers access to nuclear weapons."[39] Given Soviet propaganda attacks, noticeable non-aligned understanding for Moscow's rejection of the MLF, and allied opposition, the US quickly abandoned the idea of promoting an interim step through unilateral non-acquisition declarations by interested state parties.[40] Negotiations were additionally burdened by Bonn's insistence on Chinese Communist participation in any future agreement, notwithstanding Beijing's public refusal to participate. US arms control supporters argued in vain for the need to prioritize nonproliferation:

> If it appears that because of Alliance needs we have abandoned our efforts to prevent proliferation of national capability and are merely hoping to slow down the process, we will in effect have given a green light to states now poised at the point of decision.[41]

Below the surface, however, attitudes regarding the desirability of a nonproliferation agreement slowly started to shift. Concerns over the proliferation effects of the detonation of a nuclear device by the PRC – which finally took place in October 1964 – led to the establishment of two committees to study the problem. In January 1965, one of the two, the Gilpatric Committee, recommended a set of urgent measures aimed at inhibiting the further spread of nuclear weapons, first and foremost the conclusion of a nonproliferation agreement in advance of the formation of a multilateral NATO force. Although it gained attention and increased support amongst US officials, the nonproliferation issue remained on the back burner and the Johnson administration declined to adopt the committee's recommendations.[42]

The PRC test had an ambiguous effect on ongoing efforts to establish a global regime. On one hand, it raised concerns of an impending proliferation cascade, starting with countries potentially threatened by the Chinese bomb such as India and Japan. On the other hand, it rendered obsolete any ideas of bartering West German nuclear renunciation for a rollback of the Chinese Communist nuclear capability, which was now a *fait accompli*. However, internal US reflections on the strategic effects of further proliferation had in the meantime moved away from a more Cold War-centric perspective to reflections on the broader

18   R. Popp

consequences and the fundamental structural changes that would ensue as a result of an envisaged world consisting of multiple nuclear powers.[43] The main stumbling block, however, continued to be the MLF. With differences on this question unresolved, both the US and the USSR submitted draft nonproliferation treaties to the ENDC in August and September 1965, the latter clearly prohibiting any MLF scheme by demanding the NNWS to forsake "the right to participate in the ownership, control, or use of nuclear weapons." The Soviet language also seemed to delegitimize existing nuclear arrangements within the Atlantic Alliance as well as an alternative "software solution" to the nuclear sharing imbroglio through joint US–NATO nuclear planning.[44]

In mid-1965, one US official declared that he was not sanguine about the prospects for a universal nonproliferation agreement "even if the MLF barrier were absent."[45] With US–Soviet agreement on main NPT provisions looking more unattainable than ever, other powers stepped into the breach. US allies such as Britain and Canada now came forward with their own drafts, despite Washington's objections.[46] The Italian Foreign Minister Amintore Fanfani proposed a "moratorium" on acquiring nuclear weapons by non-nuclear states, in essence setting a time-limit for the conclusion of a NPT, after the expiration of which non-nuclear powers would regain their freedom of action.[47] Neutral states such as Sweden and India declared a strong interest in nonproliferation during tense sessions of the UN Disarmament Commission in 1965, leading in June 1965 to the adoption of a resolution sponsored by non-nuclear powers that tentatively tied a nonproliferation agreement to several other arms control measures. The eight non-aligned members of the ENDC demanded that future nonproliferation measures "be coupled with or followed by tangible steps to halt the nuclear arms race and to limit, reduce and eliminate the stocks of nuclear weapons and the means of their delivery."[48] The emerging linkage between nuclear abstention by non-nuclear powers and reciprocal actions by nuclear powers was unwelcome in both Moscow and Washington, and they quickly moved to stress that they regarded nonproliferation as a separable an unconditional measure. The "growing sentiment that the deadlock between the great powers should be broken by mobilizing the voices of the world at large" and the determination of some non-aligned powers to play a prominent role in that effort created tangible discomfort in the capitals of the superpowers.[49] The ultimate result of non-aligned efforts, however, was tolerable. UNGA resolution 2028 of November 19, 1965 defined five principles on which a future NPT agreement should be based, including measured demands such as an "acceptable balance of mutual responsibilities and obligations" and a vague reference to the aim of general and complete disarmament.[50]

With complications multiplying and a US–Soviet accord unlikely, more stress was laid on nonproliferation measures beyond an international agreement. The greatest emphasis was on strengthening the IAEA and the widest possible application of its safeguards, with the US starting off by setting an example in converting its bilateral safeguards to IAEA ones. Ahead of agreement on the NPT, the superpowers started to cooperate on strengthening safeguards after

Moscow changed course from opposition to support in mid-1963, setting the stage for the future primary role of the Agency in the NPT context. In addition, the US placed one major power reactor under IAEA safeguards in order to entice others to follow suit.[51] The first US NPT draft of August 1965 had still avoided demanding mandatory IAEA safeguards on nuclear activities, fearing that this would be an obstacle to accession to the treaty by "certain essential states," and given the public resistance of some non-nuclear states to safeguards, which they regarded to be discriminatory and intrusive.[52] The Indians had already compared the idea of imposing safeguards on "peaceful reactors" to an attempt "to maintain law and order in a society by placing all its law-abiding citizens in custody while leaving its law-breaking elements free to roam the street."[53] Despite the growing criticism, and driven by domestic pressure from the Atomic Energy Commission and US Congress, US diplomats thereafter abandoned diplomatic restraint and emphatically fought for a NPT safeguards clause which would be "simultaneously effective, credible, and acceptable."[54] Even more complicated was the question of security guarantees for non-nuclear states in a future NPT. As early as 1959, Irish Foreign Minister Aiken had introduced the idea of a collective UN defense commitment for all states renouncing nuclear weapons.[55] In the aftermath of the PRC's nuclear test, US President Johnson had promised US support to states threatened by "nuclear blackmail."[56] This assurance did not fulfill the expectations of some non-nuclear states. Foremost among them was India, which was suspected by many to be the most likely next proliferator. Catering to the non-aligned, Soviet Premier Kosygin offered in February 1966 to include a *negative* security guarantee in a future NPT (dubbed the "Kosygin Proposal"), prohibiting the use of nuclear weapons against non-nuclear states without any nuclear arms deployed on their territory.[57]

Beneath the surface, the two superpowers slowly began to synchronize their positions on the treaty's basic provisions. In preparation for the next ENDC meeting, the Johnson administration had amended the operative articles of its NPT draft, adding definitions of controversial terms such as "control," and submitted the changes to the ENDC in March 1966 in the hope of narrowing the difference between the two sides, albeit without any immediate success.[58] With a growing realization that the MLF concept was "essentially moribund," and following Soviet hints that a purely consultative nuclear planning committee with West German participation would be acceptable, negotiations entered a decisive stage by mid-1966.[59] The persisting disagreement over the wording of the basic provisions was ultimately solved through adoption of a simplified "non-transfer" clause, although this was de facto a recourse to more general language "having somewhat different meaning to both sides," as a Soviet official in Geneva conceded.[60] The sticking point remained the exact phrasing of prohibiting transfer to military alliances or groups of states, which by now referred more to a conceivable European nuclear force than a MLF. Negotiations again seemed close to breaking off at one stage, with US officials warning the Soviets that if they "wanted us to hold a public funeral for nuclear-sharing arrangements, the political price would be too high." The Legal Adviser of the State Department came

20   *R. Popp*

up with the ingenious solution of finessing the issue altogether by replacing the contentious part with the all-encompassing but indistinct phrase "to any recipient whatsoever."[61] On November 28, 1966, the Soviets finally proposed a version of Article I almost identical to the one in the final NPT, which was then accepted by US negotiators the following month.[62] Americans and Soviets also agreed on several of the so-called "underbrush" components of a future NPT, such as a withdrawal clause modeled after the LTBT and an article on treaty amendments, while being unable for now to agree on a safeguards article due to the discriminatory effect of existing EURATOM self-inspection from Moscow's perspective. The Johnson administration now intended to include a mandatory safeguards clause: "The non-proliferation treaty provides our best (and probably our only foreseeable) chance to achieve the stated US goal of a single, effective system of nuclear safeguards applied worldwide."[63]

With US–Soviet concurrence on basic provisions of a future NPT, albeit for now on an *ad referendum* basis, the path was finally cleared for drafting a comprehensive agreement and ensuring broadest possible accession. The confidential and predominantly bilateral phase of NPT negotiations now came to an end, as both sides took the agreed version of Articles I and II of the future NPT to their allies and also prepared for subsequent negotiations on the preliminary treaty text in the ENDC and at the UN. While the later and much more international character of the NPT negotiations must not be discounted, it is necessary to emphasize that the basic purpose during the negotiation history of the NPT until 1967 was nonproliferation, with neither peaceful use nor disarmament playing any meaningful role whatsoever, given the low priority of these issues for the superpowers. Nuclear disarmament and arms control, however, always formed background noise to the negotiations, and both US and Soviet officials repeatedly feared that the window for the conclusion of a NPT was closing. The growing interest by non-aligned powers was noted by both superpowers with concern, above all the tendency to link nonproliferation to other disarmament measures: "if non-proliferation was tied to such matters there might not be any treaty at all."[64] Both superpowers reacted angrily to the news that the eight non-aligned members of the ENDC were seriously considering tabling an alternative "third draft," apparently containing legally binding linkages to concrete steps on nuclear reductions and disarmament as well as safeguards for all nuclear facilities including the nuclear-weapon states (NWS) – Washington quickly exerted pressure in the capitals of the Eight in order to quell the initiative.[65]

Not only did growing international attention create a sense of urgency for the conclusion of a NPT, the fear that another power would cross the threshold before long was also a consideration. Previous attempts by historians to explain the perceptible will to come to an agreement have oscillated between two poles. The first thesis sees a predominant superpower interest, shared by most of the European allies, in codifying the existing nuclear order in Europe as part of the general move towards accepting the established Cold War settlement – with laying down West German nuclear abstention as the central impetus behind the nonproliferation agreement. The universal approach was chosen in order to avoid

Long road to the NPT   21

singling out Bonn with an openly discriminatory denuclearization obligation. If we look at the content of US–Soviet negotiations up to 1967, the centrality of the German nuclear question cannot be denied, since it was at the heart of the MLF controversy. A second and more recent interpretative strain also sees the issue of potential German proliferation as central, but points out the potential repercussions of further proliferation outside Europe on West German sensibilities, i.e., that the precarious Cold War settlement in Europe might not be endangered through nuclear-supported West German irredentism or Soviet fears about "revanchism" but as a consequence of Bonn's status concerns in the aftermath of nuclear acquisition by others. ACDA Director Foster elaborated this thinking in 1965:

> Should India, Israel, Japan or Sweden acquire an independent nuclear capability, the Federal Republic of Germany would doubtless come to feel that it had accepted second-class status by not acquiring its own independent nuclear force. In this case one of the principal objectives of NATO nuclear arrangements, that of providing a political framework in which the nuclear aspirations of the FRG could be satisfied, would no longer be tenable.[66]

Both these explanations, however, retain the (West) German nuclear status as the main explanans. While there is good reason for this emphasis, considering the centrality of the issue from the viewpoint of the main negotiating partner, the Soviet Union, it is much harder to understand why the US went to such great lengths to finalize a NPT, endangering and damaging in the process its relationship with a major ally in Western Europe.[67] This was very much the argument of the many nonproliferation skeptics within the administration at that time; they argued that the "Soviets do not want proliferation any more than we do and there is absolutely no reason to make any concessions to them in order to obtain their agreement to do something they would not do anyway."[68] With respect to the superpower dimension of the NPT negotiations, no satisfying answer has yet been given to the enigma as to why the US was willing to make the conclusion of a treaty a foreign policy priority. At least in theory, abandoning the MLF and alternative ideas for a "hardware solution" to the nuclear sharing problem might well have been sufficient to mitigate Moscow's nuclear fears regarding Germany, as well as opening a window to pursue other arms control measures. One of the domestic proponents of a robust nonproliferation stance, Robert Kennedy, argued in private for the need "to lessen the role of the atom in world politics," hinting at strategic motives transcending the confined issue of Germany's nuclear status and pointing towards more general conceptualizations of world ordering.[69] An alternative interpretation of the movement towards superpower consensus and collusion with respect to nonproliferation would point to a growing awareness in both Moscow and Washington regarding a possible future world that encompassed multiple states possessing an independent nuclear deterrent, and what this might mean in turn for military power projection and strategic influence outside their own respective world regions. Some of the documents

22   R. Popp

produced by the Gilpatric Committee illustrated this kind of thinking on the (nuclear) shadows of the future:

> The present costs of an effort to stop the spread of nuclear weapons must, however, be weighed against the costs of living in a world where proliferation has moved on: where all the Sukarnos and Ben Bellas have bombs; and where China, Indonesia, Egypt and Brazil each may have the direct capability of destroying tens of millions of American lives [...] consideration must be given to the facts that the U.S. would be faced with the threat of nuclear attack by an ever-increasing number of independent nuclear powers and that the U.S., in cutting its overseas commitments, would, in the process, reduce its influence in international affairs.[70]

It can be expected that future research on the trajectory of both US and Soviet nonproliferation policies might therefore produce some unexpected results, particularly with respect to the prevalent Cold War centrism in available accounts.[71]

On the final lap: international negotiations and the finalization of the NPT, 1967–1968

Once US and Soviet negotiators had agreed on the basic provisions of a future NPT, both sides took the next step of consulting with their major allies before they considered tabling a draft treaty at the ENDC. Illustrating the superpower domination of the process at this point, ACDA Director Foster told the German ambassador that, while the agreed language was "ad referendum," "changes would be difficult."[72] The Soviets used near-identical language vis-à-vis their East European allies.[73] The North Atlantic Council discussed the draft treaty text in early February 1967. It is hardly surprising that – apart from the French, who had signaled opposition against a nonproliferation agreement in principle and refused to even discuss the issue – the main criticism came from the West Germans and Italians. Both expressed their concerns regarding the effects of the NPT on the so-called "European clause," i.e., the nuclear status of a fully federated Europe in the future.[74] The US acquiesced, and in February 1967 transmitted to its allies a *Draft Summary of Interpretations of the NPT*. The note on interpretations argued that the NPT would neither prohibit the sharing of delivery systems nor allied consultations on defense. It also did not deal with the problem of European unity, and therefore "would not bar succession by a new federated European state to the nuclear status of one of its former components."[75] The US gave this promise despite having been informed by the Soviets that they rejected this interpretation.[76] The superpowers then negotiated a murky compromise, according to which the US would make available its interpretations to the Soviets, who thereafter would refrain from public dismissal.[77]

The other major problem during this phase of negotiations was the question of safeguards. As the Soviets refused to endorse existing EURATOM safeguards, which they regarded as de facto "self-inspection," the US tried to

Long road to the NPT   23

convince the West Europeans to accept some sort of compromise formula, such as a transition period or IAEA verification of EURATOM safeguards. The issue was complicated by a Soviet *volte face* on the safeguards issue in the aftermath of a Polish–Czechoslovak proposal in September 1966 to accept IAEA safeguards in return for the FRG doing the same. US officials feared that submitting a draft treaty without an Article III to the ENDC would make the chances of attaining meaningful safeguards later on "exceedingly slim."[78] The government in Bonn, however, argued that the proposed solution would be discriminatory to EURATOM countries.[79] Cracks in the US relationship with its allies now became visible, with West German Chancellor Kiesinger publicly referring to US–Soviet "nuclear complicity" and complaining about Washington's general neglect of timely consultations with the allies. The Italians and Dutch supported Bonn's stance. A strong anti-NPT movement emerged inside the FRG, with Finance Minister Strauss warning against subjecting the country to a "super-cartel of world powers" and former Chancellor Adenauer describing the treaty as "the Morgenthau Plan squared."[80] In late March 1967 the US presented its European allies with a draft treaty, including some minor changes to accommodate their concerns and a safeguards article based on interim IAEA verification. The new revisions did not satisfy the concerns of the allies, and Moscow and Washington therefore decided to table a draft treaty at the ENDC, albeit with a blank article on safeguards. Given that the non-Western members of the ENDC could be expected to demand non-discriminatory safeguards provisions, this was tantamount to a desertion of EURATOM countries by Washington. Strong US diplomatic pressure then brought Rome and Bonn into line.[81]

The safeguards question was also associated with the more general concern of the NNWS that the NPT, once in force, would have the effect of inhibiting their peaceful nuclear development. The issue had not received much attention in the ENDC until early 1967, and then only in reaction to the inclusion of "Peaceful Nuclear Explosives" (PNEs) in activities banned by the treaty. The Indian Representative Trivedi warned against any ideas of "non-proliferation in science and technology" directed against the developing countries.[82] None of the early NPT drafts submitted to the ENDC had contained references to peaceful use. It took the West German public campaign against the possible negative side effects of the NPT to change this picture. A FRG memorandum in April 1967 adopted many of the positions of the non-aligned Eight on the need for balanced obligations between nuclear and non-nuclear states. Furthermore, it also demanded the explicit stipulation of a guarantee for the free use of nuclear energy for peaceful purposes "without restriction."[83] In the meantime, the Mexicans had jumped on the bandwagon and proposed at the ENDC that a separate article on peaceful use be included, instead of adding to the preamble.[84] The Soviets transmitted an interim draft treaty to the US which included for the first time an article confirming the "inalienable right [...] to develop, research, production and use of nuclear energy for peaceful purposes without discrimination and in conformity with Articles I and II," the language incorporated into the final NPT's Article IV.[85]

24 *R. Popp*

The superpowers had hoped to finalize the treaty text in the ENDC by October 1967, but allied disagreements delayed progress. Following difficult negotiations, Moscow and Washington agreed to submit separate but identical drafts to the ENDC on August 24, 1967.[86] The drafts contained the basic Articles I and II as agreed between the superpowers in December 1966. Despite the US recommendation that a separate article on peaceful use should not be included, but that this should be left as a later concession to the NNWS "since it would be better for them to argue about this than to attack mandatory safeguards," the Soviets prevailed in including an Article IV on peaceful uses. As already mentioned, Article III on safeguards was left blank for now.[87] For the first time the states outside the Western and Eastern military blocs had an opportunity to inspect and debate the actual contents of the NPT, as well as to propose improvements.[88] The US and Soviet Co-Chairmen had earlier agreed that "the preamble would be a good place for amendments by non-nuclear nations," illustrating their lack of willingness with respect to genuine global consensus-building and compromise. In the end, even the final preamble of the NPT turned out to be very similar to the one in the August 1967 drafts.[89] During the ENDC deliberations which followed, the superpowers refused to give in to demands to add provisions demanding "tangible steps" toward disarmament. In response to growing criticism, the Co-Chairmen finally accepted the inclusion of a vaguely formulated article promising "negotiations in good faith" towards the cessation of the nuclear arms race, avoiding at the same time the mention of any specific measures such as the conclusion of a comprehensive test ban treaty. Also, accommodating a Mexican proposal, they added separate articles on sharing any potential benefits deriving from the development of PNEs and in support of regional denuclearization efforts.[90]

US–Soviet disagreement on a safeguards clause remained the main stumbling block. In order to facilitate compromise, Moscow abandoned its rejection of materials-based safeguards as practiced by EURATOM and moved towards acceptance of the idea that the latter could enter into an agreement on behalf of its members together with an implementation period. With Allied opposition remaining strong, the US began to support the Soviet draft as the best solution attainable, while also threatening a recourse to its previous strategy to progress to the UN First Committee with a blank Article III. Rusk warned the Germans that "we could lose control over the treaty" if an incomplete draft was presented to the General Assembly. Despite these pressures, EURATOM members decided to make their future ratification of the NPT contingent upon the conclusion of an acceptable agreement with the IAEA. They also defined minimum conditions for a safeguards clause.[91] The US and the UK tried to break the deadlock with a public announcement that they would themselves, as NWS, accept IAEA safeguards on all their nuclear activities except those of a military nature. While welcomed by the allies as a step to mitigate somewhat the discriminatory aspects of the mandatory safeguards clause, it was still not enough to facilitate consensus. Finally, the superpowers submitted a new set of identical treaty drafts on January 18, 1968, this time including a safeguards clause, creating another *fait accompli* for the European allies.[92]

With superpower agreement on the wording of Article III, the main stumbling block was out of the way. The second identical superpower drafts now included separate articles on PNE benefits, regional NWFZs, and disarmament. Regarding the latter, Moscow and Washington refused any attempts to name specific measures or timelines as a quid pro quo, but now signaled a willingness to turn the review process into an instrument to judge disarmament progress.[93] The joint US–Soviet draft treaty of March 11, 1968, however, contained only a slightly strengthened Article VI, incorporating Swedish and British suggestions.[94] The Co-Chairmen also accepted suggestions for incorporating periodic review conferences every five years. The treaty duration of twenty-five years was retained.[95] Earlier drafts had already defined a NWS as one which had manufactured and exploded a weapon or device before January 1, 1967.[96] The joint treaty was hereafter submitted to the General Assembly, formally ending the contribution of the ENDC.

With the transmission of a treaty draft, the ENDC had met the deadline of March 15, set by the UN General Assembly back in December. The main aim in the final phase was to give the impression of an open debate and to grant the opportunity for other states to file amendments, glossing over the many complaints about the stage-managed "run-around" in Geneva.[97] There was also the need to convince those states technologically capable of acquiring nuclear weapons, such as the FRG, Italy, India, and Brazil, to sign. The strategy chosen was to enlist the assistance of key countries such as Mexico, Ethiopia, and the UAR to set an example by joining at an early stage, "to separate [the] few near-nuclears from [the] overwhelming majority [of] countries having no prospect of developing nuclear weapons and whose basic objective should be enhanced security promised by [the] NPT." In advance, the superpowers had averted another danger for the NPT by convincing the sponsors of the planned conference of non-nuclear countries, based on a 1966 Pakistani initiative, to postpone it until August 1968.[98] Moscow and Washington then used the interval to railroad a resolution through the General Assembly on June 12 "commending" the Nonproliferation Treaty.[99] The final NPT text reflected several minor concessions which had become necessary in order to fend off calls for a more substantive disarmament commitment.[100] The long-standing demand for (positive) security guarantees for NNWS was "resolved" through a UN Security Council Resolution of June 19 which promised immediate action in accordance with the Charter in the case of aggression or threat of aggression with nuclear weapons. Vaguely worded and omitting any negative assurances regarding non-use, the resolution came under heavy criticism and did not satisfy the NNWS.[101] Finally, the NPT was opened for signature on July 1, 1968, and signed on the same day by the US, the USSR, the UK, and more than 50 other countries. After ratification by the three NWS and 40 additional countries, the treaty finally came into force on March 5, 1970. This was not the end of the story, however, as the whole issue of how to implement the safeguards obligations of Article III in the EURATOM area remained unresolved even after that date. EURATOM members, *sans* France, postponed ratification of the treaty until close to the first

NPT review conference in 1975, after the conclusion of safeguards agreements with the IAEA which preserved many privileges (Japan followed in 1976 after securing similar concessions).[102]

Evaluating the final phase of the NPT's completion, one cannot brush aside the difference between the way these events are remembered today and historical reality. In retrospect, the extent to which the formulation of the treaty text was a top-down driven effort is remarkable. The basic nonproliferation formula of Articles I and II was negotiated *in camera* between the superpowers, with only the veneer of a consultative process with the allies. The same was ultimately true of the safeguards clause in Article III. Most of the compensatory aspects of the final agreement, such as the articles on peaceful use, PNE services, and disarmament commitments, had already been part of the first identical US–Soviet drafts of August 1967, although not all of them were yet included as separate articles. This process resulted in a deeply one-sided and unbalanced outcome. There could not have been a bargain, as hardly any actual bargaining took place. It has to be noted, however, that the first public mention of some kind of bargain, by defining nonproliferation, peaceful use, and disarmament as the three main purposes served by the NPT, was undertaken by US officials in a number of public speeches in 1968. This was part of its "selling strategy" in order to convince fence-sitting states to accede, also by pretending ex post facto that the NNWS had "played a prominent part throughout the actual negotiation of this treaty."[103] Furthermore, while the historical record is unambiguous about the non-existence of any clearly defined quid pro quo or actual bargain during the negotiation of the NPT, this should not distract from the fact that NWS in essence accepted the bargain interpretation of the treaty at the Review and Extension Conference in May 1995 in return for indefinite extension.[104]

The ensuing debate on the character and sincerity of the alleged bargain between nonproliferation, peaceful use, and disarmament obscured another bargain inherent in the construction of the NPT, one whose components and trade-offs can be substantiated in available sources. In return for NNWS' acceptance of intrusive verification measures in the form of mandatory safeguards, the nuclear states, foremost the United States, recurrently and emphatically affirmed that the "inalienable right" to develop peaceful nuclear energy was absolute. In practice, this implied that state parties could theoretically construct the complete infrastructure for nuclear weapons construction without manufacturing an actual device, as long as they remained a party to the treaty. The content of US negotiations and consultation with its allies and other powers on treaty duration and conditions for withdrawal between 1966 and 1968 leave no doubt that leaving open the option of "nuclear latency" was an important – perhaps even the most important – selling point for the NPT. Along these lines, Washington repeatedly underscored to its allies, but also in public, that the "only technological development prohibited by the treaty" was actual nuclear weapons or devices. This meant it was allowable to have facilities producing enriched uranium, the stockpiling of fissionable material, or plutonium-fueled or fast breeder reactors, as long as these activities were under safeguards.[105] As states were "entitled under the NPT to proceed a considerable distance toward satisfying the requirements of a potentially military nuclear program," an internal US study thus predicted the continuation of proliferation under the NPT and the pursuit of civilian programs by states to the point "where a bomb can be assembled and detonated in short order."[106] As most of the so-called "near-nuclears" had no intention of acquiring an arsenal in the near future, acceding to the treaty forced no essential changes to their domestic nuclear policies. Thus nuclear latency proffered the unspoken contingency enabling the "have-nots" to accept the discrimination inherent in the NPT.[107]

Another important aspect of the final phase, one that is often overlooked, is that the superpowers in fact never managed to overcome their basic differences regarding the "European clause." In order to avoid this issue turning into a deal breaker, they decided to paper over the problem by agreeing to disagree, with the US promising its allies that a future European federation could accede to the nuclear status of one of its members while being aware that the Soviets saw such a development as being prohibited by the NPT. Hence, the basic disagreement which had stalled the conclusion of an agreement over the years was, in reality, never resolved.

Conclusion

Bearing in mind the major significance of the nonproliferation theme for international politics of the twenty-first century, it is easy, in retrospect, to exaggerate the importance of the NPT in the historical context of the Cold War. While there is no denying that the prospect of a global nonproliferation agreement was consistently high on the agenda of superpower talks for much of the 1960s, it has to be conceded that the final outcome was not too impressive. While the number of states party to the treaty increased to over 100 by 1980, this could not mask the fact that not only did the two other "legitimate" NWS as defined by the NPT – France and the PRC – stand aside, but most of the near-nuclear countries outside Europe such as Israel, South Africa, Brazil, Argentina, India, and Pakistan refused to join as well.[108] The international nuclear order, as constructed during the 1960s, was still "precarious, controversial and incomplete."[109] After all the energy and effort invested in its conception, the NPT quickly faded into the background for the remainder of the Cold War. However, despite its misconstructions and frailties, the order built during that time would form the foundation of a much more robust and near-universal nonproliferation regime in the future.

Notes

1 The author would like to thank Ursula Jasper, Jonas Schneider, and Andreas Wenger for their helpful comments.
2 There are some archival studies on the nonproliferation policies of specific states. On the US, see Shane J. Maddock, *Nuclear Apartheid: The Quest for American Atomic Supremacy from World War II to the Present* (Chapel Hill, NC: University

28   *R. Popp*

of North Carolina Press, 2010); on the UK, see Susanna Schrafstetter, *Die Dritte Atommacht: Britische Nichtverbreitungspolitik im Dienst von Statussicherung und Deutschlandpolitik 1952–1968* (München: Oldenbourg, 1999); on the USSR and West Germany, see the forthcoming monographs by David Holloway and Andreas Lutsch. For an overview, see Francis J. Gavin, "Nuclear Proliferation and Non-Proliferation during the Cold War," in *The Cambridge History of the Cold War: Volume II. Crises and Détente*, eds. Melvyn P. Leffler and Odd Arne Westad (New York: Cambridge University Press, 2010), 395–416; the most detailed work on the superpower negotiations is Hal Brands, "Non-Proliferation and the Dynamics of the Middle Cold War: The Superpowers, the MLF, and the NPT," *Cold War History* 7, no. 3 (2007): 389–423; for the emergence of the wider regime, see the contributions in Roland Popp and Andreas Wenger (eds.), "Special Issue: The Origins of the Nuclear Nonproliferation Regime," *The International History Review* 36, no. 2 (2014): 195–323.

3 George Bunn, *Arms Control by Committee: Managing Negotiations with the Russians* (Stanford, CA: Stanford University Press, 1992); Glenn T. Seaborg and Benjamin S. Loeb, *Stemming the Tide: Arms Control in the Johnson Years* (Lexington, MA: Lexington Books, 1987); for the Soviet side see Roland M. Timerbaev, *Rossiya i yadernoye nerasprostraneniye, 1945–1968* (Moskva: Nauka, 1999); the often-cited three-volume work by Mohamed I. Shaker, *The Nuclear Non-Proliferation Treaty: Origin and Implementation, 1959–1979*, 3 volumes (London; Rome; New York: Oceana Publications, 1980), is an analysis of public diplomacy rather than substantial negotiations without recourse to archival evidence. For an overview on the NPT, Ursula Jasper and James Davis, "Nuclear Arms Proliferation and the Utility of the Non Proliferation Regime," in *Human Rights, Human Security, and State Security: The Intersection*, ed. Saul Takahashi, vol. 3 (Santa Barbara, CA: Praeger, 2014), 157–180.

4 Western Working Paper, August 29, 1957, *Documents on Disarmament:* (hereafter DoDis) *1945–1959: Volume II. 1957–1959* (Washington, D.C.: U.S. Government Printing Office, 1960), 868–874; Soviet Memo, September 20, 1957, ibid., 878; David Tal, *The American Nuclear Disarmament Dilemma: 1945–1963* (Syracuse, NY: Syracuse University Press, 2008), 91–125; Maddock, *Nuclear Apartheid*, 110–124.

5 MemCon (Eisenhower, Dulles *et al.*), September 11, 1956, National Security Archive (NSArch) Collection, *U.S. Nuclear Non-Proliferation Policy, 1945–1991* (Alexandria, VA: Chadwyck-Healey, 1991) (hereafter NSArch Non-Prolif Coll.), doc. NP00274 (accessed through the Digital National Security Archive via ProQuest).

6 Radio and Television Address by Dulles, July 22, 1957, *DoDis: 1945–1959: Volume II. 1957–1959*, 826f.; Gordon Heyd Evans, "The World of Nuclear Plenty," *Bulletin of the Atomic Scientists* 19, no. 2 (1963): 26–30.

7 Eisenhower Letter to Khrushchev, March 12, 1960, Louis Galambos and Daun Van Ee, eds., *The Papers of Dwight David Eisenhower: The Presidency: Keeping the Peace*, vol. XX (Baltimore, MD; London: Johns Hopkins University Press, 2001), 1845.

8 Proposed language in Interdepartmental Working Group Draft Report, August 23, 1960, fol. "Increased Nuclear Sharing with Allies," Lot 70 D 265, Department of State, Executive Secretariat, NSC Meeting Files and Policy Reports, 11/1959–05/1966, Box 11, Record Group (RG) 59, National Archives at College Park, MD (NACP).

9 Marc Trachtenberg, *A Constructed Peace: The Making of the European Settlement, 1945–1963* (Princeton, NJ: Princeton University Press, 1999), 146–200; Susanna Schrafstetter and Stephen Robert Twigge, *Avoiding Armageddon: Western Europe, the United States, and the Struggle for Nuclear Non-Proliferation, 1945–1970* (Westport, CT: Praeger, 2004), 133–162.

Long road to the NPT 29

10 According to Trachtenberg, *A Constructed Peace*, 213ff., at least Eisenhower himself intended to let the MLF gradually evolve into an independent European nuclear force that would not be subject to a US veto, confirming some of the Soviet suspicions at the time.

11 See, for exampe, Lawrence S. Wittner, *Confronting the Bomb: A Short History of the World Nuclear Disarmament Movement* (Stanford, CA: Stanford University Press, 2009).

12 Irish Draft Res., October 17, 1958, *DoDis: 1945–1959, II: 1957–1959*, 1185f.; quoted from Aiken Address, September 23, 1959, ibid., 1478; for an analysis of the various Irish initiatives, see Shaker, *Non-Proliferation Treaty*, 1980, vol. 1, 3–24.

13 GA Res.1665, December 4, 1961, *DoDis: 1961*, 694.

14 Arms Control and Disarmament Agency (ACDA) Report "A History of Non-Dissemination Negotiations" (hereafter ACDA Report/Director), November 22, 1965, fol. "NPT – Histories," US ACDA, Director's Office NPT Files, HMS Entry UD-WX 1343-Q, Box 2, RG 383, NACP.

15 Quoted from William B. Bader, *The United States and the Spread of Nuclear Weapons* (New York: Pegasus, 1968), 36; on the gradual adjustment of Irish initiatives to Western wishes, Catherine Manathunga, "The Evolution of Irish Disarmament Initiatives at the United Nations, 1957–1961," *Irish Studies in International Affairs* 7 (1996): 97–113.

16 GA Res. 1664, December 4, 1961, *DoDis: 1961*, 693; the initiative was modelled on plans for non-nuclear-weapons-clubs circulating in European peace movements. See Alva Myrdal, *The Game of Disarmament: How the United States and Russia Run the Arms Race* (New York: Pantheon Books, 1976), 166f.

17 Maddock, *Nuclear Apartheid*, 172f.; for an example as to how the Swedish resolution was downplayed in subsequent accounts, see Shaker, *Non-Proliferation Treaty*, vol. 1, 37ff.; Bunn, *Arms Control by Committee*, 64ff.; both resolutions still receive equal treatment in early accounts. See, for example, US ACDA, *International Negotiations on the Treaty on the Nonproliferation of Nuclear Weapons* (Washington, D.C.: U.S. Government Printing Office, 1969), 4f.

18 See Rapacki Address, October 2, 1957, *DoDis: 1945–1959, II: 1957–1959*, 889–892; Khrushchev Address, January 27, 1959, ibid., 1345f.; *Izvestiya* article, August 14, 1959, ibid., 1436–1439; Statement by Soviet Government, June 25, 1959, ibid., 1423–1426; Tal, *Nuclear Disarmament Dilemma*, 121f., 147–154; James Stocker, "Accepting Regional Zero: Nuclear Weapon Free Zones, U.S. Nonproliferation Policy and Global Security, 1957–1968," *Journal of Cold War Studies* 17, no. 2 (2015): 41–49.

19 R. Scott Kemp, "The End of Manhattan: How the Gas Centrifuge Changed the Quest for Nuclear Weapons," *Technology and Culture* 53, no. 2 (2012): 272–305.

20 Memo of Meeting with the President, July 30, 1962, *Foreign Relations of the United States* (FRUS), 1961–1963, VII, 520–524.

21 Quoted from *ACDA Report/Director*, 14; cf. Rusk Memo to Kennedy, September 21, 1962, FRUS, 1961–1963, VII, 570ff.; Foster Memo, October 3, 1962, fol. "Nuclear Weapons, Non Diffusion for," National Security Files (NSF), Charles E. Johnson Files, Box 464, John F. Kennedy Presidential Library, Boston, MA (JFKL); on the Soviet interest in a NPT, see Khrushchev Message to Kennedy, n.d. (April 1963), FRUS, 1961–1963, VI, 271–279; see also the respective nonproliferation clauses in US and Soviet general disarmament proposals. See US Program, September 25, 1961, *DoDis: 1961*, 478; Soviet Proposal, March 15, 1962, *DoDis: 1962: I*, 113.

22 MemCon (Rusk, Dobrynin), May 18, 1963, FRUS, 1961–1963, VII, 702–705.

23 MemCon (Bundy, Dobrynin), May 17, 1963, FRUS, 1961–1963, V, 675; on these negotiations, Brands, "Non-Proliferation and Dynamics"; for the early support for the MLF idea, Maddock, *Nuclear Apartheid*, 154–158, 221, 228.

30 *R. Popp*

24 The Kennedy White House gave up the MLF idea in mid-1963 but decided not to back away publicly and instead to let it linger for now. See Bundy Memo to Kennedy, June 15, 1963, FRUS, 1961–1963, XII, 592–595.

25 Administrative History of the Department of State, Volume 1, Chapters 1–3: Part III: Europe, n.d. (1968/69), f. "Chapter 3," Special Files, Administrative Histories, Box 1, Lyndon B. Johnson Presidential Library, Austin, TX (LBJL), 2–8. For a summary of the MLF's manifold problems, see Bundy Memo to Ball, November 25, 1964, FRUS, 1964–1968, XIII, 121f.; on the December 1964 decision, Andrew Priest, "The President, the 'Theologians' and the Europeans: The Johnson Administration and NATO Nuclear Sharing," *The International History Review* 33, no. 2 (2011): 262–266.

26 On possible military operations against Chinese Communist nuclear installations, see William Burr and Jeffrey T. Richelson, "Whether to 'Strangle the Baby in the Cradle': The United States and the Chinese Nuclear Program, 1960–64," *International Security* 25, no. 3 (2000): 54–99; see ibid., 67f., for a direct reference to a conceivable mutual US–Soviet understanding.

27 Entry for June 21, 1963, *Journal of Glenn T. Seaborg, Vol. 26: Appendix* (Berkeley, CA: Lawrence Berkeley Laboratory, University of California, 1989–1992), PUB-625, n.p. (FOIA Request #CH-2015–01748-F by Roland Popp); editorial note, FRUS, 1961–1963, XXII, 341; see Memo, June 20, 1963, fol. "Trips and Mission, Test Ban Treaty Background," W. Averell Harriman Papers, Box 539, Library of Congress, Washington, D.C. (LOC); for the decision against sacrificing the MLF, see Summary Record of 515th NSC Meeting, July 9, 1963, FRUS, 1961–1963, VII, 779–785; but see Kennedy's remarks to Harriman in Memo for the Record, July 10, 1963, ibid., 789f.

28 Burr and Richelson, "Whether to 'Strangle the Baby in the Cradle'," 71f.; Maddock, *Nuclear Apartheid*, 211ff.; Trachtenberg, *A Constructed Peace*, 379–398, to the contrary, argues that a "near settlement" of basic Cold War issues took place in 1963.

29 Glenn Theodore Seaborg, *Kennedy, Khrushchev, and the Test Ban* (Berkeley, CA; Los Angeles, CA; London: University of California Press, 1981), 219–253; Schrafstetter and Twigge, *Avoiding Armageddon*, 85–131.

30 Gavin, "Proliferation and Non-Proliferation," 405.

31 Draft McNamara Memo to Kennedy, June 15, 1963, fol. "Nuclear Energy Matters: Nuclear Diffusion, Briefing Book, Vol. I," NSF, Carl Kaysen Files, Box 376, JFKL; cf. Meeting of Principals, July 24, 1962, FRUS, 1961–1963, Suppl. VII, VIII, IX, doc. 134; for Harriman, see Trachtenberg, *A Constructed Peace*, 383f.; Maddock, *Nuclear Apartheid*, 192f., 212f., is skeptical on the nonproliferation effect.

32 CIA Memo "The New Phase of Soviet Policy," August 9, 1963, FRUS, 1961–1963, V, 744.

33 JAEIC report-3–64 "The Test Ban and Nuclear Proliferation," April 1964, NSArch Briefing Book "The Limited Test Ban Treaty – 50 Years Later," ed. William Burr, August 2, 2013, doc. 2, at http://nsarchive.gwu.edu/nukevault/ebb433 (accessed December 20, 2015).

34 As acknowledged by the former Deputy National Security Advisor of the Kennedy administration in Carl Kaysen, "The Limited Test-Ban Treaty of 1963," in *John F. Kennedy and Europe*, eds. Douglas Brinkley and Richard T. Griffiths (Baton Rouge, LA: Louisiana State University Press, 1999), 112f.

35 Myrdal, *The Game of Disarmament*, 94ff.; another precedent for the later NPT negotiations was the active sabotage of initiatives by non-aligned powers. See ibid., xxivf., 89–92.

36 Douglas Selvage, *The Warsaw Pact and Nuclear Nonproliferation, 1963–1965*, Cold War International History Project Working Paper 32 (Washington, D.C.: Woodrow Wilson Center, 2001); Brands, "Non-Proliferation and Dynamics," 397–401.

Long road to the NPT   31

37 Maddock, *Nuclear Apartheid*, 172; Tal, *Nuclear Disarmament Dilemma*, 197ff.; on the ENDC's role, see Shaker, *Non-Proliferation Treaty*, vol. 1, 40, 69–93.

38 Ibid., 38f.; see, for example, Undén Letter to U Thant, February 16, 1962, *DoDis: 1962: I*, 38–42.

39 Tsarapkin Remarks, Verbatim Record, ENDC/PV.20729, August 13, 1964, at http://quod.lib.umich.edu/e/endc/4918260.0207.001 (accessed December 20, 2015); see also Gromyko's similar remarks in MemCon (Rusk, Gromyko *et al.*), December 5, 1964, FRUS, 1964–1968, XI, 129–135.

40 *Administrative History of the ACDA*, n.d. (1968/69), f. "Part II: Policy and Negotiations B. Non-Proliferation of Nuclear Weapons," Special Files, Administrative Histories, Box 1 and 2, LBJL (hereafter: *ACDA AdminHist*), 5; on non-aligned opinion, see Seaborg and Loeb, *Stemming the Tide*, 107.

41 Fisher Memo to Rusk, June 15, 1964, *NSArch Non-Prolif Coll.*, doc. NP00981; cf. ACDA Draft Position Paper, August 14, 1964, FRUS, 1964–1968, XI, 97–110.

42 See editorial note, FRUS, 1964–1968, XI, 110f.; See Report by the Committee on Nuclear Proliferation, January 21, 1965, ibid., 173–182; cf. Francis J. Gavin, "Blasts from the Past: Proliferation Lessons from the 1960s," *International Security* 29, no. 3 (2004): 100–135; Hal Brands, "Rethinking Nonproliferation: LBJ, the Gilpatric Committee, and U.S. National Security Policy," *Journal of Cold War Studies* 8, no. 2 (2006): 83–113; in contrast, Maddock, *Nuclear Apartheid*, 244–252, claims the near total rejection of the report by the summer of 1965. The rejection of most ACDA nonproliferation proposals in the subsequent months confirms Maddock's interpretation.

43 On similar developments in Moscow, see Brands, "Non-Proliferation and Dynamics," 403f.

44 US Draft Treaty, August 17, 1965, *DoDis: 1965*, 347ff.; Soviet Draft, September 24, 1965, ibid., 443–446; the final US draft resembled the proposal handed over to the Soviets in April 1963. See MemCon (Rusk, Dobrynin), April 12, 1963, FRUS, 1961–1963, Suppl. VII, VIII, IX, doc. 178; cf. Memo 'Analysis of Soviet Non-Dissemination Treaty', September 29, 1965, fol. "Non-Proliferation 1961–1966," ACDA Director's Office NPT Files, Box 2, RG 383, NACP; despite official adherence to the MLF, the US had started an initiative on stronger consultation on nuclear planning between NATO allies, leading to the creation of the Special Committee of NATO Defense Ministers and subsequently to the creation of the NATO Nuclear Planning Group in December 1966 which met for the first time in April 1967. Cf. State Administrative History/Europe, 8–16; Beam Memo to Rusk, November 4, 1965, FRUS, 1964–1968, XI, 262f.

45 Thompson Memo to Rusk, July 2, 1965, fol. 'DEF – DEFENSE AFFAIRS (1) July 65 …', Lot 70 D 429, Records of the Office of the Deputy Assistant Secretary of State for Politico-Military Affairs, Records Relating to Disarmament and Arms Control, 1961–1966 (G/PM:Disarmament), Box 1, RG 59, NACP.

46 *ACDA AdminHist*, 28–37; Schrafstetter and Twigge, *Avoiding Armageddon*, 152f.; David Tal, "The Burden of Alliance: The NPT Negotiations and the NATO Factor, 1960–1968," in *Transatlantic Relations at Stake: Aspects of NATO, 1956–1972*, eds. Christian Nuenlist and Anna Locher (Zurich: ETH Zurich, Center for Security Studies, 2006), 110f.

47 *ACDA AdminHist*, 48f.

48 Eight-Nations Joint Memo, September 15, 1965, *DoDis: 1965*, 425.

49 "Omnibus" Resolution, June 15, 1965, ibid., 260f.; Alva Myrdal defined the other measures as "part and parcel" of a nonproliferation agreement which would have to be fulfilled before non-nuclear powers would pledge not to acquire nuclear deterrents. See Myrdal Statement, May 10, 1965, ibid., 160; on US rejection of the "package deal," see Foster Statement, October 18, 1965, ibid., 474–482; cf. US ACDA, *International Negotiations*, 14ff., 53–56; quoted from Foster Report, June 18, 1965, FRUS, 1964–1968, XI, 214ff.

32 R. Popp

50 GA Res. 2028, November 19, 1965, *DoDis: 1965*, 532ff.; on the foregoing negoti-ations and for interpretations of the five principles, see Shaker, *Non-Proliferation Treaty*, vol. 1, 35–66.

51 On the 1963 decision, see Astrid Forland, "Coercion or Persuasion? The Bumpy Road to Multilateralization of Nuclear Safeguards," *The Nonproliferation Review* 16, no. 1 (2009): 47–64; on the Soviet change of heart, see David Fischer, *History of the International Atomic Energy Agency: The First Forty Years* (Vienna: The Agency, 1997), 249–252.

52 *ACDA Report/Director*, 25; Administrative History of the Atomic Energy Commis-sion, fol. "Volume 1, Part I, Chapters 1–7," Special Files, Administrative Histories, Box 1, LBJL, 17f.; cf. Informal Minutes of the 4th Meeting of the Committee on Nuclear Weapons Capabilities, FRUS, 1964–1968, XI, 118ff.

53 Trivedi Statement, August 12, 1965, *DoDis: 1965*, 339.

54 Quoted from Administrative History of the Department of State, Volume 1, Chap-ters 10–13, fol. "Chapter 11 (Science & Technology), Sections A-G," Special Files, Administrative Histories, Box 4, LBJL, 85; US ACDA, *International Negotiations*, 51f.

55 Aiken Address, September 23, 1959, *DoDis: 1945–1959: Volume II. 1957–1959*, 1474–1482.

56 Johnson Address, October 18, 1964, *DoDis: 1964*, 468.

57 US ACDA, *International Negotiations*, 21, 42f.; Foster Memo to Committee of Prin-cipals, July 16, 1965, fol. "DEF – DEFENSE AFFAIRS (1) July 65 …, Plans," G/PM:Disarmament, Box 3, RG 59, NACP.

58 See US Amendments to US Draft Treaty, March 21, 1966, *DoDis: 1966*, 159f.; the new US draft also changed the designation of "nuclear State" into "nuclear-weapon State" (and, analogously, non-nuclear-weapon State) to placate Indian sensibilities, anticipating the final NPT language. Cf. *ACDA AdminHist*, 52–60; US ACDA, *Inter-national Negotiations*, 33–41.

59 "Moribund" in Keeny Jr. Memo, December 24, 1968, fol. "The Non-Proliferation Treaty Volume I (#1–3)," NSF, NSC Histories, Box 55, LBJL; cf. Bundy Memo to Johnson, November 25, 1965; Foster Memo to Rusk, May 25, 1966; Keeny Jr. Memo to Rostow, June 9, 1966; MemCon (Rusk, Gromyko *et al.*), September 22, 1966, FRUS, 1964–1968, XI, 264–267, 323ff., 333f., 368–374; majorities inside US bureaucracy decisively changed with the change of heart by Secretary of Defense McNamara in favor of a NPT. See McNamara Memo to Rusk, June 7, 1966, ibid., 329f.; cf. *ACDA AdminHist*, 74–79.

60 Geneva Telegram #415 to State, July 23, 1966, fol. "The Non-Proliferation Treaty Volume II (#1–30)," NSF, NSC Histories, Box 56, LBJL.

61 The working language of September 24 committed "not to transfer nuclear weapons or other nuclear explosives or control over such weapons or explosives, directly, or indirectly through military alliances or groups of states" to any non-nuclear-weapon state. Moscow insisted on the addition of the phrase "individually or collectively." Cf. *ACDA AdminHist*, 97–111, quotation on 107; up to November 17, the Soviets resisted the "any recipient" formula. See MemCon (Rusk, Gromyko *et al.*), Septem-ber 24, 1966; MemCon (Rusk, Gromyko *et al.*), October 10, 1966, FRUS, 1964–1968, XI, 375–382, 388–391; amended Art. I working draft in McNaughton Memo to McNamara, October 15, 1966, ibid., 394–397; the "any recipient" formula prohibited the direct transfer of nuclear weapons to the UK but such a transfer was already banned by the US Atomic Energy Act, while all versions of the second sen-tence of Art. I left open the option of nuclear assistance to nuclear-weapons states, thereby protecting the Anglo-American nuclear alliance.

62 *ACDA AdminHist*, 112–123; Draft Rusk Memo to Johnson, November 28, 1966, fol. "The Non-Proliferation Treaty Volume II (#81–110)," NSF, NSC Histories, Box 56, LBJL.

Long road to the NPT 33

63 Quoted from Foster Memo to Rusk, January 11, 1967, FRUS, 1964–1968, XI, 418–421; AEC Chairman Seaborg remarked that the importance of the wider goal seemed to "outweigh the importance of preserving a special status for Euratom safeguards."; *ACDA AdminHist*, 120; cf. John Krige, "Euratom and the IAEA: The Problem of Self-Inspection," *Cold War History* 15, no. 3 (2015): 341–352.

64 MemCon (Rusk, Gromyko *et al.*), September 22, 1966, FRUS, 1964–1968, XI, 370.

65 *ACDA AdminHist*, 89f.; this would have been in line with the joint memo to the ENDC by the Eight of September 15, 1965, reiterated once again in August 1966. See Eight Nation Joint Memo, August 19, 1966, *DoDis: 1966*, 576–579; cf. US ACDA, *International Negotiations*, 43–46, 70–73.

66 Foster Memo to Committee of Principals, July 16, 1965, see above note 57; compare Brands, "Non-Proliferation and Dynamics," 39f.

67 George Ball warned in late 1965 that a Germany with denied nuclear equality might embark on adventurist policies or seek a deal with Moscow on reunification. See Ball Memo "The Dangers from a Psychotic Germany," n.d. (October 1965), fol. "I. The Nuclear Problem," Lot 74 D 272, Records of Under Secretary of State George W. Ball, 1961–1966, Box 29, RG 59, NACP.

68 McCloy Letter to Robert Kennedy, March 2, 1966, fol. "107 Correspondence: Kennedy, Robert," Series 21: Disarmament, 1944–1982, Box DA1, John J. McCloy Papers, Amherst College Archives and Special Collections, Amherst College Library, Amherst, MA.

69 R. Kennedy Letter to McCloy, April 15, 1966, ibid.; cf. the Policy Planning Council's Walt Rostow: "If nuclear proliferation occurs, the U.S. presence in both Europe and Asia will inevitably diminish."; Rostow Memo to Johnson, November 8, 1965, fol. "Dept. of State, Policy Planning, Vol. 6 (2 of 2),", NSF, Agency File, Box 52, LBJL.

70 Murray Draft Memo, December 7, 1964, fol. "Problem 2," NSF, Committee File, Committee on Nuclear Proliferation, Box 1, LBJL.

71 Gavin, "Proliferation and Non-Proliferation," 415f.; for examples of Soviet thinking along similar lines, see Brands, "Non-Proliferation and Dynamics," 403; the State Department in 1968 noticed an evolution of Soviet thinking on the benefits of a NPT over the years. Cf. State Telegram #107235 to Bonn, January 30, 1968, NSArch electronic briefing book *"The Impulse towards a Safer World": 40th Anniversary of the Nuclear Nonproliferation Treaty*, July 1, 2008, doc. 11, at http://nsarchive.gwu. edu/nukevault/ebb253 (accessed December 20, 2015); the ordering argument implied here is different from the criticism of the general hypocrisy of US nonproliferation policy forwarded in Maddock, *Nuclear Apartheid*.

72 *ACDA AdminHist*, 143.

73 MemCon, February 26, 1968, Records of the Warsaw Pact Political Consultative Committee, 1955–1990 (PCC Records), Parallel History Project on Cooperative History (PHP), at www.php.isn.ethz.ch (accessed March 1, 2016).

74 *ACDA AdminHist*, 138, 144ff.; the issue of a future European federal state had by then superseded the earlier MLF issue. Cf. Rusk Memo to Johnson, September 2, 1966; MemCon (Rusk, Brandt *et al.*), February 8, 1967, FRUS, 1964–1968, XI, 354ff., 435–439; a "total elimination of the European option" was unacceptable and "would be rejected by a large majority of the Bundestag"; extract from Bonn Telegram #820 (Hillenbrand to McGhee), July 20, 1966, fol. "Non-Proliferation," NSF, Files of Walt W. Rostow, Box 11, LBJL; cf. Lilienfeld Letter to Johnson, February 25, 1966, FRUS, 1964–1968, XI, 305ff.; the British, by contrast, were against leaving open a "majority vote European option"; British Embassy Aide-Mémoire, June 1, 1966, ibid., 325f.

75 State Telegram #141946 to Bonn, February 21, 1967, fol. "Non-Prolif. February 1, 1967 – March, Cables (1 of 6)," NSF, Files of Francis M. Bator, Box 10, LBJL; FRUS editors were unable to find this document. See FRUS, 1964–1968, XI,

34   R. Popp

445 n.2; it was clarified later that the interpretations "would form part of the negotiating history"; *ACDA AdminHist*, 188.

76 Ibid., 159; Fisher Memo to Rusk, February 25, 1967, FRUS, 1964–1968, XI, 445–448.

77 *ACDA AdminHist*, 214–218; the US had made clear that the interpretations were not intended as a formal instrument or a secret understanding. The Soviets were warned that if Moscow took an official position contradicting these interpretations later on, "very serious problems would arise which would have to be resolved"; the Soviets informed the US that they rejected any attempt to assume the right to give a unilateral interpretation to the treaty; ibid., 216; Katzenbach Letter to Clifford, April 10, 1968, FRUS, 1964–1968, XI, 573–578; see also Aufzeichnung Ruete, March 22, 1968, *Akten zur Auswärtigen Politik der Bundesrepublik Deutschland: 1968* (hereafter AAPD) (Munich: Oldenbourg, 1999), 384–388; misunderstood in Shaker, *Non-Proliferation Treaty*, vol. 1, 234f., 247ff.

78 *ACDA AdminHist*, 147.

79 Ibid., 148ff.

80 Ibid., 172ff., 178–188; State Telegram #183933 to Geneva (Rusk to Foster), April 27, 1967, fol. "Nonproliferation Treaty – April 1967 (3 of 4)," NSF, Files of Francis M. Bator, Box 10, LBJL; on Strauss, see *AAPD: 1967*, 423 n.9; for Adenauer, see Rostow Telegram #CAP67110 to Johnson, March 6, 1967, FRUS, 1964–1968, XIII, 540; cf. Leopoldo Nuti, "Negotiating with the Enemy and Having Problems with the Allies: The Impact of the Non-Proliferation Treaty on Transatlantic Relations," in *The Routledge Handbook of Transatlantic Security*, eds. Basil Germond, Jussi M. Hanhimäki, and Georges-Henri Soutou (Abingdon, Oxon; New York: Routledge, 2010), 89–102.

81 Rusk Memo to Johnson, n.d. (May 1967); Fisher Memo to Rusk, June 24, 1967, FRUS, 1964–1968, XI, 477ff., 487–492; Bonn only agreed to the tabling after US reassurances that it would prevent the negative effects of the multilateral discussions at the ENDC regarding Article III. Cf. *ACDA AdminHist*, 189–200; citation on 196f.

82 Trivedi Statement, October 31, 1966, *DoDis:1966*, 682; cf. Shaker, *Non-Proliferation Treaty*, vol. 1, 275.

83 FRG Memo, April 7, 1967, *DoDis:1967*, 179–182.

84 Remarks by García Robles, Verbatim Record, ENDC/PV.295, March 21, 1967.

85 *ACDA AdminHist*, 221; cf. Dane Swango, "The United States and the Role of Nuclear Co-Operation and Assistance in the Design of the Non-Proliferation Treaty," *The International History Review* 36, no. 2 (2014): 210–229.

86 Draft Treaty, August 24, 1967, *DoDis: 1967*, 338–341.

87 *ACDA AdminHist*, 223, 241ff.

88 The Indians had already received a draft in March 1967. Cf. ibid., 207.

89 Ibid., 121.

90 "Negotiations in good faith" was first proposed by the Mexicans. Cf. ibid., 245–262; cf. US ACDA, *International Negotiations*, 78–92.

91 *ACDA AdminHist*, 281–380; Rusk and Brandt on 323ff.; Geneva Telegram #703 to State, September 1, 1967; MemCon (Dobrynin, Foster), November 2, 1967, State Telegram #68052 to Certain Posts, November 11, 1967, FRUS, 1964–1968, XI, 502–505, 520ff., 524–529; cf. Bunn, *Arms Control by Committee*, 92–103.

92 Revised Draft Treaty, January 18, 1968, *DoDis: 1968*, 1–6; Fernschreiben Nr. 139 von Lilienfeld (Washington) an das Auswärtige Amt, January 18, 1968; Brandt Brief an Rusk, February 6, 1968, *AAPD: 1968*, 67–70, 163f.; MemCon (Dobrynin, Foster), December 26, 1967; Fisher Memo to Rusk, January 28, 1968, FRUS, 1964–1968, XI, 546f., 548f.; US Mission/NATO Telegram #1393 to State, January 18, 1968, NSArch, *40th Anniversary*, doc. 9c; cf. Bunn, *Arms Control by Committee*, 83–105.

93 "Quid pro quo" in de Palma Remarks, Verbatim Record, ENDC/PV.362, February 6, 1968; on the compromise, see Matthew Harries, "Disarmament as Politics:

Long road to the NPT 35

Lessons from the Negotiation of NPT Article VI," Research Paper (London: Chatham House: The Royal Institute of International Affairs, 2015).

94 Joint US–Soviet Draft Treaty, March 11, 1968, *DoDis: 1968*, 162–166.

95 *ACDA AdminHist*, 68–72, 90–94.

96 This was proposed by the British and Canadians and directed at the Indians in order to remove the temptation to test shortly before the opening for signature and thereby accede as a nuclear-weapon-state. Cf. *ACDA AdminHist*, 150ff., 175; see *AAPD: 1968*, 361, n.2.

97 *ACDA AdminHist*, 401ff.

98 US ACDA, *International Negotiations*, 95ff.; Memo for the Record of 584th NSC Meeting, March 27, 1968, FRUS, 1964–1968, XI, 558–561.

99 Draft Treaty, May 31, 1968; Treaty on the Nonproliferation of Nuclear Weapons, July 1, 1968, *DoDis: 1968*, 404–409, 461–465; an earlier resolution draft had "endorsed" the NPT but this was changed in response to the many criticisms directed at aspects of the treaty. Cf. ibid., 117–125; GA Res. 2373 (XXII), June 12, 1968, *DoDis: 1968*, 431f.

100 State Telegram #162528 to All Posts, May 11, 1968, NSArch, *40th Anniversary*, doc. 23b.; MemCon (Rusk, Kuznetsov), May 17, 1968, FRUS, 1964–1968, XI, 598–603.

101 Res.255, June 19, 1968, *DoDis: 1968*, 444; cf. *ACDA AdminHist*, 157, 380–395; cf. George Bunn and Roland M. Timerbaev, "Security Assurances to Non-Nuclear-Weapon States," *The Nonproliferation Review* 1, no. 1 (1993): 11–20; John Simpson, "The Role of Security Assurances in the Nuclear Nonproliferation Regime," in *Security Assurances and Nuclear Nonproliferation*, ed. Jeffrey W. Knopf (Stanford, CA: Stanford University Press, 2012), 57–85.

102 Grégoire Mallard, *Fallout: Nuclear Diplomacy in an Age of Global Fracture* (Chicago: University of Chicago Press, 2014), 235ff.; Fischer, *History of the IAEA*, 253–260.

103 See, for example, Goldberg Statements, April 26, 1968; May 31, 1968, *DoDis: 1968*, 221–233, quotation on 224; 415–422; the myth of a globally negotiated outcome has been perpetuated ever since. See, for example, Shaker, *Non-Proliferation Treaty*, vol. 1, 67f.

104 Final Document, Part I: Organization and Work of the Conference, NPT/CONF. 1995/32 (Part I); https://documents-dds-ny.un.org/doc/UNDOC/GEN/N95/178/16/PDF/N9517816.pdf (accessed March 15, 2016).

105 State Telegram #144920 to Canberra, April 11, 1968, NSArch, *40th Anniversary*, doc. 16c; Aufzeichnung Schnippenkötter, April 14, 1967, *AAPD: 1967*, 597–605; State Department Statement, February 20, 1967, *DoDis: 1967*, 97; Goldberg Statement, May 15, 1968; Foster Statement, July 10, 1968, *DoDis: 1968*, 344; 503f.; the negotiation history of the NPT is unambiguous in this respect. For a denial, see Christopher A. Ford, "Nuclear Technology Rights and Wrongs: The Nuclear Nonproliferation Treaty, Article IV, and Nonproliferation," in *Reviewing the Nuclear Nonproliferation Treaty (NPT)*, ed. Henry D. Sokolski (Carlisle, PA: Strategic Studies Institute, U.S. Army War College, 2010), 237–383.

106 Study "After NPT, What?" (authored by Richard N. Rosecrance), May 28, 1968, fol. "Atomic Energy-Armaments," Policy Planning Council: Subject Files, 1963–1973, Box 53, RG 59, NACP.

107 Closely tied to this construction is the wording of the special withdrawal clause of Art. X which leaves it to the states to define the "extraordinary events" making a withdrawal necessary.

108 Cf. the criticism in Myrdal, *The Game of Disarmament*, 171–177.

109 William Walker, *A Perpetual Menace: Nuclear Weapons and International Order* (London and New York: Routledge, 2012), 54.

3 In favor of "effective" and "non-discriminatory" non-dissemination policy

The FRG and the NPT negotiation process (1962–1966)

Andreas Lutsch[1]

The Federal Republic of Germany (FRG) never became a nuclear power and it never controlled nuclear weapons. In 1954, Bonn accepted a legal obligation vis-à-vis some of its Western allies to abstain from producing nuclear, chemical, and biological weapons on German territory.[2] This waiver seems to have provided sufficient reassurance to West Germany's allies for them to agree to the 1955 Paris Accords, thereby permitting West German admittance to the North Atlantic Treaty Organization (NATO). During 1956–1958, the Adenauer administration cautiously probed West Germany's nuclear options in terms of Western European cooperation – probably as a possible supplement to an exclusive Atlanticist nuclear policy.[3] Yet after this episode, German nuclear policy remained exclusively oriented towards NATO. During the 1960s, as the negotiations on a Treaty on the Non-Proliferation of Nuclear Weapons (NPT) progressed, West Germany's stance toward the treaty changed from rejection in the early 1960s to a rather grudging acceptance – coupled with an attempt in the second half of the 1960s to achieve a fairer balance of treaty rights and obligations. Ultimately, the FRG signed the NPT in late 1969 and ratified it in 1975.

The field lacks a precise understanding of the complexity of West German non-dissemination diplomacy and its linkages to related political and strategic processes during the 1960s.[4] Also, German non-dissemination policy is not well understood within Bonn's overall nuclear policy-making approach. This gap is particularly visible regarding the early years of the NPT negotiations, between 1962 and 1966, i.e., before Articles I and II of the later treaty were concluded. In contrast, more is known about the fact that German NPT-diplomacy intensified in early 1967 and that it had a limited impact on the treaty's provisions other than Articles I and II.[5]

Therefore, this chapter focuses on the early stage. First, it briefly reviews and offers an explanation for West Germany's ambitions in terms of the nuclear sphere of security policy since the mid-1950s. Second, it discusses how governments in Bonn perceived nonproliferation policy and the nascent nonproliferation regime in light of West German nuclear policy. Third, it inquires why Bonn proposed an almost forgotten NPT counter-scheme in early 1966 and how this proposal fitted to Bonn's nuclear policy. Finally, it explains why and to what extent West Germany's nuclear policy was transformed in late 1966.

Approaching West German nuclear ambitions

Throughout the 1960s, many believed the FRG's waiver of 1954 would not be sufficient to prevent Bonn from somehow acquiring nuclear weapons.[6] Ever since, much of the research on the origins of the NPT has seen the treaty as an effort by the superpowers – and other states – to codify especially West Germany's non-nuclear status.[7] An influential school of thought developed on the FRG and the nuclear question. This school focuses on the FRG as a "threshold state," prima facie capable in a technological, industrial, and financial sense to become a nuclear power. Regarding the latter, it is important to note that this school is totally fixated on nuclear weapons; it does not address other crucial issues in terms of nuclear power, like the availability of or the ability to procure secure and effective delivery vehicles and a reliable command and control infrastructure.[8] Authors assume or postulate explicitly that the West German government especially in the era of Chancellor Konrad Adenauer clandestinely "sought to acquire an independent nuclear deterrent," even though authors vary regarding the definition of "political will." In any case, the FRG is portrayed as a sometimes openly distrusted state that had to be prevented from "going nuclear." These authors contend that coercive actions enforced Bonn's alleged "nuclear reversal"; thus coercive actions were effective and decisive tools of nonproliferation policy against West Germany. Two coercive actions stand out. First, some pointed to seemingly credible and effective "U.S. threats of military abandonment" coupled with concurrent US assurance and protection "to obtain compliance with" US "nonproliferation demands,"[9] even though it is questionable whether the US actually "threatened" West Germany "to withdraw its security guarantees"[10] in a direct way. Second, this school of thought adheres to the narrative that the NPT thwarted West Germany's ambitions for the national nuclear option, that it froze the FRG's status as a non-nuclear-weapon state (NNWS), and that the German nuclear question was seemingly "solved" when Bonn acceded to the regime in 1969/1975.[11]

In contrast, another school of thought concentrated on a narrative which is the prevailing opinion in German historiography and which is supported by some accounts of political scientists. Basically, these authors postulate that there was "ample and growing capacity" regarding "an autonomous [nuclear] weapons acquisition program," "but no will."[12] This thesis implies that West Germany was not a case of "nuclear reversal," but a case of nuclear "renunciation"[13] or "forbearance."[14] These authors agree that we lack and that we will very likely never be able to detect unambiguous evidence which proves the contrary, and thus it has to be stated that the West German government neither decided to acquire the national control of nuclear weapons nor implemented a policy towards this end, be it with or without a formal decision-making process on government level.[15] Moreover, scholars have not identified an ambition let alone activities to make use of West Germany's fuel cycle technologies (such as heavy water reactors, enrichment and reprocessing of fissile materials) for the purpose of an indigenous production of nuclear weapons,[16] not to mention the potential illegality of involved actions considering that Bonn had waived the right to produce atomic weapons on German soil in 1954. Thus, also the thesis of a certain and/or temporary "hedging" function of West German fuel cycle technologies is not evident.[17]

In general, my view corresponds with the last-mentioned school of thought. But my view goes beyond the conventional narrative.[18] Before and after the FRG acceded to the NPT, West German governments pursued a *limited nuclear revisionism*. As an "umbrella state" and as a protégé within the framework of US extended deterrence and NATO, West Germany was discontent with the status quo and continuously sought to achieve incremental enhancements to Germany's position and influence within the nuclear order – but on a limited scale, that is without becoming an atomic power under the conditions of the Cold War, and while referring to and thus sheltering behind its legal status as a NNWS. Hence, the NPT had no nonproliferation effect regarding West Germany.

In recent years, a significant amount of government records was declassified.[19] My review of these sources revealed no German attempt to emulate British and French nuclear acquisition efforts. At least in the mid-1950s, West German thinking at the highest political level was characterized by the view that non-nuclear states were "outclassed."[20] And there is agreement that Adenauer personally never ruled out – and probably favored – that the FRG (or a reunified Germany) would eventually become a nuclear power. But in light of the available sources, there is no clear empirical nexus between such personal desires and a governmental policy to implement them, while "personal desires" should not be regarded as being equivalent to political will to acquire the national control of nuclear weapons. I argue that West German nuclear policy should be seen in the context of Bonn's orientation towards NATO and the US nuclear umbrella and that Bonn's *limited nuclear revisionism* was no end in itself. Its political core function during the 1960s was to enhance the FRG's position and influence within NATO in order to fortify the FRG's ties to the West (*Politik der Westbindung*).

Bonn's security policy was anchored in fundamental politico-military calculations. West Germany had to face a three-sided nuclear dilemma. First, in a divided Europe, the FRG faced a grave threat from the Soviet Union and the Warsaw Pact. Bonn's officials were painfully aware that Germany would serve as a main battleground of a war, perhaps nuclear war. West German policymakers were particularly "worried since the late 1950's by Soviet IR/MRBM [Intermediate Range/Medium Range Ballistic Missiles] and medium bombers targeted on Europe."[21] Any German chancellor, in the words of Helmut Schmidt, "had to remember that if the Soviet MRBMs were pointed at his country he would have to go begging to President Giscard or to Mr Callaghan or to President Carter in order to ask them to produce a counter-threat."[22]

Second, the FRG was entirely dependent upon NATO and the US nuclear umbrella. However, beginning in the late 1950s, the German leadership had to wrestle with the cardinal question of whether US extended nuclear deterrence was "absurd" and incredible.[23] And yet, nobody was able to rule out that US protection actually "worked" to deter Moscow: there were massive deployments of American troops and nuclear weapons in Western Europe, backed by the US strategic nuclear potential; the US threatened to use nuclear weapons first also below a level of conflict involving "the grand non-nuclear invasion of Western Europe";[24] and even in the face of the trend towards "nuclear parity" between the superpowers, the US "aggressively sought strategic nuclear primacy,"[25] thereby probably bolstering the credibility of its nuclear umbrella. Given these realities, West German experts and decision-makers believed even under the strained circumstances of the early 1960s that uncertainty in itself, due to the impossibility of excluding an uncontrollable spasm of nuclear escalation in conflict, might suffice to make deterrence work.[26] In Bonn, US nuclear power was regarded as indispensable to balance the threat of the Warsaw Pact. It could not be substituted.[27]

Third, the West German elites accepted the FRG's inability to provide security through nuclear acquisition. The political class perceived the FRG's status as NNWS as a fact of life, at least under the conditions of the Cold War.[28] Trying to change this status was regarded as an "impossibilité politique."[29] Such action would lead to "suicide in domestic politics."[30] Many also believed German proliferation might unleash a Soviet "preemptive attack."[31] In addition, independent of West Germany's economic prowess, decision-makers were painfully aware of the country's de facto status of a "protectorate" in terms of security policy.[32] Thus, it was unnecessary to remind West German leaders of the "simple fact [...] that Germany depends, and must depend, on collective nuclear defense," because "[i]f you would not sign [the NPT], and decided to defend yourself with your own nuclear weapons, you would (a) tear apart the Alliance [and] (b) face a very difficult period during which you might well be destroyed."[33]

Scholars have tended to exaggerate the potential value of national nuclear weapons for German security. Potential costs – isolation, loss of influence, military intervention – can very dramatically outweigh potential gains.[34] This calculation certainly applied in the case of the FRG. Notwithstanding, West German decision-makers thought the Soviet's fear of a nuclear FRG was not merely a propaganda construct.[35] Bonn had no illusions about the destabilizing effect of a West German attempt to acquire nuclear weapons. Such "endeavor[s]" would go directly against German national interests."[36] To understand the FRG's behavior, "German national interests" should not be understood in a narrow sense of territorial security, but in broader political terms. Besides the above mentioned security concerns, German proliferation had the potential to destabilize Europe. Yet stability had to be preserved as a precondition for achieving the primary "German national interest": Germany's reunification. In this respect, US support was also indispensable. Thus, from Bonn's point of view, everything needed to be done to tie German and Western European security to a credible US security guarantee.

International nonproliferation efforts and Bonn's "leveraging nuclear suspicion" strategy (1962–1964)

Especially after the Kennedy administration assumed office, the US policy community engaged in a widespread debate on the "N+1 country problem."[37] This mechanistic model implied an accelerating and quasi-automatic tendency towards further proliferation. Thus, to many US decision-makers, the spread of nuclear weapons appeared as a tide that needed to be stemmed.[38] In retrospect, it is obvious that proliferation pressures were more modest, especially when contrasted with the predictions of "generations of alarmists."[39] Nevertheless, the Kennedy administration was deeply concerned that the FRG might follow Britain and France's example and acquire nuclear weapons. Therefore, nonproliferation policy needed to be intensified, many in Washington argued.

As recently declassified documents make clear, the West German leadership repeatedly and unambiguously denied any interest to acquire the national control of nuclear weapons.[40] However, the Adenauer government felt that West Germany was massively threatened by Soviet IR/MRBMs. Bonn thought only the deployment of several hundred mobile land-based and sea-based MRBMs in Western Europe at best under West German participation could possibly counterbalance the Soviet nuclear threat. Key officials in the FRG shared the gloomy assessment of the Supreme Allied Commander Europe, Lauris Norstad, that "Western Europe would be without an adequate defense capability at the latest in 1967" if the MRBM-problem was not solved. And "then NATO would disappear."[41] Nevertheless, for political and strategic reasons, the Kennedy administration opposed any MRBM deployment in Western Europe.[42] Washington only lukewarmly supported the idea of a purely sea-based MRBM force, and insisted on a setting "truly multi-lateral in ownership and control."[43]

Policy-makers in Bonn were dismayed by what they saw as American disregard of West German security interests.[44] To gain leverage with Washington towards solving the MRBM problem, German officials started nurturing existing perceptions about the potential consequences of an insecure FRG. On the one hand, the country might eventually drift towards the East, the argument went.[45] On the other hand, it might embark upon a nuclear weapons program.[46] The Adenauer government attempted to exploit the FRG's status as a seeming "nuclear threshold state" and suspicions on the part of Bonn's allies as a source of intra-alliance bargaining power. But given West Germany's *limited nuclear revisionism* such proliferation hints did not indicate that the FRG was engaging in "nuclear hedging."[47]

Bonn's leveraging-strategy achieved mixed results. On the US side, Secretary of State Rusk reported to his British counterpart, Lord Home, that "the Germans would, sooner or later, seek to have a nuclear capacity of their own unless they were offered some alternative arrangement such as the multilateral force." Yet, London remained rather unimpressed. Apparently, their assessment of the possibilities of German nuclear policy was rather realistic.[48] Nevertheless, the German leadership accepted a very high price for this diplomatic strategy:

Federal Republic of Germany 41

distrust, suspicion, and even resentment of friend and foe alike were the consequences. Thus, this diplomatic move would ultimately catalyze numerous states' already existent predisposition towards balancing against and containing the FRG, a country whose leadership appeared to show an "increasing sign of being obsessed" with nuclear weapons.[49]

When the trend towards a nonproliferation regime materialized as a basic agenda item in superpower deliberations over Berlin and Germany and was paralleled by the adoption of the "Irish Resolution" by the UN General Assembly in late 1961, the FRG was alarmed. Because key officials of the Adenauer government referred to the "French belief that nuclear diffusion is desirable because of US unreliability,"[50] contemporary and subsequent analysts assumed that Bonn wanted to avoid the prohibition of the national nuclear option by a nonproliferation treaty. Yet, in fact, the FRG genuinely supported the Irish Resolution (UN General Assembly Res. 1665, December 4, 1961) and endorsed the principle of non-dissemination.[51] But Bonn refused to support every means of nonproliferation policy. For Bonn, nonproliferation policy could not compromise other core interests – and the superpowers' proposed NPT ideas were threatening to do just that.

Emerging until August 1962, the general design of what were to become Articles I and II of the NPT included a non-transfer/non-assistance-declaration by the nuclear powers and a non-production/non-acquisition-declaration from all other states. Yet the superpowers disagreed in regard to NATO as a nuclear alliance. The Soviets were interested in using the NPT as a means to denuclearize the transatlantic alliance, for instance by prohibiting nuclear weapons deployments on territories of non-nuclear states and any nuclear sharing arrangements.[52] Thus, Bonn rejected the NPT proposal.[53] Its de facto position remained hidden behind a diplomatic smokescreen: The FRG would commit herself to such a treaty if all other non-nuclear-weapon states in the world would do so as well.[54] Nevertheless, the West German position did not aim to preserve a "right to become a nuclear Power in the future" due to an existing plan or intention to do so. It was rooted in three politico-strategic considerations.[55]

First, the West German government strictly rejected any kind of nonproliferation settlement singling out both German states, a provision that the superpower-envisioned concept did entail at that point.[56] Second, Bonn opposed renouncing any of its nuclear options within the scope of an accord which would be legally binding between West Germany and the Soviet Union. Aware of Moscow's concern with a West German nuclear option, the FRG regarded any such waiver as an important "bargaining point" for the eventual negotiations on the German question.[57] According to the West German political concept of *Politik der Stärke* (policy of strength) towards dealing with the Soviet Union, Moscow should feel the squeeze of the German "sword of Damocles," the argument went.[58] In other words, even though German policy-makers regarded the nuclear option de facto as unfeasible, a seeming state of "nuclear latency"[59] should keep Moscow in uncertainty in regard to Bonn's intentions. Thus, the "sword of Damocles" appeared as an "*atout*," a trump.[60] Perhaps it could even be a "decisive diplomatic weapon," some suggested.[61] In any event it could not be given away without anything in return. Third, Bonn did not want a treaty that would negatively affect the "present and future nuclear defense posture of NATO."[62] The West Germans were concerned, for example, with the deployment of US nuclear weapons in the FRG and Western Europe, with existing nuclear sharing arrangements, and particularly with the deployment of MRBMs under West German participation. Given West Germany's aim to bolster its position within NATO, a superpower agreement on nonproliferation was seen as both being undesirable and dangerous. Also, when compared to other political questions, attempts to limit the spread of nuclear weapons were regarded in Bonn as of secondary importance. Nobody saw a need at this stage to propose a workable alternative to the superpower's scheme to deal with nonproliferation.[63]

After the multiple crises within NATO in late 1962 and early 1963, the Kennedy administration took concrete steps towards establishing the so-called Multilateral Force (MLF) – a seaborne MRBM-force to be owned, controlled, and manned multilaterally under the participation of interested NATO allies.[64] Given French opposition to this initiative, both West Germans and Americans thought the British held the key to success. Thus, Washington tried to win London over. Yet many in the UK felt that "the Germans should be kept quiet in other ways," i.e., through a nonproliferation agreement.[65] In response, Kennedy argued that British Prime Minister Macmillan should agree to the MLF in order to avoid negative consequences: Franco-German nuclear cooperation or an "independent nuclear effort in Germany – not now but in time."[66]

In Bonn, policy-makers were less than enthusiastic about the MLF scheme. Adenauer feared that the US had now ruled out any deployment of land-based MRBMs.[67] However, the West German government was determined to achieve a MLF agreement at the least. Political and strategic reasons spoke in its favor – "above all to participate in the strategic nuclear area in some form."[68] Thus, the German Atlanticist orientation was confirmed by the FRG's unconditional acceptance of the MLF.[69] And burgeoning détente demanded additional concessions: In late August 1963, the Adenauer government had to meet international expectations to accede to the Partial Test Ban Treaty. It did so reluctantly. A "system" of East–West relations managed by the superpowers began to emerge.[70] In October 1963, Adenauer's successor Ludwig Erhard assumed power, signaling a predominance of the Atlanticist attitude inside the FRG government.

However, starting in mid-1964, both the French government and West German "Gaullists" like Adenauer, Strauss, and others castigated the Erhard government for exclusively pinning German hopes on the US in terms of security policy – political pressure that constrained Erhard's freedom of movement. In addition, MLF-diplomacy aroused France's fury. The Warsaw Pact countries waged massive propaganda campaigns. In Britain, the Tory and the Labour governments were determined to contain German power in Europe – in late 1964, under the guise of a British counter-proposal to the MLF, the ANF. Thus, by autumn 1964, with Bonn repeatedly stating its positions both openly and behind closed doors, the perception of the FRG coveting nuclear weapons worried many. The PRC's nuclear test of October 1964 had led to a sense of exceptional urgency in the US regarding nuclear proliferation. President Lyndon B. Johnson's decision, laid down in National Security Action Memorandum (NSAM) 322 in late 1964, came as a massive blow for the Atlanticist German leadership.[71] In the critical words of the former US High Commissioner in Germany, John McCloy, the effect of NSAM 322 was "to *go easy* on the MLF, to *put the ball in the court of the Europeans* with, at best, an equivocal attitude on the part of the United States in respect of MLF."[72] Under these circumstances, Bonn feared that the US might sooner or later give preference to a nonproliferation settlement and abandon the collective nuclear force within NATO. In reaction, statements of West German leading figures became rather flamboyant. Clearly alluding to a NPT-like agreement, Foreign Minister Schröder warned Rusk that the FRG could never accept "discriminating measures."[73] In conclusion, while German disagreement with the NPT-concept was intense, the underpinning logic was much more convoluted than conventional explanations propose.

Against the NPT – in favor of an alternative regime (1965–1966)

There were clear indications in mid-1965 that a breakthrough on a nonproliferation agreement along the general lines of the 1962 design had become possible. The Gilpatric Committee had argued in its report to President Johnson for giving nonproliferation priority, even though US internal disagreements remained on how to deal with the FRG.[74] The MLF-proposal had become politically shipwrecked. But many in Bonn still hoped that triangular high-politics between Washington, London, and Bonn would lead to the establishment of a NATO collective strategic nuclear force. Within this context, the British circulated a NPT draft among the NATO allies, with the intention to table it at the formal venue for negotiations on the treaty, the Eighteen-Nation Committee on Disarmament (ENDC). The UK draft ruled out any collective nuclear force in which the participating nuclear-weapon states would not hold a veto over the use of nuclear weapons.[75] In Bonn, the Erhard government was alarmed, to say the least. Within this general context, a number of FRG attempts to secure German interests ensued.

For West Germany, the British proposal seemed to be another step in an undesirable direction. In May 1965 US Secretary of Defense McNamara had argued NATO should establish a "Select Committee" of defense ministers in order to give some non-nuclear states – and mainly the FRG – a chance to participate in nuclear consultation. Such consultations would include, inter alia, "planning for the use of nuclear forces, including the use of strategic nuclear forces."[76] McNamara had intimated that his proposal would merely be a supplement to – and not a substitute for – the continuing US offer to establish a collective nuclear force.[77] However, the Germans feared that the "Select Committee" could be played up politically to legitimize a change of US policy

44   A. Lutsch

towards a definitive abandonment of the concept to establish a collective MRBM force.[78]

Against this background, an article by William C. Foster, the director of the US Arms Control and Disarmament Agency (ACDA), in a widely read policy journal suggested that US rejection of the multilateral force option might be a prerequisite for achieving a nonproliferation treaty. In Bonn, the article was understood as inclining the balance of influence in Washington in favor of those who seemed willing to compromise with Moscow to achieve nonproliferation at the expense of a certain "erosion" of NATO.[79] The article was seen as another manifestation of the arrogance of nuclear powers, intending to fix the given hierarchy in the international state system in favor of the nuclear *beati possidentes*.[80]

The FRG's reaction was loud and public. First, Foreign Minister Schröder deliberately staged the FRG as a "role model non-nuclear weapon state," advocating that others should first emulate West Germany's 1954 voluntary renunciation. Second, he argued Bonn could abdicate nuclear "acquisition" only vis-à-vis her allies and only after German participation in a collective MRBM force had been secured. Third, he claimed the FRG would not be able to accede to a NPT. Only a reunified Germany could do so.[81] Critics of the Erhard government quickly portrayed Schröder's statement as an implicit threat: West Germany would "go nuclear" if its conditions were not met.[82] In fact, Schröder's reaction reflected the government's position since 1962 and particularly the "Sword of Damocles" strategy.

Ensuing consultations between Bonn and Washington and within NATO are revealing in regard to both West German priorities and strategy. The FRG leadership was quickly confronted with the US argument that the NPT could not be linked to the German question.[83] All the more then, the Erhard government insisted on the well-known German demand to participate in a collective nuclear force.[84] Given the anticipated consequences of strategic parity between the superpowers and the ensuing decreasing credibility of the US nuclear umbrella, Bonn was worried that Moscow might ultimately feel emboldened to blackmail West Germany.[85] The German Permanent Representative to NATO, Wilhelm G. Grewe, argued Bonn was bound to understand nonproliferation in the general context of European security: an "erosion" of NATO as a side effect of the NPT would be "catastrophic."[86] In this context, the US reaction is telling: While brushing away the other arguments, Secretary of State Rusk was quick to point out that Foster's article had no governmental endorsement and that Washington would not compromise with Moscow on a collective nuclear force.[87]

Remarkably, after Washington tabled a draft NPT in the ENDC in August 1965 – from West Germany's viewpoint, a moment marking a "new stage" of international nonproliferation diplomacy – Bonn's public reaction was ostentatiously reserved.[88] The draft was a "significant contribution." But NATO's "defense interests" should not be impaired, the West Germans argued publicly.[89] Internally, however, leading figures inside the government bureaucracy still referred to the NPT as the *Knebelungsvertrag*, implying that it would restrain only the have-nots.[90] Bonn complained to Washington that the US draft was completely imbalanced, given the nuclear powers' unconstrained freedom of action.[91] When analyzed carefully, these mixed reactions are fully consistent with West German preferences and constraints. On the one hand, the draft treaty clearly allowed for schemes for a collective nuclear force within NATO. On the other hand, it ruled out the establishment of a European nuclear force under the participation of non-nuclear states except for remote cases.[92] Especially in the eyes of German "Gaullists" it was of vital importance to preserve the full spectrum of remaining options to participate in a European nuclear force, irrespective of the currently hostile British and adverse French attitudes.[93]

In contrast to the West German government, former Chancellor Adenauer complained publicly that a NPT would be a "tragedy for Germany" because an insecure FRG would be handed to the Soviet Union on a silver platter.[94] Former Defense Minister Strauss blustered that the NPT would amount to a "military Versailles" and demanded to establish a European nuclear force immediately. The Erhard government should "not perform the role of the Atlanticist prig," Strauss argued.[95] However, these harsh criticisms were aimed at least as much at the US as they were aimed at domestic audiences in advance of the *Bundestag* elections in autumn 1965.

These fiery domestic exchanges notwithstanding, the Erhard government was confirmed in the elections. With the Soviet Union having submitted its own NPT draft – an initiative widely interpreted as attempting to denuclearize Western Europe by banning all nuclear arrangements within NATO – the FRG tried for the last time to achieve a breakthrough regarding a collective nuclear force.[96] Thus, Bonn sent a little known new scheme to the highest level in both Washington and London – a mixture between ANF-components and new elements including a long-range version of land-based Pershing missiles.[97] Subsequently, the Germans attempted to lobby the US to bring the British onboard. The Atlanticist Erhard government still had many supporters in Washington. Like their German peers, American advocates of the collective NATO force took the British Labour leaders at their word to give up the UK deterrent. This "would strike a blow for nonproliferation more significant than any piece of paper," these US officials argued.[98]

However, another fraction within the US bureaucracy advanced the opposite argument: Because the US would retain a veto on the decision to use the nuclear weapons of the collective force, the control scheme would only "dramatize that no one believes that Germans can be trusted with nuclear weapons." This might augment Bonn's nuclear ambitions instead of satisfying them, it was argued.[99] Indeed, President Johnson was very reserved towards the West German proposal.[100] Yet he advised British Prime Minister Wilson to accept the West German formula without putting pressure on London to do so.[101] On the part of the British, some argued it was "wishful thinking" to hope Bonn would be content merely with nuclear consultations,[102] with the "artichoke without the heart," as some US officials portrayed it.[103] Nevertheless, the British government "backed away" in early 1966 from its ANF-proposal, thereby removing what had been the basis for the new German scheme.[104] Thereafter President Johnson

46   A. Lutsch

seemed to act like an "honest broker" between London and Bonn, without putting pressure on either side.[105] But he continued emphasizing the "importance of the Germans finding a place in the sun."[106]

In a curious mixture of decisiveness and restraint, the Erhard administration now concluded it would not push for a collective force for the time being, but it would repel attempts to curtail Bonn's remaining nuclear options in consequence of arms control. The collective force was still seen as the only means to solve the MRBM-problem and to bolster the Federal Republic's status within NATO.[107] Corroborating this high level of uncertainty with the alliance crisis unleashed by France's final withdrawal from the integrated NATO command, the FRG leadership clearly felt a danger "that we will be steamrolled by a nonproliferation agreement."[108] West German experts did not perceive any teleology in terms of NPT diplomacy. But they did not preclude a tacit agreement between the two superpowers. As a consequence, the NPT would codify the given nuclear order. It would rule out the non-nuclear states' ability to *influence* the control of nuclear weapons through nuclear co-ownership. And it might only allow a consultative nuclear arrangement like the "McNamara-Committee" besides existing nuclear arrangements.[109] This was not an outcome the Erhard government was willing to accept, be it explicitly or silently.

Thus, to get out of the political danger zone, the Erhard government launched another – today nearly forgotten – major initiative in late March 1966: a German disarmament plan. This "peace note" included a package for all Warsaw Pact states except East Germany. It comprised offers to conclude bilateral agreements to renounce the use of force, to exchange maneuver observers, to control the export of fissile materials, and to establish a regional nonproliferation regime which should appear as "effective" and "non-discriminatory" – in contrast to the NPT.[110] Obviously, the FRG wanted to square the circle: deal constructively with the general trend of détente, behave positively on nonproliferation, reduce suspicion and distrust, and protect West German interests.[111] However, the West German government was under no illusion that its proposal had the slightest chance of being implemented. All Warsaw Pact states rejected the proposal.[112] Not even the Western powers took the initiative seriously.[113] The US approached the idea "quite reservedly."[114] Even Italy proved uninterested.[115] Ultimately, Bonn's non-dissemination initiative had very little impact.[116] In any case, the initiative documented Bonn's positive stance towards nonproliferation policy, even though the opposition to the NPT endured.

The meager result of West Germany's initiative had to be seen against the background that there was already much political momentum behind the superpowers' drive towards the NPT. Increasingly, as the Soviets signaled acceptance of existing nuclear arrangements within NATO and even some future "software" arrangement of nuclear consultations, a compromise solution appeared possible.[117] Nevertheless, even while telling the Germans that they did "not have to worry," Washington was aware that Bonn was still committed to obtaining a hardware solution.[118] Additionally, the Erhard government at no time explicitly conveyed its approval of the NPT approach.[119] It was clear in Washington that the

US would face stiff opposition "if we tried to jam down their throats the sort of agreement now proposed to us by the Russians."[120] Thus, in early December 1966, after the Erhard government had already fallen and a "grand coalition" between Christian Democrats (CDU/CSU) and Social Democrats (SPD) had been established, the FRG was still "reassured" by the US: "no decisions" had been taken on the NPT issue, "no secret deal with the Russians" had been reached, and "no positions of the alliance and options whatsoever have been abandoned."[121]

The transformation of West German limited nuclear revisionism

Despite US reassurances to the contrary, the Germans feared a superpower NPT *fait accompli* which would infringe German interests. In such a situation, even if West Germany would "formally" be consulted, she would "practically" have no other choice but to concede defeat.[122] From Bonn's perspective, this scenario materialized when the Germans received the draft Articles I and II of the NPT before the end of 1966 – draft language that would find its way almost unchanged into the ultimate text of the treaty that opened for signature on July 1, 1968.[123] However, the Grand Coalition government of CDU/CSU and SPD that governed until autumn 1969 could not agree upon a formal NPT decision. The views of the SPD- and the CSU-leadership were incompatible. The CDU-leadership was leaning towards the CSU's stance, but without sharing the CSU's more radical rejection of the NPT. In contrast, immediately after the Social Democrats (SPD) and the Liberals (FDP) formed a government the FRG signed the NPT on November 28, 1969. This policy change can be seen as a significant step towards the FRG's redefined *Ostpolitik*.

Under these circumstances, what the West Germans were left with since late 1966 was to influence the details of the future treaty to a certain amount. In mid-1968, US-President Johnson would claim "the Germans had practically written the Treaty as it stands now."[124] Starting in early 1967, Washington had been highly receptive to German demands on the specifics of the NPT language. Thus, Bonn's NPT diplomacy was surprisingly influential, given the fact that Germany – not a member of the ENDC – was not directly participating in the negoti-ations.[125] Still, Johnson's remark was a euphemism.[126] The West Germans were only allowed to influence at most secondary provisions of the treaty. Nonetheless, many of these items were complex and politically sensitive. Bonn was, for instance, influential in addressing the safeguards question pursuant to Article III, the right to use nuclear energy for civil purposes according to Article IV, and – as FRG's Foreign Minister Brandt put it – the alleged "practical lever" to disarmament in Article VI.[127] In contrast, Articles I and II – the core of the NPT – remained sacrosanct.[128] Johnson's remarks also reflected that it had become a test of stamina for American officials to listen closely to "legalistic" Germans in innumerable and redundant bilateral meetings on the specifics of the NPT to ensure that these consultations were assessed as at least partially successful by the German side.

48   *A. Lutsch*

Putting aside the specifics of NPT diplomacy since early 1967 in order to avoid a cursory and inappropriate evaluation of the German assessments, it is worth noting that the German debate on the FRG's NPT signature in late 1969 focused once again on the implications of Articles I and II. The same had been true until the turn of the year 1966–1967. The first two articles were paramount because they were seen as an attempt by the two superpowers to codify the given nuclear order on a global scale.[129] States that had tested nuclear weapons before January 1, 1967 were declared as nuclear-weapon states (NWS). All other states were supposed to accept their status as non-nuclear-weapon states (NNWS). Existing NATO nuclear arrangements were shielded, even though the NPT language of "indirect transfer of control" was in fact ambivalent. A collective nuclear force with co-ownership of nuclear weapons by NNWS was legally ruled out.[130] The participation of a NNWS (party to the NPT) in a European nuclear force would also be prohibited as long as no European federal state had been established beforehand, thereby superseding at least one of the two European NWS, France or Britain.[131] Thus, the NPT explicitly codified a new aspect of sovereignty within international law: the control of nuclear weapons had to be regarded as "measure of sovereignty and big power status symbol."[132]

The superpower compromise on the NPT was a massive setback for West German interests. However, after the US and the Soviet Union agreed upon Articles I and II, there was a general expectation especially in Washington that the FRG had to accede to the NPT "whether they like it or not."[133] In contrast, the successor to Erhard, Kurt-Georg Kiesinger, later remarked that if the FRG acceded to the NPT, West Germany would appear as a "protectorate of the US."[134] Grewe, who opposed the treaty as a matter of principle but denied any interest in a German nuclear weapons capability, criticized the NPT in early 1967: "The MLF was aimed at achieving long-term equality, the NPT is aimed at producing long-term inequality."[135] Grewe's complaints were paradigmatic for the perception of leading figures within the German administration. In the eyes of Atlanticists and "Gaullists" alike, the superpower's agreement on the first two articles of the NPT was tainted.

First, the NPT put a cap on Bonn's aim to bolster the FRG's status within NATO. The NPT relegated the FRG to a secondary position within the international state system and NATO. West Germany had gained a permanent seat within the Nuclear Planning Group (NPG), in consequence of McNamara's "Select Committee" proposal. But it was far from being self-evident in late 1966 that German "pressures for greater influence in nuclear policy" would in fact be absorbed entirely by the NPG deliberations.[136] Second, the superpowers' compromise provided no solution to the MRBM-problem from the German point of view, even though this problem had eroded German confidence in the credibility of the US nuclear umbrella for years. The failure to establish any kind of collective nuclear force in NATO contributed to a desperate feeling of insecurity "among knowledgeable people in Germany." But even if Bonn wondered "how much of Germany had to be overrun before the [nuclear] riposte would be forthcoming," it remained beyond doubt that US protection was indispensable.[137]

Federal Republic of Germany 49

According to the available evidence, the gloomy assessments of the early 1960s that NATO might collapse if the MRBM-problem remained unresolved were replaced by a consensus that NATO deterrence may well remain credible in relation to Moscow and that it would be more dangerous than ever before to doubt its credibility.[138]

If the preservation of the global nuclear status quo is to be regarded as the core objective of the NPT, then the treaty's immediate effect on the FRG was actually very low. By freezing the European nuclear order, the NPT thwarted Bonn's efforts to improve the West German *institutional position* within nuclear NATO. But the objective to increase the FRG's politico-strategic *influence* especially in nuclear NATO did *not* cease in autumn 1966 when the *position* of the FRG in nuclear NATO and in the European nuclear order was laid down. Bonn would continue to use its leverage to advance West German interests in terms of nuclear security policy and particularly within NATO's nuclear structures.[139]

Conclusion

In autumn 1966, after the superpowers had agreed on Articles I and II as the core of the NPT, West Germany's *limited nuclear revisionism* was significantly transformed. Bonn had at no time actively striven for the national control of nuclear weapons. It supported nonproliferation policy, irrespective of the fact that it had rejected the NPT as a means to deal with the non-dissemination issue. West German nuclear policy was committed to achieve two specific objectives. First, the FRG's institutional position in nuclear NATO had to be expanded by participation in nuclear arrangements. Second, the FRG's influence in nuclear NATO had to be continuously increased with the general objective to increase its credibility and to work towards a more favorable balance of risks and burdens within the alliance. Autumn 1966 brought a transformation of the FRG's *limited nuclear revisionism* in the sense that the FRG acquiesced in her *position* in nuclear NATO and the nuclear order. Thus, the FRG stopped being revisionist in this regard. But the FRG continued to be willing to expand her *influence* in nuclear matters, first of all within the structures of nuclear NATO, and especially within the Nuclear Planning Group. In this respect, West Germany remained a revisionist state and we still lack a precise understanding of Bonn's respective activities, particularly regarding the period of transition between the late 1960s and the prehistory of the NATO Dual-Track Decision of 1979.

Until the late 1960s, the political core function of German nuclear policy was to fortify the FRG's ties to the West (*Politik der Westbindung*) by bolstering the FRG's position in NATO and by expanding West German influence in nuclear matters without becoming a nuclear power. Given the politico-strategic calculation behind the FRG's *limited nuclear revisionism*, the unchanged circumstances of the Cold War, the undisputed West German *Westbindung*, and the role of the SPD in the government, there was also no "danger" after 1966 that Bonn might abandon its previous path and go nuclear. Thus, the NPT had no nonproliferation effect with regards to the FRG. The NPT was unnecessary to keep West

50   A. Lutsch

Germany non-nuclear. Even before the NPT-regime was established, any assessment of costs and benefits made the national nuclear option look unbearable. Still, the NPT can be characterized as an additional "powerful constraint"[140] which cemented the FRG's non-nuclear status. The FRG's accession to the NPT in 1969/1975 strongly fortified the already given architecture in which the security of non-nuclear West Germany was guaranteed by the US nuclear umbrella.

Notes

1   The author would like to thank the participants of the ETH conference and the Social Science Seminar at CISAC, Stanford University, for their helpful comments, in particular Erin Baggott, Barton Bernstein, Lodovica Clavarino, Lynn Eden, Francis J. Gavin, Edward Geist, Eliza Gheorghe, Siegfried S. Hecker, Elmar Hellendoorn, David Holloway, Liviu Horovitz, Jonathan R. Hunt, Ursula Jasper, Morgan L. Kaplan, Christine M. Leah, Grégoire Mallard, Leopoldo Nuti, Christian F. Ostermann, Roland Popp, Brad Roberts, Farzan Sabet, Scott D. Sagan, Nina Silove, Joseph Torigian, and Andreas Wenger.

2   Article I, protocol Nr. III on arms control, revised Brussels Pact of October 23, 1954, *Bundesgesetzblatt 1955*, Teil II, No. 7 (Bonn, 1955), 267.

3   Leopoldo Nuti, "F-I-G Story Revisited," *Storia delle Relazioni internazionali* 13, no. 1 (1998): 69–100; it is far from clear that the intended, expected or likely outcome of this attempt at cooperation would have been "a national nuclear deterrent" in the case of West Germany as some scholars contend: Harald Müller and Andreas Schmidt, "The Little-Known Story of Deproliferation: Why States Give Up Nuclear Weapons Activities," in *Forecasting Nuclear Proliferation in the 21st Century: Volume 1. The Role of Theory*, eds. William C. Potter and Gaukhar Mukhatzhanova (Stanford, CA: Stanford University Press, 2010), 124–158, here: 135; in any case, the failure to achieve the F-I-G cooperation cannot be described as "the official end to the West German nuclear weapons program"; see Nuno P. Monteiro and Alexandre Debs, "The Strategic Logic of Nuclear Proliferation," *International Security* 39, no. 2 (2014): 7–51, here: 43.

4   Compare Fred L. Kaplan, *The Long Entanglement. NATO's First Fifty Years* (Westport, CT: Praeger, 1999); Andrew Priest, *Kennedy, Johnson and NATO: Britain, America and the Dynamics of Alliance, 1962–68* (London: Routledge, 2006); Helga Haftendorn, *NATO and the Nuclear Revolution: A Crisis of Credibility, 1966–1967* (Oxford: Clarendon Press, 1996); Beatrice Heuser, *NATO, Britain, France and the FRG: Nuclear Strategies and Forces for Europe, 1949–2000* (Basingstoke: Palgrave Macmillan, 1997); Christoph Bluth, *Britain, Germany and Western Nuclear Strategy* (Oxford: Clarendon Press, 1995); Basil Germond, Jussi M. Hanhimäki and Georges-Henri Soutou (eds.), *The Routledge Handbook of Transatlantic Security* (London: Routledge, 2010); Andreas Wenger, "Crisis and Opportunity: NATO's Transformation and the Multilateralization of Détente, 1966–1968," *Journal of Cold War Studies* 6, no. 1 (2004): 22–74; Andreas Wenger, Christian Nuenlist, and Anna Locher (eds.), *Transforming NATO in the Cold War: Challenges beyond Deterrence in the 1960's* (London: Routledge, 2006); Christian Nuenlist and Anna Locher (eds.), *Transatlantic Relations at Stake: Aspects of NATO, 1956–1972* (Zurich: ETH Zurich, 2006).

5   Stephan Geier, *Schwellenmacht. Bonns Atomdiplomatie von Adenauer bis Schmidt* (Schoeningh: Paderborn, 2013); Peter Hoeres, *Außenpolitik und Öffentlichkeit. Massenmedien, Meinungsforschung und Arkanpolitik in den deutsch-amerikanischen Beziehungen von Erhard bis Brandt* (Munich: Oldenbourg, 2013); William G. Gray,

Federal Republic of Germany 51

"Abstinence and Ostpolitik: Brandt's Government and the Nuclear Question," in *Ostpolitik, 1969–1974: European and Global Responses*, eds. Carole Fink and Bernd Schaefer (Cambridge: Cambridge University Press, 2009), 244–268; Erwin Häckel, *Die Bundesrepublik Deutschland und der Atomwaffensperrvertrag. Rückblick und Ausblick* (Bonn: Europa-Union-Verlag, 1989); Uwe Nerlich, *Der NV-Vertrag in der Politik der BRD. Zur Struktur eines außenpolitischen Prioritätenkonflikts* (Ebenhausen: SWP, 1973).

6 Catherine McArdle Kelleher, *Germany and the Politics of Nuclear Weapons* (New York: Columbia University Press, 1975), 9; a German interest to obscure "remaining loopholes" was postulated recently by Michael Knoll, *Atomare Optionen. Westdeutsche Kernwaffenpolitik in der Ära Adenauer* (Frankfurt: Peter Lang, 2013), 325.

7 Francis J. Gavin, "Nuclear Proliferation and Non-Proliferation during the Cold War," in *The Cambridge History of the Cold War. Volume 2: Crisis and Détente*, eds. Melvyn P. Leffler and Odd A. Westad (Cambridge; New York: Cambridge University Press, 2010), 395–416; Hal Brands, "Progress Unseen: U.S. Arms Control Policy and the Origins of Détente, 1963–1968," *Diplomatic History* 30, no. 2 (2006): 253–285; Shane J. Maddox, *Nuclear Apartheid: The Quest for American Atomic Supremacy from World War II to the Present* (Chapel Hill: University of Carolina Press, 2010); Susanna Schrafstetter and Stephen Twigge, *Avoiding Armageddon: Europe, the United States, and the Struggle for Nuclear Non-Proliferation, 1945–1970* (Westport, CT: Praeger, 2004).

8 On C3I, see Peter D. Feaver, "Command and Control in Emerging Nuclear Nations," *International Security* 117, no. 3 (1992/93): 160–187.

9 Gene Gerzhoy, "Alliance Coercion and Nuclear Restraint: How the United States Thwarted West Germany's Nuclear Ambitions," *International Security* 39, no. 4 (2015): 91–129, quotes: 94 and 127; Monteiro and Debs, "The Strategic Logic of Nuclear Proliferation," 10, 42–47.

10 Gerzhoy, "Alliance Coercion," 92; Snyder clarified: "A complete withdrawal is hardly conceivable." Glenn H. Snyder, "The Security Dilemma in Alliance Politics," *World Politics* 36, no. 4 (1984): 461–495, quote on 467.

11 See accounts in note 9; Matthias Küntzel, *Bonn and the Bomb: German Politics and the Nuclear Option* (London; Boulder: Pluto Press, 1995); Harald Müller, "German National Identity and WMD Nonproliferation," *The Nonproliferation Review* 10, no. 2 (2003): 1–20; Müller and Schmidt, "The Little-Known Story of Deproliferation"; Marc Trachtenberg, *A Constructed Peace: The Making of the European Settlement 1945–1963* (Princeton: Princeton University Press, 1999), 234ff.; Knoll, *Atomare Optionen*, 325–337; Oliver Bange, "NATO as a Framework for Nuclear Nonproliferation: The West German Case, 1954–2008," *International Journal* 64, no. 2 (2009): 361–382; Jonas Schneider, *Amerikanische Allianzen und Nuclear Reversal. Warum manche Entscheidungsträger von Allianzpartnern der USA einer Beendigung ihrer Kernwaffenaktivitäten zustimmen und andere nicht* (Kiel: PhD dissertation, 2015), 62.

12 Horst Mendershausen, *Will West Germany Try to Get Nuclear Arms – Somehow?* (Santa Monica: RAND, 1971), 1.

13 I refer to the definitions in Jeffrey W. Knopf, "Security Assurances: Initial Hypotheses," in *Security Assurances and Nuclear Nonproliferation*, ed. Jeffrey W. Knopf (Stanford, CA: Stanford University Press, 2012), 13–38, quote on 21f.

14 T.V. Paul, *Power versus Prudence: Why Nations Forgo Nuclear Weapons* (Montreal: McGill-Queen's University Press, 2000), 11.

15 Helga Haftendorn, *Deutsche Außenpolitik zwischen Selbstbeschränkung und Selbstbehauptung 1945–2000* (Stuttgart, Munich: DVA, 2001), 94–134; Bruno Thoß, *NATO-Strategie und nationale Verteidigungsplanung. Planung und Aufbau der Bundeswehr unter den Bedingungen der massiven atomaren Vergeltungsstrategie 1952–1960* (Munich: Oldenbourg, 2006), 483f., 496; Hans-Peter Schwarz,

52   *A. Lutsch*

"Adenauer und die Kernwaffen," *Vierteljahrshefte für Zeitgeschichte* 37, no. 4 (1989): 567–593; Lawrence Freedman, *The Evolution of Nuclear Strategy*, Third edition (Basingstoke; New York: Palgrave Macmillan, 2003), 310; Kelleher, *Germany and the Politics of Nuclear Weapons*; Jeffrey Boutwell, *The German Nuclear Dilemma* (Ithaca: Cornell University Press, 1990); Jenifer Mackby and Walter Slocombe, "Germany: The Model Case, A Historical Imperative," in *The Nuclear Tipping Point: Why States Reconsider Their Nuclear Choices*, eds. Kurt M. Campbell, Robert J. Einhorn, and Mitchell B. Reiss (Washington D.C.: Brookings Institution Press, 2004), 175–217.

16 Joachim Radkau and Lothar Hahn, *Aufstieg und Fall der deutschen Atomwirtschaft* (Munich: oekom, 2013), 118–223; there is consensus in German historiography that another account is flawed because it does not display but still postulates a secret effort behind the build-up of West Germany's nuclear infrastructure in order to achieve an indigenous break-out capability under the pretext of exploiting nuclear energy for civilian purposes; cf. Tilmann Hanel, *Die Bombe als Option. Motive für den Aufbau einer atomtechnischen Infrastruktur in der Bundesrepublik bis 1963* (Essen: Klartext Verlag, 2015).

17 On the contrary thesis, see Ariel E. Levite, "Never Say Never Again: Nuclear Reversal Revisited," *International Security* 27, no. 3 (2002/2003): 59–88, here 75.

18 This view is based on my PhD dissertation *Westbindung oder Gleichgewicht? Die nukleare Sicherheitspolitik der Bundesrepublik Deutschland zwischen Atomwaffensperrvertrag und NATO-Doppelbeschluss (1961–1979)* (accepted for publication in cooperation with ZMSBw, Potsdam).

19 Even if many military aspects of nuclear history are publicly unknown, an impressive body of declassified files enables nuclear historians to understand West German governmental policies much better than ever before. The most important US files are State Department files, located at the *National Archives and Records Administration*, College Park, MD, USA [NACP]; NSC files, located at Presidential Libraries; and files from collections like the *Digital National Security Archive* [DNSA]. The *UK National Archive*, London, UK [TNA] and the *NATO Archives*, Brussels, Belgium [NATO] are of great importance as well. Most declassified German files are foreign office files, available in the *Politische Archiv, Auswärtiges Amt*, Berlin, Germany [PA AA]; formerly classified files of the chancellery and the ministry of defense are by and large inaccessible, even though some declassified files are available at two venues of the *Bundesarchiv*, Koblenz, Germany [BA] and Freiburg, Germany [BA-MA]. Selectively, formerly classified files can be found in personal papers of German politicians, which are located in private or party archives.

20 Cabinet meeting, July 20, 1956, *Die Kabinettsprotokolle der Bundesregierung* [Kab. Prot] *1956* (Munich: Oldenbourg, 1998), 486f.

21 Action Memo Hartman, Gelb and Lake, February 3, 1977, NACP, Record Group [RG] 59, Decentralized Files – Lot Files [DC-LF], Policy Planning Council [PPC], Records of Anthony Lake [AL], Box 2, TL 2/1–15/77.

22 MemCon Callaghan-Schmidt, October 18/19, 1978, TNA, Foreign and Commonwealth Office [FCO] 46/1822.

23 Schmidt's off-the-record talk with chief editors of German newspapers, October 31, 1978, *Privatarchiv Helmut Schmidt*, Hamburg, Germany, Eigene Arbeiten, 11.10.-15.11.1978, Nr. 11.

24 Speech by McNamara before the NAC, December 14, 1962, *Foreign Relations of the United States* (FRUS), 1961–1963, VIII, 442.

25 Francis J. Gavin, "Strategies of Inhibition: U.S. Grand Strategy, the Nuclear Revolution, and Nonproliferation," *International Security* 40, no. 2 (2015): 9–46, quote on 16; Keir A. Lieber and Daryl Press, "The End of MAD? The Nuclear Dimension of U.S. Primacy," *International Security* 30, no. 4 (2006): 7–44; Austin Long and Brendan Ritterhouse Green, "Stalking the Secure Second Strike: Intelligence,

Federal Republic of Germany 53

Counterforce, and Nuclear Strategy," *Journal of Strategic Studies* 38, nos. 1–2 (2015): 38–75.

26 Memo, "Gleichgewicht und Atommacht," sent by Schmückle to Knieper on October 19, 1962 on behalf of Strauss, BA-MA, BW 1/2377; see also Schelling's thesis of the "threat that leaves something to chance," Thomas C. Schelling, *The Strategy of Conflict*, Revised edition (Cambridge: Harvard University Press, 1990), 187–204.

27 See the internal high level talks on March 6, 1962, *Akten zur Auswärtigen Politik der Bundesrepublik Deutschland* [AAPD] *1962*, I, doc. 110.

28 Just a few examples: Foreign Office Instructions to Grewe, June 8, 1960, PA AA, B 130, Vol. 1987A; Strauss' remarks before the North Atlantic Council, Verbatim Record, December 17, 1960, NATO, IS-C-VR(60)51; MemCon Strauss–Rusk–Rostow, July 23, 1968, FRUS, 1964–1968, XI, 650; MemCon Kiesinger–Moro–Fanfani, February 2, 1968, AAPD 1968, I, doc. 49; MemCon Adenauer–de Gaulle, February 20, 1967, in *Adenauer. Die letzten Lebensjahre: 1963–1967. Briefe und Aufzeichnungen, Gespräche, Interviews und Reden. Vol. 2: September 1965–April 1967*, ed. Hans P. Mensing (Paderborn: Schoeningh, 2009), doc. 433.

29 MemCon Messmer–McNamara, December 1, 1961, *Documents Diplomatiques Français 1961*, II, 674; Michael Quinlan, *Thinking about Nuclear Weapons: Principles, Problems, Prospects* (New York: Oxford University Press, 2009), 34; McGeorge Bundy, *Danger and Survival: Choices about the Bomb in the First Fifty Years* (New York: Random House, 1988), 498.

30 Schwarz, "Adenauer und die Kernwaffen," 577.

31 Letter McGhee to Rusk, August 25, 1966, FRUS, 1964–1968, XV, 395; Memo Ball, October 27, 1965, *Lyndon B. Johnson Library*, Austin, TX, USA [LBJL], Papers of Lyndon B. Johnson President, National Security File [NSF], Agency File, Box 39, NATO-George W. Ball Analysis of a Collective Nuclear System; MemCon de Gaulle–Debré–Couve de Murville–Kiesinger–Brandt, September 27, 1968, AAPD 1968, II, doc. 314.

32 Memo, "Gleichgewicht und Atommacht," October 1962, BA-MA, BW 1/2377.

33 MemCon Barzel–Rostow, February 23, 1968, FRUS, 1964–1968, XV, 637.

34 Paul, *Power versus Prudence*, 148; Francis J. Gavin, "Same As It Ever Was: Nuclear Alarmism, Proliferation, and the Cold War," *International Security* 34, no. 3 (2009/2010): 7–37.

35 Memo Carstens, August 7, 1963, AAPD 1963 II, doc. 283.

36 Foreign Office circular decree, September 17, 1964, PA AA, B 43, Vol. 10.

37 Albert Wohlstetter, "Nuclear Sharing: NATO and the N+1 Country," *Foreign Affairs* 39, no. 3 (1961): 355–387.

38 Glenn T. Seaborg and Benjamin S. Loeb, *Stemming the Tide: Arms Control in the Johnson Years* (Lexington: Lexington Books, 1987).

39 John Mueller, *Atomic Obsession: Nuclear Alarmism from Hiroshima to Al-Qaeda* (Oxford: Oxford University Press, 2010), 91; Francis J. Gavin, "Politics, History and the Ivory Tower-Policy Gap in the Nuclear Proliferation Debate," *The Journal of Strategic Studies* 35, no. 4 (2012): 573–600, here 586; Gavin, "*Same As It Ever Was.*"

40 For example: telex Grewe, June 12, 1962, conv. Strauss–Kennedy, June 8, 1962, AAPD 1962, II, doc. 236; MemCon, Strauss–McNamara, May 3, 1962, NACP, RG 200, Records of Robert S. McNamara [MNR], Box 133, MemCons with Germany I–II, Vol. I, Sect. 1.

41 Norstad's conclusion before the NATO Council on October 17, 1962, telex from von Walther, October 18, 1962, AAPD 1962, III, 1741; Airgram Finletter, October 17, 1962, John F. Kennedy Presidential Library, Boston, US [JFKL], Papers of John F. Kennedy, Presidential Papers, National Security Files, Regional Security, Box 216A, MLF General 7/62–12/62; MemCon Norstad–Foertsch, November 22, 1962, Nuclear History Program archives [NHP], Bonn, doc. 113; Memo from von Walther, February 28, 1962, PA AA, B 150, Vol. 441; MemCon Strauss–McNamara,

54 *A. Lutsch*

December 15, 1961, NACP, RG 200, MNR, Box 133, MemCons with Germany I–II, Vol. I, Sect. 1.

42 See McNamara's remarks before the North Atlantic Council on December 14, 1961 for a central technical argument: US strategic nuclear forces outside Europe would more than suffice to cover targets in the Western Soviet Union, Summary Record of a meeting of the Council, NATO, IS-C-R(61)69-E. US political objections appeared to arise from proliferation concerns and because the US anticipated a deterioration of the East–West relationship: Memo von Hase, May 28, 1962, PA AA, B 150, Vol. 449.

43 Speech by President Kennedy in Ottawa, May 17, 1961, www.presidency.ucsb.edu/ws/?pid=8136 (accessed August 21, 2014).

44 Memo Sahm, June 18, 1962, PA AA, B 150, Vol. 451.

45 MemCon Strauss-Finletter, January 22, 1962, AAPD 1962, I, 196f.

46 See Adenauer's reference that the FRG's waiver of 1954 to produce nuclear weapons in Germany had to be understood as "rebus sic stantibus," MemCon Adenauer–Schröder–Rusk, June 22, 1962, FRUS, 1961–1963, XIII, 422; Adenauer–de Gaulle, July 4, 1962, DDF 1962, II, doc. 4, IV, 30; Adenauer–de Gaulle, January 21, 1963, AAPD 1963, I, 113; see also Schröder's remarks to SACEUR Norstad on July 12, 1962, AAPD 1962, II, 1261.

47 On this concept, see Levite, "Never Say Never Again," 69.

48 MemCon Rusk–Earl of Home, June 25, 1962, TNA, Ministry of Defense and Admiralty [DEFE] 11/223; McNamara–Thorneycroft discussions September 10–13, 1962, NACP, RG 200, MNR, Box 133, MemCons UK 1–22.

49 Couve de Murville to Rusk on June 20, 1962, MemCon, FRUS, 1961–1963, XIII, 417.

50 MemCon, Rusk–Strauss, June 9, 1962, FRUS, 1961–1963, XIII, doc. 140, 405.

51 Statement by Schröder before the NAC on December 14, 1961, Summary Record of a meeting of the Council, NATO, IS-C-R(61)67-E.

52 Memo Schmoller, January 4, 1963, AAPD 1963, I, 16ff.; Memo Foster, November 21, 1962, NACP, RG 59, DF-LF, Office of Politico-Military Affairs, Records Relating to Disarmament and Arms Control, 1961–1966, Box 9, DEF-DEFENSE AFFAIRS (14) 1961–1962/DEF-18–10 NONPROLIFERATION; Soviet draft of a nonproliferation agreement of March 15, 1962, *Documents on Disarmament 1962*, I, 113.

53 Letter Adenauer to Schröder, May 11, 1962, AAPD 1962, II, 918.

54 Telex Werz, September 3, 1962, AAPD 1962, III, 1491f.

55 See Rusks insinuation on the basis of unspecified "evidence," in MemCon Rusk-Earl of Home, June 25, 1962, TNA, DEFE 11/223.

56 Memo Balken, April 12, 1962, PA AA, B 150, Vol. 446.

57 See Schröder's thesis, MemCon Kennedy–Rusk–Adenauer–Strauß–Schröder, December 22, 1961, FRUS, 1961–1963, XIV, 626.

58 Letter Mertes to zu Guttenberg, August 2, 1965, *Bayerisches Hauptstaatsarchiv*, Bamberg, Germany [StA Bam.], Personal Papers Guttenberg [NLG], Vol. 50.

59 Scott D. Sagan, "Nuclear Latency and Nuclear Proliferation," in *Forecasting Nuclear Proliferation in the 21st Century. Volume I: The Role of Theory*, eds. Willam C. Potter and Gaukhar Mukhatzhanova (Stanford, CA: Stanford University Press, 2010), 80–101.

60 See Carstens' remarks to George Ball on November 16, 1964, AAPD 1964, II, 1332.

61 Letter Mertes to zu Guttenberg, July 26, 1965, StA Bam., NLG, Vol. 50.

62 Telex Werz, September 3, 1962, AAPD 1962, III, 1492.

63 Memo Lahn, October 6, 1962, PA AA, B 150, Vol. 460.

64 For the broader context of US nonproliferation concerns, see Francis J. Gavin, "The Gold Battles within the Cold War: American Monetary Policy and the Defense of Europe, 1960–1963," *Diplomatic History* 26, no. 1 (2002): 61–94.

65 Letter Bundy to Philip de Zulueta, May 10, 1963, FRUS, 1961–1963, XIII, 573.

Federal Republic of Germany 55

66 Letter Kennedy to Macmillan, May 29, 1963, TNA, Records of the Cabinet Office [CAB] 21/6044.

67 See Adenauer's remarks before the CDU/CSU parliamentary fraction on February 5, 1963, in *Die CDU/CSU-Fraktion im Deutschen Bundestag, 1961–1966*, I, 554.

68 MemCon, McNamara–Thorneycroft, December 14, 1963, NACP, RG 200, MNR, Box 133, MemCons UK 1–22.

69 Letter Adenauer to Kennedy, April 5, 1963, FRUS, 1961–1963, XIII, doc. 187.

70 Trachtenberg, *A Constructed Peace*, 352.

71 NSAM 322, December 18, 1964, FRUS, 1964–1968, XIII, doc. 65.

72 Memo McCloy, January 8, 1965, LBJL, NSF, Committee File, Committee on Nuclear Proliferation, Box 6, McCloy Memorandum, 1/8/65.

73 MemCon Schröder–Rusk, November 26, 1964, AAPD 1964, II, 1401.

74 Francis J. Gavin, "Blasts from the Past: Proliferation Lessons from the 1960s," *International Security* 29, no. 3 (2004/2005): 100–135; Hal Brands, "Rethinking Nonproliferation: LBJ, the Gilpatric Committee, and U.S. National Security Policy," *Journal of Cold War Studies* 8, no. 2 (2006): 83–113.

75 See the British NPT draft of June 1965, TNA, Foreign Office 371/181388; Memo Oncken, January 21, 1965, PA AA, B 150, Vol. 55.

76 Summary Record of a meeting of the Council, May 31, 1965, NATO, IS-C-R(65)26-E.

77 Memo Ref. II7, June 4, 1965, AAPD 1965, II, doc. 23; telex Sahm to AA, May 31, 1965, PA AA, B 150, Vol. 53.

78 Nevertheless, the German government was eager to participate in the "Select Committee." See MemCon McNamara–Erhard, June 4, 1965, LBJL, NSF, Country File, Box 185, Germany, Memos Vol. VIII, 4/65–7/65.

79 William C. Foster, "New Directions in Arms Control and Disarmament," *Foreign Affairs* 43, no. 4 (1965): 587–601, quote on 600.

80 Memo Krapf, July 9, 1965, PA AA, B 150, Vol. 56; Horst Osterheld, *Außenpolitik unter Bundeskanzler Ludwig Erhard 1963–1966. Ein dokumentarischer Bericht aus dem Kanzleramt* (Düsseldorf: Droste 1992), 214.

81 Interview with Schröder, *Düsseldorfer Nachrichten*, July 2, 1965.

82 Joachim Besser, "Schröder droht," *Kölner Stadt-Anzeiger*, July 13, 1965.

83 Telex Hillenbrand, July 26, 1965, LBJL, NSF, Country File, Box 186, Germany, Cables Vol. IX, 7/65–1/66.

84 MemCon Erhard–Harriman, July 24, 1965, AAPD 1965, II, 1249f.

85 Telex Knappstein, July 30, 1965, ibid., 1304; Memo Kaufmann, September 16, 1965, LBJL, NLJ-050–002–7-24–4.

86 Instructions for Grewe, July 24, 1965, AAPD 1965 II, 1258; Summary Record of a Meeting of the Council, July 26, 1965, NATO, IS-C-R(65)34-E.

87 Rusk was quoted in a telex by Knappstein of July 9, 1965: "There will be no non-proliferation treaty without MLF," AAPD 1965 II, 1157.

88 Telex Schnippenkötter, August 12, 1965, ibid., 1347.

89 Declaration of the Federal German Government, August 17, 1965, *Bulletin des Presse- und Informationsamtes der Bundesregierung 1965*, no. 140, 1129.

90 Osterheld, *Außenpolitik unter Bundeskanzler Ludwig Erhard*, 214. Literally translated: "Gagging Treaty."

91 MemCon Schröder-McGhee, September 13, 1965, AAPD 1965, III, 1434.

92 Article II, 1 Draft Treaty, August 17, 1965, *Documents on Disarmament 1965*, 348; see the memoranda from Theißinger, August 19, 24 and 27, 1965, BA, B 136/ 6899.

93 Letter Finletter to Rusk on July 12, 1965, FRUS, 1964–1968, XIII, 232.

94 "Adenauer: Abrüstungskonferenz eine Tragödie," *Frankfurter Rundschau*, August 20, 1965.

95 Franz J. Strauss, "Das Genfer Schelmen-Spiel," *Rheinischer Merkur*, August 27, 1965.

56   *A. Lutsch*

96   Soviet Draft Treaty, September 24, 1965, *Documents on Disarmament 1965*, 443ff.
97   See the German proposal for a "Common Nuclear Force (CNF)," undated Memo, "The Nuclear Question," LBJL, Papers of Francis M. Bator, Subject File, Box 30, Non-Prolif. August 3, 1965–July 29, 1966.
98   Memo Ball, October 27, 1965, LBJL, NSF, Agency File, Box 39, NATO-George W. Ball Analysis of a Collective Nuclear System.
99   Memo Bator, December 9, 1965, LBJL, NSF, Country File, Box 186, Germany, Cables Vol. IX, 7/65–1/66.
100   Erhard's report to the cabinet on December 22, 1965, Kab.Prot. 1965, 458.
101   Letter Johnson to Wilson, December 23, 1965, FRUS, 1964–1968, XIII, 296.
102   Telex Sir Frank Roberts, October 8, 1965, to the Foreign Office, TNA, DEFE 25/59.
103   Memo from Ball, October 27, 1965, LBJL, NSF, Agency File, Box 39, NATO-George W. Ball Analysis of a Collective Nuclear System.
104   Memo Rusk, April 11, 1966, FRUS, 1964–1968, XIII, 364; David J. Gill, *Britain and the Bomb: Nuclear Diplomacy, 1964–1970* (Stanford, CA: Stanford University Press, 2014), 76–140.
105   Memo Ruete, February 25, 1966, AAPD 1966, I, 211.
106   Memo Bator, April 4, 1966, LBJL, NSF, Country File, Box 186, Germany, Memos Vol. X, 1/66–8/66.
107   Memo Ruete, February 25, 1966, AAPD 1966, I, 216; conv. von Hassel-Lord Chalfont, military diary von Hassel, March 8, 1966, *Archiv für Christlich-Demokratische Politik*, St. Augustin, Germany [ACDP], I-157–227/1.
108   Heinrich Krone, *Tagebücher. Vol. 2: 1961–1966* (Düsseldorf: Droste, 2003), 455.
109   Letter Kolb to Stamp, January 31, 1966, BA, B 136/ 6899.
110   Note by the Federal German government, March 25, 1966, *Europa-Archiv 1966*, D174; Memo Wickert, May 24, 1966, PA AA, B 43, Vol. 82; all non-nuclear states within NATO and the Warsaw Pact should declare not to produce atomic weapons. The four atomic powers of both alliances should declare not to transfer nuclear weapons into the national control of non-nuclear states. As in the West German case, the waivers of individual states should be valid legally only vis-à-vis this state's respective allies. The German scheme for a regional nonproliferation regime would be "effective" because it would block the only possible paths toward the spread of national nuclear capabilities, if all NATO and Warsaw Pact states adhered to it. Compared to the NPT approach, it would be "non-discriminatory" because individual waivers would be declared "voluntarily" and because they would be legally valid only within the respective military alliance.
111   Government declaration by Erhard, March 25, 1966, *Verhandlungen des Deutschen Bundestages. Stenographische Berichte*, Vol. 61, 1608. Geier, *Schwellenmacht*, 388 shows a normative bias by describing the initiative simply as "stuporous."
112   Memo Lahusen, May 24, 1966, PA AA, B 43, Vol. 82.
113   Circular letter Ruete, April 1, 1966, ibid.
114   Memo Ruete, October 21, 1966, AAPD 1966, II, doc. 346.
115   Memo Schnippenkötter, November 8, 1966, ibid., doc. 363.
116   Memo Wickert, May 25, 1966, PA AA, B 43, Vol. 82.
117   Memo Foster, September 15, 1966, LBJL, NSF, National Security Council Histories, Box 55, The Non-Proliferation Treaty, Vol. II [61–80].
118   Rusk's remark according to Memo Ruete, August 8, 1966, AAPD 1966, II, 1043f.
119   Memo Carstens, September 24, 1966, BA, Personal Papers Carstens [1337]/629.
120   Memo Rostow, October 10, 1966, FRUS, 1964–1968, XV, 439.
121   Telex Knappstein, December 7, 1966, PA AA, B 150, Vol. 89.
122   Memo Schnippenkötter, December 1, 1966, AAPD 1966 II, 1570.
123   Memo Schütz, December 17, 1966, PA AA, B 150, Vol. 90.
124   MemCon Johnson-Schröder, July 25, 1968, LBJL, NSF, Country File, Box 189 (1 v. 2), Germany, Memos Vol. XV, 3/68–8/68.

Federal Republic of Germany 57

125 Hoeres, *Außenpolitik und Öffentlichkeit*, 279–344; Gray, "Abstinence and Ostpolitik."
126 See also Carl Ungerer, "Influence without Power: Middle Powers and Arms Control Diplomacy during the Cold War," *Diplomacy and Statecraft* 18, no. 2 (2007): 393–414; in contrast, Geier, *Schwellenmacht*, 216, claims that the US and the FRG secretly negotiated on the NPT "at eye level."
127 Brandt, "Sperrvertrag und Gleichberechtigung," *Sozialdemokratischer Pressedienst*, January 31, 1969.
128 Memo Schnippenkötter, July 21, 1968, PA AA, B 1, Vol. 378; Memo Keeny, December 24, 1968, LBJL, NSF, National Security Council Histories, Box 55, The Non-Proliferation Treaty Vol. I [1–3].
129 Ibid.
130 Memo Blomeyer–Bartenstein, May 16, 1968, PA AA, B 80, Vol. 806.
131 Telex Knappstein, January 13, 1967, PA AA, B 150, Vol. 94; Ralph L. Dietl, "European Nuclear Decision Making? The United States, Nuclear Non Proliferation and the 'European Option,' 1967–1972," *Historische Mitteilungen der Ranke-Gesellschaft* 24 (2011): 43–89.
132 This was McNamara's thesis. See MemCon McNamara–Walker, February 20, 1964, NACP, RG 200, MNR, Box 133, MemCons UK 1–22.
133 Memo Ball, October 27, 1965, LBJL, NSF, Agency File, Box 39, NATO-George W. Ball Analysis of a Collective Nuclear System.
134 Handwritten note Barzel, February 10, 1969, BA, Personal Papers Barzel [1371]/ 81.
135 Telex Cleveland, January 29, 1967, NACP, RG 59, CF-SN 1967–1969, Box 1728, DEF 18–6 (1/1/67).
136 Memo Hillenbrand, May 8, 1969, Gerald R. Ford Library, Ann Arbor, MI, US, Melvin R. Laird Papers, C13, NATO, 1969–1973-Documents 25–26.
137 Telex McGhee, October 21, 1966, on Erhard–McCloy talks, LBJL, NSF, National Security Council Histories, Box 50, Trilateral Negotiations and NATO: Book 1, Tabs 26–44; MemCon, FRUS, 1964–1968, XV, doc. 174.
138 Cabinet meeting, October 14, 1966, Kab.Prot. 1966, 425–431.
139 This German disposition crystallized particularly in the NPG proceedings since 1967. The summit meeting of Guadeloupe in January 1979 may be regarded as an apex with regards to Bonn's willingness to increase its influence in nuclear matters.
140 Gavin, "Blasts from the Past," 135; see also Gavin, "Strategies of Inhibition," 25ff.

4 The birth of a nuclear non-proliferation policy

The Netherlands and the NPT negotiations, 1965–1966

Elmar Hellendoorn[1]

This chapter sets out to shed light on the "birth" of Dutch nuclear nonprolifera-tion policy under *Staatssecretaris* (Undersecretary of State) Max van der Stoel (1965–1966). The chapter argues that van der Stoel's relatively brief tenure represented a decisive phase for Dutch nuclear diplomacy. Van der Stoel seized the negotiations on the Treaty on the Non-Proliferation of Nuclear Weapons (NPT) as an opportunity to assert his strong Atlanticist preferences by using idealist arguments. He firmly rejected the traditional Dutch foreign policy effort which sought to maintain an implicit European nuclear option to hedge against an eventual Euro-American split. His singular orientation on the United States meant a departure from the traditional Dutch line. While van der Stoel's Atlanti-cism was largely motivated by regional politico-strategic concerns, he sought to present it as global idealism.

Within the Ministry of Foreign Affairs (MFA) he used the arguments of inter-nationalism to exacerbate already existing tensions. He co-opted the "up and coming" progressive forces of *Directie Internationale Organisaties* (Directorate International Organizations, DIO) to overcome the entrenched position of the more conservative *Directie NAVO en WEU Zaken* (Directorate NATO and WEU Affairs, DNW) which formed the traditional core of the Dutch foreign security policy establishment. Van der Stoel's arrival at the MFA resulted in the intensifi-cation of an already ongoing bureaucratic struggle between DNW's strategists and DIO's internationalists. The main bone of contention was that the MFA's security policy establishment did not want to altogether discard the European nuclear option, as a hedge against an American departure from Europe in the future. This shows that Dutch "Atlanticism" was perhaps less deep-rooted than generally assumed. Van der Stoel, however, rejected this European option both as an obstacle to a nonproliferation agreement and as a potential wedge within the Alliance.

This contribution seeks to deepen our general understanding of Dutch nuclear nonproliferation policy by tracing these internal discussions which pre-sented a clash between two strains of thought about the dynamics and relevance of nuclear nonproliferation. The rhetoric of nuclear nonproliferation policy is often presented with strong idealistic overtones, potentially hiding politico-strategic motives. But what is actual internationalist idealism and where lie the

The Netherlands 59

politico-strategic interests? Where do the two overlap, where do they clash, and to what extent can they mutually coexist? To what extent did, and still do, internationalist approaches, often expressed in legal and multilateral terms, serve strategic objectives? Or, perhaps less commonly, to what extent are the instruments of security policy serving internationalist goals? And how often have instruments and methods become ends in themselves?

The negotiations over a nonproliferation agreement were intertwined with discussions within the North Atlantic Treaty Organization (NATO) about the establishment of a Multilateral Force (MLF). The Soviet Union had rejected nonproliferation negotiations with the United States as long as the latter considered transferring additional control over nuclear weapons to its NATO allies. Early 1965, as US enthusiasm for the MLF began to wither and in the wake of the PRC's October 1964 nuclear test, US–Soviet nonproliferation discussions were renewed.[2] The stage was set after the introduction of a US-inspired Irish resolution in the Eighteen-Nation Committee on Disarmament (ENDC) in late January 1965.[3] Under van der Stoel's aegis, the Netherlands attempted to limit the scope for multilateral nuclear sharing arrangements within NATO. This policy served two objectives: First, it was intended to prevent the development of a European nuclear force. Second, it aimed to underwrite US–Soviet nonproliferation negotiations which threatened to become deadlocked because of Soviet objections to the MLF.

It might well be asked whether van der Stoel's mix of pro-US Atlanticist "realism" and his rhetoric of internationalist "idealism," both inspired by his faith in the power of international institutions, can be considered as truly "strategic." Van der Stoel's most ardent adversaries, clustered around the security policy establishment within the MFA, took a more sceptical view: they had less faith in international law and the US role in the Atlantic alliance: it was better to keep all options open, especially the European nuclear option. This had actually been the essence of Dutch foreign policy up until that moment.

Unfortunately, very little has been written on the history of Dutch political and strategic considerations pertaining to nuclear policy, and the existing literature has no solid empirical basis due to restricted access to most of the relevant archives.[4] It is usually assumed that The Hague was a most faithful ally of Washington. Dutch fears of Franco-German dominance of the continent would have created the need for a strong tie to the United States. This account contests this thesis. Key policy-makers in The Hague never fully trusted Washington. Dutch passivity in European politics had served the implicit objective to keep Dutch options, nuclear and non-nuclear, open.

Politico-strategic requirements dominate policy-making

Up until 1965, Dutch diplomacy with regards to NATO's nuclear policy and European order had been dominated by politico-strategic reasoning. During the NATO "atomic stockpile" debate of 1956–1958, which evolved around the question of equipping European NATO forces with US tactical nuclear weapons, the

60   E. Hellendoorn

Netherlands had proposed joint nuclear planning and allied pre-delegation to NATO's Supreme Allied Commander Europe (SACEUR). This was seen as way to build stronger Euro-American ties.[5] In 1960–1961, the Dutch again went to great lengths to support Lauris Norstad, the US general serving as SACEUR, in his proposal for a NATO nuclear force – what would later become the MLF.[6] To the Dutch, further Atlantic strategic integration could offset the Franco-German axis.[7] Subsequently however, The Hague tempered its enthusiasm for nuclear sharing. The Netherlands did participate in the MLF working group of 1963–1964, but it remained uncommitted. The MLF plan was perceived as a worthless military-strategic vehicle, while it seemed to strengthen the German politico-diplomatic position in Europe.[8]

Matters affecting NATO's nuclear policy had been the *pré carré* (private preserve) of the DNW within the Ministry of Foreign Affairs' *Directoraat Generaal Politieke Zaken* (Directorate General Political Affairs, DGPZ), led by Jan de Ranitz. Joseph Luns, the Minister of Foreign Affairs, had traditionally given great leeway to his officials at DNW.[9] From the 1950s onwards, DNW had consistently favored Atlantic integration and supported European integration mainly as step towards the higher Atlanticist objective. DNW's thinking on Allied nuclear policy was largely determined by this political motive and by military-strategic reasoning. While the Cabinet was usually being informed about nuclear policy, DNW had never received much political guidance from Joseph Luns. Dutch nuclear policy was largely independent from domestic politics and determined by a small, influential group officials with access to classified nuclear information. In broad lines, this had been the situation until 1964–1965, when things started changing dramatically.

A shifting bureaucratic balance of power

As international negotiations on a draft NPT advanced throughout the mid-1960s, the Dutch approach changed dramatically. More idealistic tones began to influence Dutch nuclear diplomacy. Increasingly, domestic politics began to interfere with DNW's relative monopoly on strategic nuclear policy. As Euro-Atlantic strategy had to be reconciled with internationalist idealism, Dutch policies became less straightforward. These fundamental disagreements foreshadowed the fact that it would ultimately prove to be a complicated matter to reconcile such opposite perspectives on nuclear weapons into a single foreign policy.

While DNW was responsible for nuclear affairs within NATO, another directorate, DIO, within the *Directoraat Generaal voor Internationale Samenwerking* (Directorate General for International Cooperation, DGIS), held responsibility for multilateral disarmament issues at the United Nations. The DGIS director-general, Jan Meijer, who was a member of the Dutch Labor Party, was considered to be "an apt schemer and empire builder," and was sometimes nicknamed "Rasputin."[10] Over time, Meijer was increasingly given more leeway by Foreign Minister Luns. While Luns was a conservative member of the

The Netherlands 61

Catholic party, Meijer's bureaucratic elevation was probably an implicit concession to the Labor Party. Consequently, some considered Meijer "a natural opponent" of Jan de Ranitz at the DGPZ.[11] In stark contrast to DNW's officials, Jan Meijer's right hand at DIO's political and disarmament desk, Frans Terwisscha van Scheltinga, maintained a warm relationship with Pax Christi, a Catholic pressure group strongly in favor of nuclear disarmament.[12]

In the summer of 1965, DGIS' and DIO's position was further strengthened by the appointment of the Social Democrat Max van der Stoel as *Staatssecretaris* (Undersecretary of State) for United Nations (UN) affairs. As a consequence of a decision taken during the government's formation, Foreign Minister Luns tended to give van der Stoel great room for maneuver on disarmament policy.[13] Van der Stoel attached great importance to nonproliferation. In contrast, Luns had never shown much interest in the nonproliferation discussion.[14] Moreover, from 1960 onwards, van der Stoel had played a key role in the Labor Party's rejection of a European nuclear option, and subsequently expressed himself as an opponent of the MLF. He feared Franco-German political dominance and argued in favor of basing Western defense upon the US nuclear deterrent.[15]

DIO's scope differed from DNW: it was tasked to deal with global, multilateral fora and accordingly embraced idealistic objectives. DIO had played a key role in the drafting of the so-called *Ontwapeningsnota* (Disarmament White Paper) of 1964.[16] This public note outlined the official Dutch disarmament policy; it emphasized confidence building measures, verifiable arms control agreements, and the ultimate aim of general and complete disarmament. In the long run, the White Paper argued, balance of power politics should be replaced by peace-keeping arrangements within the framework of the UN. Consequently, small powers, like the Netherlands, also carried a responsibility to develop initiatives towards these ends.[17]

DIO's internationalists were thus bound to clash with DNW's security minded "Atlanticists," whom they privately considered a bunch of "Neanderthals."[18] The idealism of DIO brought about a more fundamental shift in Dutch nuclear policy. DNW's relative monopoly on strategic nuclear issues had guaranteed an instrumental approach to nuclear weapons. Within this mindset, nuclear weapons were a means to deter the Soviet Union. Nuclear sharing was thought to help greater Atlantic unity. In contrast, for DIO's internationalists nuclear nonproliferation, arms control, and disarmament were political ends for themselves. Moreover, idealist arguments could prove very useful in bureaucratic politics. This would later be the case when DIO's global agenda overlapped with DNW Atlantic agenda, as was the case during the NPT negotiations.

Struggling over the ANF non-proliferation clause

This conflict within the MFA had a major effect on the Dutch position on the MLF and the Atlantic Nuclear Force (ANF) discussions that were still simmering during 1965 and 1966. In 1964, Britain had advanced the ANF as an alternative to the Johnson administration's MLF proposal. In contrast to the MLF

62   E. Hellendoorn

proposal, ANF's nuclear sharing element was more limited and was aimed at opening the possibility for a disarmament treaty with the Soviet Union.[19] In June 1965, during the internal preparations for a discussion in the NATO Council on the British ANF proposal, DIO tried to impress its views on nuclear sharing and nonproliferation on the instruction to the Dutch NATO representatives. DNW officials, however, considered it "less desirable" to include a clause on non-dissemination in a potential ANF Treaty and instructed the Dutch NATO mission accordingly. DIO showed itself strongly opposed to DNW's initial guideline. The political bureau of DIO argued that the non-dissemination clause was one of the pillars of the British proposal, which was supported by the US stance, that "the treaty establishing the new arrangements should include undertakings whereby non-nuclear members would undertake not to acquire or obtain control over [nuclear weapons]."[20]

Continuing its case against the DNW's draft instructions, DIO insisted that Dutch policy should toe the official Anglo-American line. DIO believed that the adoption of such a clause in the ANF would bolster the ongoing negotiations on a nonproliferation agreement. DIO tried to reinforce its argument by adding a third point. Referring to the (informal) remarks of several senior US policy-makers, DIO was concerned that there were "active influences on American thinking which want to leave a margin for the eventual development of a European nuclear force, either coordinated or uncoordinated with the US nuclear force."[21] The DNW director was angered by the DIO memorandum, calling on the assistance of his counterpart at DIO "to assure that the tone of the correspondence between our Directorates remains business-like." In his view, MLF and ANF were already designed in such a way that they would prevent nuclear proliferation, making the addition of a nonproliferation clause "de facto redundant." He reasoned that improving NATO's nuclear arrangements and strengthening the Alliance's political cohesion would take away the main incentive for proliferation in Western Europe. While DIO seemed to put its faith in a legal solution to prevent nuclear proliferation, DNW perceived proliferation as the outcome of politico-strategic dynamics, which could not be simply altered by the adoption of some legal clause or an international treaty.

This discussion not only highlighted a different understanding of proliferation within the Dutch foreign policy establishment, it also revealed that DNW, notwithstanding its reputation of staunch Atlanticism, would not sheepishly follow the Anglo-American line. DIO's argument that the British nonproliferation clause in the ANF ("one of the pillars of the proposal") was backed up by the Americans did not persuade the DNW director. To the contrary: he called the recent "Irish resolution" on nonproliferation "effectively an American product." And, "although our government opposes nuclear proliferation, this does not entail that [the Netherlands] should copy American policy, especially on the point of non-acquisition."[22] Moreover, he was angered that, although the United States had promised to do so, there had been "no timely consultations within NATO about the Irish resolution."[23] The Irish resolution itself had already led to a vehement discussion between Terwisscha and NATO Ambassador Hans Boon in January 1965. The former embraced the idea of a non-acquisition declaration, hoping "for a positive snowball effect," while the latter rejected it, fearing to undermine the Western position.[24]

In fact, this MFA-internal discussion seems to suggest that DNW wanted to keep open a European nuclear option. Contrary to the MLF this would have been a force independent of American co-control. DNW argued that the inclusion of a non-dissemination clause would not render impossible the creation of a European nuclear force grouped around the European nuclear weapon states. In its memorandum, DIO also emphasized that a future MLF or ANF Treaty should contain an explicit clause on the maintenance of a US veto over a multilateral force. According to DIO, this would prevent the United States from untying itself from Europe's defense. However, DNW opposed writing an actual veto into a treaty. This was unnecessary, because "the idea that the US might withdraw [from Europe], while transferring control over their nuclear weapons, is diametrically opposed to previous American policy statements and cannot be considered as an obstacle [to a MLF or ANF Treaty]."[25]

DNW's dismissal of the idea that the US might withdraw from Europe was not entirely convincing. In fact, the top level of the Dutch foreign security policy establishment, doubted the wisdom of closing-off strategic options. It is illustrative that the Dutch NATO representative, Boon, was *privately* not altogether opposed to the idea of keeping European options open, "since you never know what might happen in the future."[26] This, it should be emphasized, was far from endorsing the idea of a European nuclear force – it was customary to denounce such ideas. Both DNW and its supra-organization, the DGPZ, were highly ambiguous about a nonproliferation clause, especially if it was geographically limited to Europe.[27] Simply put, DGPZ de Ranitz, like Boon, wanted to keep the European nuclear option open.

This dispute was resolved through a compromise. In early July 1965, Boon was finally instructed that the MLF-ANF Treaty should *not* contain a specific non-dissemination clause, while its participants should at the same time declare themselves in favor of a future NPT. Furthermore, according to the Dutch instructions, the eventual multilateral nuclear force should be designed to prevent nuclear proliferation in the form of national nuclear forces and therefore include a US veto, permissive action links, and safeguards against sharing technical nuclear information such as blueprints. Moreover, a future ANF should not be regarded as a step towards a European nuclear force.[28]

Separately, Boon was also instructed to discuss nonproliferation negotiations in the NATO Council. After an apparent compromise between DNW and DIO, it was agreed that nuclear proliferation should be understood as a global issue, and not just as "an aspect of East-West relations." The instruction reflected many points outlined in the 1964 disarmament note mentioned above. It suggested that the position of neutral and non-aligned countries had to be taken into account. Many of the demands of these countries were dear to DIO's internationalists. Thus, the instructions included demands for a nuclear guarantee for non-nuclear states, disarmament, and "renunciatory action," such as a Comprehensive

64 *E. Hellendoorn*

Nuclear Test Ban Treaty (CTBT), a Fissile Material Cut-Off Treaty (FMCT), nuclear disarmament, and an expansion of IAEA safeguards to all non-military nuclear facilities.

However, although the Netherlands should support these demands in principle, the DNW–DIO compromise entailed that the nonproliferation negotiations should "not be burdened" with these complicated issues. With regards to the MLF-ANF controversy, Boon was instructed to "be aware" that difficulties might be created by Russian opposition to NATO's plans. Simply put, Boon was left to his own devices and he could act upon his own authority, and freely "discuss the matter in the NATO Council."[29] DNW had accepted some of DIO's rhetoric, while blocking DIO from actually setting the agenda.

Slowly converging positions in Washington and The Hague

Once the final compromise on instructions for Boon had been reached, DIO immediately began to advocate a change of the overall policy. DIO now argued that the successful conclusion of a nonproliferation agreement should be considered a *precondition* to the establishment of a multilateral nuclear force. This approach would have rendered a non-dissemination clause within an agreement on multilateral nuclear forces expendable. For DIO, only this sequence could secure a global NPT agreement.

In contrast, DNW cast doubt on the principal willingness of the USSR to sign a nonproliferation agreement in case the MLF/ANF plans were postponed. To the contrary, DNW saw "more reason to assume that the USSR would agree to such a treaty once the ANF was established."[30] Therefore, DNW strongly opposed DIO's proposition. "The alternative DIO-story [...] is not usable. [...] DIO's conclusion that a nonproliferation agreement should be established before the MLF/ANF is *unacceptable*."[31] The most plausible explanation for this dispute between DIO and DNW seems to be found in bureaucratic politics. By arguing to give nonproliferation initiatives precedence over NATO's nuclear affairs, DIO was attempting to establish an internationalist framework for the Dutch Atlanticist (strategic) nuclear security policy. A success of this strategy would have provided DIO with a significant gain in authority over DNW, an important tactical victory within the bureaucratic infighting.

Reports arriving in The Hague from Washington indicated that the DNW–DIO debate was similar to disagreements within the US administration. On the one hand, the US State Department was formulating NATO policy. On the other hand, the Arms Control and Disarmament Agency (ACDA) was in charge of US nonproliferation initiatives. When Carl Schurmann, the Dutch Ambassador to Washington, met State Department official Robert Schaetzel in July 1965 to discuss MLF and nonproliferation issues, the differences within the US government were evident. In a recent article, the ACDA Director William Foster had suggested to abandon the MLF-idea in order to facilitate the nonproliferation negotiations with the USSR.[32] In his conversation with Schurmann, Schaetzel called Foster's article "second rate rehash." The ACDA "school of non-proliferators" wanted "to achieve a treaty at any price." Those people "consider the illusion of progress as important as progress itself," Schaetzel concluded. He argued that one of the very few realistic approaches to nonproliferation would be lost by disbanding the MLF-concept. He considered the MLF non-negotiable, and made it clear that the State Department did not see the MLF as bringing about additional proliferation.[33]

By August 1965 the Dutch learned that the United States and the Soviet Union might move out of the existing stalemate at the ENDC, the official venue for the negotiations on nonproliferation.[34] Subsequently, Richard Freund, ACDA's Deputy Assistant Director, met with DIO's Terwisscha van Scheltinga to discuss the ENDC. Freund argued it was likely that the Soviets would try to achieve a NPT even if a nuclear arrangement within NATO was agreed upon.[35] However, he admitted that such a "nuclear arrangement" would have to be something other than a multilateral force: the Russians had "implied" that a NATO select committee on nuclear planning (i.e., something other than a hardware sharing option) was compatible with a non-proliferation agreement.[36] This potential progress on the negotiations forced the Dutch to reach internal agreement on a common position.

Van der Stoel takes charge

In late July 1965, van der Stoel became Undersecretary of State for UN affairs. Previously, he had been the international secretary of the Labor Party, and after being a Labor member of parliament (1967–1973) went on to become minister of Foreign Affairs from 1973–1977 and again in 1981–1982. Van der Stoel was certainly no pacifist dreamer. Ultimately, he would be considered as a "realistic idealist," and as a strong-minded Atlanticist.[37] Yet in the mid-1960s, before assuming office, van der Stoel, and with him the entire Dutch Labor Party, had become a declared opponent of the MLF. He perceived the MLF as a step towards a European nuclear force, a development which could lead to a Euro-American split. Nonproliferation, on the other hand, was a core element of Labor's "active peace policy" or "socialist international policy." Van der Stoel considered nonproliferation a key step towards mutual East–West disarmament, which might, in the long run, lead to world peace and the creation of an international legal order.[38]

As the international negotiations on a nonproliferation treaty began to gain traction, van der Stoel was fully aware that the Dutch government could no longer entertain such disparate internal positions. The DNW–DIO stalemate within the MFA had to be resolved in order for the Dutch to be able to effectively influence the course of the nonproliferation negotiations. Therefore, van der Stoel requested both directorates to draft memoranda on the extent to which a regional nonproliferation agreement – such as an ANF clause – would limit the chances for a global nonproliferation treaty.[39]

This exercise proved to be a reiteration of earlier discussions. DIO argued once again in favor of a nonproliferation clause within a potential multilateral

66 E. Hellendoorn

force treaty. In contrast, DNW claimed that Western Europe should not indefinitely deny itself the right to nuclear weapons given that it might become threatened by new nuclear weapons states in the future. The proliferation problem had to be addressed by improving the overall security situation of those states which might develop nuclear weapons. Most important, DNW argued, the Netherlands should be careful not to adopt an exposed position within the MLF–ANF discussions. For the DNW officials, the Dutch aims could be best achieved by not explicitly expressing a position on the nonproliferation clause.[40] By according equal weight to DIO's and DNW's opinion, van der Stoel had elevated the internationalists, diminishing the relative weight of DNW.

Independent of this bureaucratic debate, van der Stoel entertained his own views on these issues – views that proved decisive in shaping the Dutch position. On the one hand, he was highly skeptical about the multilateral force idea as he worried that any European nuclear force would bring about a Euro-American "decoupling" in security affairs. For van der Stoel, the main Dutch interest in a MLF–ANF agreement would be the establishment of "stronger mutual bonds between America [sic] and Europe." Therefore, he strongly favored a nonproliferation clause in an eventual MLF–ANF treaty. He argued any such treaty would have to prevent the abandonment of the US veto. Such a step would forestall the potential transfer of the nuclear capabilities from a NATO nuclear force to a European regional organization within the alliance, which would exclude the United States.[41]

On the other hand, van der Stoel felt that a credible nuclear arrangement within NATO was required in order to prevent future West German nuclear demands. He believed that a software solution might serve this purpose. Such a software solution would give participating NATO member states a certain degree of influence upon Allied nuclear strategy, but would grant them no direct control over the strategy's execution. This alternative notion of Allied nuclear sharing would also serve as an escape route in case the anti-MLF opposition within NATO blocked any progress on a hardware solution. In addition, van der Stoel seemed to believe that the US was currently developing similar ideas.[42]

Moving onto the international stage

As soon as van der Stoel established his authority over the nonproliferation and MLF–ANF discussions, he started presenting the Dutch government's positions internationally. For instance, van der Stoel repeatedly met the British Secretary for Disarmament Affairs, Lord Chalfont, who was to ultimately become his regular sparring partner – if not an ally – on nuclear issues. The British preference for the inclusion of a strong nonproliferation clause in a MLF or ANF treaty had always been close to that of DIO and van der Stoel. Thus, when van der Stoel and Chalfont first met on October 21, 1965, they agreed that the MLF still seemed to be "the hardest nut to crack." This might be achieved by establishing crisis management and contingency planning mechanisms within NATO.[43]

The Netherlands 67

In subsequent talks with the US State Department, Robert Schaetzel tried to persuade van der Stoel. When van der Stoel mentioned that the Soviets argued that the MLF was an obstacle for the nonproliferation talks, Schaetzel replied that the US would "not let the Soviets dictate the terms of negotiation." Schaetzel asked van der Stoel whether the Netherlands could play a key role in achieving a European consensus.[44] Although van der Stoel might have preferred to let the MLF–ANF issue rest, the US negotiating strategy dictated that there should be substantial progress on the establishment of a nuclear arrangement within NATO before a NPT could be realized.

Back in The Hague, however, DNW urged caution and argued there seemed very little room for maneuver within the MLF–ANF negotiations. Dutch NATO representative Boon was thus instructed that it was not up to the Netherlands to develop "new initiatives."[45] In early February 1966, van der Stoel and Chalfont met on the margins of disarmament talks in Geneva. Chalfont thought that the Russians were not willing to move forward as long as there was uncertainty about NATO's future nuclear arrangements. In order to achieve progress on non-proliferation, "a real solution of NATO's nuclear issues should be found." He considered that the Russians might accept some compromise solution – more than a purely consultative solution, but less than a hardware formula.[46] Van der Stoel agreed, but he was at the same time increasingly worried that even such a solution might still leave the European nuclear option open.

Plotting against the European nuclear option

By early 1966, van der Stoel was becoming increasingly concerned that a nuclear arrangement within NATO might not indefinitely prevent – or might even facilitate – the development of a European nuclear option. He wanted to prepare an offensive against this option. However, before he could stage such an offensive on the international stage, he had to put his house in order and further establish his authority over the "old guard" of NATO policy, DNW. In November 1965, he had done so by first threatening the replacement of Hans Boon, the independently operating NATO Ambassador, charging him with insubordination in a private letter. Angrily, van der Stoel wrote Boon that he was "amazed and disappointed" that the latter had not taken a sufficiently forceful position against West German propositions to develop a European option.[47]

At the same time, van der Stoel requested DGPZ to draft new instructions for upcoming NATO discussion on nonproliferation. Although van der Stoel did probably consider it too early to unfold an initiative in NATO, he made it absolutely clear that the Netherlands "should not oppose" the prohibition of transferring of nuclear weapons to "an association of states" (which would allow the creation of a European nuclear force). He legitimized this by arguing that "the Dutch position vis-à-vis the Soviet Union and the non-aligned countries would be strengthened if we [as NATO] show us proponents of stringent nonproliferation obligations."[48] Van der Stoel had moved decisively: he set the margins of

68   E. Hellendoorn

the Dutch position and made it clear that he would not tolerate any transgression thereof on the part of Boon and DNW.

The matter became urgent when the American draft nonproliferation treaty seemed to allow for a European nuclear force based upon a majority vote, a proposition deemed "unacceptable" by van der Stoel.[49] On February 5, 1966, the US submitted a revised draft to its NATO partners. The accompanying explanation maintained that the new text was designed "to make explicit [that] the intent of the US draft Treaty [was] not to transfer nuclear weapons to a non-nuclear state, or for that matter, to several non-nuclear states acting together." Also, the US text stated that "the new language would not extend to an association which included a nuclear state." In other words, the draft still allowed for the transfer of nuclear weapons to create a European nuclear force.[50]

In The Hague, DIO was very much worried, as it expected that the Americans would forward this draft directly to the Soviet negotiating team in Geneva, without first consulting their NATO allies.[51] Meanwhile, the State Department informed the Dutch Ambassador in Washington that the US thought that Germany's interest in a separate European nuclear force was actually increasing. This information "horrified" The Hague.[52] Nevertheless, when Foreign Minister Luns spoke with Lyndon B. Johnson on February 14, 1966, the US President explained that "he did not want to be perceived as imposing a solution on his European partners."[53] Did Johnson put the ball in the Dutch court? Van der Stoel certainly thought so.

Absent US willingness to tackle the issue, the Dutch MFA felt it now had to reveal its genuine position within the MLF–ANF negotiations. The Hague deemed it necessary to act in order to change the US draft treaty so that it would exclude a European option based upon majority voting. Therefore, in early March 1966, van der Stoel instructed Boon to suggest the elimination of the language prohibiting the transfer of nuclear weapons "into the control of any association of non-nuclear-weapon states" and argue for its replacement with "or into the control of any association of states".[54] The subsequent Dutch intervention of March 2, 1966 led to considerable bewilderment amongst NATO partners. However, the Dutch found some support in Britain. The British disarmament secretary, Lord Chalfont, agreed that it should be possible

> to exclude the possibility of a European nuclear force which would allow the majority of the non-nuclear states to decide on the use of nuclear weapons, without the veto-power of nuclear partners. *But*, it *could not* exclude the possibility of a federal Europe with its own nuclear force, if France and the UK would be part of such a federal Europe.[55]

An Italian diplomat in The Hague was dispatched to the Dutch MFA to find out what the Netherlands really intended. The Italians wanted to know whether the Dutch were trying to rule out an MLF or ANF. The DIO official who received the Italian diplomat answered that The Hague opposed the possibility that a decision to use MLF–ANF nuclear weapons could be taken by a group of non-nuclear-weapon states. Therefore, the nuclear states contributing the weapons should be legally prohibited from forfeiting their veto. The Dutch argued that a European Nuclear Force (ENF) could only be the "military crown" of a future European political union. Short of that, a multilateral option was only acceptable as a "composite" nuclear force, wherein the participating nuclear-weapon states would maintain their veto.[56]

Backlash from taking the initiative

The United States was not pleased by the Dutch intervention. In private bilateral discussions, Washington critiqued The Hague's insistence on excluding the possibility of abandoning the veto power of nuclear-weapon states within a multilateral force as solely "an academic issue." The Dutch replied they feared Franco-German hegemony. Such an undesirable outcome could only be prevented by ensuring continued US participation and coresponsibility in Europe's security, the Dutch officials argued.[57]

Nevertheless, from Washington's perspective, the uncertainty within NATO about a nuclear arrangement subsequent to the Dutch intervention weakened the US position in the negotiations with the Soviet Union. The FRG had countered the Dutch proposal by stating it was willing to accept only a non-production clause, thereby – implicitly – rejecting a non-transfer clause.[58] Conversely, Britain had supported the Dutch. Samuel De Palma (Deputy Director at the ACDA) told Schurmann, the Dutch Ambassador to Washington, that "the current [negotiation] situation is even more disadvantageous than some years ago when Moscow might have accepted some sort of a MLF."[59] De Palma thereby implied that the Dutch activism had weakened the US hand vis-à-vis the Soviets.

NATO Ambassador Boon also weighed in. He had opposed van der Stoel's nonproliferation policy, given that it was limiting Europe's capability to defend itself if need arose. By summer 1966, the US–Soviet nonproliferation talks were deadlocked: the Soviets demanded language clearly prohibiting the creation of any kind of MLF-ANF or European nuclear force. Under these circumstances, Boon alluded that the Dutch position on non-transfer was not dissimilar to the Soviet one. Thus, with a certain irony, he concluded that such NATO concessions to the USSR would be no real sacrifice for the Netherlands. In his coded message to van der Stoel, Boon moreover warned that

> states like Egypt, Japan, India and Pakistan will perceive future self-imposed constraints on NATO's nuclear armaments as undermining the Alliance's firepower, and will therefore be encouraged to develop their own nuclear capability, providing them with greater prestige on the world scene.[60]

Boon thus tried to appeal to the concern about global proliferation in order to weaken the enthusiasm for a non-transfer clause.

In The Hague, DNW was glad to employ the US chagrin over the Dutch intervention within its bureaucratic infighting against DIO. When DIO argued in

70   E. Hellendoorn

favor of starting a discussion within NATO to define "proliferation," DNW decidedly refused to cooperate with this "self-defeating" policy proposal: "Such a discussion within NATO would probably lead to a broad definition [of proliferation], as the Soviets are hoping for," DNW argued.[61] In other words, a fixed definition of proliferation would compromise NATO's room for maneuver and thus help the Soviet Union.[62]

This renewed divergence between DIO and DNW was illustrative of the two fundamentally opposed worldviews and approaches to nuclear politics. While DIO's internationalists hoped to manage the spread of nuclear weapons through definitions and legalistic solutions, DNW's strategists were much more concerned with the long-term contextual consequences. The latter felt that it would be impossible to forecast such long-term developments and therefore equally impossible to manage "unknowns" through specific technical-legal solutions, as suggested by the former. These two opposed ways of thinking about nuclear proliferation almost inevitably led to stalemates and bureaucratic strife.

Van der Stoel used the opportunity to try to finally bury all multilateral force proposals. "The MLF-ANF was no longer of essential importance for the West" and could be dropped "if the Soviet Union would be prepared to sign the nonproliferation treaty," he argued. On the other hand, there should be no concessions to the Soviet Union on the point of "consultative arrangements like the special committee [on nuclear planning]."[63] In September 1966, Boon received his instructions. Most important was that the amendment prohibiting the transfer of nuclear weapons "into the control of any association of states" would be maintained.[64] During the NATO Council of October 19, Boon intervened accordingly, explaining:

> The proposed amendments do not rule out the MLF/ANF or similar concepts provided that the participating nuclear-weapons states maintain an effective veto on the use of the nuclear weapons they have brought in. This does not imply that the Netherlands wishes to choose in favor of such a concept at a moment when this matter is not the subject of active discussion at least within the Alliance. On the contrary the continuation of the studies undertaken by the Special Committee on the possibilities of giving substance to the sharing of responsibilities on the nuclear field through consultative arrangements is a matter which is of active interest.[65]

The Dutch proposal was widely supported, amongst others by the British, Norwegian, Belgian, Danish, and Canadian representatives.[66]

The impact of this proposal on the American position in its negotiations with the Soviet Union should not be overestimated. During US–Soviet meetings on September 24, 1966 (thus preceding the NATO consultations), Washington had already proposed the phrase "not to transfer control *to any recipient whatsoever*" as a concession to the Soviet Union.[67] This language would be accepted by the Soviets and in the end included in the NPT. The Netherlands were informed about this US–Soviet breakthrough during a NATO Council meeting on October

19. In the meanwhile, the Dutch had – mistakenly – believed that they could still affect the non-transfer language.[68] Van der Stoel's tenure ended as the Cabinet fell on November 22, 1966.

Conclusion

Van der Stoel's tenure as Undersecretary of State at the Ministry of Foreign Affairs marked the beginning of a new phase in Dutch nuclear diplomacy. Traditionally, a conservative security policy establishment had dominated Dutch strategic nuclear policy-making. The general policy of these strategists had been aimed at maintaining a strong NATO, and it had generally been pro-US. However, The Hague had never fully trusted Washington and it therefore had to keep some options of European "proliferation" open. Van der Stoel presented a purer form of Atlanticism, which entailed a profound suspicion of Franco-German continental entanglements, while putting greater faith in institutional set-ups. Van der Stoel successfully set out to break the de facto monopoly of the security-policy establishment over Dutch NATO and nuclear policies. He endorsed progressive internationalists within the MFA to set a more "idealist" nuclear policy agenda. Since these internationalists strongly opposed the idea of a European nuclear force, van der Stoel could use the idealist agenda as a smoke screen for unmitigated Atlanticism.

The rise of van der Stoel's variety of Atlanticism and his empowerment of internationalists led to an increase of Dutch activity in the NATO debate on nuclear sharing and nonproliferation. The Hague confronted its allies with a diplomatic offensive to limit nuclear sharing arrangements as much as possible. Ironically, van der Stoel's position resembled the Soviet one, causing American irritation. Anglo-Dutch relations were much warmer and van der Stoel found his main ally in London. Further research would have to point out what NATO members privately thought about the Dutch stance and to what extent it influenced them. However, it appears that the NPT negotiations inclined Dutch nuclear diplomacy more than vice versa. Van der Stoel used the negotiations to reorient Dutch security policy. The internal struggle over Dutch nuclear nonproliferation policy reveals how the conflict between two worldviews can lead to serious stalemates and be self-undermining. It seems that more energy was spent on bureaucratic infighting than effective policy execution. It would be interesting to see whether other states were confronted with similar internal transformations during the NPT negotiations, and whether the effect of these negotiations was greater on the thinking on nuclear weapons within many states than the other way around. Ultimately, it begs the question to what extent contemporary nonproliferation policy-making is affected by similar tensions between geopolitical and more idealistic motivations, and how often are the latter a fig-leaf for the former.

72 E. Hellendoorn

Notes

1 The author would like to thank Roland Popp, Liviu Horovitz, and Duco Hellema for their valuable comments.
2 Hal Brands, "Non-Proliferation and the Dynamics of the Middle Cold War: The Superpowers, the MLF, and the NPT," *Cold War History* 7, no. 3 (2007): 389–423.
3 "Code, PV (Permanente Vertegenwoordiging) New York (De Beus no. 46), Nonproliferatie atoomwapens, ref. no. 1089, 25–01–1965, Confidentieel," Nationaal Archief (NA) 2.05.313/23999 NPV (Non-Proliferatie Verdrag) Onderhandelingen 1965. *Het Nationaal Archief*, Den Haag, Netherlands.
4 Files pertaining to the DIO-desk are located in the National Archives and fully open to the public. These, however, do not contain the documents on discussions about and within NATO. Most of the relevant files about strategic nuclear policy-making are still guarded by the MFA. For the Dutch position on the NPT, see L.M. Van der Mey, "Non-proliferation of Nuclear Weapons," in *The Politics of Persuasion: Implementation of Foreign Policy by the Netherlands*, eds. Philip Everts and Guido Walraven (Aldershot: Avebury, 1989), 118–132; on the MLF, see Duco Hellema, *Dutch Foreign Policy: The Role of the Netherlands in World Politics* (Dordrecht: Republic of Letters, 2009), 203–208; or Ine Megens, "Trouw maar terughoudend. De Nederlandse houding tegenover de gezamenlijke kernmacht voor de NAVO," *Transaktie* 27, no. 4 (1998): 469–493; or Alfred van Staden, *Een trouwe bondgenoot: Nederland en het Atlantisch bondgenootschap (1960–1971)* (Baarn: In den Toren, 1974), 97–109.
5 "Memo, BZ/DWS/NE (Buitenlandse Zaken, Directie Westelijke Samenwerking, NAVO en Europese defensieaangelegenheden) to DWS, De politieke betekenis der modaliteiten waaronder de USA nucleaire wapenen voor tactisch gebruik aan de Atlantische bondgenoten zal stellen, no. 570, 14–09–1957, Zeer geheim," "Code, NL Embassy W'ton (Van Voorst no. 81) to BZ, ref. no. x1476, 20–11–1957, Zeer Geheim," "Memo, BZ/DNW/AN (Directie NAVO- en WEU-zaken, Bureau Algemene NAVO- en WEU-Zaken) to DNW, Aantekening bij telegram x 1281, 25–06–1958," ABZ II DAV (Archief Ministerie van Buitenlandse Zaken, Codearchief 1955–1965, Directie Atlantische Samenwerking en Veiligheidszaken) 531 Atoomwapens onder NAVO.
6 On the Norstad Proposal, see Ralph Dietl, "In Defence of the West: General Lauris Norstad, NATO Nuclear Forces, and Transatlantic Relations, 1958–1963," *Diplomacy and Statecraft* 17, no. 2 (2006): 347–392, esp. 362.
7 For such Dutch considerations, see "Memo, BZ/DNW, MRBM's voor NATO, July 18, 1960, Top Secret," ABZ II DAV 535 Atoomwapens onder NAVO 1 July 1960 t/m 1961.
8 Duco Hellema, *Dutch Foreign Policy: The Role of the Netherlands in World Politics* (Dordrecht: Republic of Letters, 2009), 203–208.
9 This chapter will argue that many of the DNW officials were in fact no convinced "Atlanticists."
10 Marc Dierikx, "'Mister Ontwikkelingshulp.' Jan Meijer (1914–1997),' in *In dienst van Buitenlandse Zaken. Achttien portretten van ambtenaren en diplomaten in de twintigste eeuw*, eds. Bert Van der Zwan, Bob de Graaff, and Duco Hellema (Amsterdam: Boom, 2008), 145–156; quote on 147; Interview with Wim van Eekelen, May 29, 2013.
11 C.A. van der Klaauw, *Een diplomatenleven. Memoires* (Amsterdam: Bert Bakker, 1995), 85f.
12 The influence of societal movements on Dutch nuclear non-proliferation policy falls outside the scope of this contribution. Sam Rozemond quoted in Chris Ruitenfrans, "Het beste met de wereld voor," *Trouw*, November 28, 1998.
13 The Cabinet of Prime Minister Cals (1965–1966) declared upon assuming office that it attached "special importance to the broad field of disarmament," see *Handelingen*

The Netherlands 73

Tweede Kamer, 1964–1965, no. 36, April 27, 1965, 1309, Albert Kersten, *Luns. Een politieke biografie* (Amsterdam: Boom, 2010), 360f; in the Dutch system there is the Minister of Foreign Affairs, with Undersecretaries of State. This is an informal political position, without representation in the Cabinet, but with great bureaucratic authority and relative independence from the Minister. Next to van der Stoel, there was *Staatssecretaris* Leo de Block for European affairs.

14 Interview Wim van Eekelen, May 29, 2013.
15 Frank Zuijdam, *Tussen wens en werkelijkheid. Het debat over vrede en veiligheid binnen de PvdA in de periode 1958–1977* (PhD Thesis, Universiteit van Amsterdam, 2001), 56–59, 102–121, 128–131; see also Hans Smits, *De bom in de vuist. De Partij van de Arbeid tussen afschrikking en atoompacifisme* (Amsterdam: Uitgeverij Raamgracht, 1984), 86.
16 Buitenlandse Zaken, *Ontwapening, veiligheid, vrede. Nota betreffende het onwapeningsvraagstuk* (Den Haag: Staatsuitgeverij, 1964).
17 Ibid., 10–14.
18 Interview with a former DIO official, The Hague, June 13, 2012.
19 See Susanna Schrafstetter and Stephen Twigge, "Trick or Truth? The British ANF Proposal, West Germany and the US Nonproliferation Policy 1964–1968," *Diplomacy and Statecraft* 11, no. 2 (2000): 161–184; John Young, "Killing the MLF? The Wilson Government and Nuclear Sharing in Europe, 1964–1966," *Diplomacy and Statecraft* 14, no. 2 (2003): 295–324.
20 "Memo, BZ/DIO/PI (Directie Internationale Organisaties, Afdeling Politieke en Internationale Veiligheidszaken), to DNW/MS (Afdeling Militaire Samenwerking), ANF/ MLF en niet verspreiding van kernwapens, no. 42/65, June 14, 1965," ABZ III (1965–1974) DAV 1245 MLF en nonproliferatie nov 1964 October 1965.
21 Ibid. The remarks DIO/PI referred to were the following: Robert Schaetzel (September 27, 1963 in Ditchley), "The [MLF] would also inevitably make easier the eventual development of a European nuclear force"; Lyndon B. Johnson (November 8, 1963 in Brussels), "A united Europe may one day acquire control of the multilateral nuclear missile fleet"; Robert Bowie (December 3, 1963 in WEU Parliament): "Such a force might evolve in either of two ways: it might become an integrated Atlantic force with the United States still a member but without a veto. Or it might develop into an integrated European force without the United States as a member"; Walt Rostow (June 24, 1964 in WEU Parliament), "We have wished to leave the structure of the MLF sufficiently flexible to adjust as Europe moves towards unity"; McGeorge Bundy (NSA Advisor, December 1964, TV interview), "We are willing to consider the suggestion that this agreement should have in it a clause which says somewhere if and when Europe is fully unified and has a political authority that could take an enormous decision of this kind, then the arrangements perhaps ought to be opened to review."
22 "Memo, BZ/Chef DNW to Chef DIO, ANF/MLF en niet verspreiding van kernwapens, no. 56/65, June 15, 1965," ibid.
23 "Code, BZ/DIO (Luns no. 43) to GNV Parijs, niet-verspreiding van kernwapens, ref. no. x598, February 2, 1965, Confidentieel," ABZ III DAV 763 Voorkoming verspreiding van kernwapens jan-aug 1965.
24 "Memo, BZ/DIO/PI to Chef DIO, Niet verspreiding van kernwapens (Ierse resolutie), no. 10/65, January 29, 1965," NA 2.05.313/23999 NPV Onderhandelingen 1965.
25 "Memo, BZ/Chef DNW to Chef DIO, ANF/MLF en niet verspreiding van kernwapens, no. 56/65, June 15, 1965," ABZ III DAV 1245 MLF en nonproliferatie November 1964–October 1965.
26 A former colleague of Boon said that Boon, as a historian, took a longer view of potential developments. Also, interview with Wim van Eekelen, May 29, 2013.
27 "Memo, BZ/DNW/PN to Chef DNW via DNW/PH, Ierse ontwerpresolutie ENDC-Commissie, no. 32, 22 January 1965," ABZ III DAV 763 Voorkoming verspreiding van kernwapens jan-aug 1965. In June 1965 a report reached The Hague that US State

74   E. Hellendoorn

Department official Vincent Baker had suggested that the NATO countries would make a non-acquisition statement, but with the caveat that "changed international circumstances" might force a revision of such statement. DGPZ scribbled in the margin of the report that "any *public* announcement of potential nuclear proliferation would be a step back." The word "public" implied that DGPZ was not at all convinced that there should be a *secret* or implicit understanding amongst NATO partners that a non-acquisition statement should be revisable (emphasis added). It seems that DGPZ would only accept a public declaration of intent not to proliferate, if it was coupled with a secret understanding within NATO that such a statement would be revisable. "Memo, BZ/GNV Parijs/Van Barneveld Kooy to Ambassadeur [Boon], Non-proliferatie verdrag, no. 65/81, June 17, 1965," ABZ III DAV 763 Voorkoming verspreiding van kernwapens jan–aug 1965.

28 "Code, BZ/DNW/MC (afdeling Militair-economische aangelegenheden en civiele defensie) (Luns no. 52) to GNV Parijs, [Britse ANF voorstellen], ref. no. 3485, July 2, 1965, Geheim," ibid.

29 "Code, BZ/DIO/PI/DNW/PN (Luns no. 70), niet-verspreiding van kernwapens, ref. no. 3692, July 15, 1965, Confidentieel," ibid.

30 "Memo, BZ/DNW to DIO/PI, MLF/ANF en non-proliferatie, no. 67, July 14, 1965," "Memo, BZ/DIO to DNW, Uw memo no. 67 betreffende MLF/ANF en non-proliferatie, no. 109/65, July 15, 1965," ABZ III DAV 1245 MLF en nonproliferatie nov 1964–okt 1965.

31 Emphasis added. "Memo, BZ/DNW/MC to Wnd Chef DNW, Gedachtenwisseling met DIO over ANF/MLF, July 17, 1965," ibid.

32 William C. Foster, "New Directions in Arms Control and Disarmament," *Foreign Affairs* 43, no. 4 (1965): 587–601.

33 "Code, NL Embassy W'ton (Schurmann no. 442), niet verspreiding van kernwapens; het Gilpatric rapport, ref. no. 5583, 09–07–1965, Geheim," ABZ III DAV 1245 MLF en nonproliferatie nov 1964–okt 1965.

34 "Code, NL Embassy W'ton (Van Baarda no. 518) to BZ, ontwapening, ref. no. x6410, 12–08–1965, Geheim," ibid.; nonetheless, there were still doubts in Washington about the seriousness of the Kremlin. In his talks with Dutch diplomat van Baarda, Freund wondered whether the Russians were really committed to a non-proliferation treaty and a test ban. He suspected that they wanted to use the negotiations to sow discord inside the Western camp and also to stir up the Non-aligned against the West.

35 "Code, NL Embassy W'ton (van Baarda no. 596) to BZ, ontwapening, ref. no. 7292, 13–09–1965, Confidentieel," ibid.

36 "Code, GNV Parijs (Boon no. 382), Bijzondere raadszitting 17 september: agendapunten 20e VN assemblee, ref. no. 7485, 17–09–1965, Confidentieel," ibid.

37 Maarten Kuitenbrouwer, "Een realistische idealist. Max van der Stoel (1973–1977, 1981–1982)," in *De Nederlandse ministers van Buitenlandse Zaken in de twintigste eeu*, eds. Duco Hellema, Bert Zeeman, and Bert Van der Zwan (Den Haag: Sdu Uitgevers, 1999), 243–256.

38 Zuijdam, *Tussen wens en werkelijkheid*, 128–131.

39 "Memo, van der Stoel to DGIS & DGPZ via S, no. 5/65, 30–08–1965," ABZ III DAV 763 Voorkoming verspreiding van kernwapens jan-aug 1965.

40 "Memo, BZ/DIO/OV (Bureau Ontwapening en Internationale Vredesvraagstukken), Enige argumenten ten gunste van een regionaal non-proliferatie commitment zoals voorgesteld in het ANF-project, September 10, 1965," "Memo, BZ/DNW/PN, Argumenten contra opname van non-proliferatie paragrafen in een ANF-overeenkomst [undated, around September 10, 1965], Vertrouwelijk," ibid.; "Memo, BZ/de Ranitz to Z via S, Niet-verspreiding van kernwapens, no. 207, September 13, 1965," ABZ III DAV 764 Voorkoming verspreiding van kernwapens sept 1965–mrt 1966.

41 This would also serve as "a counterweight" against the foreseen European clause of the NPT.

The Netherlands 75

42 "Memo, van der Stoel to M, no. 27/65, September 22, 1965," ABZ III DAV 1245 MLF en nonproliferatie nov 1964–okt 1965.

43 "Code, NL Embassy London (De Beus no. 522) to BZ [Onderhoud van der Stoel-Chalfont], ref. no. x8488, 21–10–1965, Confidentieel," ibid.

44 "Code, NL Embassy W'ton (Schurmann no. 751) to BZ, Bezoek staatssecretaris van der Stoel aan Washington, Nucleaire problematiek, ref. no. 79567, November 11, 1965, Geheim," ABZ III DAV 1246 MLF en nonproliferatie nov 1965–feb 1967.

45 At the same time, however, DNW warned that "we should be careful not to be confronted with nuclear arrangements which we did not help to prepare." "Code, BZ/DNW (Celer no. 4) to Brussel, Bonn, London, Rome, W'ton, GNV+Parijs, Nucleaire samenwerking, ref. no. 412, 26 January 1966, Geheim," ABZ III DAV 578 Atoomwapens onder NAVO 1966–1968.

46 "Code, PV Genève (Kaufmann no. 16) to BZ, ENDC Genève, ref. no. 2115, 08–02–1966, Confidentieel," ABZ III DAV 1246 MLF en nonproliferatie nov 1965–feb 1967.

47 "Letter, van der Stoel to Boon (NL Ambassador NATO), cc. Luns, Den Haag, November 6, 1965," NA H.N. Boon 2.21.183.09/93 Correspondentie; during earlier NATO consultations, the West German side had underscored that a European clause should be guaranteed and that a nonproliferation treaty should be coupled with progress on Western European integration as well as on the German question. Although the Dutch officially considered nonproliferation the priority, Boon personally seemed to appreciate the German remarks. "Code, GNV Parijs (Boon no. 382), Bijzondere raadszitting 17 september: agendapunten 20ᵉ VN assemblee, ref. no. 7485, 17–09–1965, Confidentieel," ABZ III DAV 1245 MLF en nonproliferatie nov 1964–okt 1965.

48 "Memo, van der Stoel to DGPZ via S, no. 53/65, 02–11–1965," ABZ III DAV 764 Voorkoming verspreiding van kernwapens sept 1965–mrt 1966.

49 The majority vote would relinquish the American veto. "Code, BZ/DNW/PN (Luns no. 229) to NL Embassy W'ton & PV New York, Niet-verspreiding van kernwapens, ref. no. x6764, 19–11–1965, Confidentieel," ibid.

50 "Memo, BZ/DNW/PN to DNW, Gewijzigd VS-concept non-proliferatieverdrag, no. 28, February 7, 1966," ibid.

51 "Memo, BZ/DIO/OV to DIO/PI, Voorgenomen tekstwijzigingen in Amerikaans ontwerp non-proliferatie verdrag, no.[…]/66, February 17, 1966," ibid.

52 "Code, NL Embassy W'ton (Schurmann no. 98) to BZ, nuclear sharing, ref. no. x2384, 16–02–1966, Geheim," ABZ III DAV 578 Atoomwapens onder NAVO 1966–1968.

53 "Code, NL Embassy W'ton (Schurmann no. 88), Nucleaire samenwerking, ref. no. 2298, February 14, 1966, Geheim," ibid.

54 Cited in van der Mey, "Non-proliferation," 118–132.

55 Emphasis original. "Memo, BZ/DIO/OV (Terwisscha van Scheltinga), Notulen van het gesprek van de Staatssecretaris van Buitenlandse Zaken, Mr. M. van der Stoel met de Britse 'Minister of State' voor ontwapeningsaangelegenheden, Lord Chalfon op 7 maart 966, DIO/OV-53113–2487GS, 25–03–1966, Geheim," NA ABZ III 25955 Onderhandelingen NPV I 1965–1967.

56 "Memo, BZ/DIO/PI to Chef DIO, DGIS, DGPZ, Non-proliferatie verdrag, March 24, 1966," ABZ III DAV 764 Voorkoming verspreiding van kernwapens sept 1965–mrt 1966.

57 "Memo, GNV Parijs/van der Kun to Ambassadeur (Boon), Gesprek met De Palma en Baker, no. 1721, March 7, 1966," ABZ III DAV 764 Voorkoming verspreiding van kernwapens sept 1965–mrt 1966.

58 "Code, NL/BZ/DNW/PN/DIO/PI to NL Embassy Bonn, Duits vredesoffensief, ref. no. 2739, April 19, 1966, Confidentieel," ABZ III DAV 1246 MLF en nonproliferatie nov 1965–feb 1967.

76   E. Hellendoorn

59 "Code, NL Embassy W'ton (Schurmann no. 325) to BZ [Gesprek met Depalma], ref. no. 5836, May 26, 1966, Geheim," ibid.

60 "Code, GNV NAVO (Boon no. 1161) to BZ, Non-proliferatie en NAVO, ref. no. x7519, 22–07–1966, Geheim," ibid.; although this might have seemed a rather hypothetical argument at the time, the nuclear historian Frank Gavin makes a similar argument: Frank Gavin, *Nuclear Statecraft: History and Strategy in America's Atomic Age* (Ithaca, NY: Cornell University Press, 2012), 120–133.

61 "Memo, BZ/DNW to DGPZ, Non-proliferatie en NAVO, no. 54, August 11, 1966," ABZ III DAV 1246 MLF en nonproliferatie nov 1965–feb 1967.

62 Bureaucratic infighting ensued once again at this point. However, DNW estimated that (the international lawyer) van der Stoel would back up DIO's proposal and overrule DNW. DNW decided to stall, dragging its feet when it had to return the draft instructions to DIO, trying to lift it over the summer. DNW, backed up by DGPZ de Ranitz, refused to comment or sign off the paper. In doing so, they tried to prevent Boon being instructed in time for the upcoming NATO discussion so that, for the time being, he would not have to intervene according to van der Stoel's policy. De Ranitz hoped he could delay matters because van der Stoel was poised to leave for his summer holiday. "Memo, BZ/Chef DIO to Chef DNW, Non-proliferatie en nucleaire samenwerking in NAVO, no. 180/66, August 10, 1966" and "Memo, BZ/de Ranitz (DGPZ) to DIO, Ontwerp non-proliferatie verdrag, no. 464, 04–08–1966," ABZ III DAV 765 Voorkoming verspreiding van kernwapens apr–nov 1966.

63 "Memo, BZ/van der Stoel to DGPZ via S, Non-proliferatie, no. 145/66, 10–08–1966," ibid.

64 There is no archival evidence that the US requested The Hague to put forward this language. "Code BZ/DIO/OV-DNW/PN to GNV Parijs, Non-proliferatie en NAVO, ref. no. x6152, September 7, 1966, Geheim," ibid.

65 "Letter, GNV Parijs to Minister van BZ (DWN/PN) [Interventie tijdens de Raadsdiscussie van 19 oktober], Parijs, October 20, 1966, Vertrouwelijk," ABZ III DAV 765 Voorkoming verspreiding van kernwapens apr–nov 1966.

66 "Code, GNV Parijs (Boon no. 1659) to BZ, Non proliferatie, ref. no. x10305, October 19, 1966, Confidentieel," ibid.

67 "Memcon, Rusk/Gromyko, September 24, 1966, Secret," FRUS, 1964–1968, XI, doc. 153.

68 "Code, GNV Parijs (Boon no. 1659) to BZ, Non proliferatie, ref. no. x10305, October 19, 1966, Confidentieel."

5 "A turning point in postwar foreign policy"

Italy and the NPT negotiations, 1967–1969

Leopoldo Nuti

This chapter explores Italy's nuclear policy-making during the final phase of the negotiations leading to the conclusion of the Treaty on the Non-Proliferation of Nuclear Weapons (NPT). The chapter deals with a time-frame starting in late 1966, when the Italian government was first apprised of the new US draft of the treaty, and concluding with the Italian signature in January 1969. The chapter's main goal is to provide a plausible explanation for the Italian hostile reaction to the US proposal, thereby filling a significant gap in the historical literature. Other than my own, the only other available accounts are the contemporary works of the opponents or the supporters of the treaty. My research has been able to provide a more rounded account thanks to the increasing availability of a variety of Italian, US, and British primary sources.[1] This chapter, in particular, is based on the personal papers of Aldo Moro and Amintore Fanfani (respectively stored in the *Archivio Centrale dello Stato* (Central State Archives) and in the Italian Senate's Historical Archive), the papers of the *Ufficio Disarmo* (Disarmament Office) of the Italian Foreign Ministry (at the Ministry's Historical Archive); the newly declassified US Arms Control and Disarmament Agency (ACDA) Director's Office NPT files (Record Group 383) and the records of the Department of State (Record Group 59) at the National Archives at College Park, Maryland, as well as on a number of collections from the British National Archives at Kew.[2]

The chapter proceeds as follows. The first section places the negative Italian assessment of the treaty in the context of the nuclear policies pursued by the previous Italian governments, as well as in the more general framework of Italy's postwar foreign policy. It emphasizes Italy's strive for parity among Western European states as its main foreign policy driver. The second section addresses the tense confrontation between Rome and Washington, and the protracted attempt to alter the content of the initial US draft, as the government became concerned that the NPT would relegate Italy to a permanent lower-level status among European powers and jeopardize its technological aspirations. The third section investigates the parallel efforts to bolster Italy's nuclear capabilities in the fields of nuclear naval propulsion and uranium enrichment – efforts pursued with increasing determination as the signature of the treaty was perceived as unavoidable. The fourth section looks at the final phase of the

78   *L. Nuti*

negotiations, as well as the last-minute attempts to delay the signature. Finally, the conclusion discusses the possible explanation for the Italian decision to sign the treaty regardless of the perplexity and resentment it engendered.

Italian foreign policy after the Second World War and the challenges of nuclear sharing

The Second World War had a shattering impact on Italian foreign policy. The magnitude of the disaster of 1943, when the country found itself split in two separate entities occupied by enemy powers at war with each other, made clear to the postwar generation of Italian policy-makers that for a long time their country would remain in an enfeebled condition.[3] At the same time, the issue of the country's ranking in the international hierarchy of powers had been central to its foreign policy since its birth, and it could not be easily ignored or dismissed by post-1945 political forces. There was a yawning gap between the powerlessness of the Italian state that was reassembled in the last two years of the Second World War and the heritage of a political mindset which regarded parity with the other European powers as the inescapable goal of Italian foreign policy.

Step by step, Italian diplomats learned the game of multilateralism and reached the conclusion that the best possible option to regain the country's standing within the international system was to play an active role in all the international organizations the Western world was establishing under US leadership. The core element of this policy was a close relationship with the United States. Washington played a dual role as the main guarantor of both Italy's external security and the stability of its domestic politics. What was even better, the US also promoted a federalist version of European integration, one that perfectly matched Italy's aspirations to a status of parity with its Western European counterparts and one that prevented the return to traditional balance of power logics. NATO and European integration quickly became the twin pillars of Italy's postwar foreign policy.

The gradual nuclearization of NATO's strategy throughout the 1950s, however, challenged the very premises of Italy's policy by threatening to reintroduce a hierarchy inside Western Europe. With the Alliance increasingly relying on nuclear deterrence to guarantee the security of its members, Italian decision-makers believed that only those countries which had access to atomic weapons would ultimately be able to take the crucial decisions for NATO's future. By the mid-1950s the Italian government seemed to have reached the conclusion that for the time being the safest way to meet this predicament would be through a close cooperation with NATO and the US, thereby employing the multilateral approach as the core conceptual and operational framework towards preventing the country's marginalization within the international system. Between 1955 and 1959, therefore, the steady acceptance of the deployment of US nuclear weapons on Italian soil evolved into a regular pattern that formed the basis for Italian nuclear policies for the next ten years. At the same time, there was a parallel attempt to explore whether any nuclear cooperation might be possible within a

European framework, an alternative which would be repeatedly investigated, particularly when the US approach seemed to falter.[4]

Italy's US-centered policy was based on the expectation that Washington would increasingly share parts of its arsenal with the Western European allies – an expectation that was perceived as realistic given the growing number of nuclear weapons that the US armed forces had been deploying overseas since the mid-1950s. After 1955, Italy began to host a vast array of American nuclear delivery systems, such as the tactical Corporal and Honest John rockets, the anti-aircraft Nike-Hercules missiles, dual-use artillery, and atomic demolition munitions. Most important were the Jupiter missiles installed in Southern Italy in 1960 under a dual-key system which gave the Italians the tangible impression that they were actually sharing the control of a crucial weapons system. The political significance of this choice, in the Italian eyes, could only be one:

> This [the Jupiters' deployment] clearly marks an increase in the help we offer to the US and it marks an increase in the risks which our country will run into, in case of war. We may even say that for the time being we are closer to the nuclear club than France is, not because we produce the warheads but because we host them on our territory. This, I believe, is a very strong argument for both thwarting the attempt to build a [tripartite] directorate in NATO and for demanding a more active Italian participation to the shaping of the Alliance's common policy.[5]

Both the Jupiters' withdrawal in 1963 and the Kennedy administration's overall wavering attitude on nuclear sharing were perceived as somewhat ominous signs by Italian diplomats. Nevertheless, the Italian government continued to hope that a multilateral path to a nuclear status remained open. When the US proposed a sea-based NATO Multilateral Force (MLF), the Italian navy took it seriously enough to overhaul one of its main ships, the cruiser *Garibaldi*, and equip it with four special Polaris launching pits. At the same time, in December 1962, the Italian Minister of Defense, Giulio Andreotti, officially asked his US counterpart for assistance to develop a nuclear propulsion capacity for the Italian fleet "within the framework of the profitable military cooperation between the two countries."[6]

From 1963 to 1965, as the negotiations on the MLF evolved through many ups and downs, the Italian government continued to state its interest in it and elaborated a number of ambitious proposals to take advantage of it in case the multilateral fleet was ever going to be created. Time and again, Italian diplomats would outspokenly tell their US counterparts "that the Italian claim to great power status should be reflected in some way in the MLF structure," that the US should help Italy "in this important matter of prestige," and that the future force should be militarily significant in order to "provide an opportunity to raise Italy's international status."[7] Status concerns also determined Italian reactions to alternatives to the MLF, such as the idea of a NATO Select Committee. While initially regarded with much suspicion as potentially threatening to relegate the MLF to

80 *L. Nuti*

the backburner, Italian decision-makers also saw benefits in the US proposed Select Committee, as nuclear consultation promised to fill a crucial gap in Alliance military planning. According to the Italian representative to the Atlantic Council, Adolfo Alessandrini, the proposal might not only help to reinforce the cohesion of NATO, but would also give the allies a welcome opportunity to influence the formulation of US overall strategy. Italian participation in nuclear planning or in MLF alternatives, such as the British proposal of an Atlantic Nuclear Force (ANF), he argued, would bring the country closer to equal status vis-à-vis its allies, an objective that seemed all the more urgent given the fears of being excluded from core decision-making inside the Western alliance. Trilateral negotiations between Washington, Bonn, and London that were taking place around that time – officially to discuss offsetting the cost of US and British forces in West Germany – were regarded with great suspicion in Italy. They were seen as a potential nucleus for an exclusive, restricted nuclear consultation group at the expense of Italian aspirations – "a tragic mistake, not only insulting Italy but capable of producing most serious repercussions there," in the irate words of the Italian ambassador in Washington, Sergio Fenoaltea, who passionately pleaded with the State Department to immediately stop these conversations.[8]

Italian interest in a hardware solution involving US nuclear sharing, however, was still very strong as late as 1966, even if the government in Rome was aware that its chances were shrinking. What mattered was that the principle of parity be preserved and that the door to a multilateral nuclear option not be closed by any of the disarmament solutions that were simultaneously being discussed at the Eighteen-Nation Committee on Disarmament (ENDC) in Geneva. The point was made unmistakably clear by Prime Minister Aldo Moro to Foreign Minister Amintore Fanfani in June 1966:

> I would like to be sure that we are holding firm on the point we have made until now, namely that any collective nuclear force projects, such as the multilateral or any similar ones, [...] cannot be considered as [nuclear] dissemination and would not therefore meet any obstacle in Geneva in any of the proposals we make ourselves or we support, when made by someone else.[9]

While the MLF negotiations were dragging on, therefore, the Italian delegation in Geneva was tasked with maintaining a precarious balance between supporting the principle of nonproliferation and the right to set up a collective nuclear-sharing arrangement, whatever form it might take.[10] Thus all the Italian initiatives in Geneva were conceived with the specific purpose to give the utmost flexibility to any disarmament measures that the ENDC might adopt. Any future nonproliferation agreement had to be compatible with an arrangement for nuclear-sharing promoting Italian aspirations to a higher standing inside NATO. Balancing these somewhat conflicting goals was not easy, but it was seen as all the more necessary to secure the survival of the Alliance as well as of Italy's basic foreign policy goals.

Italy 81

Italian reactions to the New US NPT draft, late 1966–early 1967

At the December 1966 NATO Ministerial Council, US Secretary of State Dean Rusk confidentially disclosed a new preliminary draft of Articles I and II of the envisaged treaty on nuclear nonproliferation to the Secretary General of the Italian Foreign Ministry, Egidio Ortona, who reacted with "extreme perplexity."[11] In the following month and a half, as other articles of the US draft were gradually revealed, Ortona's personal bewilderment turned into a wave of collective indignation that opened one of the most serious crises in the history of postwar Italian foreign policy. The crux of the matter, as an internal Foreign Ministry note remarked, was the transformation of the US position on Article I. Until early November 1966, the US stance had seemed to leave room for some form of nuclear-sharing arrangement. The draft shown to Ortona by Rusk, on the other hand,

> would radically innovate the previous American positions, as it would drop both the possibility of any nuclear sharing inside an alliance, and the possible creation of a European nuclear force. This would be tantamount to accepting, by and large, the Soviet position.[12]

Before the US government finalized its thinking on the matter, therefore, Ambassador Fenoaltea was instructed to inform Secretary Rusk on the three principles "on which Italy attached considerable importance," namely:

1 The Treaty should contain nothing which would stand in the way of political integration of Europe, provision should be made specifically for gradual movement toward European unity. Italy will oppose any formulation which permits a European nuclear force only after complete unity has been established.
2 The treaty should include as signatories all states on the threshold of becoming nuclear powers, and also Italy's neighbors, including Yugoslavia and other states of the Mediterranean basin.
3 Provision should be made for peaceful uses of nuclear energy.[13]

These three issues formed the core of the Italian opposition during the following months. A fourth item was added when a possible text for Article III (safeguards) was disclosed at the end of January 1967: the Foreign Ministry defined it "as harmful as it could be," arguing that it would introduce an absolute discrimination between nuclear and non-nuclear countries and it would also "cause the gravest damage to the European Community" by denying any validity to European Atomic Energy Community (EURATOM) safeguards.[14]

Besides the formal objections, however, there were important *political* reasons for the visceral Italian resentment. These reasons were expressed with extreme candor to Ambassador Reinhardt a few days later by an Italian "top

82   L. Nuti

diplomat" who defined them as his own personal views. In the subsequent months, however, they would be repeated time and again in the internal Foreign Ministry memos:

> US draft would give Europe to De Gaulle. It would make France paramount in Europe as only nuclear power on continent: and would show that De Gaulle had been right to make his own national nuclear force while others, who had stuck to the interests of NATO and Atlantic partnership in hope of showing to De Gaulle that had been wrong, would be relegated to second-class status.[15]

The Italians left the US in no doubt about the severity with which they regarded the change in the US position. It was a veritable watershed, Ortona told ambassador Reinhardt, and

> the more Italians studied the draft treaty, the deeper became their concern with regard for its implications for the future of Italy and Europe. They felt it constituted for Italy *a turning point in postwar foreign policy*, and he said *he had never seen* [PM] *Moro so oppressed* by the gravity of a decision he was called upon to make [my emphasis].[16]

Translating this dismay into a coherent policy, however, proved quite difficult. NATO Secretary General Manlio Brosio noted that in the Foreign Ministry "Everybody is aware of the gravity of the thing and would like to oppose it, but no one knows how. They hesitate to align Italy with Germany alone." Fanfani, Brosio added, seemed cautious and inclined to gain time by raising objections or asking for clarifications, hoping that eventually the US might realize that it was not in Italy's interest to sign the new treaty.[17] The US, however, was insisting that Italy define its position as early as possible and was not willing to accept the Italian stalling strategy. In early February 1967, therefore, a first restricted meeting took place at the Foreign Ministry to define the Italian position. It concluded that it would be preferable not to tie Italy's hands forever. Italy should adhere to a treaty only for a limited period of time, at least until the nuclear states had given ample evidence of their determination to reduce their arsenals.[18] The new draft, it was concluded in a subsequent meeting, had "dangerous implications for the principles which for many years had shaped Italian policy on European and Atlantic issues," and it tried to stabilize the international system "at the expenses of the non-nuclear countries" and above all of those states "which have reached, or are very close to, the so-called nuclear option," thus enshrining forever what was just a temporary difference. It would also give France "a clear cut political and military hegemony inside any eventual European political association limited to continental Europe," thereby encouraging the Gaullist policy of excluding Britain from the Community.[19]

The Italian position led to a rather tense bilateral confrontation when it was revealed to Secretary Rusk a few days later. After repeating his instructions almost verbatim, Ambassador Fenoaltea officially asked Rusk to modify the unlimited duration of the treaty, replacing it with a five-year period at the end of which a new conference would decide whether the treaty would remain in force or not. Rusk rebutted that he was "disappointed" by the Italian refusal of the principle of nonproliferation, and bluntly asked whether Italy thought it was desirable to stop the current trend of nuclear proliferation: yes or no? If the answer was no, it would be necessary to draw the logical consequences.[20] A subsequent written US response rejected the Italian arguments in more detail, but ignored the *political* rationale behind the Italian opposition. The whole negotiation, therefore, threatened to become a *dialogue des sourds*, in which both sides knew quite well what the main issue at stake was, but never dared to openly discuss it.

With the bilateral negotiations with Washington temporarily stalled, the Italian government summoned a meeting of the Supreme Defense Council, the highest security body in the country. On February 20, 1967, the Council was opened by Fanfani with the momentous statement that the NPT issue was "of an exceptional gravity which deserved the greatest attention."[21] After a critical survey of the negotiations, the President of the Republic, the social-democrat Giuseppe Saragat, commented that the problem was "of vital importance" for Italy. He then warned the participants to be careful lest Italy be the only country to pay a price for nonproliferation, and launched into a violent tirade

> Everything we heard worries us. At our border, France is a nuclear power. And if the French bombs do not bother Russia, they bother us. We had tried to come out of a heavy situation through the multilateral force. At least that gave us some joint management of nuclear strategy. Now the multilateral force is gone and in its place we have this non-proliferation agreement. The US are getting along with the USSR behind our back. And if other countries, such as Israel and Egypt, arm themselves with these weapons, we, who are the most important power in the Mediterranean, in what conditions will we find ourselves? [...] As for the inspections, is it conceivable that we be reduced to the rank of Egypt at the time of the capitulation treaties? That we be submitted to the pressure and the blackmail of others?[22]

A gloomy debate ensued, with all the participants taking a very pessimistic view on the proposed treaty. Criticism ranged from strategic to technical and technological reasons. Prime Minister Moro, a quintessentially cautious and moderate statesman, warned that the US text "blocked any chance of any major development in a European sense" and that the "condition of disparity which the draft imposed on the non-nuclear countries made the treaty unacceptable." However, he suggested that Italy should not follow a line of "absolute denial" at the negotiations in Geneva, but one of cautious and sustained pressure to obtain a substantial modification of the treaty. In spite of some additional strident criticism from Saragat, this is the conclusion that the Council eventually adopted and the Italian representative in Geneva was instructed accordingly.[23]

84 *L. Nuti*

Interestingly, the official minutes do not contain any hint that the Council ever discussed a possible national nuclear option if the government opted for an outright rejection of the treaty, but the personal recollections of two of the participants – Fanfani and Minister of Interior Paolo Emilio Taviani – do.[24] Perhaps someone proposed radical solutions during the discussion but these were eventually expunged from the official record. What matters, however, is the final result: out of a very tense confrontation and a hostile general attitude against the treaty, Fanfani was instructed to take a critical stance against the US draft, but also to keep negotiating.[25]

In the following months Italian diplomacy closely followed these instructions, surprising the Lyndon B. Johnson administration with its stubborn opposition. In the North Atlantic Council, in particular, the Italian delegate refused to pledge Italy's support for the new draft the US intended to table at the ENDC negotiations.[26] A similar hostility was displayed in a number of bilateral talks with members of the Johnson administration, such as ACDA Director William Foster and Vice-President Hubert Humphrey. President Saragat was the most eloquent critic of the treaty, telling Humphrey that Italy,

> could have a bomb in four years if it started to build one now or could have had one now if it had started earlier. Italy does not [...] want to have a bomb [...] doesn't want to involve itself in a nuclear force and doesn't want to get in the nuclear club. Hence, Italy doesn't need reins to keep it in line. Given this situation, Italy wanted a treaty which would not be unfair to countries which do not [...] want their own nuclear arms. [...] Italy as a leading industrial power in the Mediterranean basin cannot accept a position of inferiority to Mediterranean countries of a lesser industrial capacity.[27]

Foster was also given an aide memoire which contained a long list of clarifications, a document which was so detailed as to raise many doubts in Washington about Italy's ultimate intentions.

The only opening in this gloomy picture seemed to come from a meeting between Fanfani and the US ambassador to NATO, Harlan Cleveland, in early March 1967. The Italian foreign minister impressed Cleveland with his suggestions to make the draft treaty more balanced by reinforcing the disarmament pledge of the nuclear countries, as well as to have the NPT guarantee the validity of the EURATOM safeguards and avoid their replacement with ones from the International Atomic Energy Agency (IAEA). Both proposals, Cleveland concluded, should be seriously considered as they presented "significant opportunities" for accommodation with the US position without jeopardizing the goals of the treaty.[28] Fanfani's confidential demarche, however, remained an isolated episode, as all other Italian declarations regarding the NPT continued to be highly critical. By early April 1967 the Foreign Ministry officially informed the State Department that the Italian government still had three major reservations, each one encompassing a whole cluster of different problems.[29] Confidentially, the US ambassador in Rome was told that a

Italy 85

number of key diplomats were encouraging the Foreign Minister to stick to such a rigid position.[30]

In order to break the impasse, in April 1967 Rusk wrote to Fanfani that the US was willing to meet some of the Italian requests, such as the guarantee of a steady supply of nuclear fuel, and that it was also ready to accept international safeguards on its own civilian nuclear plants if this could reduce the perception of the NPT as too discriminatory. Fanfani's reply expressed his appreciation for the US efforts, but retained a non-committal attitude.[31] A similar stance was displayed by Prime Minister Moro when he met US President Johnson a few days later at the funeral of Konrad Adenauer. "This nuclear problem," Moro concisely summed up the issue, "was essentially a political one." He felt that the treaty "in its present form might have very serious repercussions on European politics and that furthermore it could have a negative effect on the Atlantic alliance." After Johnson tried to reassure him in his most effusive language that the US would never do anything against the interests of its allies, and of Italy in particular, Rusk chimed in stressing the importance of preventing proliferation. Moro, however, concluded that as much as he was worried by "a possible proliferation," he was also concerned by the danger "that might be caused by the treaty in its present form [and] all efforts should be made so as to avoid any such danger."[32] Nor was the tone of the public debate any more encouraging, since most newspapers seemed to share the bewilderment of the government.[33] Only the Communists, some of the Socialists, and the tiny Republican Party took an outspoken position in favor of the NPT. The most conspicuous support came from Italian physicists, who in early March 1967 circulated an appeal inviting the government to support a nonproliferation agreement without any further hesitations.

Countermeasures? The Italian government, nuclear naval propulsion, and uranium enrichment

The stalling strategy towards the NPT negotiations was accompanied by a number of new initiatives regarding scientific and technological cooperation with Italy's European partners. This approach might have reflected Italy's aspirations to play a larger role in civilian nuclear matters as it saw itself faced with impending restrictions on military affairs. Joint enrichment projects and naval propulsion, in particular, became the subjects of a protracted diplomatic activity from 1967 on.[34]

The interest in participating in a joint project on uranium enrichment was the result of the convergence of a number of factors, all coming to a head concomitant with the NPT negotiations reaching a turning point in the summer of 1967. Plans for a joint European nuclear enrichment plant had been discussed before, but they had never gone very far for a variety of reasons. Now several critical factors were spurring a number of European countries to reconsider this option. In May 1967, the EURATOM Commission approved a memorandum which officially recommended the creation of a European enrichment plant.[35]

86   L. Nuti

At the same time, a major technological breakthrough was emerging, one that was going to have a dramatic impact on the whole world of uranium enrichment. By the mid-1960s it was becoming increasing clear that the commercially uncompetitive method of centrifugal isotopic separation might soon become a lot cheaper – and easier to reproduce – than the more expensive gaseous diffusion technique used until then. By early 1967, the British, the Dutch, and the West German governments had all independently reached this conclusion and started negotiations that would eventually lead to the 1970 treaty of Almelo and the establishment of their joint consortium, Urenco.[36]

The Italian government watched these developments with apprehension. Its civilian nuclear program had gone through several ups and downs, but by the mid-1960s it had grown to a respectable size, with three operating power reactors, two small research reactors, a pilot reprocessing plant under completion, and a large number of ambitious, albeit highly controversial, research projects.[37] Its main structural problem remained the fact that the *Comitato Nazionale Energia Nucleare* (CNEN) was under the control of the Ministry of Industry, rather than an authoritative, and largely independent, agency modeled after the United Kingdom Atomic Energy Agency (UKAEA) in Great Britain or the *Commissariat à l'Energie Atomique* (CEA) in France. The unfolding of this flurry of European projects, however, spurred the Italian nuclear elite into action. In June 1967, the CNEN approved a document which encouraged the intensification of all activities related to the mid- and long-term procurement of uranium supplies, including the participation in international initiatives and the definition of a clear-cut national policy.[38] In the following months, both the specialized press and a number of relevant political figures started mentioning the idea of a European enrichment plant. Two individuals were particularly outspoken in their support for a European project: Achille Albonetti, the Director of the CNEN International Relations Division, who in the last months of 1967 began to publish a number of articles praising the idea of a European separation plant,[39] and Giulio Andreotti, the new Minister of Industry, who remained very much concerned with Italy's nuclear activities.[40] Thus, the CNEN started exploring the opportunity to cooperate with Great Britain in the field of centrifugal separation, including the possible Italian participation in the tripartite arrangement with the West Germans and the Dutch.[41]

Neither the European enrichment plant nor the Italian participation in the future Urenco would ultimately be successful.[42] After long negotiations, Italy was not admitted into the British–Dutch–West German project and instead entered the field of uranium enrichment by accepting to participate in the French initiative for the expansion of the site of Pierrelatte, what would later be called EURODIF (*European Gaseous Diffusion Uranium Enrichment Consortium*). In the context of this chapter, however, it is important to highlight the coincidence in 1967 of the upsurge in interest for uranium enrichment with the progress of NPT negotiations. This strong interest in enrichment technology was certainly influenced by rapidly evolving economic and technological factors, but the impact of the concerns engendered by the NPT should not be underestimated.

Italy 87

In April 1967, for instance, an internal Foreign Ministry memo warned that the current NPT draft would impose a number of severe controls on any Italian initiative in the field of uranium enrichment or of plutonium reprocessing.[43]

A similar rationale probably explains the almost simultaneous initiative to develop an Italian nuclear-propelled surface vessel. After Andreotti's formal request for US assistance to develop an Italian nuclear submarine in December 1962, the negotiations with the US dragged on for several years. In 1966, the Italian navy formally dropped the idea and signed an agreement with the CNEN for the development of a nuclear propelled *surface* ship. This was clearly done with the hope that such a change would eliminate any US resistance to providing the necessary assistance. Shortly after the project was launched Albonetti inquired whether the US could provide the enriched uranium necessary to both complete a critical test of the ship's engine and to guarantee a regular supply of fuel for its reactor. The US State Department, however, made it clear that the civilian and military dual-use nature of the vessel was still likely to raise strong Congressional opposition, and suggested that the Italian navy's participation in the project be replaced through an entirely civilian agency.[44] The CNEN replied with a detailed memo which included almost all the guarantees the US had requested, but specified that the participation of the Italian navy was necessary because only the Defense Ministry could supply the required funding for the project.[45]

Initially the State Department assessed the Italian memo in moderately favorable terms, but when Albonetti and Admiral Luigi Tomasuolo eventually made an exploratory trip to Washington they met with stiff resistance.[46] The negative outcome of their inquiry spurred the CNEN to find elsewhere the required low-enriched uranium. By July 31, 1967, Albonetti wrote to his counterpart in the UKAEA, J.L. Croome (Director of the Authority's Overseas Relations Office), officially inquiring about the price of the materials necessary for "the performance of a critical experiment, the irradiation tests of fuel elements, the fabrication of the first reactor core."[47] At the same time, similar requests were sent to the Atomic Energy Commission (AEC) in the United States and the CEA in France.

The Italian request sparked a long and heated debate within the British government, which found itself "caught in the cross fire of [its] European Common market and Anglo-American interests."[48] Inside the British government, all sides saw an obvious linkage between a nuclear fuel supply to Italy, the parallel negotiations on the NPT, and the joint enrichment plants. A denial, a British internal memo concluded, "would be interpreted by the Italians as discriminatory and against their interests. Their willingness to sign a Non-Proliferation Treaty would hardly be enhanced."[49] This assessment turned out to be remarkably accurate. Not only was resentment against the US growing within the Italian nuclear establishment, but the Johnson administration's attitude reinforced the temptation to look elsewhere for fuel supply. When Albonetti went to London to discuss the matter with his British counterparts, he stated that the Italians

88   *L. Nuti*

felt that they could not be entirely dependent on others for supplies of enriched materials for nuclear ships, whether for marine or naval purposes. Privately off the record, he added some fairly intemperate remarks about the attitude of the Americans [...] he had also made enquiries in France and he thought that the French would be prepared to supply their requirements in exchange for plutonium derived from [the Italian plant in] Latina.[50]

Albonetti's temperament might be the best explanation for his outburst, but his anti-American attitude was widely shared, as the US refusal to provide "even" the supply for the nuclear-propelled ship had "sunk deeply" into the conscience of the Italian nuclear industry, forcing "both industry and the government to come to the proper conclusion that Italy must look to itself in this regard and not be in a position to be dependent on others."[51]

Eventually, the nuclear fuel negotiations with the US State Department and the UK Foreign Office became strictly interwoven with the parallel discussions on centrifugal enrichment, and many in London thought it necessary to compensate the likely Italian exclusion from the trilateral consortium by meeting their demands for the ship's fuel.[52] After clearing the matter with the US, the British government finally extended its formal offer at the end of November 1968. For a number of reasons, no Italian reply came until August 1969. At that point Albonetti surprisingly replied that the CNEN and the Italian navy were no longer interested in the British offer, as they had decided to accept another one, "considered more convenient" – clearly the one of the French CEA.[53] While the French side of the negotiations is still classified, it is not difficult to imagine that the final decision to accept one offer instead of the other can probably be explained not only by the economically attractive offer made by the CEA, but also by the fact that France was going to accept Italy as a partner inside EURODIF, while the British could not do the same with Urenco. To this day, Albonetti remembers with a clear *Schadenfreude* the somewhat baffled reaction of both the English and the Americans when he told them that the CNEN had decided to accept the French offer.[54]

Reluctantly accepting "a dose of castor oil"

While strengthening its profile in the field of nuclear technology and negotiating with the Americans a possible revision of the initial draft treaty, Italy was also discussing the impact of the NPT with some of the most outspoken opponents of the agreement. The most significant talks were those with the West Germans, who were clearly sharing Italian feelings about the NPT.[55] After some rather cautious initial encounters, the Italians suggested that from a tactical point of view it would be better to present their points of view on the NPT separately, and possibly even using different rationales for their criticisms.[56] Rather than presenting a common front, the two countries should therefore develop a close consultation and division of labor – a suggestion fully approved by the West Germans, who declared a preference for "a de facto parallelism to an organized bilateralism."[57] By the late spring 1967, the consultations reached their climax in two lengthy meetings between Prime Minister Moro and FRG Chancellor Kurt-Georg Kiesinger. Both leaders openly expressed their disappointment with the American proposal and pledged to continue their close cooperation in trying to protect NATO from any possible negative consequences emerging from the treaty.[58]

At the same time, Italian diplomats also consulted with some Asian powers that shared their skepticism towards the NPT. By the end of April 1967, the Secretary General of the Foreign Ministry, Roberto Gaja, had two long discussions with the Indian Foreign Secretary, C.S. Jha, and two days later with a Japanese delegation led by Ambassador Nishimura, Head of the Japanese Atomic Energy.[59] These conversations seem to indicate the Italian intention to try to modify the text of the treaty rather than simply delay or postpone its inevitable entry into force. The Italian behavior during the remaining of 1967 and all of 1968, however, does not allow to draw such a clear-cut conclusion. When the US presented a new draft at the Atlantic Council in June 1967, all the members of the alliance agreed that the new text could be tabled at the next session of the ENDC in Geneva, but also continued to withhold their formal support. Fanfani, however, took the oppportunity to tell Cleveland that he was now more optimistic as he believed that the worst was over and that the strongest resistance against the treaty had been overcome.[60]

When the new session of the ENDC opened shortly thereafter, however, that same Fanfani surprised everyone by presenting yet another list of sweeping requests, including the unexpected demand that the nuclear countries pledge to transfer part of their nuclear fuel to the non-nuclear states at a special price – a proposal which was judged by the US an "unworkable and unrealistic grandstand play for non-aligned audiences."[61] A few days later, the diplomatic offensive continued with another formal demand, this time delivered by Ambassador Ortona in the form of a written aide-memoire which raised the issue of introducing more flexibility in the treaty, either by altering its duration or by defining an "appropriate and satisfactory procedure" to introduce any future amendments.[62] The permanent nature of the treaty continued to be targeted, culminating with the amendement formally presented at the ENDC by the new Italian representative at the Conference, Caracciolo, which asked that the duration of the treaty be limited to a fixed number of years.

At the end of 1967, a working group of the Ministry of Foreign Affairs drew a balance sheet of the negotiations and noted that the new US draft had accepted a number of Italian requests, such as introducing an explicit pledge to engage in future negotiations to disarm, as well as limiting the safeguards only to nuclear fuel.[63] Yet many issues remained unresolved, noted another internal memo in early 1968, stressing as particularly important the limitation of the duration of the envisaged treaty, the security of supply of nuclear fuel, and the right to experiment with peaceful nuclear explosions.[64]

While the Foreign Ministry retained this guarded attitude, a foreign policy debate in the Italian Senate displayed an increasing support for a quick

90 *L. Nuti*

conclusion of the NPT negotiations. Spurred by some stinging criticism, Fanfani openly supported a rapid conclusion of the treaty, admitting that a quick conclusion might be preferable to any future improvements obtained through a prolongation of the negotiations. His statement, however, was almost immediately contradicted when a US diplomat in Rome was confidentially told the opposite.[65] This alternation continued throughout the first months of 1968. When Caracciolo presented three more amendments in Geneva, Rusk himself penned an irritated response, noting that the US had already met many Italian requests and did not see how many more it could accept. Yet the pressure continued, and eventually some of the late Italian requests found their way into the treaty.[66] Article VIII and Article X.2, in particular, established that every five years there would be a review conference and that the treaty would remain in force for a period of twenty-five years, at the end of which a conference would decide whether or not to prolong it indefinetely.[67] The request for an explicit right to conduct "peaceful nuclear explosions," on the other hand, was repeatedly denied, while the issue of fuel supply, and of the safeguards it should be submitted to, continued to remain unresolved. Eventually, the Italian delegation to the ENDC approved the presentation of the draft treaty to the United Nations General Assembly (UNGA) and, subsequently, Italy voted in favour of the approving UNGA resolution.[68] After the UN vote, however, the Italian Foreign Ministry gave the Ambassador in Washington a "problematic and unrealistic task," namely to ask the Johnson administration to slow down the submission of the treaty to the US Senate until a compromise on the issue of safeguards could be found between the EURATOM and the IAEA.[69] Clearly, US Ambassador Gardner Ackley remarked, Italy still regarded the treaty as a heavy dose of "castor oil": "principle good, effects bad."[70]

In the late spring of 1968, the Italian political system experienced a serious shock which created an uncertain political setting and made it even more difficult for any government to formulate a consistent position on the NPT. After the May 1968 elections, the center-left coalition met an unexpected defeat which jeopardized its future. While the Christian Democrats only suffered minimal losses, the Socialist Party lost over 5 percent. On the other hand, the main opposition force, the Italian Communist Party, increased its representation by almost 2 percent, a marginal victory which nonetheless strengthened the forces which supported the treaty. When the US, the USSR, and the UK signed the NPT on July 1, 1968, however, the domestic crisis in Italy was still far from being resolved. The caretaker government led by Giovanni Leone could only take the unusual decision to submit the treaty to the Italian parliament, and open up a debate, *before* the government signed it. A long, tense, and often harsh discussion ended with the creation of a strange majority in which the Christian Democrats, the Socialists, the Communists, and the tiny Republican Party supported the treaty, the Neo-Fascists and the Monarchists opposed it, and the conservative Liberals abstained from taking a position. Between the votes of the Chamber of Deputies (July 18, 1968) and of the Senate (July 26, 1968), the new Foreign Minister, Giuseppe Medici, met with Ambassador Ackley and told him

Italy 91

that his government was finally ready to sign the NPT, even if Italy remained "unhappy with the treaty."[71]

Just when it appeared as if the long charade was almost over, the Soviet invasion of Czechoslovakia offered a wonderful opportunity for a "pause for reflection." The Soviet action, the Italian government noted immediately, "jeopardized the entire basis of the treaty," which was rooted in the principle of détente. Just when the government was about to sign, therefore, the Prague crisis forced it to reconsider.[72] Needless to say, the pause was exploited once again for renewed initiatives meant to strengthen the Italian negotiating position, and perhaps postpone the signature indefinitely. Thus, Italy flirted with the idea of an alternative international body to the IAEA for managing the future nonproliferation regime. Yet at the same time the Foreign Ministry let it be known that it would be interested in a possible seat on the IAEA's Board of Governors. Italy also supported the convocation of a conference of non-nuclear states to define a common position towards the treaty, and launched a (largely unsuccessful) initiative to synchronize its possible signature with those of twelve other "significant" non-nuclear states, from India to Brazil, China, Japan, Israel, West Germany, and Australia.[73] Not surprisingly, the US took a sharply critical view of all of these moves.[74] The animosity, however, was mutual: in a highly confidential talk, an Italian diplomat revealed that the Foreign Ministry was still in "an acute anti-American phase" and that many of his colleagues "were looking forward to a new US administration to display a more sympathetic attitude toward NATO and European problems."[75]

Finally, the solution came with the creation of a new center-left government led by the Christian Democrat Mariano Rumor and with the Socialist Pietro Nenni as Foreign Minister. Nenni, who had consistently spoken in favor of the treaty since 1967, made it clear that he wanted to sign the NPT right away and he did so on January 28, 1969. It should be noted, however, that the signature was also accompanied by a long protocol listing no less than twelve reservations. Nor was the saga over, as Italy would ratify the treaty only six and a half years later, in May 1975, after another vitriolic debate. The signature, therefore, only marked the win of the first round by the supporters of the treaty.

Conclusion

Why did the Italian government eventually sign the NPT in January 1969? First of all, as the Foreign Ministry itself noted in a number of internal memos, many of the Italian requests had been met, and the treaty looked far more acceptable in 1969 than it had done in early 1967. This defanged much of the initial criticism and made it more difficult to oppose the treaty on technical terms. At the same time, the growing parliamentary support for the principle of nonproliferation made it also difficult to oppose the treaty on *political* terms, as almost none of the key political leaders of the center-left wanted to be perceived as an implicit supporter of a national nuclear option. This left the difficult task of opposing the treaty to a number of highly placed bureaucrats (from Albonetti at the CNEN to

Gaja, Ducci, and others in the Foreign Ministry). Subsequent to the signature, these bureaucrats formed a strong coalition and continued their protracted resistance against the treaty. Finally, the expected success of some of the negotiations on nuclear enrichment and nuclear naval propulsion might have made it more tolerable to sign a nonproliferation agreement, since when (and if) it would come into force Italy was likely to have strengthened its nuclear standing in both fields. The sum of these circumstances, coupled with a growing international pressure, made it possible for Nenni to do what his predecessors had been reluctant to do.

Two conclusions can be drawn from the new documentary evidence presented in this chapter. The first – and obvious – one is that Italy deeply resented the NPT and saw it as a crucial turning point in the postwar era. For most Italian political leaders, the NPT opened up a historical transition, marking the end of their faith in multilateralism and in the supranational approach to European integration. What is all the more remarkable is that the opposition to the treaty was not coming from a radical and nationalist right, but was actually shared among the moderate forces of the center-left. Those who had ample reservations about the treaty were mostly Christian Democrats and even some Socialists – not to mention the Social Democratic President of the Republic, Giuseppe Saragat. Their concern did not stem from any particular militarist aspiration, but was the result of the most deeply rooted ambition of Italian foreign policy, namely to achieve a parity of status with the other European countries. Until the emergence of the NPT, the Italian political elite seemed to share the belief that such an outcome was still possible, and that the West would be able to forge a community in which even the most guarded national secrets could be shared.

A second conclusion addresses the contribution that the study of the Italian case can offer to our understanding of how countries approach the issue of nuclear proliferation. Did Italy negotiate in good faith or did it simply try to buy time, hoping that the NPT would die of natural causes, just like the MLF did before? The evidence does not seem to provide a clear-cut answer on which to build a strong case. Most protagonists were reluctant to speak out openly, and even in the confidential documents of the time, each one of them seems to try to portray himself as the only moderate, rational actor, while blaming the others for their crypto-nationalism – Fanfani being the past master in performing this role.

Faced with an unpleasant choice, Italy probably tried to follow many parallel courses of action – all at once. Such an ambiguous behavior seems to be consistent with Ariel Levite's intuition that the nonproliferation choice of any given country is better described as a blurred and gray process, rather than the clear trespassing of a demarcation line by a rational actor taking a formal, irreversible stance. Furthermore, Levite argues, the ambitions of a potential proliferator can best be restrained by converting them into a posture of nuclear hedging, as non-nuclear states are more likely to approve a formal limitation of their sovereignty if they are reassured by the fact that they can remain close to a nuclear option.[76] This model seems more apt to describe the Italian posture than Itty Abraham's *nuclear ambivalence.* Abraham's paradigm is also very useful in understanding

Italy 93

the Italian behavior as it stresses the inevitable dual nature of all nuclear programs and concludes that the resistance to any external control does not necessarily imply a hidden military aspiration.[77] In the Italian resistance to the NPT, however, there was a military dimension, albeit probably not a strictly national one. Italy bargained hard to obtain as many changes as possible in the initial draft, it tried to postpone to the most possible distant future the moment of truth, it attempted to strengthen its nuclear capabilities by probing the limits of what could and could not be done within the NPT, and it tried to the very end to keep open a European military nuclear option

Notes

1 Leopoldo Nuti, *La sfida nucleare. La politica estera italiana e le armi atomiche, 1945–1991* (Bologna: Il Mulino, 2007); a short English summary of the book's main points can be found in Leopoldo Nuti, "Italy's Nuclear Choices," *UNISCI Discussion Papers* 25 (2011): 167–181.
2 I owe the customary debt of gratitude to William Burr for pointing out to me that the ACDA collection had just been opened to researchers a few days before my fall 2013 trip to College Park.
3 On the events of 1943 and their consequences, see Elena Aga Rossi, *Una nazione allo sbando. L'armistizio italiano del settembre 1943 e le sue conseguenze* (Bologna: Il Mulino, 1993) and Ennio Di Nolfo and Maurizio Serra, *La gabbia infranta. Gli alleati e l'Italia dal 1943 al 1945* (Roma: Laterza, 2010); on the foundations of post-Second World War Italian foreign policy, Ennio Di Nolfo, Romain H. Rainero, and Brunello Vigezzi, eds., *L'Italia e la politica di potenza in Europa, 1945–1950* (Milano: Marzorati, 1988).
4 I have repeatedly investigated the Franco-Italian–German (FIG) nuclear agreements, in particular in "Le role de l'Italie dans les negociations trilaterales 1957–1958," *Revue d'Histoire Diplomatique* 104, nos. 1–2 (1990): 133–158 and "The F-I-G Story Revisited," in *Dividing the Atom. Essays on the History of Nuclear Proliferation in Europe*, eds. Leopoldo Nuti and Cyril Buffet. A Special Issue of the Journal *Storia delle Relazioni Internazionali* 13, no. 1 (1998): 69–100. See also my forthcoming "Extended Deterrence and National Ambitions: Italy's Nuclear Policy, 1955–1962," in *Journal of Strategic Studies* 39, no. 4 (2016): 559–579.
5 Alberto Rossi Longhi al Presidente del Consiglio, November 24, 1958, *Archivio Storico Ministero Affari Esteri*, Rome, Italy (ASMAE), *Amb. Parigi. 1951–1955*, b. 80.
6 Letter from American Embassy Rome (Gannett) to the Dept. of State (Conroy), December 20, 1962, *National Archives and Records Administration*, College Park, MD, USA (NACP), Record Group 59 (RG 59), Lot file 67 D 516, NATO Affairs 1959–1966, Box 9, f. Italy (May 1964–1965).
7 MemCon (Fenoaltea-Smith), October 23, 1964, and MemCon (Fenoaltea, Petrignani, Rusk, Spiers, Smith), October 24, 1964, ibid.
8 MemCon (Fenoaltea, the Under Secretary), December 30, 1965, ibid.
9 PM Aldo Moro to FM Amintore Fanfani, June 25, 1966, *Archivio Aldo Moro* (AAM), *Archivio Centrale dello Stato*, Rome, Italy (ACS), b. 54, f. NATO, sub folder (sb) "Questioni generali." Moro was so concerned with this issue that a month later he expressly repeated the instructions to the Italian ENDC delegation not to mix the MLF with the NPT negotiations: Appunto per la Segreteria Generale da parte del Consigliere Diplomatico alla Presidenza del Consiglio (Pompei), August 10, 1966, in AAM, ACS, b. 93, f. TNP.

94   *L. Nuti*

10 "L'Italia e i negoziati per il trattato di non-diffusione delle armi nucleari," 31, type-written document by Amb. Emilio Bettini, Head of the Disarmament Office of the Italian Foreign Ministry, ASMAE, fondo Bettini, b. 7.

11 Egidio Ortona, *Anni d'america. Vol. III, La Diplomazia (1967–1975)* (Bologna: Il Mulino, 1989), 48.

12 Evoluzione della posizione americana nei riguardi di un accordo di non-disseminazione delle armi nucleari, (undated, but probably late December 1966), ACS, AAM, b. 93, f. TNP.

13 MemCon (Fenoaltea, Rusk, and others), January 25, 1967, "Draft Non-Proliferation Treaty," NACP, RG 383 (Records of the Arms Control and Disarmament Agency), Director's Office NPT files, Box 4, f. NPT-Italy 1967–1968.

14 Internal note attached to a letter from Secretary General Gaja to Diplomatic Counsellor Pompei, February 1, 1967, ACS, AAM, b. 93, f. TNP.

15 Telegram 4085 from US Embassy Rome (Reinhardt) to the Secretary of State, February 7, 1967, NACP, RG 383, Director's Office NPT files, Box 4, f. NPT-Italy 1967–1968.

16 Telegram 4087 from US Embassy Rome (Reinhardt) to the Secretary of State, February 7, 1967, ibid.

17 Manlio Brosio, *Diari NATO 1964–1972* (Bologna: Il Mulino, 2011), 366.

18 Entry of February 4, 1967, *Diario Fanfani*, in *Archivio Storico del Senato della Repubblica*, Rome, Italy (ASSR), Carte Fanfani.

19 Appunto, Accordo di non-disseminazione nucleare, February 5, 1967, ASMAE, Fondo Bettini, b.1.

20 Tel. 133734 from the State Dept. to Embassy Rome, February 8, 1967, "Italian Views on Non-Proliferation Treaty," NACP, RG 383, Director's Office NPT files, Box 4, f. NPT-Italy 1967–1968; the Italian delegate to the North Atlantic Council restated the same arguments, MemCon, February 10, 1965, ibid.

21 Seduta del 20 febbraio 1967 del Consiglio Supremo di Difesa, *Archivio Storico della Presidenza della Repubblica*, Rome, Italy (ASPR), Verbali delle Sedute del Consiglio Supremo di Difesa.

22 Ibid.

23 Ibid.

24 Entry of February 20, 1967, ASS, *Diario Fanfani*, and Tel. 13257 from AmEmbassy Paris to State Dept., March 1, 1967, NACP, RG 383, Director's Office NPT files, Box 4, f. NPT-Italy 1967–1968; Paolo Emilio Taviani, *Politica a Memoria d'uomo* (Bologna: Il Mulino, 2002), 217.

25 Entry of February 20, 1967, ASS, *Diario Fanfani*; M. Brosio, *Diari NATO*, March 1, 1967, 374.

26 The rigid position taken by the Italian Ambassador to NATO is highlighted (with much satisfaction) by Brosio in the pages of his journal. See the entries from February through April 1967, 367–392.

27 Tel. 5101 from AmEmbassy Rome to State Dept., April 1, 1967, NACP, RG 383, Director's Office NPT files, Box 4, f. NPT-Italy 1967–1968.

28 Tel. 13788 from AmEmbassy Paris to State Dept., March 7, 1967, ibid.; entry of March 1, 1967, ASS, *Diario Fanfani*.

29 Tel. 167791 from the State Dept. to AmEmbassy Rome, April 3, 1967, NACP, RG 383, Director's Office NPT files, Box 4, f. NPT-Italy 1967–1968.

30 Tel. 398 from AmEmbassy Rome to the State Dept., April 13, 1967, ibid.

31 Telegram 177013 from the Dept. of State to the Embassy in Rome, April 18, 1967, and Fanfani to Rusk, April 19, 1967, ibid.

32 Tel. 12810 from AmEmbassy Bonn to the Dept. of State, April 26, 1967, ibid.

33 Aldo Garosci, "Le difficoltà di un trattato ineguale," *L'Avanti!*, March 5, 1967.

34 Both were mentioned in the aide-memoire given to Foster: Appunto "Considerazioni preliminari sulle risposte americane al questionario tecnico da noi consegnato al Signor Foster," April 8, 1967, ASMAE, Fondo Bettini, b. 1.

35 Susanna Schrafstetter and Stephen Twigge, "Spinning into Europe: Britain, West Germany and the Netherlands: Uranium Enrichment and the Development of the Gas Centrifuge 1964–1970," *Contemporary European History* 11, no. 2 (2002): 256; Jean-Pierre Davier, *Eurodif 1973–1993. Histoire de l'enrichissement de l'uranium* (Bruges: Fonds Mercator, 1993), 319; Tel. 6869 from AmEmbassy Brussels to the State Dept, June 21, 1967, NACP, RG 59, CFPF 1967–1969. b. 2897, f. AE 11–2 EURATOM.

36 R.B. Kehoe, *The Enriching Troika: A History of Urenco to the Year 2000* (Marlow: URENCO, 2002); John Krige, "The Proliferation Risks of Gas Centrifuge Enrichment at the Dawn of the NPT," *The Nonproliferation Review* 19, no. 2 (2012): 6.

37 For a highly critical analysis of the Italian civilian program, see Mario Silvestri, *Il costo della menzogna. Italia nucleare, 1945–1968* (Torino: Einaudi, 1968); for an updated (and less biased) appraisal, Silvio Labbate, *Il governo dell'energia. L'Italia dal petrolio al nucleare (1945–1975)* (Firenze: Le Monnier, 2010).

38 Labbate, *Il governo dell'energia,* 108f.

39 Silvestri, *Il costo della menzogna,* 379ff.

40 Ibid., 376f.

41 "Italy and the Centrifuge Organization," note by G.P.C. Macartney, August 30 1972, *UK National Archives*, Kew, United Kingdom (UKNA), FCO 55–933 Participation of Italy in Tripartite Centrifuge Arrangement.

42 Ibid.

43 Appunto "Considerazioni preliminari sulle risposte americane al questionario tecnico da noi consegnato al Signor Foster," April 8, 1967, ASMAE, Fondo Bettini, b.1.

44 Tel. 135835 from the State Dept. to the Embassy in Rome, February 13, 1967, NACP, RG 59, CFPF 1967–68, f. DEF 12 IT.

45 Airgram A-932 from the Embassy in Rome to the Dept. of State, "Italian request for nuclear fuel," April 14, 1967, NACP, RG 59, CFPF 1967–68, b. 1560, f. DEF 12 IT.

46 Silvestri, *Il costo della menzogna,* 385f.; see also *The Department of State during the Administration of President Lyndon B. Johnson. Volume I: Administrative History,* Chapter 3, Part D, Bilateral Relations with Western Europe – Italy, DDRS, 1985/2834.

47 Letter from A. Albonetti to J.L. Croome, July 31, 1967, UKNA, EG 8, f. 43 "Export of Enriched Uranium for Italian Nuclear Ship."

48 Letter from M. Michaels to M. Palliser, March 11, 1968, UKNA, EG 8, f. 44 "Export of Enriched Uranium for Italian Nuclear Ship"; Letter from Robert Press (Cabinet Office) to J.L. Croome, UKAEA, August 23, 1967, UKNA, EG 8, f. 43 "Export of enriched uranium for Italian nuclear ship."

49 Memo attached to a letter from J. Mcadam Clark to G.E. Hall, October 17, 1967, UKNA, EG 8, f. 43.

50 Letter from J.L. Croome to G.E. Hall, October 31, 1967, UKNA, EG 8, f. 43.

51 Airgram A-672 from Amembassy Rome to State Dept., December 22, 1962, NACP, RG 59, CFPF 1967–69, b. 1560, f. DEF 12 IT.

52 Letter from Fred Mulley to the Secretary of State for Defence, November 8, 1968, UKNA, EG 8, f. 44.

53 Letter from A. Albonetti to Mr. C. Allday, August 5, 1969, in UKNA, EG 8, f. 44; see also Letter to Chairman Holifield, JCAE, September 15, 1969, NACP, RG 59, CPFP 1967–69, b. 1560, f. DEF 12 IT.

54 Personal interview, fall 2013.

55 Leopoldo Nuti, "Negotiating with the Enemy and Having Problems with the Allies: The Impact of the Non-Proliferation Treaty on Transatlantic Relations," in *The Routledge Handbook of Transatlantic Security*, eds. Jussi Hanhimäki, Georges-Henri Soutou, and Basil Germond (London: Routledge, 2010), 89–102.

56 Tel. 117 aus Rom, February 14, 1967, *Politisches Archiv des Auswaertiges Amtes*, Berlin, Germany (PAAA), Bestand 150.

96 *L. Nuti*

57 Aufzeichnung: Italienische Haltung zu den Europa-Fragen, March 23, 1967, PAAA, Bestand 150.

58 Aufzeichnung, April 28, 1967, and Aufzeichnung, June 5, 1967, both PAAA, Bestand 150.

59 Appunto, April 26, 1967, and Appunto, April 28, 1967, ASMAE, Fondo Bettini, f. 1.

60 Tel. 20212 from AmEmbassy Paris to Dept. of State, June 15, 1967, *Lyndon B. Johnson Presidential Library*, Texas, USA (LBJPL), Personal Papers of F. Bator, Box 31.

61 Tel. 467 from US Mission Geneva to Dept. of State, August 9, 1967, NACP, RG 383, Director's Office NPT files, Box 4, f. NPT-Italy 1967–1968.

62 Handed to the Secretary by Amb. Ortona at the end of meeting on August 21, 1967, ibid.; see also E. Ortona, *Anni d'America. Vol. III*, 49–53.

63 Attività svolta dal gruppo di lavoro per le questioni del disarmo durante il 1967, ASMAE, Fondo Bettini, b. 6

64 Appunto. Le trattative sulla non-proliferazione, January 29, 1968, ASMAE, Fondo Bettini, b. 6.

65 Tel. 2432 from AmEmbassy Geneva to Dept. of State, February 1, 1968, NACP, RG 383, Director's Office NPT files, Box 4, f. NPT-Italy 1967–1968.

66 In March Ortona complained that the Italian proposals were not being taken seriously: Memorandum of conversation, March 11, 1968, ibid.

67 George Bunn, Charles Van Doren, and David Fischer, *Options and Opportunities: The NPT Extension Conference of 1995*, PPNN Study 2 (Southampton: The Mountbatten Centre for International Studies, 1991), 6–8.

68 Ortona, *Anni d'America. Vol. III*, 96–98.

69 Ibid., 96.

70 Tel. 5425 from Rome to the State Dept., April 12, 1968, NACP, RG 383, Director's Office NPT files, Box 4, f. NPT-Italy 1967–1968.

71 Tel. 7285 from AmEmbassy Rome to the Dept. of State, July 26, 1968, ibid.

72 Tel. 8837 from AmEmbassy Rome to the Dept. of State, October 10, 1968, ibid.

73 "Appunto: firma del TNP," December 31, 1968, ASMAE, Fondo Bettini, b. 5.

74 The State Department mercilessly defined this as "the season of the silly initiatives"; INR Report no. 721, September 24, 1968.

75 MemCon, "NNC and NPT," October 9, 1968, NACP, RG 383, Director's Office NPT files, Box 4, f. NPT-Italy 1967–1968; the hope that a new administration might take a different attitude is explicitly discussed in an internal Foreign Ministry memo: "Appunto: il prossimo cambio di amministrazione negli Stati Uniti e i suoi eventuali effetti sul trattato di non proliferazione," November 28, 1968, ASMAE, Fondo Bettini, b. 5.

76 Ariel E. Levite, "Never Say Never Again: Nuclear Reversal Revisited," *International Security* 27, no. 3 (Winter 2003): 59–88.

77 Itty Abraham, "The Ambivalence of Nuclear Histories," *Osiris* 21, no. 1 (2006): 49–65.

6 Nonproliferation under pressure
The nuclear debate within the Warsaw Pact, 1965–1968

Laurien Crump-Gabreëls

During the second half of the 1960s, the nuclear question caused acrimonious debates within the Warsaw Pact (WP). Conventional wisdom has it that the Eastern European alliance was just an "empty shell" or a "Soviet transmission belt," and can hardly explain such intra-alliance dissent.[1] In contrast, this chapter argues that the members of the Warsaw Pact used their alliance as a platform to further their own interests. Similar to the developments within the North Atlantic Treaty Organization (NATO), the WP debate on what would ultimately become the Treaty on the Non-Proliferation of Nuclear Weapons (NPT) exposed the divergent interests of the Eastern alliance's members and their attempts to alter the course of history towards their own ends.

This chapter's main focus is on the nuclear debate within the Warsaw Pact, from the Political Consultative Committee (PCC) meeting in January 1965 up to the conclusion of the NPT in July 1968.[2] The chapter traces the negotiations and discussions during this period by examining the available evidence from various WP meetings, as well as analyzing the relevant bilateral negotiations. Since the end of the Cold War, political documents from Eastern European archives have become widely accessible. Soviet documents are, however, not so easily available, and the same applies to various military sources. Therefore, the diplomatic bargaining process rather than the military implications of the NPT take center-stage here. The emphasis is placed on the views and efforts of the non-Soviet Warsaw Pact (NSWP) members, an input that has generally been considered virtually non-existent. New evidence from archives in Eastern Europe nevertheless shows that the Warsaw Pact gradually turned into an instrument for the NSWP members of the Eastern alliance to assert their own national interests.[3]

Within WP discussions on the merits of a nonproliferation treaty, most allies regarded the NPT as a satisfactory solution to counter the Multilateral Force (MLF) project within NATO and to preclude a nuclear option for the Federal Republic of Germany (FRG). East German and Polish leaders were particularly determined to curb the FRG's potential nuclear ambitions. Conversely, the Romanian leadership was not so easily persuaded. Striving to expand its own scope for maneuver – both within and outside the alliance – Bucharest constantly demanded involvement in the superpowers' negotiations.

98   *L. Crump-Gabreëls*

Romania's objections were initially facilitated by its bilateral understanding with the People's Republic of China (PRC): Having adopted a neutral stance vis-à-vis the emerging Sino-Soviet split in the first half of the 1960s, the Romanian leaders were loath to antagonize Beijing. Further, the Romanians also wanted to constrain the influence of the superpowers, and thus had little interest in "a nuclear monopoly" of the US and the Soviet Union (SU), as they saw it.[4] Finally, unlike most other WP countries, Romania did not perceive an immediate threat from West Germany, nor did it have Soviet nuclear warheads stationed on its soil. Therefore, almost up to the NPT's conclusion, Romanian objections threatened to hijack any Warsaw Pact decision-making on the treaty. At the last moment, however, Bucharest reversed course, when it could no longer delay the conclusion of the NPT.

This chapter addresses a glaring hiatus in the nonproliferation historiography. Studies on the nuclear debate within NATO abound.[5] Yet Douglas Selvage has so far been the only one to cover this field from the WP perspective in his landmark study on *The Warsaw Pact and Nuclear Nonproliferation*.[6] His paper, however, only deals with the period 1963 to the beginning of 1965, and therefore primarily examines the East German and Polish stance on the MLF with a specific focus on the German Question, rather than the nonproliferation debate at large. Moreover, the discussions between the Kremlin and its Polish and East German allies on a potential NPT took place outside the official framework of the WP. Between July 1963 and December 1964 its members never even met – the Romanian leadership vetoed all East German proposals to convene the WP in order to prevent the East German allies from using the WP as a "transmission belt" for their national interests.[7] During 1963–1964, discussions on nonproliferation thus only took place at the *bi*lateral level. The impact of the NPT debate on the *multi*lateral dynamics of the WP will, however, be central to this chapter. More attention will also be paid to the motives behind Romania's dissent. Although Selvage deals with the Romanian stance at the PCC meeting in January 1965, his findings are based on Polish and East German sources and therefore contribute little to our knowledge of Bucharest's motives.

In contrast, the Romanian stance on nonproliferation has been researched in depth by Eliza Gheorghe. Nonetheless, her work focuses on how the Romanian leaders courted American favor for nuclear supplies by mediating in the Vietnam War and by exploiting their country's image as "maverick" within the Soviet bloc.[8] She therefore neither mentions the WP context, nor the Chinese influence on the Romanian leadership at that time. In fact, the Sino-Romanian collusion – which inspired the Romanian stance halfway through the 1960s – has not yet been studied at all. Hal Brands' attempt to assess the nonproliferation debate on "both sides of the Iron Curtain" does not remedy this gap either, since he has not conducted any archival research in Eastern Europe.[9] Brands rightly concludes that "[w]ithin both NATO and the Warsaw Pact, the imperatives of alliance unity and the limits of hegemonic influence enabled smaller powers to exert considerable pressure on US and Soviet policy."[10] The empirical evidence upon which he bases this claim is, however, very minimal in regard to the Eastern European side, and he has to draw heavily upon Selvage's article. A reconstruction of the nonproliferation debates within the Warsaw Pact therefore serves to shed a new light on both the NPT negotiations and on the dynamics within the alliance.

This chapter proceeds as follows. First, it addresses the history of the Warsaw Pact from its foundation in May 1955 onwards. It explains why the Polish and East German leaders attempted to use the WP as an instrument to influence the Soviet–American negotiations on the NPT, and how the Romanian leadership thwarted Polish and East German interests by vetoing any proposal to convene the WP in the first half of the 1960s. The Romanians used the Sino-Soviet split to distance themselves from the alliance in order to assert their autonomy. The chapter continues to show how this clash of interests led to a stalemate in a WP meeting in January 1965, during which a proposal for a nonproliferation treaty was discussed. Although all other allies agreed to the proposals, the Romanians vetoed it and secretly colluded with officials from the PRC in order to increase their leverage over their allies.

The chapter proceeds to show how the Romanian dissidence on this issue led to a divide in the alliance between Romania and the rest, which the Kremlin attempted to remedy by sending its deputy foreign minister to Bucharest in February 1967 and by inviting the Romanian leadership to Moscow a month later. Despite these Soviet efforts, the Romanians refused to yield and suggested convening a Warsaw Pact meeting to discuss the NPT instead. The chapter concludes with this meeting, which took place in March 1968, during which the Romanian dissidence threatened to paralyze the alliance. The other WP members chose to isolate Romania and close ranks. The Romanian leadership ultimately signed the NPT, but it had changed the dynamics in the WP in the process.

The WP challenge to Soviet influence

When the Warsaw Pact was founded on May 14, 1955 following West Germany's accession to NATO five days earlier, officials immediately stigmatized the Soviet alliance as a "cardboard castle."[11] The Eastern alliance, which consisted of the Soviet Union, the German Democratic Republic (GDR), Poland, Czechoslovakia, Hungary, Bulgaria, Romania, and Albania, superficially looked like NATO, with the Political Consultative Committee (PCC) resembling the Atlantic Council, and the Warsaw Treaty mirroring the Atlantic Treaty. In fact, however, it hardly played any role in the Soviet bloc's foreign policy during the first five years of its existence. Its sole official organ was the PCC, which only met twice in this period, and apparently merely served to rubberstamp Soviet decisions. Nevertheless, these circumstances changed in the early 1960s, when the Soviet Union came under pressure from both the incipient Sino-Soviet Split and the Second Berlin Crisis.[12]

Soviet First Secretary Khrushchev faced a huge challenge from the superpower struggle over the status of West Berlin, which was occupied by the Western allied forces, but located in the middle of Eastern Germany. On the one hand, he had to prevent the Cold War from escalating because of a disagreement about the status of half a city. On the other hand, he had to keep East Germany's First Secretary, Walter Ulbricht, at bay by taking seriously his concerns about the status of Berlin. Ulbricht was particularly concerned about the status of Berlin, since West Germany showed an increasing interest in nuclear sharing in NATO through MLF. Combined with the already existing conundrum related to the potential reunification of the two German states, the situation was critical. The so-called "German Question" thus became increasingly difficult to solve.

Poland and the GDR demanded more leeway both towards the resolution of the German Question and regarding the potential nuclearization of the FRG. Selvage argues that the Polish First Secretary Władysław Gomułka and his East German colleague Walter Ulbricht attempted to exercise considerable influence during the early nonproliferation negotiations between Soviet First Secretary Nikita Khrushchev and US President Lyndon Johnson. According to Selvage, Khrushchev had embarked on a so-called "Rapallo policy" in the first half of the 1960s, an approach under which the Soviet Union tried to improve its relations with the FRG at the expense of Polish and East German interests. Under pressure from the Sino-Soviet split, Khrushchev aimed towards some form of rapprochement with the West. He was even willing "to concede West German access to nuclear weapons through NATO as the price for a nonproliferation agreement with the United States."[13] This policy change led to severe protests from Ulbricht, who was primarily worried about the repercussions for the potential recognition of the GDR, and Gomułka, who was furious about the repercussions West German nuclearisation would have on the balance between NATO and the Warsaw Pact.

When the Kremlin – under pressure from the Sino-Soviet split – attempted to give priority to rapprochement with the Americans by decoupling the MLF from an agreement on nonproliferation in October 1963, both Ulbricht and Gomułka put a halt to Khrushchev's enthusiasm, as Selvage argues. Gomułka immediately phoned Khrushchev in order to demand the arranging of a PCC meeting to discuss the official WP stance on the MLF and he wrote him a critical letter.[14] Meanwhile, Ulbricht attempted to pressurize his allies into convening the PCC from January 1964 onwards so as to gain a stake in the meetings of the Eighteen-Nation Committee on Disarmament (ENDC). The ENDC was the multilateral body where the treaty was being negotiated under the aegis of the United Nations. Although several WP members, such as Poland and Romania, were members of the ENDC, the GDR was not a member, since its existence was not recognized outside the communist world. Both Ulbricht and Gomułka intended to use the Warsaw Pact as an instrument to check Soviet unilateralism on nuclear issues, and to demand a greater input. This intention was, however, thwarted by another WP member, namely Romania.

The Romanian leadership had begun to chart an increasingly independent course in the 1960s. The Romanian First Secretary, Gheorghe Gheorghiu-Dej, had resisted Soviet attempts to designate Romania as the provider of raw materials within the Council for Mutual Economic Assistance (COMECON). The Romanian leadership therefore regarded institutions such as the COMECON and the WP as an obstacle to Romania's autonomy. For the same reason, in the wake of the Cuban Missile Crisis, Romania had declared itself "neutral" in case of a hypothetical war between the SU and the US, as Raymond Garthoff recalled.[15] The Romanian leadership also refused to take sides within the Sino-Soviet split, and maintained contacts with both the SU and the PRC. By doing so, the Romanian leadership wanted to underline that the Kremlin could by no means dictate its foreign policy. Thus, the increasing hostility between the SU and the PRC, its former ally, had also put the Kremlin in a precarious position.

The Romanians were prepared to take a risky stance during the Sino-Soviet Split, and flirted with the Chinese communists in order to distance themselves from the Soviet grip. Unlike Albania, they did not openly defect to the PRC's side, but cultivated their contacts with the Kremlin too. The Romanian leadership even successfully increased its prestige by acting as a "mediator" between the PRC and the Soviet Union in a vain attempt to remedy the increasing tensions. Its role as mediator, who rose above both parties, underlined Romanian autonomy and increased its scope for maneuver. This gave the Romanian leadership the clout to formulate a so-called "Declaration of Independence" in April 1964, in which it declared all communist parties equal, apparently in order to alleviate Sino-Soviet tensions. The declaration in fact undermined Soviet supremacy and emphasized Romania's reluctance to participate in organizations such as the COMECON and the Warsaw Pact. Soviet influence within Eastern Europe had diminished to such an extent that it could now openly be challenged.[16]

Romania feared that its increasingly independent foreign policy would be constrained by its WP membership. Thus, the Romanian leaders vetoed Ulbricht's attempt to convene the PCC from January 1964 in order to close ranks on MLF. This meant that the PCC was not convoked at all between July 1963 and January 1965. The East German zeal to convene the PCC was thus checked by the Romanian leadership in pursuit of its own particular goals. This marks an interesting development in the politics of the Warsaw Pact: not only were NSWP members limiting Soviet freedom of action, but they also started to expand their own scope for maneuver at the expense of their allies. The Romanians in particular controlled the extent to which the alliance could serve as a transmission belt for their peers' interests, notably those of the GDR.

Meanwhile, the Soviet leadership was caught in the double predicament of both the Sino-Soviet Split and the Second Berlin Crisis. With the PRC aggressively charting its own course and West Germany striving to acquire enhanced control over nuclear weapons, the Kremlin saw itself forced to maintain unity within Warsaw Pact ranks at all costs. Consequently, the NSWP members started to use the alliance as an instrument through which they could assert their own interests by either (1) playing the PRC and the Soviet Union off against one another, or by (2) using the Soviet predicament in the second Berlin Crisis as leverage over the Kremlin. Given this vulnerability, the Soviet leadership was compelled to accommodate the interests and viewpoints of its East European allies to a much greater degree than before.

102　L. Crump-Gabreëls

Romania versus the rest

The Soviet predicament was further complicated by the PRC test detonation of a nuclear device on October 16, 1964. Although the Chinese nuclearization had been expected for some time, the nuclear question had now become particularly acute.[17] Both superpowers faced new dilemmas: On the one hand, the United States was now confronted with two nuclear Communist powers. On the other hand, the PRC and the Soviet Union had grown so far apart during the Sino-Soviet split in the early 1960s that Beijing's nuclearization was equally disturbing to the Kremlin. The "Cold War in the Communist world" could now go nuclear too.[18]

While the nonproliferation negotiations between the superpowers had been stalled over different views on the MLF, the PRC's nuclear test highlighted their common concerns. Mainly, if the PRC's test were to become a precedent for other countries' nuclear ambitions, such a development would severely disturb the balance of power for the Soviet Union and the United States alike. The PRC's detonation therefore provided an extra impetus to the superpowers' ambitions to both adopt arms control measures and consult their allies on nonproliferation. Moscow now had to take its allies' concerns over NATO nuclear sharing seriously and, therefore, had to cease from accommodating Washington over MLF. At the same time, the Kremlin could afford to push Washington a little harder on this very issue, since the US administration had also come under increased pressure to come to an agreement with Moscow. This meant that Leonid Brezhnev, who had only succeeded Khrushchev as General Secretary of the Communist Party of the Soviet Union (CPSU) on October 14, 1964, finally conceded that the "MLF [...] was incompatible with a nonproliferation agreement."[19] The Kremlin was again in line with its Polish and East German comrades. Khrushchev's ouster created a window of opportunity for the East Germans, and Ulbricht immediately renewed his campaign to convene the PCC to discuss MLF.

This time the Romanian leadership agreed to convene the PCC on the conditions that the WP's deputy foreign ministers would assemble first in December 1964 and that the PCC meeting itself would be postponed until January 1965. The deputy foreign ministers could thus prepare the PCC meeting in a multilateral framework, instead of relying on a Soviet agenda. The nuclear question had, accordingly, triggered the de facto creation of a new organ within the WP, since the deputy foreign ministers had never convened before. It had also spurred the initiative of the NSWP members, who had decided to convene without prior agreement by the Kremlin, while even setting the agenda. The deputy foreign ministers took no decisions in December 1964, since the Romanian representatives insisted on a mere preliminary discussion and vetoed any potential decision. But the mere fact that all NSWP members had a stake in defining the parameters of the incumbent PCC meeting showed that the Soviet Union could no longer call the shots – nuclear or not – within the WP. It was therefore no coincidence that Walter Ulbricht suggested in a letter on January 13, 1965 to link the discussion on the MLF to nonproliferation. He had even appropriated the initiative by attaching a draft nonproliferation treaty.[20] The Warsaw Pact would prevent the Soviet Union from going it alone on nuclear policy issues.

Meanwhile, the Kremlin needed the support of its WP allies more than ever. The Soviet leadership faced the hard task of improving its links to Beijing in order to create a united front against US "aggression" in the Vietnam War, while at the same time cultivating its relations with the Johnson administration with the aim of formulating a common nonproliferation policy. The Romanian leadership exploited the Kremlin's precarious position to the full. Romanian attempts at mediating in the Sino-Soviet split in the spring of 1964 had intensified so much that representatives from the Romanian leadership met on an almost weekly basis with Liu Fan, the PRC's ambassador in Bucharest. It was, therefore, part of a broader strategy to ask the Chinese opinion on developments within the Warsaw Pact, notwithstanding the fact that the PRC's leadership had already been fully excluded from the alliance since 1961.

The Romanians were keen to discuss their preparations for the PCC meeting in January 1965 with their comrades from the PRC. The Sino-Romanian collusion was particularly provocative so briefly after the PRC's detonation of a nuclear device in October 1964, which was not welcomed within the WP. In early January 1965, several meetings took place between Liu Fan and the Romanian politburo member Emil Bodnaras, who was considered a specialist on Asia. Bodnaras indicated Romanian support for the October 1964 Chinese proposal for total disarmament and promised to oppose any Soviet attempt to turn the WP meeting against the PRC. The PRC leadership clearly feared that a united WP stance on an NPT would be regarded as a post factum condemnation of the PRC's newly acquired nuclear status.[21] Meanwhile, the Romanian leadership intended to use Bejing's stance on the NPT as leverage over its allies at the PCC meeting.

The Romanians did so with relish. The day before the PCC convened on January 19, 1965 in Warsaw, the Romanian delegation already stood its ground in an informal bilateral meeting with Walter Ulbricht. The East German leadership occupied the opposite extreme of the spectrum in terms of an NPT, which it regarded as an essential instrument to thwart the MLF and to curb suspected West German nuclear ambitions. Ulbricht desired to defend the East German proposal on nonproliferation, which he also wanted to present to the UN, thus using it as an instrument to allow for the unprecedented participation of the GDR at the UN. He accordingly tried to use the WP as a direct instrument for de facto East German recognition. The Romanian leadership nevertheless warned Ulbricht that the problem should not be raised at the UN, since it might be used "in order to condemn China."[22] The Romanian leadership had called Ulbricht's bluff: on nonproliferation they would continue to side with the PRC.

During the actual PCC meeting, the protagonists did not budge. All leaders apart from Romania's Gheorghiu-Dej were united in their support for Ulbricht's proposal to present a proposal for an NPT to the UN. Brezhnev strongly supported Ulbricht, but also stressed the need for coordination with the PRC. By

104   L. Crump-Gabreëls

backing the PRC's proposal for a disarmament conference, Brezhnev hoped to repair Moscow's relations with Beijing.[23] Brezhnev thus trod his ground carefully. In contrast, Gheorghiu-Dej went much further and praised the merits of the PRC's nuclear test, while ignoring the East German proposal on nonproliferation altogether.[24] Both Gheorghiu-Dej and the Romanian foreign minister Corneliu Manescu questioned the legitimacy of the WP to act as a body representing all socialist countries. This was, in fact, an insidious move to rob the WP of its relevance. Manescu added that a nonproliferation treaty would lead to a nuclear "monopoly" of the existing nuclear powers.[25] This argument had a particularly interesting dimension to it, since there is evidence that the Romanian leaders intended to keep their own nuclear options open.[26] Thus, no agreement on a nonproliferation treaty could be reached at the PCC meeting.

The Romanian stance during the meeting strikingly echoed the conversations between Bodnaras and Liu Fan. The Romanian representatives went to great lengths to both serve the PRC's interests and assert their autonomy. Poland's Gomułka strongly criticized the Romanian objections, arguing that the NPT was *not* targeted against the PRC, since the PRC had already become a nuclear power.[27] Gomułka also ridiculed the proposal for total disarmament as unacceptable to the West.[28] The other allies rallied against the Romanian representatives too. All other WP members had a genuine interest in the NPT, which would finally put an end to the greatly dreaded MLF. The Czechoslovak First Secretary Antonín Novotný appealed to unity so as to avoid the image of a disunited WP in the Western press.[29] Gheorghiu-Dej riposted with an appeal to the right of an autonomous opinion. The Romanian autonomy was, however, questioned by both Gomułka and Brezhnev. Both suspected Romanian collusion with the PRC.[30] The Romanian reliance on Beijing's position indeed seemed rather servile. The PRC's stance on nonproliferation nevertheless suited Romanian purposes. It helped Bucharest to maintain its scope for maneuver within the WP.[31]

During a final meeting of first secretaries to fine-tune the communiqué, Gomułka managed to formulate a compromise that satisfied his Romanian comrades. Gheorghiu-Dej agreed to the formulation that "[t]he creation of MLF, in any form, means the proliferation of nuclear arms and, especially, the access of those arms to West German militarists."[32] The Romanian delegation had thus succeeded in limiting any mentioning of the issue of proliferation to the MLF, thereby undermining the East German initiative for a treaty on nonproliferation. The Romanian leadership had accordingly compromised the position of the six other WP members, all of whom had favored a proposal for an NPT. It had, at the same time, ensured that "no document would be adopted against China," as Bodnaras had promised Liu Fan.[33] Meanwhile, Ulbricht's proposal for an NPT was not even mentioned in the communiqué, let alone approved, even though all other WP members were strongly in favor. The potential condemnation of the PRC at the UN had provided the Romanians with a useful instrument to maintain their autonomy at the expense of all their allies.

The Sino-Romanian collusion continued after the PCC meeting. The Romanian delegation even provided the PRC ambassador with all confidential documents related to the PCC meeting, such as the minutes, Ulbricht's letter, the draft communiqué, and the draft nonproliferation treaty. In a meeting with Liu Fan Bodnaras described the PCC meeting as a "battle" in which a "massive attack" had been carried out against the Romanian delegation, with Gomułka showing "the most combative attitude." He emphasized the triumphant role of the Romanian delegation, which had fought against the nuclear monopoly of the "monstrous club" of the traditional nuclear weapon powers, and which had determined the contents of the communiqué.[34] Bodnaras' self-congratulatory account corresponded to the proceedings of the meeting, to the extent that it was solely due to Romanian objections that the draft NPT was neither approved nor mentioned in the communiqué. Moreover, the actual minutes show that Gomułka indeed seemed the only party leader who managed to stand up to Romanian obstinacy. Brezhnev was at most reduced to the role of an arbiter, but did not seem able to seize the initiative. Nor was he able to push through the East German proposals, even though he vehemently supported them, and possibly helped to draft them. As the Romanians emphasized, "no decision was taken, because we opposed it."[35]

The Soviet leadership, nevertheless, went ahead with the proposal for a nonproliferation treaty, and presented it in its own name at the UN assembly in October 1965. Since the PCC meeting in January 1965, the Kremlin had become still more determined in its stance against the MLF.[36] The Romanian dissent had not stopped the Kremlin from presenting a proposal for an NPT. Thus, in nuclear terms, the Romanian obstinacy was of little importance. However, it had ensured that such a proposal could not be presented in name of the Warsaw Pact.[37] Although the other allies supported the treaty, the Romanian stance had prevented the Soviet leadership from using the WP as an instrument to bestow extra legitimacy on its own proposals. The lack of unity within the Eastern alliance had thus become painfully evident. It did, however, ensure that the Romanians – and the other WP members – could maintain the maximal scope for maneuver in terms of foreign policy. The WP could not be used to bind its members to Moscow's foreign policy goals or, indeed, to those of any other member. For the other allies the Romanian quest for autonomy came at a price: a common WP move would have been in the interest of most WP allies, and the Romanian delegation had undermined exactly that.

The Romanian U-turn

In the subsequent period, the division between Romania and the six other WP members deepened. In March 1965, Gheorghiu-Dej died and was succeeded as General Secretary by politburo member Nicolae Ceauşescu, who took an even more aggressive stance against the Kremlin.[38] Acrimonious discussions between Romania and the other WP members on a declaration on the Vietnam War dominated the PCC meeting in Bucharest in July 1966. According to the records, the Warsaw Pact became divided between "one" and "the six," who mused on ways to neutralize Romanian dissent.

106   L. Crump-Gabreëls

Nevertheless, in the summer of 1966, the PRC leadership embarked on the so-called "Great Proletarian Cultural Revolution," which contained a radical program of persecuting and killing "revisionists." This sealed the Sino-Soviet split, and prevented the Romanians from playing the SU and the PRC off against one another anymore. The Kremlin no longer had to pretend to take the PRC's interests to heart, and the connection with the PRC had ceased to be useful for the Romanians. In order to underline their autonomous foreign policy program, the Romanian leadership turned westwards instead. In January 1967, Bucharest established diplomatic relations with the FRG. This step went clearly against established WP policy, and against the explicit interests of both Poland and the GDR.

Meanwhile, the superpowers had drawn closer on the NPT, and had agreed in early October 1966 on a "no transfer" clause in Article I of the treaty, which meant that nuclear warheads would not be transferred to either non-nuclear states or to alliances which involved non-nuclear states.[39] Ultimately, this agreement rendered the MLF de facto impossible. Conversely, this development meant that it was now a still more urgent priority for both superpowers to get their allies on board. The Soviet leaders therefore asked their WP allies for input on the treaty, and consulted all of them in October 1966. In February 1967, the Kremlin even sent deputy foreign minister Alexander Soldatov to Bucharest in order to ask for Romanian input, questions, and observations on the negotiations with the US. Soldatov underlined that the SU had already supported several proposals on nuclear disarmament, as the Romanians had wished. The US administration had proposed that the current draft of the nonproliferation treaty would be presented at the ENDC – of which Romania was a member – in Geneva, but the Soviet leaders had insisted on previous consultations with their allies.[40] While the Romanian leadership kept Soldatov for several weeks in the dark on its position, the other WP members had already sent their observations to the Kremlin and agreed to the draft.[41] The de facto burial of MLF had satisfied *their* interests.

Brezhnev still coveted Romanian approval and invited Ceauşescu and Maurer to a bilateral summit meeting in Moscow in March 1967.[42] He emphasized the importance of socialist unity, especially considering the disunity in the West on nonproliferation, where France and the FRG still strongly disagreed with the treaty. Brezhnev therefore welcomed a Romanian proposal to convene a PCC meeting to discuss the nonproliferation treaty. Thus, the Romanian leadership had made a U-turn: after trying time and again to thwart the convening of PCC meetings, Bucharest had now itself suggested convening such a meeting. Unable to control the bilateral consultations between the Kremlin and the other WP members, the Romanian leadership obviously wanted to put its stamp on the entire process within a multilateral forum. Therefore, in April 1967, Soviet and Romanian foreign ministry officials collaborated in Moscow on a draft treaty. In May 1967 the Soviet and American leadership presented a new draft treaty at the ENDC in Geneva, which even included several Romanian proposals, inter alia, in relation to complete disarmament. This was something the Romanians considered of great importance, since it would have terminated the atomic monopoly of the nuclear powers.

The Warsaw Pact   107

Two weeks after the ENDC had begun to examine the new draft treaty, Romania's Ceauşescu officially proposed in a letter dated January 31, 1968 to convene the PCC for NPT related discussions.[43] Ceauşescu was particularly vexed that the issue had been treated in greater depth within NATO than within the WP.[44] The matter had not been discussed within the PCC since January 1965, when the Romanian delegation had thwarted the deliberations. The other NSWP members had been reluctant to support another Romanian initiative, which could have well resulted in the paralysis of the WP, and had therefore shelved the Romanian proposal in 1967. The "six" were, after all, already united on the question of the nonproliferation treaty, with which they agreed in its current form.[45] This time, they accommodated Romanian wishes despite these objections, since they feared that the Romanians would otherwise block future meetings.[46] Moreover, the matter had become very urgent, since the ENDC planned to submit the draft treaty for final approval to the UN General Assembly on March 15, 1968. The other WP allies therefore desperately hoped to forestall Romanian dissent within the ENDC.

The Romanians had already "sharply attacked" the current draft treaty at the ENDC in Geneva on February 6, 1968.[47] Ceauşescu therefore wanted to discuss "strictly necessary amendments" with his allies before the final treaty was submitted for approval to the UN. The Romanian leadership proposed to include "obligations that the nuclear-weapon states take steps toward nuclear disarmament"[48] as well as a review conference after five years, and a security guarantee of nuclear countries not to attack non-nuclear-weapon states with nuclear weapons.[49] The proposed Romanian amendments met with little sympathy at a meeting of WP deputy foreign ministers in East Berlin on February 26–27, 1968. All other delegations strongly supported the draft treaty as it stood, in which a great number of Romanian amendments, such as the more general one on disarmament, were already included, as the Soviet delegate Kuznetsov emphasized. The other delegations feared that the Romanians wanted, once again, to delay the conclusion of the NPT by splitting the socialist vote within the ENDC, which was exactly what the Romanian deputy foreign minister, Gheorghe Macovescu, threatened to do.[50] The "six" nevertheless refused to be blackmailed, and the meeting ended inconclusively.

The persistent division between "the six" and "the one" hardly boded well for the subsequent PCC meeting, which was to take place in Sofia on March 6–7, 1968. The other WP delegations had drawn their conclusion from the PCC meeting in Bucharest in July 1966, where the Romanians had dominated the entire meeting with countless amendments on a Vietnam Declaration. The allies had carefully studied the Romanian proposed amendments to the nonproliferation treaty in order to successfully refute them.[51] A particularly detailed Bulgarian report considered the Romanian proposal on total disarmament "unrealistic" and anachronistic, since it "goes beyond the scope and goals of the nuclear nonproliferation treaty," and seemed based on outdated 12-year-old Soviet proposals.[52] Moreover, the Romanian proposal to limit inspections to states which could use nuclear energy for military purposes would imply that "some states could

108 _L. Crump-Gabreëls_

avoid the controls of the International Atomic Energy Agency and begin nuclear-weapons production." Also, the proposal to hold a review conference every five years, which would enable countries to withdraw from the treaty by announcing "the extreme circumstances that threaten its interests" to the UN, "would bring considerable instability to the treaty," the Bulgarian report argued.[53]

Under the pretext of "sovereign equality" and "non-interference in domestic affairs," the Romanian proposals clearly served to maintain the utmost scope for maneuver in Romanian foreign policy. The Romanian leaders therefore did not intend to "sign a treaty at any price."[54] The East German leadership was particularly worried that the Romanian amendments would thwart the NPT altogether. That would play into the hands of the FRG: Bonn was a strong opponent of the NPT because it believed it would deliver the final blow to the MLF, which it coveted. The NPT was thus of particular importance to the GDR, exactly because it would weaken the position of the FRG. Moreover, the Romanian proposal that nuclear-weapon powers should never attack a non-nuclear-weapon state would undermine East German security by protecting West Germany even though nuclear weapons were stationed on its soil.[55] The other WP members shared this concern. Brezhnev even emphasized in a private conversation with Ceaușescu that "West Germany would thank us" if the Romanian proposals were accepted.[56]

During the actual meeting "the six" attempted to avoid antagonizing the Romanian delegation by praising the socialist nature of the proposals, but calling them "unrealistic," since the NATO-members would never accept them. Brezhnev repeated time and again that a lot of Romanian proposals had already been included in the draft treaty. The atmosphere soon turned sour, since Ceaușescu declared that the Romanian leaders "would present their proposals [...] in Geneva, [...] at the forthcoming session of the UN, in their whole foreign policy and in their public program as well," whereas the "six" feared that the amendments "could lead to the postponement or even failure of the treaty." The Romanian dissidence thus threatened to prevent the conclusion of the treaty, which the other WP members considered "a victory for the socialist states, primarily for the Soviet Union, and a new phase in our offensive against imperialism's positions."[57] Not only had the treaty been negotiated at length with all WP members, but the Soviet leadership had also succeeded in drafting a treaty that was acceptable to the US and most of its allies, even though it would definitively prevent the MLF. The treaty thus represented a peaceful solution to an issue that had caused much unrest in the WP in the first half of the 1960s.

This time, however, "the six" were resolved not to yield to Romanian pressure. The other WP members had also become more self-conscious about dealing with Romanian dissidence. The Romanian _Alleingang_ (unilateralist attempt) on nuclear issues exhausted its allies' patience. The "six" now decided to sign a declaration _without_ Romania, in which they strongly supported the Soviet draft for a nonproliferation treaty.[58] Although they did not sign the declaration in the name of the Warsaw Pact, but as six individual states, it clearly signaled to the West that the vast majority of the alliance did _not_ support the Romanian amendments. The same applied to the communiqué, which only mentioned that nonproliferation had been discussed in an atmosphere that was "frank and comradely."[59]

It was a blow to the Warsaw Pact that the disagreements between Romania and the rest were made public for the first time in the history of the alliance, but the declaration of "the six" had also served to undermine the Romanian position. Although Ceauşescu triumphantly stated upon his return to Bucharest that the PCC "must be satisfied with this role, and not the role up to now, to approve everything the Soviet Union does," his allies were not at all pleased with the way the Romanians disapproved of almost everything in the WP.[60] Ceauşescu was, in turn, not amused when the Bulgarian First Secretary, Todor Zhivkov, told him about the separate declaration.[61] Without any Soviet pressure, the other NSWP members had rallied behind the Kremlin in supporting a treaty that they genuinely deemed to be in their own interest. According to the Hungarian premier Jeno Fock, the separate declaration might enable "the six" to "have a greater impact on the Romanians [...] without causing a schism in the Warsaw Treaty."[62] In the eyes of the other WP members, it was not the Soviet leadership, but the Romanian leadership that threatened to undermine their interests. On a great number of issues the interests of the six WP countries simply coincided. The main gain of the PCC meeting consisted in the fact that "the six" had found a way to bypass Romanian dissidence.

At the very last moment, the Romanian leadership nevertheless decided to join "the six." After it had continued to argue during the negotiations at the UN that the NPT did not cater for the "interests of non-nuclear states," Bucharest radically changed its course in June 1968, when it became clear that an overwhelming majority of UN members supported the treaty.[63] The Romanian delegation suddenly contributed constructively to the negotiations, and claimed "that Romania was never against the treaty, but had an active part in its perfection and improvement."[64] This statement went beyond mere rhetoric, since, from Bucharest's perspective, some of its proposals on disarmament and the provisions for withdrawal were in fact included in the NPT.[65] The treaty thus catered for two important Romanian concerns: It challenged the nuclear monopoly of the nuclear powers and confirmed the national sovereignty of each participant.

When the conclusion of the nonproliferation treaty had become irreversible, the Romanian leaders wanted to share in its success. Since the Cultural Revolution the Romanian leadership no longer needed to take the Chinese position into account anyhow. The Romanian delegation therefore ultimately decided to sign the nonproliferation treaty on July 1, 1968, together with sixty-two other states.[66] At the final hour, the WP had united on the NPT, in shrill contrast to NATO.

Conclusion

The nuclear question stimulated a lot of debate within the Warsaw Pact and forced Moscow to consult with its allies. In this respect, the NPT negotiations had a similar effect in both the WP and NATO. Nevertheless, within the Eastern

110 *L. Crump-Gabreëls*

European alliance, the NPT negotiations' emancipatory effect was even more striking, defying the standard view of the WP as a mere Soviet transmission belt. Nonproliferation negotiations initially spurred the East German leader Ulbricht and his Polish comrade Gomułka into action, since both of them had a vested interest in preventing the MLF, and both attempted to prevent Khrushchev from approving a nonproliferation treaty that did not exclude nuclear sharing. In the first half of the 1960s, the debate on the NPT nevertheless took place at the bilateral level, outside of the multilateral framework of the WP. The Romanian leaders had successfully prevented the PCC from convening between July 1963 and January 1965, as they did not want Ulbricht to use the alliance as a transmission belt for *his* foreign policy interests.

The Romanian leadership had, however, agreed to a meeting of the WP's deputy foreign ministers in December 1964, which was an unprecedented compromise. Bucharest also raised the nuclear debate to the multilateral level, where NPT issues would be discussed again at the PCC meeting in January 1965. This summit was, however, paralyzed by Romanian dissent. Conversely, the Romanians subsequently changed their strategy, and actively lobbied for the convening of a PCC meeting on nuclear nonproliferation in 1968. The nuclear question thus contributed to a watershed in the proceedings of the WP: whereas all previous PCC meetings had been convened by the Soviets in Moscow, the one on the MLF in January 1965 was the first one to be initiated by an NSWP member (Ulbricht) in an NSWP capital (Warsaw). This accordingly paved the way for the Romanian leadership to host the next PCC meeting in Bucharest (July 1966), and to convene the one after that (March 1968) on the issue of the NPT.

The main non-Soviet protagonists within the nuclear debate were the Polish leader Gomułka and his East German comrade Ulbricht on one side, and the Romanian leadership on the other. The Poles and East Germans had a great vested interest in the NPT, since it would definitively thwart the MLF. In contrast, the Romanian leadership strove to maintain the utmost flexibility in its foreign policy, and therefore attempted to thwart a consensus on the NPT time and again. Meanwhile, the other WP members were also in favor of the NPT, which they, too, considered an instrument to keep West German nuclear ambitions at bay. The WP thus began to be divided into a group of "six" against "one" in the second half of the 1960s. The Romanian dissent caused an action–reaction dynamic, which compelled the other members of the Eastern alliance to formulate their stance more clearly and thus, inadvertently, contributed to their self-consciousness.

This division between "the six" and "the one" also applied to other areas of foreign policy, such as the Romanian stance on the Sino-Soviet split, the Vietnam War, and diplomatic relations with the FRG. It was also apparent during the Prague Spring of 1968, where Romania was the only WP member that joined neither the multilateral deliberations on the situation in Czechoslovakia, nor the military intervention in Czechoslovakia in August 1968. In fact, the first multilateral meeting about the Prague Spring took place in Dresden at the end of March 1968, shortly after the PCC meeting where Romania had been isolated. The

Romanian dissent was, however, all the more potent in the nuclear debate, where the other six feared that Romania, as a member of the ENDC, might prove a serious obstacle to the conclusion of the NPT. Since the Romanian dissent was, nevertheless, not limited to the issue of nonproliferation, it seemed part of a broader strategy, namely to maintain the utmost scope for maneuver in foreign policy, and to defend Romanian sovereignty and autonomy at all costs.

Likewise, the Romanian dissent had less of an impact on the NPT than on the functioning of the Warsaw Pact. The NPT was concluded in July 1968, when the Romanian leadership toned down its criticism and signed it after all. Although Romania could have caused a permanent breach in the WP by refusing to sign the treaty, it could not have prevented the conclusion of the NPT. The fact that "the six" signed a declaration without Romania in March 1968 indicates that the Romanians would be isolated, rather than compelled to concede. There is no evidence that the SU would or could have forced Romania to sign the NPT; there is, on the other hand, evidence that the Kremlin even kept the "French option," namely to allow Romania to withdraw from the WP's military structures, open.[67] The Romanian attitude to the NPT was, indeed, very similar to the French one, which regarded the NPT "as an effort to maintain superpower hegemony."[68]

Unlike the French, the Romanians did, however, participate in the treaty negotiations, and even managed to exercise a limited amount of influence. The Romanian dissent did not fundamentally change the shape of the NPT, but the treaty ultimately did include proposals from Romania on complete disarmament and national sovereignty, which the Romanians considered of importance. More-over, Bucharest's initiatives had compelled Brezhnev to take the interests of his allies seriously and to consult them frequently. The Romanian approach also paid off in the form of subsequent WP reforms, which were concluded in March 1969. The newly created committee of the defense ministers and a military council had to function according to intergovernmental, rather than supra-national, procedures, in order to safeguard the sovereignty of the WP members. This had been hotly contested for four years, and finally agreed on Romanian insistence. The input of the NSWP members as autonomous agents had now been formalized.

The Romanian signature of the nonproliferation treaty in July 1968 therefore does not testify to any Soviet pressure, but to a genuine desire to avoid further isolation. Since the final treaty already contained a great number of Romanian proposals, Bucharest would have undermined its own interests with a refusal to sign at the last moment. The evolution of the treaty thus illustrates a new course in Soviet foreign policy: whereas the NSWP allies had not been involved at all in the Limited Nuclear Test Ban Treaty that was concluded in August 1963, they had been elaborately consulted on nonproliferation. The Kremlin had gone out of its way to involve the Romanian leadership in the negotiations. The Romanian signature should therefore be regarded as an acknowledgement of its input, rather than a confirmation of Soviet hegemony. The eventual WP consensus regarding the NPT came at a price for the Kremlin: the multilateralization of the Warsaw Pact.

112   *L. Crump-Gabreëls*

The Romanian leadership failed to sabotage the nonproliferation treaty altogether, but it succeeded in challenging the Kremlin in the nuclear arena. It had increased its scope for maneuver by dominating the nonproliferation debate inside the WP to a large extent. Although Ulbricht and Gomułka had already attempted to block any Soviet unilateralism on the MLF, the Romanian leaders had succeeded in demanding active involvement in the negotiations of the nonproliferation treaty. In all these cases the nuclear question emancipated the NSWP members from the Soviet grip. The nuclear problem proved to be such a hotly contested issue that it caused the first public division between the one and the six, and indeed almost caused a schism in the WP. It thus challenged the concept of the WP as a "Cardboard Castle," and proved a catalyst for further multilateralization of the alliance. The Kremlin maintained its nuclear monopoly within the Warsaw Pact. It did, however, lose its monopoly on deciding on Soviet bloc foreign policy.

Notes

1 Andrzej Korbonski, "The Warsaw Treaty after Twenty-five Years: An Entangling Alliance or an Empty Shell?" in *The Warsaw Pact: Political Purpose and Military Means*, eds. Robert W. Clawson and Lawrence S. Kaplan (Ohio: Rowman & Littlefield, 1982), 3; and Clawson and Kaplan, *The Warsaw Pact*, x.
2 Some of the arguments in this article can be found in Chapter 5 of my monograph *The Warsaw Pact Reconsidered: International Relations in Eastern Europe, 1955–1969* (London; New York: Routledge, 2015), 170–211.
3 I have done particularly extensive research in the archives in Bucharest and Berlin.
4 For the Romanian attitude towards the superpowers, see Elena Dragomir, "The Perceived Threat of Hegemonism in Romania during the Second Détente," *Cold War History* 12, no. 1 (2012): 116.
5 Helga Haftendorn, *NATO and the Nuclear Revolution: A Crisis of Credibility, 1966–1967* (Oxford: Oxford University Press, 1996); and Anna Locher, *Crisis? What Crisis? NATO, de Gaulle, and the Future of the Alliance, 1963–1966* (Berlin: Nomos, 2010).
6 Douglas Selvage, *The Warsaw Pact and Nuclear Nonproliferation, 1963–1965*, Cold War International History Project (CWIHP) Working Paper No. 32 (Washington, D.C.: Wilson Center, 2001).
7 For the East German use of the WP as a "transmission belt" for its foreign policy interests, see Douglas Selvage, "The Warsaw Pact and the German Question, 1955–1970: Conflict and Consensus," in *NATO and the Warsaw Pact: Intrabloc Conflicts*, eds. Mary Ann Heiss and S. Victor Papacosma (Ohio: Kent State University Press, 2008), 179f.
8 Eliza Gheorghe, "Atomic Maverick: Romania's Negotiations for Nuclear Technology, 1964–1970," *Cold War History* 13, no. 3 (2013): 373–392; and "Romania's Nuclear Negotiations Postures in the 1960s: Client, Maverick and International Peace Mediator," *Romanian Nuclear History Project Working Paper* 1 (2012), www.roec.ro/romanias-nuclear-negotiations, accessed August 27, 2013.
9 Hal Brands, "Non-Proliferation and the Dynamics of the Middle Cold War: The Superpowers, the MLF, and the NPT," *Cold War History* 7, no. 3 (2007): 389–423.
10 Ibid., 411f.
11 NATO officials cited in Vojtech Mastny and Malcolm Byrne (eds.), *A Cardboard Castle? An Inside History of the Warsaw Pact 1955–1991* (Budapest; New York: Central European University Press, 2005), 1.

The Warsaw Pact   113

12 The Sino-Soviet split denotes the schism between the Soviet Union and the People's Republic of China after Nikita Khrushchev started charting a more liberal course in Eastern Europe (from 1956 onwards), while Chairman Mao Zedong became increasingly radical. In April 1960 the schism became public at a Romanian Party Congress in Bucharest. Subsequently, the relationship between the Soviet Union and the PRC became increasingly hostile, which also resulted in the withdrawal of Soviet advisers from the PRC and the cancellation of the PRC's observer status within the Warsaw Pact in 1961. The second Berlin Crisis (1958–1962) centered around the status of West Berlin. The crisis was largely resolved by the building of the Berlin Wall in August 1961.

13 Selvage, *The Warsaw Pact and Nuclear Nonproliferation*, 2.

14 See ibid., 3–9.

15 Raymond L. Garthoff, "When and Why Romania Distanced Itself from the Warsaw Pact," in *Cold War Crises*, ed. James Hershberg, CWIHP Bulletin no. 5 (Washington, D.C.: Wilson Center, 1998), 111.

16 This was a Romanian manifesto on the equality of Communist parties in order to defend its autonomous stance within the Soviet bloc. See Dennis Deletant and Mihail Ionescu, *Romania and the Warsaw Pact: 1955–1989*, CWIHP Working Paper no. 43 (Washington, D.C.: Wilson Center, 2004), 72.

17 Brands, "Non-Proliferation and Dynamics," 401.

18 Cf. the subtitle of Lorenz Lüthi's book: *The Sino-Soviet Split: Cold War in the Communist World* (Princeton: Princeton University Press, 2008).

19 Selvage, *The Warsaw Pact and Nuclear Nonproliferation*, 14.

20 Letter from Ulbricht to WP leaders, January 13, 1965, *Stiftung Archiv der Parteien und Massenorganisationen der DDR im Bundesarchiv*, Berlin, Germany (SAPMO-BArch), DY 30/3388, 69ff.

21 Meeting between Bodnaras and Liu Fan, January 1, 1965, *Arhivele Naţionale Istorice Centrale ale României*, Bucharest, Romania (ANIC), Romanian Workers' Party Central Committee (RWP CC), International Relations (IR), 4/1965, 1–12; and meeting between Bodnaras and Liu Fan, January 9, 1965, ANIC, RWP CC, IR, 4/1965, 15–19.

22 Meeting between Gheorghiu-Dej, Maurer, and Ulbricht, January 18, 1965, ANIC, RWP CC, IR, 15/1965, 103–111.

23 Minutes of the PCC, January 19–20, 1965, ANIC, RWP CC, IR, 15/1965, 29 for the altered and erased paragraph.

24 Ibid., 77.

25 First session of the editorial committee, January 19, 1965, ANIC, RWP CC, IR, 16/1965, 224.

26 Gheorghe, "Atomic Maverick," 373–392.

27 "Polish Minutes of Discussion at the Political Consultative Committee (PCC) Meeting in Warsaw," January 20, 1965, Parallel History Project on Cooperative Security (PHP); www.php.isn.ethz.ch/collections/colltopic.cfm?lng=en&id=17921&navinfo=14465 (accessed August 26, 2013).

28 "Romanian Minutes of the PCC Meeting," January 20, 1965, PHP, www.php.isn.ethz.ch/collections/colltopic.cfm?lng=en&id=17921&navinfo=14465 (accessed August 26, 2013); also minutes of the PCC, January 19–20, 1965, ANIC, RWP CC, IR, 15/1965, 3–91.

29 Ibid., 11.

30 "Polish Minutes of Discussion at the PCC Meeting in Warsaw." January 20, 1965, PHP, 7, 9.

31 Gheorghe argues that the Romanian status as "maverick" also helped the Romanians in obtaining certain concessions from the West, perhaps even concerning nuclear equipment. See "Atomic Maverick," 399.

32 Minutes of the PCC, January 19–20, 1965, ANIC, RWP CC, IR, 15/1965, 88.

33 Meeting between Bodnaras and Liu Fan, January 9, 1965, ANIC, RWP CC, IR, 4/1965, 15–19.

114   *L. Crump-Gabreëls*

34 Meeting between Bodnaras and Liu Fan, January 27, 1965, ibid., 36ff.
35 Meeting between Maurer, Bodnaras and Liu Fan, January 28, 1965, ibid., 49–50.
36 Brands, "Non-Proliferation and Dynamics," 401.
37 Meeting between Bodnaras and Liu Fan, October 28, 1965, ANIC, RCP CC, IR, 4/1965, 222; the Romanians also wrote a report on their position on nonproliferation in which they expressed agreement with the Chinese position. Cf. Memo on a Non-proliferation Treaty, August 1965, ANIC, RCP CC, IR, 38/1965, vol. I, 99–107.
38 Dumitru Preda *et al.*, eds., *România – Republica Federală Germania. Începutul relațiilor diplomatice 1966–1967,* vol. I (Bucharest: Editura Enciclopedica, 2009), XXIV.
39 Brands, "Non-Proliferation and Dynamics," 408.
40 "TOP SECRET. Information on discussions with A.A. Soldatov, Deputy of the Minister of Foreign Affairs of the USSR, on the Problem of Nonproliferation of Nuclear Arms," February 27–28, 1967, ANIC, RCP CC, IR, 113/1967, 21, 27. The ENDC had again resumed its work on February 21, 1967.
41 Meeting between Soldatov and Manescu, March 6, 1967, ANIC, RCP CC, IR, 113/1967, 28–29.
42 "Minutes of the Discussions at the Highest Level between the CPSU and the RCP, Moscow, March 17–18, 1967," ANIC, RCP CC, IR, 14/1967, 38.
43 "Letter by the General Secretary of the PCR (Nicolae Ceaușescu) to the First Secretary of PZPR (Władysław Gomułka) Proposing to Summon the PCC," January 31, 1968, PHP, www.php.isn.ethz.ch/collections/colltopic.cfm?lng=en&id=18012&navinfo=14465 (accessed August 26, 2013).
44 "East German Criticism of the Romanian Amendments to the Soviet Draft of a Non-proliferation Treaty," March 4, 1968, PHP, www.php.isn.ethz.ch/collections/colltopic.cfm?lng=en&id=17992&navinfo=14465 (accessed August 26, 2013).
45 "Minutes of the Extraordinary Plenary Session of the Central Committee of the Romanian Communist Party," March 1, 1968, ANIC, RCP CC, C 31/1968, 40.
46 "Memo by the Hungarian Foreign Minister (János Péter) on the Romanian Proposal to Convene the PCC," February 5, 1968, PHP, www.php.isn.ethz.ch/collections/colltopic.cfm?lng=en&id=18010&navinfo=14465 (accessed August 26, 2013).
47 "Memo about the Conversation between Comrade Walter Ulbricht and Comrade diplomat Abrassimov," February 13, 1968, SAPMO BArch, DY 30/3390, 41–43.
48 "Draft Commentary on Romanian Position at the PCC Meeting to the CC of the Bulgarian Communist Party Plenary Meeting," March 6, 1968, PHP, www.php.isn.ethz.ch/collections/colltopic.cfm?lng=en&id=17988&navinfo=14465 (accessed August 26, 2013).
49 "Minutes of the Extraordinary Plenary Session of the Central Committee of the Romanian Communist Party," March 1, 1968, ANIC, RCP CC, C 31/1968, 43.
50 "East German Minutes of the Berlin Meeting of Deputy Ministers of Foreign Affairs Preparatory to the PCC Meeting," February 26, 1968, PHP, www.php.isn.ethz.ch/collections/colltopic.cfm?lng=en&id=17996&navinfo=14465 (accessed August 26, 2013). Cf. *Politisches Archiv des Auswärtigen Amtes*, Berlin, Germany (PA AA), Ministerium für Auswärtige Angelegenheiten der DDR (MfAA), G-A 552.
51 "Draft Commentary on Romanian Position at the PCC Meeting to the CC of the Bulgarian Communist Party Plenary Meeting," March 6, 1968.
52 "Minutes of the Plenary Session of the Central Committee of the Bulgarian Communist Party – Report on the PCC Meeting by the First Secretary (Todor Zhivkov)," March 14, 1968, PHP, www.php.isn.ethz.ch/collections/colltopic.cfm?lng=en&id=17966&navinfo=14465 (accessed August 26, 2013).
53 "Draft Commentary on Romanian Position at the PCC Meeting to the CC of the Bulgarian Communist Party Plenary Meeting," March 6, 1968, PHP, 7–8.
54 "Minutes of the Extraordinary Plenary Session of the Central Committee of the Romanian Communist Party," March 1, 1968, ANIC, RCP CC, C, 31/1968, 45.

The Warsaw Pact 115

55 "East German Evaluation of the Romanian Position on the Soviet Proposal of a Non-proliferation Treaty," February 26, 1968, PHP, www.php.isn.ethz.ch/collections/colltopic.cfm?lng=en&id=17994&navinfo=14465 (accessed August 26, 2013).

56 "Discussion between Comrades Nicolae Ceaușescu and Ion Gheorghe Maurer, and Comrades Leonid Brezhnev and Alexei Kosygin, March 6, 1968," ANIC, RCP CC, IR, 38/1968, 115.

57 "Report to the Hungarian Party Politburo and Council of Ministers on the PCC Meeting," March 9, 1968, PHP, www.php.isn.ethz.ch/collections/colltopic.cfm?lng=en&id=17967&navinfo=14465 (accessed August 26, 2013).

58 "Statement Supporting Soviet Draft Nonproliferation Treaty," March 9, 1968, PHP, www.php.isn.ethz.ch/collections/colltopic.cfm?lng=en&id=17974&navinfo=14465 (accessed August 26, 2013).

59 "Communiqué on Soviet Draft Nonproliferation Treaty," March 9, 1968, PHP, www.php.isn.ethz.ch/collections/colltopic.cfm?lng=en&id=17970&navinfo=14465 (accessed August 26, 2013).

60 "Protocol Nr. 10 of the Session of the Executive Committee of the R.C.P. on March 8, 1968," ANIC, RCP CC, C, 34/1968, 11.

61 "Note about a Conversation between Comrade N. Ceaușescu and T. Zhivkov on the Evening of 7.III.1968 (Sofia)," ANIC, RCP CC, IR, 38/1968, 91.

62 "Minutes of the Hungarian Party Politburo Session," March 8, 1968, PHP, 5.

63 Diplomatic Report from Bucharest, SAPMO-BArch, May 23, 1968, DY 30/IVA2/20/374, 322.

64 Diplomatic Report from Bucharest, SAPMO-BArch, June 20, 1968, DY 30/IVA2/20/374, 419.

65 "Treaty on the Non-Proliferation of Nuclear Weapons (NPT)," July 1, 1968, www.un.org/disarmament/WMD/Nuclear/NPTtext.shtml (accessed August 28, 2015).

66 Francis J. Gavin, "Nuclear Proliferation and Non-proliferation during the Cold War," 410, in *The Cambridge History of the Cold War: Volume II. Crisis and Détente*, eds. Melvyn Leffler and Odd A. Westad (Cambridge, MA: Cambridge University Press, 2010), 395–416.

67 "Memo of Results of the Chiefs of General Staff Meeting regarding Reorganization of the Warsaw Treaty," March 1, 1968, in *A Cardboard Castle?*, eds. Mastny and Byrne, 249ff.

68 Brands, "Non-Proliferation and Dynamics," 410.

Part II

Global and regional dynamics in negotiating the NPT

7 Unusual suspects down under

Australia's choice for the nonproliferation treaty

Christine M. Leah[1]

Australia has always had a complex and conflicted relationship with the bomb. Within this broader trend, in the late 1960s, Australia's attitude towards the nascent Treaty on the Non-Proliferation of Nuclear Weapons (NPT) was largely influenced by four divergent political constraints: (1) the aspiration for a nuclear weapons capability; (2) the concern that the NPT would impede Australia's access to and development of nuclear technology; (3) the desire to limit the further proliferation of nuclear weapons in its region; and (4) the attachment to US extended nuclear deterrence. For many decades it has been assumed that Australia's final decision to ratify the NPT in January 1973 was mainly due to specific American security assurances.[2] This "nuclear umbrella" – or "extended nuclear deterrence" – is indeed often cited as one significant factor constraining the spread of nuclear weapons by obviating the need for US allies to possess their own nuclear deterrent.[3]

In contrast, this chapter argues that Australia's decision-making was in fact much more convoluted. It argues that US security assurances ultimately played only a small role in Canberra's decision to ratify the treaty. Australia sought a nuclear capability because it saw other Asian powers (notably Communist China, Japan, and Indonesia) as existential threats, and neither the United Kingdom nor the United States seemed eager to offer specific assurances that their nuclear forces would be used to defend Australia. When the NPT came along, Canberra voiced concern over whether the treaty's verification system could truly prevent its northern neighbors from going nuclear. However, this flexibility was also advantageous for Australia, allowing it to hedge during negotiations up until the early 1970s. NPT proponents argued that Australia's ratification would better the relations with Washington and compel potential foes to also ratify. However it was only because Asia had become relatively stable that the government ratified the treaty in 1973. This coincided with the decline of the bomb lobby in domestic political circles and a new political leader who was adamant that Australia should not become the, by then, seventh nuclear-weapon state.

The overwhelming majority of historical work on Australia and nuclear weapons was completed by Wayne Reynolds and Jim Walsh in the late 1990s.[4] This chapter builds on that research and presents new declassified material from

120   *C.M. Leah*

the National Australian Archives – a very open and accessible source for researchers. As a result of recent regulation changes, researchers have access to a relatively rich source of primary material.[5] Nevertheless, readers need to be aware that a great number of files are still to be cleared for public access. Little is publicly known on key issues, like for instance, Great Britain's thinking about the role of its nuclear weapons in potentially defending its colonies against aggression and invasion, or the details of French military nuclear assistance to Australia. Still, building on three years of archival research and interviews with former and current government officials, this chapter attempts to provide a more nuanced perspective on Australia's early non-proliferation policies.

The chapter proceeds as follows. First, it provides an overview of the regional security setting after the Second World War, and the mentality of Australian leaders, who were unused to navigating the Asian security environment without Anglo-Saxon "great and powerful friends." Second, it summarizes Australia's nuclear acquisition attempts first with the help of London, then through Washington, and then by using its own resources and technology to achieve an independent nuclear capability. Third, it canvasses debates between different government departments and political parties as to what Australia's nuclear future should look like. Fourth, it presents the main points of contention regarding the NPT and how these should be resolved. Fifth, it shows what domestic and international changes facilitated the ultimate decision to ratify the NPT in 1973. Finally, the last section asks what might happen next. Given that stability and order in Asia is coming under increasing pressure, what are the different ways Australia's attitudes towards nuclear weapons could evolve over the next few decades, and what would shape the outcome?

Regional security setting

Colonized by the British in 1788, and the Aboriginal population essentially stripped of their land and lifestyle, *Terra Australis* became a tiny white, Anglo-Saxon outpost surrounded by a myriad of different Asian populations.[6] Even well after Federation was declared in 1901, the descendants of the first British settlers still clung very strongly to the idea that they were part of a larger British nation.[7] Yet given subsequent advances in technology and military power, the peoples of Australia became much more aware of their surrounding geography and their vulnerability to potential threats from Southeast and mainland Asia.[8] The experiences of the Second World War fighting in the Pacific against Asian forces and the subsequent significant contraction of British sea power played an important role in defining Australia's security perceptions. By the 1950s, Australia saw itself suddenly faced with the prospect of navigating a region that was not dominated by a Western maritime power anymore. Distance and isolation from the United Kingdom had now become a significant part of the Australian mentality and how it saw its position in the world.[9]

Indeed, when the Indonesian National Revolution proclaimed independence from the Netherlands in 1945, Australia saw this as a further erosion of the

Australia 121

West's presence in Asia – a presence that its people had always lived with. For the still fledgling Australian nation, Indonesia was a new wild child on the block: a bankrupt economy, a powerful communist party waiting in the wings, and an unpredictable Sukarno as its leader, a man who would not tolerate the remaining Dutch presence in West New Guinea.[10] Sukarno's aggressive stance would lead to a policy of *konfrontasi* in the 1960s, an Indonesian military response – assisted by the Soviet Union – to the proposal to integrate Malaya, Singapore, North Borneo, and Brunei into the Federation of Malaysia.[11]

The difficult security situation around Indonesia, coupled with the communist revolution in China, the outbreak of the Korean and Indochina Wars, and the lingering wariness about Japan exacerbated Australian security concerns. The outbreak of the Vietnam War and the contraction of British forces East of Suez also contributed to this sense of insecurity. The Australia–New Zealand–United States (ANZUS) Treaty had been signed in 1951, but Canberra was still focused on keeping the British in the region. Australians felt that the United States was not committed to ANZUS in the same way it was devoted to Western Europe through NATO, and thus believed Washington would not be keen to increase its commitments in Asia. Australians saw this US reluctance as the main reason why Washington had opposed a UK inclusion in the ANZUS Treaty, an attempt to avoid a commitment to defend British interests in Hong Kong or Malaya.[12] Ultimately, it was not until the late 1950s that the United States came to be considered Australia's primary defense partner.[13] And during the first two decades after the Second World War, Australian strategic elites saw Southeast Asia resembling much less like what was becoming the European Economic Community and a lot more like the Balkans before the First World War. The dominant perception was that a powerful Indonesia could take advantage of its weaker neighbors, they themselves plagued with internal domestic instabilities.[14]

Exploring nuclear options

As detailed histories of Australia's nuclear weapons pursuit persuasively argue, the security concerns outlined above, combined with very weak conventional capabilities, pushed Australian policy-makers towards exploring nuclear weapons options. Although there are no Cabinet documents explicitly stating that it was official government policy to seek a nuclear *weapons* capability, it is clear that as early as 1945 senior officials sought to provide the country with a certain level of latency, should the need for such a capability eventually arise.[15] It should be noted here that personal leadership styles mattered – and continue to matter – a lot in Australia. Security policy was not much debated, even within the Cabinet, and these issues were deemed more of a matter for the Prime Minister and the Minister for External Affairs. This helps to explain the sometimes more apparent fluctuations in Australian proliferation policy. From 1956 onwards, there were various pushes from within the Air Force, the Department of Defence, and the Australian Atomic Energy Commission (AAEC) to develop an Australian nuclear weapons capability. While the AAEC presented a plan for domestic technology

122   C.M. Leah

development, this approach was rejected in favor of the Department of Defence's preference to procure nuclear weapons from the British.

Towards the end of the 1940s, British officials were looking for a suitable test site for the emerging UK missiles program. Since the US was not keen to let Britain test on American soil, London approached Canberra on this issue. The new Australian Prime Minister Robert Menzies responded positively to British requests. A formal agreement was reached in 1951. Given the still intense feelings of loyalty towards the mother country, Canberra wanted to be a responsible contributor to the still prevalent concept of "Empire Defense." Prime Minister Menzies described the Labor's opposition to this cooperation as "clearly [a policy] of suicide, and a lonely suicide at that."[16] As the Australian Ambassador to the United States Howard Beale would note in later years:

> it would, in this situation, have been against our own interest, and brutally ungenerous as well, to have refused the assistance requested. [...] There are times when a nation must stand up and be counted; for Australia this was such a time.[17]

One major result of the UK–Australia cooperation was the Woomera rocket range, stretching from Adelaide about 1,250 miles across the desert to the West Australian coast. Britain was both producing the weapons for testing and further development and providing equipment and scientific personnel. Australia was providing all the local technical support. Canberra's intention was to develop variants of the British technology for its own national defense.[18] The partnership for testing missiles eventually led to cooperation in testing nuclear warheads. Towards this end, an initial decision was taken in 1953. Starting in 1956, a total of nine explosive devices were detonated in the Australian desert, more specifically on the Maralinga and the Monte Bello islands.[19]

In the end, the bilateral cooperation did not yield decisive results towards providing Australia with a nuclear weapons capability. The British government wanted to postpone any agreement for the transfer of nuclear technology to Australia until after Washington formalized its own cooperation with London. Thus, the UK was dragging its feet in negotiations on the supply of missiles or actual warheads to Australian authorities, wary of the implications of sharing conventional and nuclear military technology with Canberra in regard to the relations with Washington. Eventually, the US Congress passed the McMahon Act, which barred the UK from sharing with Australia any information obtained from the United States. Thus, British–Australian nuclear cooperation eventually came to a halt in 1957. The UK started testing at the US Nevada Test Site and eventually concluded that the conversion of Australia's Maralinga into an underground testing facility was too expensive a redundancy. Dissatisfied with this cooperative approach, Australia continued to engage in domestic nuclear research towards acquiring a nuclear weapons capability.[20]

By the end of the 1950s, the Australian government had already initiated a large uranium mining project. While the authorities concluded that Australia had

Australia 123

no immediate need to build nuclear power stations, nuclear technology was quickly deemed too important to be ignored. If Australia was to keep up with progress overseas – namely in the UK and Canada – then it would have to be active in research and development. Hence, the AAEC ordered the establishment of the Lucas Heights reactor, which went critical in 1958. It was a ten-megawatt reactor moderated by heavy water and initially fuelled with highly enriched uranium. The AAEC also engaged in research on enrichment technology, particularly on gas centrifuges and laser techniques. Agreements were concluded with both Canada and France towards sharing centrifuge technology.[21]

A leading figure within the Australian scientific community and one of the three head commissioners of the AAEC was Philip Baxter. He was a driving force behind the research activities at Lucas Heights, and soon became the key adviser to the Prime Minister's Defence Committee. Around 1966, the Minister of National Development proposed that Australia construct a nuclear power reactor. This was initially opposed, but after John Gorton became Prime Minister in January 1968 and after the discussions surrounding the NPT began, the government launched a program to build a 500-megawatt nuclear power reactor at Jervis Bay. Towards this end, Australia signed a secret agreement to collaborate on nuclear enrichment with France.[22] Starting in 1965, proposals had even been made for a 300-megawatt reactor power station in the Snowy River, a separate project to Jervis Bay. The assessment of Ernest Titterton – professor of nuclear physics at the Australian National University and a strong voice in favor of a nuclear capability – was that this facility would have been able to produce sufficient plutonium for fifty twenty-kiloton nuclear bombs per year.[23] However, many argued these nuclear facilities would be costly and, by 1968, Washington was pushing Canberra towards signing the NPT.

Domestic nuclear disputes

Given intense regional security dynamics, the late 1960s saw the apogee of public debate on Australia's nuclear future. The PRC's first nuclear test in October 1964 was a cause of great concern in Australia. In Canberra's assessment, Beijing's nuclear acquisition greatly increased the risk of nuclear retaliation and had the potential to expand any regional conflict into a global war.[24] Further, there was quite a bit of distress about Japan and Western Germany going nuclear in reaction to the PRC. Shortly after, officials in the Sukarno government began to publicly announce Indonesia's intentions and capabilities to build a nuclear bomb. The Indonesian military even claimed it had completed research into a ballistic missile capability, and that it could produce such a weapon if the necessary funds were made available.[25] Sukarno himself argued that "the more countries that are in possession of atomic and nuclear bombs, the stronger the guarantee that would be given that these weapons of the modern world would not be used."[26] The US intelligence community appeared persuaded that Indonesia was committed to nuclear acquisition.[27] Within this context, many Australian decision-makers seriously considered a national nuclear option.

124 *C.M. Leah*

Part of the rationale behind a national nuclear weapons capability was the belief that such arms would become commonplace. They were, after all, considered to be modern instruments of war and deterrence. Already in 1962, the Australian government's statement at the United Nations reflected these views. In a letter to the UN Secretary General on the question of the circumstances under which Australia would formally renounce a nuclear weapons capability, the government responded that it "seriously doubts the effectiveness of regional agreements for the limitation of nuclear weapons."[28] In the same vein, Canberra also argued that further proliferation would only worsen Australia's security situation, especially given the absence of any firm British or US security guarantees. Such argumentation suggested that Australia saw few other options than acquiring its own nuclear deterrent.[29] For instance, AAEC's Philip Baxter went even a bit further, stating that he found "it very hard to be unduly concerned about what is called proliferation of nuclear weapons," and that such proliferation in some situations – such as the Middle East – "might even be a contribution to world stability."[30]

By contrast, there were also Australian officials pushing for a limit to further proliferation.[31] Nonetheless, even within these circles, policy-makers were rather concerned with regional proliferation, than with the continuous nuclear possession by the great powers.[32] Both the government headed by Robert Menzies and the succeeding prime ministers had few objections to the UK or US possession of nuclear weapons. "There is an advantage for the world in having nuclear and thermo-nuclear weapons in the hands of the United States, the United Kingdom and the Soviet Union, and in no others," argued Menzies.

> These Great Powers [...] are sufficiently informed about the deadly character of these weapons to find themselves reluctant to cause a war in which they are used. The possession of these violent forces is, in the case of these great nations, a deterrent not only to prospective enemies but to themselves.[33]

Even proliferation by France was not seen in Australia as inherently destabilizing for NATO or the defense of Western Europe.[34]

The unclear US stance in regard to the security of its allies was an additional concern for Australian decision-makers. As I detail in another publication, the Americans were not very keen to lay out the details of any nuclear security guarantee to Australia. This fact made many officials in Canberra – especially within the Department of Defence, the AAEC, and pro-nuclear lobbies within both the Menzies and the Gorton governments – even more skeptical about the credibility of the ANZUS alliance.[35] In fact, it was Robert McNamara himself who said that it would be "entirely natural" and "an obvious thing to happen" for Australia to acquire nuclear weapons in response to China's new nuclear capability.[36] Another US official commented that, given China's nuclear capability, if he had been given the chance again, he would not have recommended offering assurances that the US would respond with nuclear weapons if Australia were

Australia 125

attacked.[37] In contrast, Washington simply continued to assert that US conventional forces would be sufficient to deter hostile actions against Australia by Beijing or Jakarta.

Within this context, quite a few Australian politicians and bureaucrats expressed strong views towards the acquisition of a nuclear deterrent. For instance, AAEC's Philip Baxter's view that the threat of use of atomic weaponry was a better alternative to sacrificing thousands of young soldiers found support in the armed services. It was also supported early on by John Gorton, who would ultimately become prime minister in 1968. Gorton was not an enthusiast of the "forward defense" concept that had governed so much of Australia's defense policy since 1945 – contributing forces overseas in support of great power ambitions. His view was that Australia should focus its resources on "continental defense," which implied a strong build-up of modern air and naval reconnaissance and strike forces, able to deter threats from great powers in Asia. Before becoming the leader of the government, Gorton expressed the concern that Southeast Asia might "have a war of the kind we saw in Korea" and that Australia must therefore have troops available at "a moment's notice." He believed that since such a war could go "from worse to worse," Australia would require its own atomic weaponry.[38] Neither the United Kingdom nor the US could ultimately be trusted. "I should like to see us have inter-continent [*sic*] missiles of our own and have our own bomber aircraft, capable of delivering our own bombs should we find that necessary," Gorton argued.[39]

It is also worth noting some of the more colorful statements made during this time by various other politicians. "The best defensive weapons are nuclear weapons, and it is time that Australia developed its own," argued a senator.[40] "We do not have to use it. Other countries have it and do not use it. It is the greatest deterrent in this world," he added.[41] Another senator thought that "Australia will have to have the means of using nuclear weapons whether they are produced here or not" in response to a Chinese test.[42] "Until we have the atom bomb in Australia, until we can manufacture it ourselves, we will never be safe," agreed another. "Indonesia will have it sooner or later."[43] Others were concerned about US security guarantees, arguing Washington would not sacrifice Los Angeles for Sydney. "If we run any risk of atomic attack, I believe it is in our interests to have the weapons with which to reply."[44]

The NPT debate

This was the setting in Australia when the negotiations towards a global non-proliferation treaty entered the decisive phase.[45] Given the pressures and constraints outlined above, many within the Department of Defence, the Menzies and Gorton cabinets, and the AAEC argued it made very little sense for Australia to sign a treaty that would deprive it of the nuclear option – now or in the future. Still, there were others – especially in the Department of Foreign Affairs and Trade – who were much more in favor of signing the NPT. They believed that not doing so would weaken the US alliance and isolate Australia from the rest of the international community. Australia's abstinence from the Treaty could also strengthen the hand of the treaty's opponents in Japan.[46] A vociferous internal debate ensued.[47] Before the matter was ultimately settled under the Labor Prime Minister Gough Whitlam, the debate circled around the treaty's verification mechanism, the NPT's constraints upon latent capabilities, Australia's role within the international system, and the validity of Washington's security guarantees.

Many Australian officials were skeptical of the different provisions of the proposed treaty. One issue of concern was the efficiency of the NPT's envisioned verification mechanism. The first Australian speech to the UN regarding the NPT was in May 1968, and contained no hint of belief that the superpowers would seek to reduce their own stockpiles. It expressed concerns over the treaty's potential harmful effects on nuclear research in Australia.[48] Indeed,

> [i]f signatories are permitted to do nuclear work quite close to the stage of actually exploding a device, the undesirable industrial restraints on Australia may not be great. But if the controls go a long way back in the production process, Australia might be shut out of a lot of research and development.[49]

In addition, the speech at the UN betrayed some preoccupation with China's standing outside the treaty; a feeling this measure of arms control was a "European" measure, a symbol of a *détente* which "excludes China."[50]

The main concern was that, if proliferation continued, Australia would find itself increasingly vulnerable to nuclear blackmail, since the United States might become less and less keen to defend its ally in a more proliferated world.[51] Hence, Australian policy-makers worried that under the planned treaty, states would be able to divert material from peaceful to military purposes, and interpret their safeguard agreements based on their own interests.[52] Baxter's assessment was that safeguards would be extremely difficult to administer in practice, and that the IAEA had been born in the "wild optimism" of the 1950s.[53] For Titterton, the NPT was a "worthless and ineffective bit of paper," and cheating the NPT was possible in many ways. Thus, he argued that Australia should not sign away its nuclear weapons options in exchange for an ineffective control system.[54]

An additional issue given serious consideration was the question of potential industrial espionage. If inspectors had access at all times and to all places, this would be problematic in what was seen as a highly competitive nuclear industry.[55] A further concern was the expected duration of the treaty: one report noted that 25 years would be too long given the potential technological and geopolitical changes during such a long time period.[56] Some states might hedge by preparing for the post-Treaty situation, whether from ambition or anxiety. In this way "the stabilizing objective of the Treaty could be defeated."[57] For the AAEC "the Treaty would consolidate existing inequalities in nuclear weapons competence amongst the non-nuclears thus placing certain countries for the indefinite future at an advantage in this respect under the withdrawal clause."[58]

Australia 127

Given these concerns, the ability of Australia to reduce its lead time by producing basic radioactive fissile materials (allowed under the NPT's Article IV) and subsequently withdraw from the treaty was given consideration.[59] As a result, they recommended that Canberra should try to secure from London a "recognition of an obligation to allow Australia the right of access to United Kingdom nuclear weapon 'know how' [...] in the event of important countries in the general Pacific and Indian Ocean areas acquiring nuclear capability."[60] In 1969, Baxter wrote that the growth of the domestic nuclear industry would provide a basis from which Australia, should it at any point in the future consider nuclear weapons essential for providing security, could "move with the minimum delay to provide such means of defense."[61]

A US delegation concluded after a discussion with AAEC officials that "the political rationalization of these officials was that Australia needed to be in a position to manufacture nuclear weapons rapidly if India and Japan were to go nuclear."[62] As a consequence, Australia's aim within the NPT negotiations was to ultimately enable the country to achieve a short lead time towards assembling the various components of a weapons program.[63] Therefore, it is no surprise that the Australian negotiators insisted that the ban of the right to "manufacture" was to come in "just short" of fabricating a device.[64]

It was a majority in the Department of External Affairs that was mostly in favor of signing. A departmental report argued that signing would align Australia with the great majority of the international community who support genuine steps towards the limitation of armaments; that the treaty would be an important link in relations between the Soviet bloc and Western countries; that as a non-nuclear power, it was a vital Australian interest that the emergence of new nuclear powers should be restrained; and that Australia's signature of the treaty, which was strongly desired by the United States, would reinforce its association with the Washington and enable Canberra to give further support to the US position vis-à-vis encouraging Asian countries to sign and ratify. Besides, if Australia did not sign, it would be like saying that Germany, Italy, Japan, Indonesia, India, and others should not sign either.[65] Thus, AAEC officials made it clear to a US delegation that Australian ratification would be conditional on the assent to the treaty "by particular states considered to be capable of establishing a nuclear capability in a short time, for example India, Japan, and perhaps West Germany."[66]

Although many were skeptical in regard to US security guarantees, officials in Canberra were still hopeful that Washington would extend a nuclear umbrella over Australia, however ill-defined this assurance might be.[67] Some policy-makers even expressed hope in regard to a nuclear sharing agreement with Washington, and suggested the US might reconsider its stance towards ANZUS and start treating it as a counterpart to NATO.[68] In conclusion, policy-makers in Canberra did not want the already weak security guarantee to be compromised in any way. During the negotiations, they informed the US government that Australia "could not even contemplate signing the NPT if it were not for an interpretation which would enable the deployment of nuclear weapons belonging to an

128 *C.M. Leah*

ally on Australian soil."[69] Somewhat settling these concerns, a report by the AAEC noted that ratification of the NPT "would not prevent the use by Australia's allies of nuclear weapons in Australia's defense, nor would it prevent Australia from building or acquiring missile or satellite delivery systems." Regarding its provisions for countries not to accept nuclear weapons or their control, the NPT "would not prevent us from agreeing to the stationing in or passage through our territory of weapons under the control of another power."[70]

Coming to a decision on the NPT

The section above shows that there was not one agreed-upon strategy vis-à-vis NPT negotiations within Australia's political elites. However, over the subsequent years, an altered domestic and international setting facilitated the eventual ratification of the NPT in 1973. At the domestic level, a change in government from the Liberals to Labor and a weakening of the nuclear-weapons lobby within the bureaucracy paved the way towards NPT ratification. At the international level, new strategic assessments about China and Indonesia's military capabilities and political intentions concluded that neither was likely to invade Australia or threaten it with nuclear weapons. And a majority of policymakers (some with hesitation) concluded that an attack on Australia by any major power was unlikely to occur outside the context of a general world war, and in which case it would be one of the last targets in a strategic nuclear exchange. However, even within this more benign environment, Australia's decision appears to have been significantly eased by the awareness that it could quite comfortably hedge its technological bets within the internationally accepted framework of the NPT.

In late 1972, the Labor party came into office. Labor had been a long-standing supporter of the NPT. The new Prime Minister, Gough Whitlam, did not seek advice on whether or not to ratify the treaty. For him, this decision was already an established Labor priority. In comparison to the Liberal party, Labor had a more internationalist philosophy. Its general stance was that nuclear weapons were harmful to international security. For instance, Labor saw nuclear testing as detrimental to the environment and to human health. French testing in the Pacific in the 1970s did nothing to help change this attitude. Hence, Canberra under Labor became increasingly concerned and opposed to above-surface testing. In the early 1970s, together with New Zealand, Labor helped organize a meeting of sixteen Pacific nations to declare opposition to the French tests, and cosponsored a resolution that condemned nuclear tests generally. Labor also made sure that Australia was active in disarmament forums. For example, in 1975 Australia began to endorse nuclear weapon-free zones.[71] Nevertheless, Whitlam's government remained committed to US extended nuclear deterrence and did nothing to endanger Washington's ability to provide a nuclear umbrella.[72]

In addition to this government change, by the early 1970s, the powerful lobby within the bureaucracy in favor of a nuclear weapons option had been significantly weakened. Not only did the Department of External Affairs have more

Australia 129

influence with the Whitlam government, but close links had also developed between the defense authorities and the Department of External Affairs. There was also much closer contact between External Affairs and the joint planning committee. As such, where there had been much less coordination between foreign and defense policies before, such coordination increased somewhat by the beginning of the 1970s.[73] This contributed to the decline of the influence of the military in the formulation of defense policy.[74] Also, when the Whitlam government came to power, many public servants within the Departments of the Defence and External Affairs who had lobbied for the bomb were replaced with those who supported Labor's steadfast policy of Australia ratifying the NPT.[75] Over at the AAEC, the influence of Philip Baxter diminished, and he left the organization in 1975. His departure and the demise of the Jervis Bay project under the Whitlam government led the AAEC to focus on uranium mining for export instead.[76]

These domestic political and bureaucratic changes were accompanied by a transition to a more benign regional security environment. By the end of the 1960s and beginning of the 1970s, China was no longer considered a direct threat to Australia, as it was not seen as having the military capabilities to expand to such a degree. Also, China was opening up to the world economically, and by this time, especially after the Soviet–Chinese *mésentente*, Communism was no longer perceived as a massive and coherent force bent on world domination. In the words of the prominent Australian academic, the late Coral Bell, "Australian opinion, like the American, followed the US opening to China with astonishment, relief, pleasure, and fascination. The sense of a new epoch was very strong."[77] Therefore, already in 1968, more "moderate" voices within the Defence Department argued that "no threat of conventional attack on Australia or its Territories is foreseen that might require the use of nuclear weapons for defense."[78]

Nonetheless, even under these more benign circumstances, defense officials stressed that Australia should "maintain its freedom to reduce the lead time for the development of such a capacity from the present period of from seven to ten years" and noted that such hedging appeared likely to be "possible under the Non-Proliferation Treaty, but satisfaction of this score should be a factor in any consideration of Australia's becoming a party to that Treaty."[79] Other policy-makers, however, were still reluctant to commit to the treaty. Concerned with the US nuclear umbrella, they argued that "we may find it imperative at some future time to have our own nuclear deterrent against for instance a possible Chinese attack and or nuclear blackmail."[80] Even after Australia ratified the NPT, the 1975 main guidance document of the defense establishment noted that "opportunities for decision open to the Australian government in future would be enlarged if the lead time for the acquisition of a nuclear weapons capability could be shortened." Thus, the document recommended the government to invest in the further development of civilian nuclear technology.[81]

130   *C.M. Leah*

Conclusion

Subsequent to Australia's NPT ratification, the question of a nuclear weapons capability essentially disappeared, both in public debate and within the government. According to Professor Paul Dibb, a long-serving senior official within the Department of Defence, and Dr. Richard Brabin-Smith, former Chief Defence Scientist, there was generally little government interest or expertise in nuclear matters throughout the 1970s and 1980s.[82] Australia promoted measures aimed at supporting nuclear arms control and disarmament, but also enhancing the strength of extended deterrence in both Europe and the Asia-Pacific.[83]

Nevertheless, experts within both academia and the bureaucracy repeatedly advised successive governments of the need to maintain "acceptable lead times" regarding nuclear technology. In 1975, for instance, an influential think-tank published a report on the economic, technical, political, and strategic conditions required for Australia to wield a credible nuclear deterrent. The report concluded that for so long as favorable geopolitical circumstances endured, Australian interests could be better served by a modest build-up of its conventional forces.[84] According to journalist Brian Toohey, even the Hawke government (1983–1991) accepted a defence planning assessment that argued Australia should be in a position to develop nuclear weapons as quickly as any neighbour that seems to be pursuing such a goal.[85]

Nuclear weapons have been central to Australia's sense of security since the dawning of the atomic age in 1945. Sometimes this phenomenon has been implicit, at other times it has been explicit. But the fact remains that Australia has always had a complex and conflicted relationship with the bomb. Indeed, once the NPT was proposed, it was far from clear that Canberra would sign and then ratify it. There was no clear path to that final decision in 1973; policy-makers across the spectrum had to juggle and push for competing interests, including existential threats from Asia, the credibility of extended deterrence, the alliance with the US, the desire to look like a "good" international citizen, and the technological and scientific capabilities to hedge against future possible threats. Debates over these issues coincided with significant shifts in both the domestic political scene and the regional security landscape. These two phenomena led to a (if reluctant and tenuous) conclusion that no power would threaten Australia without incurring retaliation by its powerful friends.

Additional research into the period of the late 1970s to the early 1990s in the Australian National Archives might yield interesting insights into how policy-makers thought about Western European strategic dynamics, including negotiations over the NATO Nuclear Planning Group, the Mutual and Balanced Force Reductions talks, the Intermediate Nuclear Forces Treaty, and the Conventional Forces in Europe Treaty. Nevertheless, what will be interesting to see is how the relationship between these issues evolves now that Australia is facing a much more unstable strategic environment. The US, China, India, Pakistan, and now even South Korea and Japan, are jockeying for power and increasing capabilities for their national defense, and, to some extent, to "contain" Chinese activities

Australia 131

and provocations in the South China sea. These are very different conditions to the early 1970s – the foundational context for Australia's NPT ratification. Asia is no longer a peaceful region, and American military dominance is coming under increasing pressure. Australia is trying to accommodate these changes by contributing more to US defense efforts, including ballistic missile defense programs, and looking to procure a more credible submarine fleet.

Currently, signs of Australia's attempts to accommodate these strategic alterations are noticeable. The Australian Labor Party's decision to allow uranium sales to India is a glaring illustration of the relevance of the NPT coming into question in this part of the world. "International practice has changed," Martin Ferguson, the Mining Minister, told an interviewer. He said it was hypocritical for Australia to sell uranium to China and Russia but not to the largest democracy in the world. He said that "India is an emerging economy; it's one of the ten largest economies in the world with huge purchasing power [...] India is not a rogue state."[86] Still, currently this issue is being debated in parliament between those who would see India being given preference as a non-NPT member, and those who would not.[87] But these are long-term (though fundamental) evolutions, rather than revolutions, in Australia's strategic environment. On the one hand, an Australian Prime Minister is unlikely to question the country's adherence to the NPT anytime soon. On the other hand, it is also clear that Asia is becoming increasingly unstable, with an increasing potential for conflict, especially between the US and China.

In a future military conflict with China, Australia would be highly vulnerable to long-range missile attack, including those carrying nuclear payloads. Despite Australia being a continental power, almost all its population is concentrated in a half-dozen major cities; easy targets for small numbers of warheads. In a high-intensity conflict between the United States and China, it is not inconceivable that Beijing may seek to coerce Canberra with long-range nuclear missiles as a step up the escalation ladder, demonstrating to Washington its capacity to conduct nuclear strikes over intercontinental ranges. In such an eventuality, extended nuclear deterrence may hardly seem credible. Retaliating on Australia's behalf would demonstrably mean accepting large-scale nuclear attack by China on the continental United States. In that situation, the most effective means for Australia to insulate itself from long-range nuclear attack is to develop its own reliable long-range nuclear deterrent. And whilst this is not necessarily the most desirable prospect, it is still one the Asian region should nonetheless be prepared for.

Notes

1 The author is grateful to Jim Walsh for providing a number of archival documents on Australia's nuclear history.
2 See "Australia" in *Preventing Nuclear Dangers in Southeast Asia and Australasia* (London: IISS, 2009); Andrew O'Neill, *Asia, the US and Extended Nuclear Deterrence: Atomic Umbrellas in the Twenty-First Century* (New York: Routledge, 2014); Steven Pifer, Richard C. Bush, Vanda Felbab-Brown, Martin S. Indyk, Michael

132   *C.M. Leah*

O'Hanlon, and Kenneth M. Pollack, *U.S. Extended Nuclear Deterrence: Considerations and* Challenges (Washington, D.C.: Brookings Institution, 2010).

3 See Kurt M. Campbell, Robert J. Einhorn, and Mitchell B. Reiss, (eds.), *The Nuclear Tipping Point: Why States Reconsider their Nuclear Choices* (Washington D.C.: Brookings Institution Press, 2004).

4 Jim Walsh, "Surprise Down Under: The Secret History of Australia's Nuclear Ambitions," *The Nonproliferation Review* 5, no. 1 (1997): 1–20; Jacques E.C. Hymans, *The Psychology of Nuclear Proliferation: Identity, Emotions, and Foreign Policy* (Cambridge, MA: Cambridge University Press, 2006); for a comprehensive review of the history of efforts, assessments, bureaucratic processes and debates on the nuclear option in Australia, see Walsh, "Surprise Down Under"; Richard Broinowski, *Fact or Fission? The Truth about Australia's Nuclear Ambitions* (Melbourne: Scribe Publications, 2003); Wayne Reynolds, *Australia's Bid for the Atomic Bomb* (Melbourne: Melbourne University Press, 2000); Wayne Reynolds, "Rethinking the Joint Project: Australia's Bid for Nuclear Weapons, 1945–1960," *The Historical Journal* 41, no. 3 (1998): 853–873; Michael Carr, *Australia and the Nuclear Question: A Survey of Government Attitudes, 1945–1975* (Unpublished MA Thesis, University of New South Wales, 1979).

5 Under the current Archives Act 1983, researchers are permitted to access Commonwealth government records that are in the open access period. Following amendments to the Act approved by Parliament in May 2010, the open access period for Commonwealth records as defined by the Act will begin after twenty years instead of the previous thirty years. The open access period for Cabinet notebooks will begin after thirty years, instead of fifty years.

6 John Hirst, *Freedom on the Fatal Shore: Australia's First Colony* (Melbourne: Black Inc, 2008).

7 Up until 1901 there were six separate self-governing British colonies in Australia. These were Queensland, New South Wales, Victoria, Tasmania, South Australia, and Western Australia. In 1901 the colonies collectively became the Commonwealth of Australia. Fred Alexander, *Australia since Federation: A Narrative and Critical Analysis* (Melbourne: Nelson's Australian Paperbacks, 1969).

8 Alan Watt, *The Evolution of Australian Foreign Policy, 1938–1965* (Cambridge, MA: Cambridge University Press, 1967).

9 See Geoffrey Blainey, *The Tyranny of Distance: How Distance Shaped Australia's History* (Melbourne: Sun Books, 1982); or Garfield Barwick, "Australia's Foreign Relations," in *Australia's Defence and Foreign Policy*, ed. John Wilkes (Sydney: Australian Institute of Political Science, Angus & Robertson, 1964), 3–44.

10 Howard Beale, *This Inch of Time: Memoirs of Politics and Diplomacy* (Melbourne: Melbourne University Press, 1977), 156ff.

11 For a more detailed discussion of Australia–Indonesia relations during the late 1950s and early 1960s, see James Angel, "Australia and Indonesia: 1961–1970," in *Australia in World Affairs: 1966–1970*, eds. Gordon Greenwood and Norman Harper (Vancouver: University of British Columbia Press, 2002), 352–376.

12 Coral Bell, *Dependent Ally: A Study in Australian Foreign Policy* (Oxford: Oxford University Press, 1988), 49.

13 Beale, *Inch of Time,* 167.

14 Arthur L. Burns, in *Australia's Defence and Foreign Policy* (Sydney: Australian Institute of Political Science, Proceedings of 30th Summer School. Angus and Robertson), 60.

15 Prime Minister Ben Chifley believed that Australia should seek to cooperate with the United Kingdom in nuclear matters for "defence and commercial purposes." The Minister for External Affairs Dr Herbert V. Evatt directly cabled British Prime Minister Atlee requesting that Australia participate in Empire nuclear research and development. Cable from Chifley to Bruce, September 4, 1945. *National Archives of Australia*, Canberra, Australia (NAA): A461/2, C373/1/4.

Australia 133

16 Cited in Coral Bell, *Dependent Ally,* 83.
17 Beale, *Inch of Time*, 87.
18 Cf. Reynolds, *Australia's Bid for the Atomic Bomb.*
19 Lorna Arnold, *A Very Special Relationship: British Atomic Weapon Trials in Australia* (London: Her Majesty's Stationery Office, 1987).
20 On the end of the bilateral cooperation with Britain, see Reynolds, *Australia's Bid for the Atomic Bomb.*
21 Ibid.
22 Ibid.
23 Cited in ibid., 194.
24 Memorandum, May 12, 1960, "Disarmament – Australian Defence Principles. Report by the Defence Committee," NAA: A1838/269. 36/42.
25 Statement by Indonesian Brigadier-General Hartono, Director of the Army Equipment Department. Cited in an inward cablegram from the Australian Embassy in Jakarta, November 17, 1964, "United Nations – Nuclear Weapons – Policy and Capability of Certain Powers," NAA: A1838, CS 919/12/10, Part 1.
26 Inward Cablegram, Department of External Affairs, I43178, 1965. In "United Nations – Nuclear Weapons – Policy and Capability of Certain Powers – Indonesia," NAA, A1838, CS 919/12/10 Part 1.
27 US State Department, "Addendum INR Contribution National Intelligence Assessment 4–65. The Likelihood of Further Nuclear Proliferation," November 4, 1965, National Security Archive Electronic Briefing Book No. 155, National Intelligence Estimates of the Nuclear Proliferation Problem, The First Ten Years, 1957_1967, doc 11b, http://nsarchive.gwu.edu/NSAEBB/NSAEBB155 (accessed August 10, 2015).
28 Senator Frank McManus, "Should We have the Bomb?" *The Australian*, November 15, 1967.
29 Christine M. Leah, *Australia and the Bomb* (New York: Palgrave Macmillan, 2014).
30 Cited in Brian Martin, *Nuclear Knights* (Canberra: Rupert Public Interest Movement), 53.
31 For an overview of these domestic debates, see Christine Leah and Rod Lyon, "Three Visions of the Bomb: Australian Thinking about Nuclear Weapons and Strategy," *Australian Journal of International Affairs* 64, no. 4 (2010): 449–477; see also, *Archives of the Department of Foreign Affairs and Trade*, Canberra, Australia (ADFAT): Unregistered document; Report by the Joint Planning Committee at Meetings Concluding February 2, 1968, Department of Defence File No. 67/1017, Report No. 8/1968, An Independent Australian Nuclear Capability – Strategic Considerations, 1 (Top Secret AUSTEO). One reason cited was the increase in risk that something would go wrong. Letter from Howard Beale to John Foster Dulles, April 22, 1958, A1838/269. 10/30.
32 Letter from A.H. Tange to The Acting Secretary, Department of Defence. "Procurement of Nuclear Weapons for Australian Forces," January 22, 1958. NAA: A7942/1. 19/23.
33 Robert Menzies, Ministerial Statement on Defence, Commonwealth of Australia Parliamentary Debates (House of Representatives), September 19, 1957.
34 Draft report (undated), "Political Implications of French Nuclear Test." NAA: A1838/2. 16/24.
35 Leah, *Australia and the Bomb.*
36 Report, "History of Australian Policy towards the Acquisition of a Nuclear Weapons Capability, a U.S. View," in "Non Proliferation of Nuclear Weapons," NAA: A1838, CS TS919/10/5, Part 1.
37 Inward Cablegram from Australian Delegation to the United Nations, New York, November 30, 1967. Discussions with Fisher – Deputy Director, Arms Control Agency. In "Non proliferation of nuclear weapons," NAA: A1838, CS TS919/10/5 Part 1.

134 *C.M. Leah*

38 John Gorton, Commonwealth of Australia Parliamentary Debates (Senate), May 8, 1957.
39 Ibid.
40 Reginald Turnbull, Commonwealth of Australia Parliamentary Debates (Senate), August 25, 1964.
41 Ibid., 216.
42 George Branson, Commonwealth of Australia Parliamentary Debates (Senate), September 2, 1964.
43 Reginald Turnbull, Commonwealth of Australia Parliamentary Debates (Senate), May 6, 1965.
44 Frank McManus, Commonwealth of Australia Parliamentary Debates (Senate), May 16, 1962 or James Richardson, "A Limit on H-Bombs, or a Scramble?" *Sydney Morning Herald*, July 24, 1969.
45 E.M. Burns, "The Nonproliferation Treaty: Its Negotiation and Prospects," *International Organization* 23, no. 4 (1969), 788–807; Brad Roberts, "From Nonproliferation to Antiproliferation," *International Security* 18, no. 1 (1993): 139–173.
46 ADFAT: Unregistered document. Memo from James Plimsoll. "Draft Treaty on Non-Proliferation of Nuclear Weapons." March 12, 1968.
47 For a discussion of this, see Leah and Lyon, "Three Visions of the Bomb," 449–477.
48 Statement by the Australian Ambassador the UN, Patrick Shaw, to the First Committee of the General Assembly, May 17, 1968, reported in *Current Notes in International Affairs*, 206, 210.
49 ADFAT: Unregistered document. From Plimsoll, March 12, 1968.
50 Alex Bellany, *Australia in the Nuclear Age: National Defense and National Development* (Sydney University Press: Sydney, 1972), 109.
51 ADFAT: Unregistered document. Report of the Defence Committee provided by G.L. Prentice (Secretary), March 18, 1968.
52 Draft Cabinet Submission from Paul Hasluck, Minister of External Affairs, Draft Treaty on the Non-Proliferation of Nuclear Weapons, February 19, 1968, Attachment to memorandum from M.R. Booker, First Assistant Secretary, Div II, External Affairs, to Paul Hasluck, Minister of External Affairs, February 21, 1968, "Non-Proliferation of Nuclear Weapons, 919/10/5" NAA: A1838, CS TS919/10/5.
53 J.P. Baxter, "Ten Years of Nuclear Progress: A Survey," in *Atomic Power: A Review*. Papers presented at the symposium held at the UNSW, November 7, 1963 (Sydney: University of New South Wales, 1963)
54 Brian Martin, *Nuclear Knights*, 31.
55 ADFAT: Unregistered document. Report of the Defence Committee provided by G.L. Prentice (Secretary), March 18, 1968.
56 Ibid.
57 Ibid.
58 ADFAT: Unregistered document. Report of the Defence Committee provided by G.L. Prentice (Secretary), March 18, 1968.
59 ADFAT: Unregistered document. Report by the Joint Planning Committee at Meetings Concluding February 2, 1968, Department of Defence File No. 67/1017, Report No. 8/1968, An Independent Australian Nuclear Capability – Strategic Considerations, p. 1 (Top Secret AUSTEO).
60 Report for Cabinet by R.G. Menzies [then Minister for External Affairs], Undated (1961), "Nuclear Tests Conference: Control Posts in Australia," NAA: A5818/2. V6. 1/22.
61 "We'll Spend $500m on Nuclear Power 'by Year 2000'," *The Australian*, July 14, 1969.
62 MemCon, Consultations with Australians on NPT and Status of Interpretations on Articles I and II, United States Arms Control and Disarmament Agency, April 24, 1968; National Security Archive, "The Impulse towards a Safer World": 40th

Anniversary of the Nuclear Nonproliferation Treaty, doc. 16d., www.gwu.edu/~nsarchiv/nukevault/ebb253/index.htm (accessed August 10, 2015).
63 Personal communication with Wayne Reynolds, March 30, 2012.
64 Ibid. See also MemCon, Consultations with Australians on NPT and Status of Interpretations on Articles I and II, April 24, 1968.
65 ADFAT: Unregistered document; Memo from M.R. Booker, First Assistant Secretary, Division II, External Affairs, to the Minister for External Affairs, Draft Treaty on the Non-Proliferation of Nuclear Weapons, March 7, 1968, 2–3 (Secret); ADFAT: Unregistered document. Memo from James Plimsoll. "Draft Treaty on Non-Proliferation of Nuclear Weapons," March 12, 1968.
66 AAEC, Commentary on the NPT, February 23, 1968, "Non Proliferation of Nuclear Weapons," NAA: A1838, TS919/10/5, Part 2.
67 Comment by Bill Pritchett, April 22, 1968, "Non Proliferation of Nuclear Weapons," NAA: A1838, CSTS919/10/5, Part 8.
68 Memo from J.P. Quinn, December 20, 1957, to Mr. Plimsoll. NAA, A1838/269. 30.32.
69 MemCon, Consultations with Australians on NPT and Status of Interpretations on Articles I and II, April 24, 1968.
70 AAEC, Commentary on the NPT, February 23, 1968.
71 See Henry S. Albinski, *Australian External Policy under Labor: Content, Process and the National Debate* (Queensland: University of Queensland Press, 1977), 14–253.
72 See Dora Alves, *Anti-Nuclear Attitudes in New Zealand and Australia* (Washington D.C.: National Defense University Press, 1985), 47; and letter from E.G. Whitlam to W.E. Rowling, October 7, 1975, cited in *Documents on Australian Defence and Foreign Policy, 1968–1975*, eds. Richard J. Walsh and George Munster (Hong Kong: J.R. Walsh and G.J. Munster, 1980), 128.
73 On this, see Brian D. Beddie, "Some Internal Problems," in ibid., 126–139.
74 Sir Arthur Tange, *Defence Policy-Making: A Close-Up View, 1950–1980. A Personal Memoir* (Canberra: Australian National University EPress, 2008), 25.
75 For a more detailed discussion of this, see Reynolds, *Australia's Bid for the Atomic Bomb.*
76 For a review of the AAEC's activities in the late 1960s and beyond, see Alice Cawte, *Atomic Australia: 1944–1990* (Kensington, NSW: Kensington University Press, 1992); Richard Leaver, *Australian Uranium Policy and Non-Proliferation* (Canberra: Australian National University, 1988); Ann Moyal, "The Australian Atomic Energy Commission: A Case Study in Australian Science and Government," *Search* 6, no. 9 (1975): 365–381.
77 Coral Bell, *Dependent Ally*, 110.
78 1968 Strategic Basis, para 229. NAA. Strategic Basis papers were guidance documents prepared by the defense establishment and endorsed by a majority of defense or Defence chiefs of staff or defense committees. They would outline the environment, challenges and opportunities informing Australian defense policy and provide recommendations to the government of the day.
79 1968 Strategic Basis, para 229.
80 Report from the Department of External Affairs, March 26, 1971. "NPT – Developments since the Treaty's Entry into Force." In "Nuclear – Non Proliferation Treaty," NAA: A1838, CS 919/10/5.
81 1975 Strategic Basis, 70.
82 Discussion with Professor Paul Dibb and Dr. Richard Brabin-Smith, Canberra, March 12, 2012.
83 For a more detailed discussion of this, see Leah, *Australia and the Bomb.*
84 *An Australian Nuclear Weapons Capability* (United Services Institution of the Australian Capital Territory, Canberra, 1975).

136 *C.M. Leah*

85 Cited in Brian Martin, "Proliferation at Home," *Search* 15, no. 5–6 (1984).
86 Transcript of interview with Mining Minister Martin Ferguson, http://minister.ret.gov.au/MediaCentre/Transcripts/Pages/ABCNewsradioInterviewMariusBenson.aspx (accessed January 20, 2012). On legal issues of the Australia–India uranium sales agreement under the NPT, see Kalman Robertson, "The Legality of the Supply of Australian Uranium to India," *Security Challenges* 8, no. 1 (2012): 25–34.
87 See, for example, submission by Crispin Rovere, in Proof of Committee Hansard, Joint Standing Committee of Treaties, May 18, 2015, Melbourne. Commonwealth of Australia, http://parlinfo.aph.gov.au (accessed August 10, 2015).

8 Between idealism, activism, and the bomb

Why did India reject the NPT?

A. Vinod Kumar

Why would a country with a remarkable record of activism towards halting the spread of nuclear weapons decide to reject a treaty fashioned specifically for this objective? India's decision to stay out of the Treaty on the Non-Proliferation of Nuclear Weapons (NPT) remains a puzzle that has yet to be conclusively explained. An official narrative has emerged over the past decades on why India refused to accept the NPT.[1] In a nutshell, the Indian government termed the treaty as "discriminatory" for failing to enshrine a balance of obligations and responsibilities between the nuclear-weapon states (NWS) and the non-nuclear-weapon states (NNWS). Thus, India contended that the treaty was not a credible instrument towards the elimination of nuclear weapons, and was instead sustaining a world of nuclear "haves" and "have-nots."

While many of these arguments have been subsequently confirmed by developments within the NPT regime, it remains unclear whether such ideational factors were the primary reason for India's decision to remain outside the treaty. For that matter, there are not many competing views on what factors drove India's decision. Rather, the official government position is widely accepted as a consensual national perspective. Few academic studies have inquired whether the NPT decision was driven by considerations of national interest, by ideological perspectives, or by an assortment of both. A historical analysis of the decision-making process and geopolitical conditions during the years when the NPT was being negotiated may throw up many indicators on why the declared rationale may not have been the paramount reason for India's NPT decision. For, many behavioral patterns pertaining to India's strategic thinking and its responses to the security environment of that period remain as key explanatory gaps in the understanding of the decision-making process.

Some studies point to how most of NNWS preferred to accede to the NPT not on the basis of the "vague" promises of disarmament, but on their value judgments of individual gains, including the prospect of mitigating the presence of nuclear weapons in their neighborhoods and accessing resources for peaceful uses of nuclear energy.[2] India, while placing the centrality of disarmament as its ideational objective, was also deeply concerned about the security implications of nuclear weapons introduced in its neighborhood. Contrary to the sentiments of many NNWS that were comfortable with the status quo of existing arsenals in

138 *A. Vinod Kumar*

the hands of a few even while supporting the disarmament cause, India could not seemingly accept the reality of its rival (China) possessing nuclear weapons and a nonproliferation treaty limiting its own options to deal with this challenge. India's eventual NPT decision seems to be an outcome of this peculiar dichotomy – of wanting a disarmament end-goal, but not at the expense of its security interests – a conundrum that probably defined Delhi's complex positioning on issues like pathways to disarmament, the feasibility and prudence of security guarantees, as well as securing the right to undertake peaceful nuclear explosions (PNEs), among others. An underlying conflict was seemingly at work with the leadership caught between its ideological commitments and the pressure of policy realism to keep options open within a looming threat environment.

Therefore, the quest to understand India's NPT decision has to take into account some questions and inferences on India's approach to various structural issues that were integral to the NPT construction process. First is the perceptible inconsistency on the issue of disarmament. Why did India challenge the validity of Article VI as a durable disarmament roadmap, despite its earlier position that disarmament could realistically be pursued only in a phased manner? Was it the absence of preambular provisions for measures like, for instance, stockpile elimination, ending fissile materials production, or a comprehensive test ban that caused India's minimal faith in the NPT as a route to nuclear disarmament? Second is the issue of security guarantees and the complexities of India's activism. Why did India reject Resolution 255 of the UN Security Council (UNSC) despite seeking assurances from the nuclear powers? Why did India engage Moscow and Washington if it perceived a conflict with its non-alignment ideals? Was seeking a China-centric guarantee from the nuclear powers India's real objective?

Third is the extent of the impact of the Chinese challenge, imprinted on the Indian psyche through the 1962 border war and amplified by the 1964 nuclear test. The circumstantial role of this threat matrix on India's NPT decision has largely been confined to conjectures without substantive empirical evidence on whether India perceived the NPT as a hindrance in preparing a nuclear quid pro quo to the Chinese nuclear challenge. Did India see it as untenable to sign the Treaty when China was not party to the NPT negotiations and yet qualified as a NWS? Relevant to this context is the Indian domestic debate on pursuing a nuclear weapons program or keeping this option open. A number of questions arise on this correlation: Why India did not prefer to test before 1967? Did the leadership misjudge the implications of the NPT on its strategic calculus, or did elites keep false hopes of a balanced treaty? And did a late realization drive the eventual NPT decision?

Fourth is the enigma surrounding India's nuclear test of May 1974, and its linkage to the NPT decision. During the negotiations within the Eighteen-Nation Committee on Disarmament (ENDC), India had vouched for securing the right to PNE as inherent to peaceful uses of nuclear energy, despite very few articulations on how this technology will be used. The timing of the 1974 test, four years after the NPT entered into force, and the branding of it as a peaceful explosion, raised speculations as to whether it was a technological demonstration of India's weapons capability with the intention to keep all options open. Considering the fact that India had abstained and not voted against the NPT resolution at the United Nations General Assembly (UNGA), it could also be speculated whether India had considered accession to the NPT after undertaking the PNE.[3]

These issues point to the broad picture of ideational and political difficulties that marked India's nuclear policy-making during this period. Adding to it was a complex mixture of bureaucratic incertitude, regional security impulses, domestic politics, scientific activism, and absence of collective and informed strategic wisdom, which could have caused an incoherent understanding on what the NPT augured for India's strategic future, and the role nuclear weapons could have played in it. However, the decision to undertake a nuclear explosion some years later could be hinting at a larger game plan with an intrinsic link to the NPT decision – the initiation of India's nuclearization phase, by building a sustainable nuclear infrastructure that could anchor a self-reliant nuclear energy program and provide the flexibility of exercising a nuclear weapons option, if and when necessary.

A major part of the available literature examined the core issues in their complexities and entirety, though not precisely pointing to a tipping point on what led to the NPT decision. T.T. Poulose put together a compilation of analyses in 1978, at a time when the aftermath of the PNE and resistance to the NPT began to play out on India's external relations.[4] This compilation analyzes the debates on issues like safeguards, PNE, and security guarantees, but also justifies the Indian arguments on discrimination, inequity, and disarmament. Writing in the same volume, G.G. Mirchandani offers an insightful glimpse in the domestic debate on nuclear weapons and the political confusion on the options to deal with the Chinese threat while sustaining the Nehruvian way.[5] J.P. Jain produced two volumes capturing the disarmament and nonproliferation debates, along with a superlative collection of relevant documents.[6] Another important analysis was done by Ashok Kapur in 1976, which provided an extensive survey of India's diplomatic endeavors, an overview of various schools of thought within the establishment, and an analysis on how the core issues were dealt with at the negotiating table.[7] Departing from the tenor of the publications of the early years is a variegated collection by K. Subrahmanyam, published from the late 1960s onwards. Subrahmanyam largely focused on the feasibility of the nuclear weapons option, the arguments in favor or against it, and his own analysis of the strategic environment, which gives indications of a potential strategic scheme.[8] However, the most comprehensive book detailing the evolution of India's nuclear program has been by George Perkovich, which attempts to explain through a large collection of oral narratives the major milestones and policy shifts in India's nuclear history. Published soon after the 1998 tests, Perkovich's book charts the course towards weaponization, but spares little on key decisions like the NPT.[9]

Most of this literature provides the analytical framework within India's nuclear discourse, but does not explain the actual considerations weighed by the

140 *A. Vinod Kumar*

leadership in its decision-making. Adding to this lacuna is the problem of minimal access to official records in India, especially pertaining to nuclear policy. Most of the accessible records are confined to parliamentary debates and diplomatic documents, which propel the official position without shedding light on the strategic program or its impelling connection with the NPT question. A holistic explanation of the NPT decision, hence, may still remain beyond convincing reach. Nonetheless, the rest of the chapter will continue this quest through two inquisitions: (1) understanding India's approach to the treaty construction process; and (2) examining the underlying factors that determined India's approach to the NPT.

India and the quest for a disarmament instrument

India's nuclear diplomacy running up to the NPT decision and the PNE can be divided into two decade-long phases: First, the 1954–1964 timeframe, when the idealism of India's first prime minister, Jawarharlal Nehru, shaped the country's grand strategy. Second, the 1964–1974 interval, when the country's leadership had to decide between the Nehruvian ideals and pursuing realistic options towards strategic policy-making. The defining turning points were Nehru's death in May 1964 and China's nuclear test on October 16, 1964. China's nuclearization exacerbated the debate over the path India should pursue to secure its national interest. As a counterfactual, it could be argued that, had he been alive, Nehru might have signed the NPT considering the fact that he had supported the Limited Test Ban Treaty (LTBT) despite it being a partial measure. However, it could also be premised that Nehru could have opposed the NPT, had he been alive to witness the Chinese test and had sensed the treaty's discriminatory character.[10] This incertitude of choices reflected the predicament of India's leadership in managing national interests without compromising on Nehruvian ideals.

The first phase, which could be described as an era of idealism, began with Nehru's 1954 proposal for a standstill agreement to halt nuclear testing.[11] Although there are indicators suggesting Nehru was also receptive towards keeping the nuclear weapons option open, the public statements he made throughout his life were profound expressions of his disarmament vision, echoing the intensifying superpower arms race and their propensity to monopolize the affairs of the atom.[12] Nevertheless, Nehru's disarmament dogma seemed to be a mix of idealism, pragmatism, and a bit of surrealism. While Nehru sounded pragmatic in his affirmations that disarmament could only be achieved in a phased manner, he suggested ambitious timelines like four to five years for nuclear abolition to be accomplished.[13] Also, Nehru's vision for general and complete disarmament by prohibiting all conventional as well as biological and chemical weapons, and his exaggerated claims on the impact of nuclear testing, seemingly carried a tenor of idealistic pretentiousness.[14] Considering the wide extents of his idealistic formulations, an inherent feature of his internationalism, it may be relevant to understand whether the leadership of the day could have mulled the merits of accepting a treaty that did not come close to the disarmament vision that Nehru articulated.

India 141

Nonetheless, the prospect of a grand disarmament agreement was a key ideational objective that shaped India's initial positions when various proposals – Ireland's draft resolution for measures the treaty's "non-acquisition" and "non-dissemination" and the US and Soviet drafts for a disarmament treaty – were debated at the UNGA and ENDC.[15] While supporting these proposals, India felt that all such measures should form the building blocks of a disarmament treaty.[16] India's policy-makers envisaged a comprehensive instrument that included obligations for the nuclear powers to curb stockpiles, end weapons production, and facilitate eventual nuclear elimination – a position India maintained throughout the NPT negotiations. The US–Soviet Joint Statement on Agreed Principles for Disarmament Negotiations of September 1961, while sustaining this pursuit, made little headway, as the superpowers could not agree on a common draft for a disarmament treaty.[17] Regarding nuclear testing, India warned that "if they go on testing, others will soon follow suit."[18] India's skepticism was driven by the fact the superpowers did not provide for a disarmament timeline or "progressive squeezing to zero," besides suggesting different reduction targets.[19] India, instead, called for "full-blooded (and verifiable) measures" from the beginning.[20] However, with the US–Soviet talks failing, the first decade of India's nuclear diplomacy largely ended with the consolation of the LTBT entering into force in 1963.

The second phase began on the eve of the first Chinese test, with Indian Prime Minister Lal Bahadur Shastri exhorting the Cairo conference of Non-Aligned States to build pressure on China to desist from testing.[21] In Geneva, India's representative V.C. Trivedi cautioned the ENDC about the Chinese plan for an "Asian bomb," and called upon the Committee to "prevent this proliferation" by proceeding to a disarmament treaty with measures to "prohibit the manufacture, acquisition, receipt or transference of these weapons."[22] This was probably the first time when "proliferation" crept into the Indian lexicon, with Trivedi warning of the possible widening of the nuclear club.[23] That India still hoped for a disarmament treaty to emerge from the ENDC negotiations was illustrated by its partial support for the Soviet's Gromyko plan, which entailed maintaining limited stockpiles for a "minimum deterrent" or a "nuclear umbrella."[24] India supported this plan for its "positive step of substantial cuts from the first stage," but not without warning that "minimum deterrent" implies that these limited arsenals could actually be used in certain circumstances.[25]

The diplomatic overdrive, which intensified after the Chinese test, coincided with the emergence of the pro-bomb lobby within the country – initially propelled by the right-wing parties and later joined by voices from other parties, media, and the nascent strategic community.[26] At the pro-bomb forefront was the Bharatiya Jana Sangh, a party which had demanded the production of nuclear weapons soon after the 1962 war with China.[27] Besides building pressure for a nuclear deterrent, the lobby also sought withdrawal from the LTBT in light of China's non-adherence.[28] Adding to the clamor was the statement by Homi Bhabha, the head of India's Atomic Energy Commission (AEC), that a nuclear weapon device could be readied in 18 months.[29] The government's measured

142   *A. Vinod Kumar*

response to these nuclearization demands was that although India had the technological capability to develop such weapons, it would use nuclear energy only for peaceful purposes; this policy, however, was not to be seen as static and would be reviewed based on the security environment, the government stated.[30] This approach illustrates the dilemmas confronting the Indian leadership since 1964 – its hope for a disarmament instrument that could address its security concerns without having to compromise on its moralistic standing or change the peaceful nature of its nuclear program.

A foremost implication of China's test was the shifting of the discourse from the disarmament imperative to the urgency of establishing an instrument to prevent wider dissemination of nuclear technology. India returned to the ENDC in mid-1965 with a new set of priorities including the call for nuclear powers to reduce and eliminate their arsenals, the need to address the "security" concerns of non-weapon-states, and the demand for an equitable framework of safeguards that would not inhibit the right of nuclear "have-nots" to access and develop peaceful nuclear energy resources. Ashok Kapur describes a trend in this new diplomacy as embodying the emergence of new schools of thought within the government.[31] The first school, represented by R.K. Nehru, reiterated traditional "world-order concerns" and the necessity of achieving general and complete disarmament. The second school, led by Trivedi, spearheaded a revisionist shift towards a deterrent role for India, matching the domestic mood for a nuclear response to the Chinese challenge. Eventually, Kapur argues, it was a third school – as a synthesis of the first two – which represented India's positions in the transitional phase between the Chinese test and emergence of the NPT draft text.

The new negotiating position, articulated by B.N. Chakravarty at the UNDC and Trivedi at the ENDC, expounded the Indian conception of a potential non-proliferation treaty. It included: (1) an undertaking by nuclear powers not to transfer nuclear weapons or technology (non-dissemination); (2) an undertaking not to use nuclear weapons against countries which do not possess them (non-use); (3) an undertaking through the UN to safeguard the security of countries threatened by a nuclear-armed state (security guarantee); (4) tangible progress towards disarmament including a comprehensive test ban, complete freeze on production of nuclear weapons and delivery means, and substantial reduction in stockpiles; and (5) an undertaking by non-nuclear powers not to acquire or manufacture nuclear weapons (non-acquisition).

The US and Soviet delegations submitted individual drafts for a non-proliferation treaty after formal negotiations began in June 1965.[32] The Indian response to the drafts was that any commitment by the non-weapon-states to forego nuclear arms had to be simultaneous with the renunciation by nuclear powers of further production and reduction of stockpiles. Trivedi spearheaded the debate by defining the concept of proliferation in order to point out that the main issue is about "the proliferation that has already taken place."[33] Placing the onus on the nuclear powers, he argued that "a non-proliferation agreement is an agreement to be entered into by nuclear powers not to proliferate," and that "a prohibition applies first to those who are in a position to proliferate, and only secondarily to those who may subsequently be doing it." Besides seeking to introduce the dimension of "vertical proliferation" into the debate, Trivedi's statement that "no international treaty will be acceptable which dictates only to non-nuclear countries while those possessing nuclear weapons do not assume prior commitments" indicated the hardening of India's position.[34]

Two developments that influenced the NPT negotiations at this stage were Resolution 2028 and the Fanfani proposal for a partial non-proliferation treaty. On September 15, 1965, India joined seven other non-aligned nations to submit the Eight-Nation Joint Memorandum, which listed five principles for a potential non-proliferation treaty.[35] Through Resolution 2028 (XX) of November 19, 1965, the UNGA accepted these principles as basis for the treaty's negotiations. It is worthwhile to note that India constantly pointed to the inconsistency of subsequent NPT drafts with Resolution 2028 as a reason for its opposition, though many countries that had voted for the resolution later overlooked this aspect and supported the treaty. With the US and Soviet drafts focusing only on "non-dissemination" and de-emphasizing disarmament measures, Italian foreign minister Amintore Fanfani proposed a phased program for nonproliferation. India added to the Italian proposal by suggesting that the first stage should be a "partial non-proliferation treaty," wherein nuclear powers would cease all production and begin reductions, while a comprehensive treaty with undertaking by NNWS not to acquire or manufacture them was to be the second stage – in Trivedi's words: a situation where "haves" reduce their arsenals and become "have-nots."

While these proposals failed to muster support, the subsequent debates until March 11, 1968 – when the US–Soviet joint draft was introduced at the ENDC – were dominated by the arguments of the NNWS that the available text promoted a fragile nonproliferation instrument that allowed the existing nuclear powers to further proliferate. The "have-nots" argued that the draft did not entail a disarmament mechanism, nor account for existent menacing stockpiles, while at the same time heaping prohibitions upon non-nuclear states. The superpowers responded that the aim of the treaty should be to check the further spread of nuclear weapons, and hence tying up nonproliferation to other measures could cause an impasse that could affect all objectives.

Thus, the threat of a deadlock was effectively exploited by the superpowers to drive a wedge among the NNWS, before alluring them with the promise of uninhibited access to nuclear energy resources.[36] Ultimately, this strategy proved effective, given that the eventual division among NNWS appears to have been driven by countries like Brazil and India, on the one hand, who demanded credible measures towards disarmament and, on the other hand, states like Mexico and Sweden, who accepted the good faith promises of the nuclear powers. As the NPT was opened for signature, the dominant sentiment that determined the support of over ninety-five countries was that having a treaty was better than having none, while many felt that no agreement on disarmament was possible without an agreement to prevent the further spread of nuclear weapons.[37]

144   A. Vinod Kumar

India's approach to the draft treaty: between interests and idealism

To US government officials, the Indian decision to abstain rather than vote against the NPT at the UNGA was puzzling and suggested that India may either accede at a later point or might be expecting some further amendments.[38] Minister of State for External Affairs, B.R. Bhagat, explained the government's decision in the Indian parliament: "Our abstaining in UN parlance does not mean watering down our stand. It only means that we do not subscribe to the principles underlying the treaty."[39] Though India sought to stand on a moral high ground by terming the treaty as discriminatory, its positioning on many of the structural issues embodied an evident struggle between its ideational calling and securing its own national interests, as displayed in the many political and diplomatic endeavors it pursued at and outside the negotiating table.[40] In the final debates on the treaty text, India projected its opposition on three core issues: (1) absence of proper disarmament pathways; (2) security guarantees for non-weapon states; and (3) the constraints being placed on the right to access and develop peaceful resources of nuclear energy, including PNEs. Though it could be assumed that all these factors had a bearing on India's NPT decision, the domestic debate and decision-making process was a scene of many confusing signals and inconsistent policy postures.

Orthodoxy on disarmament – was it genuine?

Government officials repeatedly stated that India would only accept a treaty that included a credible disarmament obligation.[41] Days after the US–Soviet joint draft was presented, Indira Gandhi exclaimed: "The present draft treaty does not promote disarmament. Measures which do not involve an element of self-restraint on the part of all states cannot form the basis for a meaningful agreement to promote disarmament."[42] There might be a handful of reasons for India's lack of confidence on the NPT evolving into a vehicle for disarmament. First, China was neither a party to the NPT negotiations, nor committed to accede to the treaty. Any disarmament process, hence, would not cover the fledging Chinese arsenal as long as Beijing stayed out of the treaty.

Second, the ability of the NPT to facilitate disarmament was in question as there were no preambular provisions for the liquidation of stockpiles, for a reduction process, or for incremental steps like a test ban or a production freeze for fissile materials. India rejected the references to the "cessation of nuclear arms race" and "effective measures for disarmament" as mere pious declarations. Third, the validity of Article VI was doubted by India which felt that the undertaking to pursue disarmament in good faith lacked any legal obligations and had no verification mechanism. An interesting aspect is the revelation that the reference to "negotiations in good faith" was specifically added to "entice" India.[43] Nevertheless, India might have been justified in stating its non-confidence on such proposals, which it could have seen as perfunctory.

Therefore, a combination of ideational and strategic factors seems to have prompted India to employ the disarmament argument as a key reason to oppose the Treaty. Challenging the weak disarmament fundamentals in the treaty text added legitimacy to the Indian position and marked a logical conclusion to its decade-long activism seeking a comprehensive disarmament instrument. By contributing to the disarmament movement at various forums in the subsequent years – including at the Special Sessions of Disarmament (SSODs), India also attempted to maintain a moral high-ground.[44] In 1987, India advanced a landmark proposal – the Rajiv Gandhi Action Plan (RGAP) – which conceived of total elimination by 2010.[45] Such initiatives, even many years after the NPT rejection, signified a pattern in India's policy postures: seeking to uphold its commitment to a nuclear weapons free world; projecting an alternate route to disarmament and total elimination; and underlining its orthodoxy on disarmament as key logic of rejecting the NPT.

Security guarantees – what was the real objective?

Following the passage of the NPT in the UNGA, the nuclear powers submitted a resolution – UNSCR 255 – at the Security Council on June 19, 1968. This resolution enshrined a commitment by nuclear powers to provide immediate assistance to any NNWS within the treaty which was a victim of an act or object of a threat of aggression involving nuclear weapons.[46] India rejected this commitment with a pontifical assertion that "real security comes through disarmament."[47] This position was the outcome of India's complicated approach towards the issue of security guarantees: On the one hand, India wanted the nuclear powers to institutionalize guarantees through the NPT. On the other hand, India opened negotiations with the superpowers in an attempt to seek assurances on the Chinese threat.

The oscillation in Indian positions was evident in many statements throughout the NPT negotiations. B.K. Nehru told the ENDC in March 1964: "It is all well to ask a person not to defend himself, but that somebody has to take on that defense and that can only be the international community." External Affairs Minister, Swaran Singh, elaborated further in May 1966: "To bring about an atmosphere of non-proliferation, the non-nuclear powers should be assured that they will not suffer by foregoing nuclear weapons." It was clear that the Chinese nuclear challenge was the main driver for India's campaign to seek security guarantees. While US President Lyndon Johnson offered to respond to requests from Asian nations in the event of a nuclear threat from Communist China, Prime Minister Shastri responded by saying that "China alone could not do much damage to India, for any kind of atomic war might become global," thus hinting that nuclear powers will have to intervene in such an eventuality.[48] Shastri discussed the issue with British premier Harold Wilson and stated at his London press conference that "it was for the nuclear powers to discuss some kind of guarantee," while also clarifying that India was not seeking any "special guarantee" for itself, but assurances to cover all non-weapon-states.[49]

146   *A. Vinod Kumar*

However, the process of devising a suitable security guarantees instrument had befuddled India as well as the superpowers. US Ambassador to India Chester Bowles exhorted Washington to "being alert to any opportunities that might come our way to assure India that if she were blackmailed or attacked by China with or without nuclear weapons, we would not stand on sidelines."[50] India had, though, taken the position at ENDC that a multilateral security guarantee should come under the auspices of the UN along with an undertaking of non-use against non-weapon states. Trivedi defined it as including a *passive* assurance (against use or threat of use) and an *active* assurance (protection through alliances).[51] The breakthrough came when Soviet representative Kosygin suggested that the NPT could include an undertaking on non-use of nuclear weapons against non-nuclear-weapon states. The Soviets reportedly conveyed to Indian envoy L.K. Jha that India would be protected against a nuclear attack if it renounced the right to produce nuclear weapons and signed the NPT.[52] A draft of the Soviet declaration was carried by Jha to Washington for discussion with President Johnson, who was advised by his aides to "strengthen his [Jha's] hand in New Delhi against the hawks who want to go nuclear."[53] The Johnson administration, constrained by a constitutional problem of giving a guarantee to India only as a formal treaty with Senate's approval, preferred the Soviet proposal of "acting through the UNSC if a non-nuclear NPT state is subject to a nuclear threat or attack."[54]

The eventual Indian approach to these proposals and UNSCR 255 was, though, confounding. Confusion prevailed within the government on whether to accept "big power guarantees," with Swaran Singh declaring such assurances as a "moral obligation of the world."[55] Shastri told the Parliament in May 1965 that he did not find any "encouraging response" to his call for "eradicating the menace of nuclear weapons," thus conflating "security" with "disarmament." A moral justification that was propped up to overlook the Soviet and US proposals was that these alternatives could undermine India's non-alignment policy.[56] Foreign minister M.C. Chagla told the Rajya Sabha that "such assurances could be multilateral or unilateral, but could be accepted only if they do not impinge on our non-alignment policy."[57] The nuclear powers did not hide their rancor, with a US diplomat, William Foster, publicly remarking: "Indians had great pride in their non-alignment. It is very difficult to work out a way in which both positions can be met simultaneously."[58]

A presumable logic of India's paradoxical approaches could be that it did not want to be bound by any commitment that could constrain its nuclear weapon option. The actual concern voiced by Indian policy-makers has been whether such guarantees would "deter" China and whether there would be immediate reprisal from the nuclear powers in the event of a nuclear attack.[59] The tenuous nature and unreliability of superpower assurances has been under-lined by various sections in the government, with Indira Gandhi herself doubting whether strategic interests would allow the nuclear powers to fulfill these guar-antees.[60] Rejecting UNSCR 255 after endorsing Moscow's UNSC proposal, and demanding guarantees within the NPT's text after initially seeking protection, underlined the notion that India was tentative on the issue of security guarantees and did not see political feasibility in seeking assurances from the nuclear powers. This ambiguity, though, enabled India to use the issue as another red herring to oppose the treaty. Conversely, rejecting the UNSC guarantee also implied the intention to keep other national security options open for the long haul.

The PNE conundrum

The struggle during the NPT negotiations was most vigorous on the question of the so-called "peaceful nuclear explosions" (PNEs), and the right to access or develop this technology. India consistently insisted that PNEs would be an inherent part of the peaceful applications of nuclear energy and any attempt to deny it amounted to impinging on sovereignty. Trivedi said: "there is full justification for preventing proliferation in weapons, but it had never before been suggested that there should be non-proliferation in science and technology."[61] He contended that countries should be allowed to conduct controlled fusion experiments for peaceful purposes, while fission applications for weapons should be prohibited.[62] In contrast, the US delegation argued that PNE was a "highly-sophisticated weapon" as the "science and technology behind a nuclear explosive device were inseparable from those behind nuclear bombs."[63] Any non-weapon-state that conducted a nuclear explosion, the US argued, would be regarded as having acquired the basic technology for producing nuclear weapons. Washington, in turn, proposed that nuclear powers could share the PNE technology for peaceful purposes with NNWS at "affordable costs." India rejected this proposal terming it an "atomic commercial super-monopoly."[64] India's diplomats argued that "the civil nuclear powers cannot tolerate an atomic apartheid in their economic and peaceful development."[65]

These contentions apart, the manner in which the two sides looked at this technology reveals many paradoxical patterns. Well before the US hardened its position on PNEs, a discussion paper from its Atomic Energy Commission talked of including Plowshares projects – the development of techniques to use nuclear explosives for peaceful purposes – along with other areas of cooperation with India to counterbalance the impact of China's test.[66] In January 1965, US Presidential science adviser Jerome Wiesner had reported Bhabha's interest in the Plowshare program and suggested that the Indian decision against developing nuclear weapons had to be supported by gains in peaceful nuclear technology. US ambassador Bowles also talked of persuading India not to produce nuclear weapons by "creating sense of pride on part of Indian people in their own scientific capacity and prowess."[67] A diplomatic cable to Washington suggests the areas of technical cooperation as including "the possibility of a small satellite, Plowshare experiments, and collaborative research on thorium fuel and fast reactors."[68] There were also reports that the US had supplied a small amount of plutonium for research purposes to India in December 1966. Even Vikram Sarabhai, who succeeded Bhabha as DAE chief and was known to be anti-bomb,

148   *A. Vinod Kumar*

had demanded the right to undertake PNEs.[69] In his criticism of the NPT text, India's envoy Husain stated that "we must develop and utilize it in every form that make possible not only great civil engineering projects but also to speed up the progress of our peoples."[70]

This review makes clear the complexity of India's position in relation to PNEs. On the one hand, India made a strong distinction between PNEs as peaceful applications, and its demand that all other forms of nuclear testing be banned. On the other hand, Delhi made only broad references to the application of this technology for developmental projects. In the late 1950s, Bhabha had talked about utilizing atomic explosions for civil engineering projects, under IAEA supervision.[71] The project, termed Subterranean Nuclear Explosion Program (SNEP), was sanctioned by Shastri, and was assumed to be the beginning of the Indian PNE effort similar to the US Plowshare approach.[72] Two public expositions on PNE applications came after the 1974 test. In a September 1974 paper, Trivedi talked of devising new methods of exploiting oil resources as well as deposits of low-grade copper and other minerals using underground nuclear explosions.[73] This idea was reiterated by Rikhi Jaipal, a former Indian diplomat, in a 1977 article, where he argued that "the significance of this technology lies in its [*sic*] applications in the simulation of higher yields of gas and petroleum and tapping of geothermal heat from 250 hot springs, besides exploiting low grade nonferrous ores, dealing with granite overburdens, earth-moving operations, deepening of harbors and linking of rivers."[74] Pointing to experiments by advanced countries, Jaipal argued that the opposition to PNE was a political posture and was dominated by the arms control angle.

Assuming that the SNEP was an attempt to develop PNE technologies, it should also be assumed that India was progressing on this front even while the NPT negotiations were ongoing. Yet, the government remained non-committal until November 1972, when Indira Gandhi told the Parliament that the "AEC is constantly reviewing progress in the technology of underground nuclear explosion both from theoretical and experimental angles, and assessing its economic value."[75] Nine months before the 1974 test, the minister in charge of atomic energy, K.C. Pant, confirmed that studies were being done, stating that "we have to identify the broad applications which are viable," and that "the technology is in part conditioned by the allotment application."[76] The emphasis in both statements was on experiments and economic applications, thus trying to suggest that India would be using this technology only for peaceful purposes. However, Raja Ramanna, a key figure in the 1974 test, later mentioned how Indira Gandhi, while approving the PNE, had "decreed that the experiment should be carried out for the simple reason that India required such a demonstration."[77] While the exact meaning of these words is yet to be discerned, the reasons for such a demonstration six years after rejecting the NPT remains an enduring mystery. Did India refuse to sign the NPT in order to secure this right? What did India gain from this demonstration and why were no further PNEs undertaken? An argument persists that India described its nuclear test as a PNE, as the plutonium came from the spent fuel of a heavy water reactor built with Canadian assistance

India 149

for peaceful purposes.[78] Nonetheless, with no "allotment application" identified after the test, the PNE continues to be treated as a demonstration of India's weapon capability, which nevertheless occurred seven years after the nuclear club was closed.

India's NPT decision: keeping the nuclear option open?

The previous section listed the many reasons that India officially advocated opposition to the final NPT text. It is clear from various pieces of evidence that India's position on most of these core issues had innate complexities and paradoxes, a conclusion that raises the fundamental question – were the contentions so onerous for India to warrant its rejection of the treaty? As described earlier, there was sufficient space for dialogue, compromise, and adjustments on the core issues, some of which India pursued in the course of negotiations before proceeding to a rigid opposition. What prompted this turnaround and what weighed in the minds of the leadership when the NPT decision was made? Though India started its decade-long phase of nuclear diplomacy with the conception of a comprehensive disarmament instrument, the Chinese nuclear tests conducted throughout the 1960s had a deep-rooted impact on India's strategic psyche and decision-making process. While this linkage has been understated in India's public expositions, it could be premised that the raging domestic pressure to build a strategic response to China had a decisive influence on the leadership's thinking. Despite minimal evidences to prove that the eventual NPT decision was solely based on the China factor, the Chinese tests triggered intense debates in the Indian parliament, with the government consistently assuring members that the threat to India's security was constantly assessed and that all suitable actions for the defense of the country would be taken.[79]

The first to react to the first Chinese test of 1964 was then Information Minister Indira Gandhi: "India is in a position to produce the bomb within 18 months. But I think we should use atomic energy for peaceful purposes only."[80] Shastri reiterated India's decision not to produce nuclear bombs, but assured the parliament in November 1964 that this stand need not be regarded as a permanent or static policy.[81] After China's third test in May 1966, Indira Gandhi, as the newly appointed prime minister, declared that "we are increasing our know-how and that China cannot attack any country with impunity."[82] Swaran Singh, for his part, assured the Lok Sabha that the policy (of making a bomb) was kept under constant review and that the government intended to develop the know-how and technical capability, a statement described by B.G. Varghese, then information advisor to the Prime Minister, as "perhaps the first public commitment, howsoever vague, to developing a nuclear option."[83] However, while stating that "we should try to develop the know-how *completely*," Swaran Singh added that "this is the best way under the present circumstances to develop the know-how, but to continue to stick to our policy that such development should be for peaceful purposes."[84] While many of these statements were meant to placate the pro-bomb lobby, the government was unwilling to commit on

150　*A. Vinod Kumar*

whether it was willing to consider the weapon option at some stage.[85] In the meantime, the evolving nature of the NPT text began to force a subtle change in this approach, with the government telling the parliament that not just China but other factors – including the progress made at the disarmament negotiations – have to be taken into consideration for any decision.[86] This was an indication that the government continued to keep hope on the ENDC to produce a durable non-proliferation instrument that would set the stage for a disarmament pathway.

The leadership was thus seemingly exploring a two-pronged approach: First, it was hoping that a credible treaty would emerge out of the ENDC negotiations. Second, it sought to manage the pro-bomb lobby by assuring them of a proactive policy to meet the Chinese threat. Both these approaches, though, were belied with the NPT text evolving in a manner that was seen as detrimental to Indian interests. On the one hand, a nonproliferation treaty without the expected disarmament fundamentals, provisions for reductions and elimination, or enshrined security guarantees belied India's hope of an international legal instrument providing a firewall against the fledging Chinese arsenal. On the other hand, signing the treaty could have meant India having to forego the right to pursue its own security alternatives. The eventual outcome seems to have been an effort to explore a third option, a sort of middle path – one that did not look like compromising on the ideational position, even while securing the space to exercise strategic flexibility. What did this middle path entail – a strategic program or something short of it?

Leaning towards the bomb?

The genesis of Indian thinking in favor of exploring a nuclear deterrent dates back to the Nehruvian times. Analysts like Bharat Karnad have pointed to Nehru's "awe" for the atom's gigantic manifestations after the Hiroshima-Nagasaki bombing and his interest in General Claude Auchinleck's formulation of an Indian nuclear force.[87] Karnad also claimed that Nehru had conceived of a two-tier nuclear program – civilian-cum-military program christened *Janus-faced* – and that Bhabha had requested permission to undertake a nuclear test after the 1962 war with China.[88] While these assertions remain debatable, Nehru's public advocacy of disarmament had shaped the policy direction for his successors, Shastri and Indira Gandhi. Despite his stand against nuclear weapons, Shastri's sanctioning of the SNEP has been interpreted as his tacit consent to build an infrastructure with an inherent military character.[89] However, it was Indira Gandhi's struggle to maintain a balance between the Nehruvian path and catering to the pro-bomb clamor that defined the dilemmas of policy-making during the crucial years of 1966–1968. M.G.K. Menon, who succeeded Bhabha as head of the Tata Institute of Fundamental Research (TIFR), later talked about Bhabha indicating the possibility of joining the Indira cabinet (implying potentially dramatic changes in the nuclear program).[90]

B.G. Varghese mentions a core group which was mandated to prepare a paper on various aspects of a nuclear weapons program.[91] Subsequently, in an AEC meeting of 1966, where Vikram Sarabhai was named its new Chairman, a tentative approval was given for the study of a nuclear weapons program and delivery systems.[92] By the time of Bhabha's demise, the nuclear weapon debate had attained new dimensions, with various studies conducted on the cost and feasibility of a weapons program. Subrahmanyam writes about three schools that shaped this debate: the first school opposed India's nuclearization, the second demanded a full-fledged credible deterrent, and the third favored a "crash program" of weapons and delivery means for a limited mission.[93] Costs were a major factor in relation to Bhabha's estimate of Rs18 lakh being intensely debated (and contested by some scientists), along with those estimates done by Subrahmaniam Swamy and others.[94] The US State Department quotes Bhabha making an estimate of ten million dollars for developing and testing a crude device.[95] A 1964 US Intelligence Estimate states that India had capabilities for plutonium separation and could produce and test its first device in one to three years after a decision, which was to be determined by factors like the pace of the Chinese program and assurances from the superpowers.[96]

With pressure building up in the country, Indira Gandhi, in an interview for *Le Monde*, stated that "we may find ourselves having to take a nuclear decision any moment and it is therefore not possible for us to tie our hands."[97] Sarabhai had remarked to Robert McNamara in April 1967 that "if disarmament is not going to be the next step, then India is reluctant to give up the option of building the bomb."[98] Jha is also reported to have stated that "the nuclear technology India has developed is threatened by serious curtailment if India adheres to the NPT."[99] Another major indication of the proactive thinking was Gandhi's statement to the Rajya Sabha in November 1967 that "our policy is constant under review and first consideration is to safeguard national security."[100] Later, she declared in the Lok Sabha that "we will now be driven by our self-enlightenment."[101] In many subsequent debates, the government also emphasized that "when exposed to nuclear blackmail, India will take full account of its national security needs."[102]

The significant point, though, is that none of these statements indicated a leap towards a nuclear weapon program. Rather, Gandhi said in the same Lok Sabha speech of April 1968 that the "government do not propose to manufacture nuclear weapons, based on a decision taken many years ago, which is unrelated to the NPT."[103] There are many facets to this position. On the one hand, the government's rejection of the NPT enabled it to moderate the pro-bomb pressure building up in the country. On the other, India conveyed to the world its intention to maintain strategic autonomy – by rejecting a "discriminatory treaty" as well as security alliances, and maintaining its right to access and develop the whole spectrum of peaceful uses of nuclear energy. However, the continuing Chinese tests and the persistent pressure for a strategic response had required the government to devise a new strategy that provides some strategic balancing without compromising on its ideational standing.[104] This entails a middle path, which could be described as the initiation of the nuclearization phase.

152 *A. Vinod Kumar*

Towards nuclearization?

Besides the different schools of thought that influenced India's diplomatic strategy and propelled the bomb demand, there was a predominant view that vouched for a middle path – of exercising a nuclear option. It implied the establishment of a self-reliant and advanced nuclear infrastructure that could provide for a sustainable nuclear energy program, and enable a shift to a military version if and when the need arose. Though there are many votaries to this approach (which some could term as latent weaponization), a definitive direction was provided by Sarabhai who announced a plan on May 25, 1970, which, at first glance, looked like a blueprint for expanding nuclear energy and space research.[105] A closer look, though, reveals it to be the game plan to build an advanced infrastructure of nuclear, space, and electronics, all with clear dual-use implications. The plan included projects like advanced thermal reactors to lower cost for plutonium production, fast breeder reactors, heavy water facilities, gas centrifuge technology and development of uranium mines, among others, for the nuclear sector, and construction of facilities for solid propellant, rocket fabrication and in-flight guidance, and communication and remote sensing satellites, in the space domain.

The fact that many of these capabilities later ended up in the strategic as well as the integrated guided-missile development program (IGMDP) is testament to the origins of this nuclearization phase in the late 1960s, charted through a common vision of Bhabha and Sarabhai.[106] The nuclearization strategy had patent impulses: (1) the strong ideational rooting of the Indian political system of that period made it hard for the government to reverse its anti-bomb posture and launch a strategic program; and (2) the pro-bomb pressure that could not be subdued as Chinese nuclear tests intensified in the 1960s, followed by development of intermediate-range missiles and satellite systems. The government needed to negate the pro-bomb pressure with a proactive policy, and (3) the NPT could be the only major impediment for a shift from a passive state of nuclear energy development to an active phase of nuclearization. Signing the treaty could have invariably limited India's options and maneuvering space.

Subrahmanyam describes this as part of a multi-faceted strategy that was to define India's nuclear policy from the 1970s. It includes: (a) reliance on the general deterrence exercised by superpowers; (b) a weapon program or a program of "peaceful" or a plutonium explosion (even by risking violation of safeguard agreements); (c) research and development with regard to atomic energy, space, and electronics to reach "a balanced weapons capability" as early as possible; and (d) the pursuit of security within a treaty with one of the superpowers.[107] Subrahmanyam had opined that this strategy should be entwined with India's disarmament campaign and effort to achieve abolition of nuclear weapons. While a friendship treaty was signed with the USSR a few years later, the plutonium/peaceful explosion came through the PNE in 1974 even as the disarmament crusade continued throughout the 1970s and 1980s. Assuming that this was the larger game plan that propelled India's NPT decision, it also explains the intention behind the PNE (as a validation/demonstration of the technological capability) and why India did not test before 1967 (political decision not to develop nuclear weapons). Though it is difficult to postulate whether India could have galloped towards a nuclear weapon program right after the PNE, the immediate conditions after the test – namely its international condemnation, the withdrawal of support by US and Canada to the civilian program, the establishment of denial regimes like the Nuclear Suppliers Group (NSG), as well as the domestic political turmoil – had limited India's nuclear decision-making choices in the immediate years after the PNE.

Conclusion

There is logical pattern to which India's NPT decision had eventually evolved, and it seemed to be an outcome of considered strategic choices and circumstances. The shift of momentum from disarmament talks to a nonproliferation treaty, the rapidly expanding Chinese program, and the domestic pressure for a strategic response, all had pushed India's leadership to a point where policy choices were limited. A major factor that constrained the leadership was the burden of idealism carried over with pride from the Nehruvian days. The period between October 1964, when the Chinese first tested, and early 1968, when the final treaty draft was debated, was one of turmoil (marked by deaths of Shastri and Bhabha), leadership change (Indira Gandhi as PM and Sarabhai as head of the nuclear establishment), which added to the incoherent appreciation of how the strategic environment was evolving, how the treaty draft was shaping up, and the realistic choices that could be exercised.

Between the time when NPT negotiations started in June 1965, and January 1967, India had lost the window of undertaking a nuclear test, and qualifying as a nuclear-weapon-state, having been mired in ideational and political confusions. The principled position against nuclear weapons, which was consistently reiterated, did not enable a proper appreciation of implications of missing this testing window. The leadership hoped that the treaty would emerge as a strong instrument of disarmament and would enable it to maintain its ideational status, without having to change the peaceful nature of its program or shifting to a strategic option. Much of the NPT text evolved in the latter half of 1967, and by the time the final draft came up in early 1968, it was too late for India's realization that the treaty may be a fragile edifice without substantive structures to move towards the disarmament end-goal. With the Chinese threat intensifying every passing year and domestic pressure mounting, it became clear for the leadership that signing the NPT would amount to grave disadvantages for India's strategic future. The weak disarmament fundamentals of the treaty were, thus, a saving grace which enabled India to officially reject it using the moral argument. Having to deal with all-round pressure on various fronts, the prudent choice before the leadership was to stay out and empower itself to meet the inimical strategic environment, without progressing towards an active weaponization initiative. The nuclearization strategy acted as the perfect middle path, which

154 *A. Vinod Kumar*

was validated by events of subsequent years. Though the future of the treaty was hard to predict in the 1970s, its subsequent failure to anchor a durable disarmament process and the emergence of two nuclear rivals in India's neighborhood largely justified Delhi's decision to reject the treaty and exercise the nuclearization option.

While many of these aspects may remain debatable due to the absence of sufficient documentary evidence to conclusively substantiate the "nuclearization" thesis or to falsify it, the positive aspect of India's decision is that its argument on false disarmament hopes has been validated by the treaty's functional history. The record of India's interaction with the NPT is also unique, considering that it was the only state that opposed the treaty and managed to maintain its position over the last 45 years. Most countries which had voted against and those which abstained on the treaty resolution ended up acceding to the NPT, while Pakistan remained an interesting case of a state voting for the resolution and preferring not to accede. Another aspect to consider is of how India's ideational positions evolved in the course of the negotiations. India initially wanted a comprehensive disarmament treaty that incorporated non-dissemination measures. When a nonproliferation treaty was becoming a reality, India wanted it to be comprehensive enough to include suitable disarmament structures. Eventually, India's original goal of a grand instrument that would lead to a world without nuclear weapons remains unfulfilled, a fact that enabled it to justify its rejection of the NPT. That India's arguments on the discriminatory nature of the NPT and its lopsided structure have been proven in the subsequent decades also helps Delhi to maintain the official narrative on why the treaty was unacceptable.

Notes

1 The UNGA adopted the draft treaty through Resolution 2373 (XXII) on June 12, 1968 by 95 votes in favor, four against, and the remaining 21 abstaining.
2 For a recent review of the relevant literature, see Liviu Horovitz, "Beyond Pessimism: Why the Treaty on the Non-Proliferation of Nuclear Weapons will not Collapse," *The Journal of Strategic Studies* 38, no. 1–2 (2015): 126–158.
3 According to B.G. Varghese, there were suggestions for adhering to the NPT for a limited period, as staying out could have been construed as future intent to build nuclear weapons. B.G. Varghese, *First Draft* (New Delhi: Tranquebar, 2010), 128.
4 T.T. Poulose (ed.), *Perspectives of India's Nuclear Policy* (New Delhi: Young Asia Publications, 1978).
5 G.G. Mirchandani, "India and Nuclear Weapons," in *Perspectives of India's Nuclear Policy*, ed. T.T. Poulose (New Delhi: Young Asia Publications, 1978).
6 J.P. Jain, *Nuclear India*, 2 volumes (New Delhi: Radiant Publishers, 1974).
7 Ashok Kapur, *India's Nuclear Option: Atomic Diplomacy and Decision Making* (New York: Praeger Publishers, 1976).
8 Subrahmanyam's articles include: "India: Keeping the Option Open," in *Nuclear Proliferation Phase II*, eds. Robert M. Lawrence and Joel Larus (Lawrence, KS: University Press of Kansas, 1974); "A Strategy for India for a Credible Posture against a Nuclear Adversary," The Institute for Defence Studies and Analyses, New Delhi, 1968; cf. Special Issue of IDSA Journal 3, no. 1 (1970).
9 George Perkovich, *India's Nuclear Bomb: The Impact on Global Proliferation* (Berkeley, CA: University of California Press, 1999).

India 155

10 See glimpses of this debate in Jagat S. Mehta, *Rescuing the Future* (New Delhi: Manohar, 2008).

11 Jawaharlal Nehru made this proposal in the Lok Sabha on April 2, 1954, which was forwarded by the Indian representative to the UN Secretary General in a letter (DC/44 and Corr.1); the letter called for "...'Standstill agreement' in respect, at least, of these actual explosions, even if arrangements about the discontinuance of production and stockpiling, must await more substantial agreements among those principally concerned." Official Records of Disarmament Commission, April–June 1954. DC/44 and Corr. 1, April 8, 1954; at the ninth session of the General Assembly, India submitted a revised draft resolution to this effect to the First Committee (A/C.1/L.100/Rev.1), which was referred to the Disarmament Commission by the 497th Plenary Meeting of the General Assembly on November 4, 1954. The resolution is available at www.un. org/en/ga/search/view_doc.asp?symbol=A/RES/809(IX); also see the debate at the 497th meeting, and Indian submissions at http://repository.un.org/bitstream/ handle/11176/298887/A_PV.497-EN.pdf?sequence=1&isAllowed=y (accessed in January 2016).

12 The closest that Nehru had indicated about a future consideration of nuclear weapons was his statement that "if one has these fissionable materials and resources, then one can make a bomb, unless the world will be wise enough to stop (its) production." See Nehru's statement of May 24, 1957 on Nuclear Explosions Resolution (and his speeches on disarmament) in *Documents on India's Nuclear Disarmament Policy*, Volume I, eds. Gopal Singh and S.K. Sharma (New Delhi: Anamika Publishers & Distributors, 2000); also see arguments by Bharat Karnad on Nehru's approach towards nuclear weapons in *Nuclear Weapons and Indian Security: The Realist Foundations of Strategy* (New Delhi: Macmillan India, 2002).

13 Jawaharlal Nehru's Speech at the UNGA on October 30, 1960, in Singh and Sharma (eds.), *Documents on India's Nuclear Disarmament Policy*.

14 India demanded the addition of chemical and biological weapons and small arms in order to make the disarmament process comprehensive. See debates of ENDC/P.V.37, May 15, 1962 and ENDC/P.V.47, June 1, 1962; quoting a Western scientist, Nehru told the Parliament on May 2, 1962 that the ongoing atmospheric tests would cause over three million deaths, in terms of genetic damage. Nehru's speech is included in Singh and Sharma (eds.), *Documents on India's Nuclear Disarmament Policy* n. 12; documents pertaining to India's statements at the ENDC have been collected from a variety of sources, including the Foreign Affairs Records at the Ministry of External Affairs (MEA) Library, http://mealib.nic.in/?2588?000 and the declassified documents from the Archives and Records Management (A&RM) Division of MEA, some of which have been released to the National Archives of India, www.mea.gov.in/images/pdf/national-archive-new.pdf.

15 Ireland submitted drafts on "non-dissemination" and for measures against "relinquishing control or transferring information on nuclear weapons manufacturing" in 1959 and 1960, but these were opposed on each occasion by one of the superpowers. The eventual UNGA resolutions were 1664 (Question of Disarmament) and 1665 (Prevention of Wider Dissemination of Nuclear Weapons).

16 Ashwani Kumar Chopra, *India's Policy on Disarmament* (New Delhi: ABC Publishing House, 1984); also see William Epstein, *The Last Chance: Nuclear Proliferation and Arms Control* (New York: The Free Press, 1976).

17 See text of Joint Statement on Agreed Principles, https://disarmament-library.un.org/ UNODA/Library.nsf/1cf71faffad96cd38525796500789846/d0276def8b6fad0f85257 a130054e158/$FILE/A-4879.pdf (accessed June 2014).

18 ENDC/P.V. 34, May 9, 1962.

19 While the Soviets suggested a four-year period, the US talked of a phased programme wherein the first stage of a three-year period would be used to freeze

156 *A. Vinod Kumar*

production of nuclear weapons, the second stage to make major inroads into stockpiles, and the third for total elimination. See debates of ENDC/P.V.49, June 5, 1962.

20 ENDC/P.V.30, May 3, 1962.
21 Chopra, *India's Policy on Disarmament*.
22 ENDC/P.V.174, March 12, 1964.
23 Also, in a letter to the UN Secretary General dated October 10, 1964, India's representative, B.N. Chakravarthi, requested that an item entitled "Non-proliferation of nuclear weapons" be inscribed in the agenda for the Nineteenth session of the UNGA.
24 ENDC/P.V. 212, September 1, 1964.
25 Statement by B.K. Nehru at ENDC/P.V.212 and 216, September 15, 1964.
26 Mirchandani, "India and Nuclear Weapons."
27 The Jan Sangh had passed this resolution at its Bhopal session of December 1962.
28 See Raj Krishna, "India and the Bomb," *India Quarterly*, New Delhi, April–June 1965.
29 Bhabha's declaration was made in an All India address on October 24, 1964. See Jain, *Nuclear India II*; also see "Bhabha: India Can Make Atom Bomb in 18 Months," *National Herald*, October 5, 1964.
30 Poulose, *Perspectives of India's Nuclear Policy*.
31 Kapur, *India's Nuclear Option*.
32 While the US draft talked of prohibiting transfer of nuclear weapons into "national control" of any non-weapon state or actions that leads to increase in number of states with possessing nuclear weapons or assisting in their manufacturing, the Soviet draft emphasized the prohibition of transfers of technology, weapon or control to states that do not possess nuclear weapons.
33 Trivedi defined "proliferate" as "reproduce itself, grow by multiplication of elementary parts," ENDC/P.V. 223, August 12, 1965.
34 Trivedi contended that "further proliferation is only the consequence of existing or continuing proliferation, and prevention should be of all types of proliferation." ENDC/P.V. 232, September 14, 1965.
35 The five principles included:

> (a) the treaty should be void of any loopholes which might permit states to proliferate; (b) it should embody acceptable balance of mutual responsibilities and obligations; (c) the treaty should be a step towards general and complete disarmament, particularly nuclear disarmament; (d) there should be acceptable and workable provisions to ensure its effectiveness; and (e) it should not adversely affect the right to conclude regional treaties to ensure total absence of nuclear weapons in respective territories.

> The joint memorandum on non-proliferation (ENDC/158) was submitted to the 233rd meeting of UNGA by Brazil, Burma, Ethiopia, India, Mexico, Nigeria, Sweden and the United Arab Republic. See Disarmament Commission, (Official Records) Supplement for January to December 1965, New York 1966.

36 Epstein, *The Last Chance*.
37 Ibid.
38 A conversation between the US Secretary of State and Soviet diplomats notes India as expected to abstain on the Treaty vote. See MemCon, May 17, 1968, *Foreign Relations of the United States* (FRUS), 1964–1968, XI, doc. 239; William Foster reported to be working with India on its reservations and that he expected India to sign the Treaty. Cf. Memo for the Record of the 584th Meeting of the National Security Council, March 27, 1968, ibid., doc. 229.
39 Rajya Sabha debate on Nuclear Non-Proliferation Treaty, July 25, 1968, www.idsa. in/npihp/documents/RS_25-July-1968.pdf (accessed August 2015).

40 In statements to ENDC (P.V.370, February 27, 1968) and the First Committee (1567th meeting, May 14, 1968), India's representative M.A. Husain argued that India will not sign a treaty that does not conform to Resolution 2028, and that "a viable treaty should impose equal obligations on all, confer same benefits of security and progress."

41 A collection of the Rajya Sabha Q&A and debates, at www.idsa.in/npihp/document.html (accessed August 2015).

42 Statement to the Lok Sabha, March 14, 1968.

43 Memo from Kreisberg to Ambassador, "India's Attitude toward the Nuclear Non-proliferation Treaty (NPT)," November 12, 1973, FRUS, 1969–1976, E-8, doc. 151.

44 India's statements included: Morarji Desai, "Quest for Peace," Speech at the Special Session of the United Nations General Assembly, New York, June 9, 1978; P.V. Narasimha Rao, "Disarmament: An Urgent Concern," Statement made at the Second Special Session on Disarmament on June 11, 1982, www.indianembassy.org/policy/Disarmament/disarm12.htm (accessed March 2009).

45 Also known as the Comprehensive Plan for Phased Elimination of all Nuclear Weapons; Text of RGAP available at Annex I of the *Report of the Informal Group on Prime Minister Rajiv Gandhi's Action Plan for a Nuclear-Weapons-Free and Non-Violent World Order 1988*, released on August 20, 2011, www.pugwashindia.org/images/uploads/Report.pdf (accessed October 2014).

46 Text of Resolution available at www.un.org/en/ga/search/view_doc.asp?symbol=S/RES/255(1968) (accessed August 2015).

47 Swaran Singh stated at 1582th First Committee Meeting of October 6, 1967 that "security lies in disarmament, not in 'protection'," and that the possessor should be denied license to increase "instrument of threat." UNGA 22nd Session, A/C.ljPV.JS82, http://daccess-dds-ny.un.org/doc/UNDOC/GEN/NL7/407/38/PDF/NL740738.pdf?OpenElement (accessed June 2015).

48 *The Hindu*, November 1, 1964, quoted by A.G. Noorani, "India's Quest for a Nuclear Guarantee," *Asian Survey* 7, no. 7 (1967): 490–502.

49 *The Times* (London), December 5, 1964.

50 Telegram to Komer of the National Security Council Staff, January 8, 1965, FRUS, 1964–1968, XXV, doc. 83.

51 First Committee 1469th meeting, November 17, 1966, UNGA 21st Session, A/C.l/SR.1469, http://daccess-dds-ny.un.org/doc/UNDOC/GEN/NL1/548/69/PDF/NL154869.pdf?OpenElement (accessed June 2015).

52 Varghese talks of Jha communicating the message from Kosygin that if India signed the NPT, China would not be able to blackmail India because any threat would invite international reprisals through the UN, with Soviet support. See Varghese, *First Draft*; Kosygin's message was also conveyed by Jha to P.N. Haksar, the Principal Secretary to Prime Minister Indira Gandhi, in which Jha mentioned the Soviet insistence that India should sign NPT to qualify for the guarantee. See Notes by L.K. Jha to the Prime Minister's Secretariat, Nehru Memorial Museum and Library, New Delhi, India, P.N. Haksar Papers, IIIrd Installment, Subject File No. 111 (1967–1973).

53 MemCon (Johnson, L.K. Jha, B.K. Nehru *et al.*), April 19, 1967, FRUS, 1964–1968, XXV, doc. 440; also see telegram from Rostow to Johnson, ibid., doc. 438.

54 There was talk of including language enabling intervention even without UNSC sanction. MemCon (Rusk, Gromyko), June 23, 1967, FRUS, 1964–1968, XI, doc. 198.

55 Following discussion of Kosygin's proposal in Delhi, Jha was sent not just to Washington, but also to London and Paris with objective of a seeking formal guarantees from all nuclear powers to come to the aid of non-weapon states subjected to a nuclear threat. However, it is not clear how the Indian government viewed the potential of a nuclear threat from the then established nuclear-weapon states, thus inherently defining this campaign as an effort to seek assurances against a Chinese nuclear threat.

158　*A. Vinod Kumar*

56 The conflict between India's non-alignment policy and its effort to seek security guarantees from the superpowers was widely debated in the Indian parliament. While groups like the Swathantra Party were in favor of seeking an American nuclear umbrella, most members cutting across party lines felt that the nuclear-weapon states, fearing a Chinese retaliation against them, may not come to India's rescue in the event of a Chinese attack. Interestingly, Swaran Singh stated in the Rajya Sabha in May 1966 that "non-alignment does not come in the way of taking all possible steps to safeguard our integrity and protect our country." Debate on Call Attention Notice given by B.K.P. Sinha on "Hydrogen bomb explosion by China," of May 11, 1966 (unpublished document).
57 Statement of June 13, 1967, available at www.idsa.in/npihp/documents/RS_13-June-1967.pdf (accessed August 2015).
58 *The Times of India*, April 6, 1967, quoted by A.G. Noorani, "India's Quest for a Nuclear Guarantee."
59 Quote from M.C. Chagla, ibid.
60 Statement to Lok Sabha, Debate on Foreign Affairs, March 14, 1968.
61 First Committee, 1436th Meeting, October 31, 1966.
62 First Committee, 1443rd Meeting, November 7, 1966.
63 First Committee, 1448th Meeting, November 9. 1966.
64 ENDC/P.V.370, February 27, 1968.
65 ENDC/P.V.298, 23 May 23, 1967.
66 Perkovich, *India's Nuclear Bomb*.
67 See above note 54.
68 Telegram from the Embassy in India to the Department of State, January 21, 1965, FRUS, 1964–1968, XXV, doc. 85.
69 Sarabhai made this demand to the US envoy in Delhi. See "India wants a 'Complete Freeze' on Current Posture of Nuclear Powers," *US Mission to Geneva Cable 3048 to State Department*, April 3, 1968, available at www.gwu.edu/~nsarchiv/nukevault/ebb253/doc14.pdf (accessed July 2014).
70 See above note 40.
71 See Document 5 in Jain, *Nuclear India*.
72 See Perkovich, *India's Nuclear Bomb*. P.K. Iyengar also alluded to this in an interview with the author in October 2011.
73 V.C. Trivedi, "India's Approach towards Nuclear Energy and Non-Proliferation of Nuclear Weapons," Working Paper presented at the Divonne meeting organized by the Arms Control Association and Carnegie Endowment for International Peace, September 9–11, 1974.
74 Rikhi Jaipal, "The Indian Nuclear Explosion," *International Security* 1, no. 4 (1977): 44–451.
75 Statement to Rajya Sabha on December 7, 1972, available at http://idsa.in/npihp/documents/RS_7-December-1972.pdf (accessed August 2015).
76 Debate in Rajya Sabha, August 2, 1973, available at http://idsa.in/npihp/documents/RS_2-August-1973iii.pdf (accessed August 2015).
77 Raja Ramanna, *Years of Pilgrimage* (New Delhi: Viking, 1991).
78 Canadian assistance ended after India refused to subject all facilities to safeguards and restrain from any more PNEs. See CIA, Directorate of Intelligence Report, "India's Nuclear Procurement Strategy: Implications for US," December 1982, available at http://digitalarchive.wilsoncenter.org/document/116902 (accessed May 2015).
79 See Rajya Sabha debate on the Chinese program at www.idsa.in/npihp/documents/RS_2-August-1966.pdf (accessed August 2015).
80 Mirchandani, "India and Nuclear Weapons."
81 Ibid.
82 See Indira Gandhi's response to Rajya Sabha questions, referred in Mirchandani, "India and Nuclear Weapons." Also see Gandhi's submissions during the debate on

India 159

"Nuclear blast by China" in Rajya Sabha on August 2, 1966, www.idsa.in/npihp/documents/RS_2-August-1966.pdf (accessed in October 2014).

83 Varghese, *First Draft*.

84 In the Rajya Sabha debate days after the third Chinese nuclear test, members demanded development of nuclear weapons as a means to address the Chinese nuclear challenge and, therefore, not depend on the guarantees of other nuclear-weapon states to come to India's aid in the event of a Chinese attack. Swaran Singh replied that "if we feel that we can be protected by others, it will not be a wise step or way of thinking," though adding that the government policy was under constant review. Debate on Call Attention Notice given by B.K.P. Sinha on "Hydrogen Bomb Explosion by China," of May 11, 1966 (unpublished document).

85 During the debate of May 1966, a Rajya Sabha member, Akbar Ali Khan, noted the shift in the government policy:

> While fully appreciating the reasons for the policy, I feel that the slight that the policy will be under constant review is a matter of some satisfaction … so far as our preparedness is concerned at what stage it is. The government should satisfy us that so far as the preparedness and knowhow is concerned, we are in a position to do so if we decide to embark on that project.

Singh replied that "it is recognized that we are one of the countries capable of becoming an atomic (weapon) power in a reasonably short time" (ibid.).

86 *Times of India*, May 11, 1966, quoted by Noorani, "India's Quest for a Nuclear Guarantee."

87 Karnad, *Nuclear Weapons and Indian Security*.

88 Karnad made this reference at an IDSA-NPIHP conference in New Delhi in October 2012.

89 Varghese asserts that "Shastri had approved a project to develop the necessary technology for a bomb, but had stopped short of agreeing to a test," Varghese, *First Draft*; on the other hand, in a message on Wiesner's visit to India, Ambassador Bowles talks of Shastri stating to Wiesner that if nuclear weapons were ever made in India it would not be during a Ministry headed by him. See Telegram 2055 from Embassy in Delhi, January 21, 1965, State Department Central Files 1964–1966, SCI 7 US, Record Group 59 (RG 59), National Archives and Records Administration, College Park, MD (NACP).

90 Bhabha died in a plane crash the day the Indira government took over. Menon made the revelation in a lecture at the Dr. Homi Bhabha Birth Centenary Symposium organized by the TIFR in 2008. See Dipan K. Ghosh and Arun K. Grover, eds., *Tribute to a Titan* (Mumbai: Indian Physics Association, 2009).

91 The other members of the group included Homi Sethna, S. Gopal, Romesh Thapar, Pitamber Pant and K. Subrahmanyam. While Subrahmayam was given the task of covering the security dimensions, Gopal was supposed to spell out the diplomatic implications and Sethna covering the technological aspects. Subrahmanyam and Gopal opined during these deliberations that a US guarantee would be less effective and could not be relied upon once China's capability increases. See Varghese, *First Draft*.

92 Varghese also quotes Sarabhai telling him in December 1966 that "a decision had been taken to go ahead with an Intermediate Range Ballistic Missile (IRBM) project, so as to ensure a credible nuclear option." Ibid.

93 K. Subrahmanyam, "The Path to Nuclear Capability," Special Issue of *IDSA Journal* 3, no. 1 (1970).

94 Swamy talked of producing around 200 bombs by 1970–1971 using plutonium from all facilities (including those that were under safeguards). Speech to the Jana Sangh Parliamentary Study Group, August 19, 1968.

95 Cf. FRUS, 1964–1968, XXV, doc. 85.

160   *A. Vinod Kumar*

96 National Intelligence Estimate Number 4–2-64, "Prospects for a Proliferation of Nuclear Weapons over the Next Decade," October 21, 1964, available at http://digitalarchive.wilsoncenter.org/document/115994 (accessed May 2015).

97 *The Hindu*, May 6, 1967, quoted by Noorani, "India's Quest for a Nuclear Guarantee."

98 A.G. Noorani, "India's Nuclear Guarantee Episode," *Frontline* 18, no. 2 (2001).

99 Ibid.

100 See statement at http://idsa.in/npihp/documents/RS_21-November-1967.pdf (accessed August 2015).

101 Lok Sabha Debate on Foreign Affairs, April 5, 1968.

102 See Rajya Sabha debates at www.idsa.in/npihp/documents/RS_2-August-1973iii.pdf and www.idsa.in/npihp/documents/RS_26-November-1970-i.pdf (both accessed August 2015).

103 See Lok Sabha Debate on Foreign Affairs, April 5, 1968.

104 The pro-bomb pressure continued even after rejecting the NPT. Following the Chinese satellite test of April 1970, two major conferences were organized in Delhi (May 7–10), first by a Parliamentary Committee and another by two leading think tanks, where an overwhelming consensus emerged in favor of a weapon program.

105 Press handout reproduced in Special Issue of *IDSA Journal* 3, No. 1 (1970).

106 Bhabha and Sarabhai were instrumental in preparing the initial framework of India's space program (which Sarabhai headed), besides drawing a blueprint to develop an electronics R&D ecosystem.

107 Subrahmanyam, above note 8.

9 Non-nuclear Japan?

Satō, the NPT, and the US nuclear umbrella

Fintan Hoey

In 2009 the Japanese Liberal Democratic Party (LDP) were ousted from power by their rivals, the Democratic Party of Japan (DPJ). This was the first time the LDP had lost office following an election, and this defeat ended the party's almost uninterrupted dominance of Japanese political life since its founding in 1955. The DPJ had campaigned in part on a pledge of greater government transparency and moved to open files relating to a series of secret Cold War-era security agreements which successive Japanese governments had concluded with the United States. These agreements included allowing the US to transport nuclear weapons through Japanese territory and to deploy such arms in an emergency. In many cases, both historians and the public had already known of these due to archival releases in the US. However, the subsequent releases by the Japanese Diplomatic Archive added a further dimension and rounded out the picture.[1] Nonetheless, there has been no systematic opening of material related to Japan's exploration of an independent nuclear weapons option. The limited source base available comes from leaks to the media or from specific declassification requests by researchers. While we now know a great deal about certain aspects or events, there remain significant gaps in our knowledge.

Japan was in a strange and unique position with regard to the Treaty on the Non-Proliferation of Nuclear Weapons (NPT). On the one hand, it was and remains the only country to have been attacked with nuclear weapons. The country also experienced a significant domestic backlash against nuclear energy and weapons when a Japanese fishing boat, the Dai Go Fukuryū Maru (Lucky Dragon), was exposed to the nuclear fallout from the US Castle Bravo thermonuclear test at the Bikini Atoll in March 1954.[2] Understandably, these experiences deeply affected the Japanese psyche and left the Japanese people averse to nuclear arms, the so-called "nuclear allergy." However, such traumatic events should not be taken to mean that all Japanese completely rejected nuclear technology, but only that this technology, particularly weapons, had the ability to rouse intense domestic opposition.[3] Indeed, by the early 1960s Japan was considered one of the main proliferation threats along with West Germany, India, South Africa, Brazil, and Israel. Not only did Japan have the basic technologies and know-how to develop nuclear weapons, but it was also faced with the mounting threat of Communist China's own nuclear weapons program. There

162   *F. Hoey*

were also significant worries expressed by elites over Japan's relegation to the status of a second-tier power were it to forego the development of a nuclear weapons capability.

Ultimately, Japan would come to rely upon the extended nuclear deterrence provided by its US ally and would also agree to sign and ratify the NPT. This ultimate result was foreshadowed by the 1967 articulation by Prime Minister Satō Eisaku of the "Three Non-Nuclear Principles" in which Japan foreswore the production and possession of nuclear weapons and barred the introduction into Japan of nuclear weapons by another country.[4] Despite this statement, Japan's non-nuclear status remained a grey area. During the Cold War, successive Japanese governments concluded (and subsequently concealed) arrangements supporting the US extended deterrent over Japan in contravention of the Three Non-Nuclear Principles. Moreover, Japan has been declared the "most salient example" of nuclear hedging, as it has been keeping alive the option of rapidly developing a nuclear arsenal through its advanced missile and civilian nuclear power programs.[5] While Japan's policy choices may appear contradictory and muddled, this chapter argues they are the result of a number of conflicting priorities, including security exigencies, US alliance constraints, Washington's nonproliferation pressures, and Japanese public opinion.

How and why Japan's nuclear policy took this course is a fascinating and important episode in Japan's postwar foreign policy. Despite this, Japanese nuclear decision-making has only recently begun to attract scholarly interest. This lack of interest may be due to the assumption that Japan's choices on nuclear weapons were to some extent inevitable given its history and its (less than accurate) reputation as the quintessential "non-nuclear" state.[6] Recent scholarship on this question challenged such assumptions and showed the complex interplay between domestic politics and international diplomacy which led to the adoption of Japan's policy on nuclear weapons.[7] However, historians disagree sharply on the extent to which negotiations over the reversion of Okinawa from US back to Japanese control contributed to Japan's eventual adherence to the Non-Proliferation Treaty. One view argues that Prime Minster Satō Eisaku formulated Japan's nuclear policy in the context of the reversion of Okinawa.[8] Another vehemently disagrees, arguing that while Satō himself may have connected the nuclear debate and Okinawa, he was alone in this. Rather, the wider international environment, not least the pressures of US nonproliferation policy, account for Japan's decision.[9]

Building on these contributions and on earlier research on US–Japanese relations under the leadership of Satō, this chapter challenges some of the key assumptions and conclusions, while offering fresh insights into the link between the NPT and the US nuclear umbrella.[10] Japan did make a series of nuclear-policy choices which were not inevitable, but were based on a particular reading of Japan's security needs and on the political imperative of securing the reversion of Okinawa from US control. Prime Minister Satō was definitely a crucial player within this context, and he steadily moved away from favoring an independent Japanese nuclear weapons capability and towards a growing reliance on the nuclear guarantees as provided by the US. However, the historical record shows that Satō went too far too early by declaring the "Three Non-Nuclear Principles" and in fact scrambled to regain freedom of action subsequent to this off-the-cuff statement. Moreover, Satō miscalculated when attempting to link Japan's accession to the NPT with securing US agreement to return Okinawa and remove US nuclear weapons from the island. Despite these missteps, Satō put in place the foundation for Japan's policies on nuclear weapons which have lasted to the present era: adherence to the NPT, a nuclear hedging strategy, and the reliance on the US extended deterrent.

Japan's early nuclear options

During the Second World War, Japanese atomic scientists working to build a bomb achieved success in producing some fissionable material, but lack of resources prevented them from developing Uranium 235 in sufficient quantities to produce a chain reaction.[11] After Japan's surrender, the occupation authorities forbade all nuclear research.[12] The United States ended its occupation of Japan in 1952, but ensured the continued presence of its military forces through the simultaneous conclusion of a bilateral Mutual Security Treaty. The US also retained full administrative rights over the Ryukyu Islands (of which Okinawa is the largest) so as to maintain full freedom of action regarding its massive military presence there.[13] In line with the Eisenhower administration's doctrine of "massive retaliation," beginning in the 1950s Okinawa became host to both strategic and tactical nuclear weapons.[14] The islands of Iwo Jima and Chichi Jima, which had also remained under direct American control following the end of the occupation, were used to store nuclear weapons to resupply bombers and submarines in the event of a general war.[15]

A year after the 1954 Lucky Dragon incident, US plans to deploy "Honest John" dual-use surface-to-surface missiles to Japan were greeted with huge protests leading to an assurance that they would only be fitted with conventional warheads.[16] Indeed, between 1955 and 1965 the US deployed an "impressive infrastructure" of nuclear capable weapons, minus their nuclear components, to Japan.[17] Combined with port calls by nuclear armed ships – which were a "legal inch away from Japanese territory" – the US was able to include Japan in its nuclear war planning, while denying it was introducing nuclear weapons into the country. State Department diplomats cautioned their military colleagues that such acrobatics were necessary so as to insulate the ruling conservatives in the LDP from widespread criticism.[18] Indeed, conservative leaders, including two prime ministers, Hatoyama Ichirō and Kishi Nobusuke, found it politically expedient to join the chorus of opposition to the introduction of nuclear weapons in Japan, despite not personally sharing these views. Moreover, under the terms of the alliance, Japanese policy-makers were powerless to enforce any nuclear ban, a fact they acknowledged in private conversations with US officials.[19]

Japanese politicians also attempted to push back against popular feeling. In 1954, Japan embarked on a civilian nuclear program under the US "Atoms for

164   *F. Hoey*

Peace" initiative.[20] In 1956, Kishi noted that Japan's postwar "peace constitution" – by which Japan renounced the right of belligerency and of maintaining an offensive military capability – did not prevent Japan from developing tactical nuclear weapons. The resultant negative reaction forced Kishi to backtrack from this stance.[21] He spent much of his term in office (1957–1960) negotiating a major revision of the treaty of alliance in order to give Tokyo a greater overall say as well as a veto over the introduction of nuclear weapons into Japanese territory. However, a secret understanding ensured that the US could continue to dock nuclear armed warships at Japanese ports without the need to engage in prior consultation with Tokyo.[22] Japanese leaders continued to mislead the public and made the disingenuous claim that no nuclear weapons entered any part of Japanese territory.[23] Kishi's efforts to force ratification of the revised treaty through the Diet resulted in massive protests and his early resignation in 1960. His successor, Ikeda Hayato, stressed economic growth and played down security issues, but was himself forced to quit in 1964 due to ill-health. He was succeeded as prime minister by Satō Eisaku, Kishi's younger brother, who would play a crucial role in formulating Japan's approach to nuclear weapons.[24]

The nuclear umbrella

Japanese nuclear policy decisions in the 1960s were deeply affected by a gathering international consensus towards nonproliferation and especially by US attitudes in this regard. The global proliferation of nuclear weapons was viewed with intense alarm by the administrations of US presidents John F. Kennedy and Lyndon B. Johnson.[25] By the end of 1964 both France and China had developed independent deterrents and were, from the point of view of US anti-proliferation efforts, lost causes. India and Japan were thought most likely to be next in this proliferation "chain reaction" (a term used in a State Department memo apparently without humor intended). Though not viewed as necessarily damaging to American interests – after all, an Indian and/or Japanese bomb would be pointed at Beijing – the main fear was the effect such proliferation would have on Pakistan, Israel, and Egypt.[26] Dean Rusk, who served under both Kennedy and Johnson as Secretary of State, felt the best way to prevent states from developing independent deterrents was to share nuclear weapons with them – a form of killing proliferation *with* proliferation.

To this end, Rusk proposed "a US-supplied Far Eastern nuclear stockpile" open to Japan and India. This mirrored a similar nuclear sharing proposal, the Multilateral Force (MLF), which the State Department was then advocating within the administration and with Washington's NATO allies to satisfy West Germany's aspirations to great power status, but also to prevent Bonn from developing an independent nuclear weapons capability.[27] Though such an "Asian MLF" was not without its critics and skeptics within the administration, including Defense Secretary Robert McNamara who questioned whether Japan or India could ever possess a sufficient deterrent capability, the option was definitely taken seriously.[28] In the immediate aftermath of the PRC's nuclear test in

October 1964, the Defense Department proposed a series of drastic steps to forestall the development of independent deterrents by two countries in Asia, presumably India and Japan, considered most likely to react to Beijing's actions. These steps included offering to store nuclear weapons and delivery systems on the country's territory, train its personnel, and place weapons under joint control. The goal of these creative plans was to ensure that were proliferation to occur it would not take place beyond the United States' "guidance and influence."[29] The memo, in common with other estimates and within the US government at the time, noted the anti-nuclear feeling in Japan, but also that the prospect of a Chinese Communist bomb was inducing elite opinion to the idea of a nuclear weapons program.

One such member of the elite, newly installed Japanese Prime Minister Satō Eisaku, told the US ambassador in Tokyo in late 1964 of his desire to see Japan develop nuclear weapons since "if [the] other fellow had nuclear [weapons] it was only common sense to have them oneself." The ambassador, former Harvard professor Edwin Reischauer, immediately dispatched a worried cable to his superiors noting that the new man "lives up to his reputation of being less judiciously cautious" than his predecessor and was in need of "more guidance and education" from the US to dissuade him from such dangerous plans.[30] The embassy had earlier counseled that in light of the PRC test Japan needed to be assured of the validity and range of America's deterrent power in East Asia and the Pacific.[31]

In due course, when Satō met with Johnson two weeks later, the US president assured him that "if Japan needs our nuclear deterrent for its defense the United States would stand by its commitment and provide that defense."[32] Though the United States had provided Japan with a security guarantee since the end of the postwar occupation in 1952, there had been no specific assurance of an extended nuclear deterrent until this point. Apparently satisfied by this Satō noted that his remarks to Reischauer about his desire to see Japan have its own deterrent was of a personal nature and did not represent official Japanese policy.[33]

It is unclear whether or not Satō was stating his actual intentions. One view argues that Satō had no intention of embarking on the development of an independent Japanese deterrent but rather adopted this line in order to secure from the United States an unambiguous acknowledgement of extended deterrence.[34] This is difficult to accept since Satō would have had no way of knowing the US would respond in this way. An incredibly cautious politician, he was most likely keeping his options as open as possible.[35] In any case, his ready acceptance of this extended deterrent meant that US draft plans to share nuclear weapons with Japan were not pursued any further. However, the US plans remain of interest given that they show how serious the United States saw Japan as a proliferation threat and the great lengths Washington was considering in order to prevent this. The US plans also show the strong connection between providing security (whether through an extended deterrent and/or placing weapons under joint control) with nonproliferation policies.[36]

166 *F. Hoey*

The three non-nuclear principles

While finding a way to articulate a workable posture on nuclear weapons was crucial for Satō, his main domestic and foreign policy priority remained the reversion of the Ryukyu archipelago – of which Okinawa is the main island – to Japanese control. In fact, his quest for reversion would ultimately play a crucial role in his approach to nuclear weapons. Okinawa had been the site of a vicious and bloody battle between Japanese defenders and US marines at the close of the Pacific War. Following Japan's defeat, the island became an important US military base. After the end of the occupation in 1952, the United States continued to administer the territory, though Japan retained "residual sovereignty."[37] At the start of his tenure, Satō became the first Japanese prime minister to visit Okinawa, where he declared that until it returned "to the fatherland, the post war era will not be over."[38]

In an attempt to settle this unfinished business, Satō journeyed to the United States in late 1967 to further negotiations on the reversion of Okinawa to Japanese control. Satō secured some limited movement on the issue but he was left in no doubt that the United States would only countenance reversion if its bases on Okinawa were unaffected and Japanese attitudes towards defense issues "matured." This meant tackling and reversing the widespread popular distrust and opposition to the US–Japanese alliance. To this end Satō spoke in the Diet in December 1967 in defense of both Japan's limited self-defense forces and the mutual security treaty with the United States. These, he noted, safeguarded the country and were fully consistent with the postwar "peace" constitution. Satō then stated that Japan's nuclear policy was also informed by the constitution and that Japan would "not possess nuclear [weapons], nor will we produce them, nor will we allow nuclear [weapons] to be introduced [into Japan]. These are the three principles with respect to nuclear weapons." Crucially, Satō made a point of underlining the importance of the US nuclear guarantee which was an essential element of Japan's nuclear strategy, though he did not connect this to the prohibition on introduction.[39]

Scholars disagree over Satō's reasons for articulating these principles. One view is that they were off-the-cuff, another that he wished to push back against the nuclear taboo by singling out nuclear *weapons* and thereby normalize nuclear *power generation*.[40] They can also be seen as a way of making his strong defense of Japan's limited military and its alliance with the US more palatable to the public. Indeed previous Japanese governments had signaled, to the public at least, opposition to an independent deterrent and to the presence of nuclear weapons on Japanese territory (while also turning a blind eye to nuclear-armed ships in Japanese ports). Furthermore these were general principles and not hard and fast rules. Nevertheless, the opposition was not prepared to make life easy for Satō and demanded they be passed as a Diet resolution thus giving them greater enforceability. Satō opposed this since not only would this have tied the hands of future governments it would have also severely complicated negotiations over Okinawa.

Japan 167

In response, Satō sought to recapture the initiative in early 1968 and delivered a speech on the "Four Pillars of Nuclear Policy." The Three Non-nuclear Principles now formed one of the pillars along with reliance on US extended deterrence, global nuclear disarmament, and the peaceful use of nuclear power. In this way he hoped to reconcile the idealism of Japan's amorphous anti-nuclear sentiment with the pragmatism of relying on the US extended deterrent.[41] Satō had initially hoped to completely omit the third principle – the ban on the introduction of nuclear weapons – but this was retained at the behest of the LDP's General Affairs Committee. Some of its members, including future Defense Agency Director and Prime Minister Nakasone Yasuhiro, opposed reliance on the US, since it placed Japan in a secondary position and also ruled out for the future the acquisition of an independent deterrent.[42] Satō clearly opposed its retention and later told Reischauer's successor as US ambassador that the non-introduction principle was "nonsense."[43] Why then was it retained? For once Satō faltered in his attempt to walk the narrow path between ensuring Japan's security and paying heed to popular distrust of US nuclear power. He may also have realized too late the crucial link between "nuclear introduction" and the maintenance of the nuclear umbrella.

By this time Satō's thinking regarding an independent deterrent had become more conflicted. Just three months prior to articulating the Three Non-Nuclear Principles he privately told an astounded aide: "I should just come out and say that nuclear weapons are necessary and then resign."[44] This statement has been interpreted by some as an indication of Satō's persistent misinterpretation of the seriousness of US proliferation concerns.[45] What is more likely is that this episode illustrates how torn Satō was on the issue, with regard to the US nuclear umbrella, an independent Japanese deterrent, and popular opinion. It seems that Satō was still intent on keeping his options as open as possible. In any case, his internal divisions on the issue reflected the mood of the nation.

Exploring nuclear policy options

Satō's acceptance of the US nuclear umbrella and his promulgation of the Three Non-Nuclear Principles and the Four Pillars of Nuclear Policy did not completely put to bed the question of an independent nuclear deterrent. Japanese attitudes towards nuclear weapons, at both the popular and elite levels, were in flux and often contradictory. Public opinion was opposed to Japan acquiring nuclear weapons and all the more opposed to the presence of US nuclear weapons on Japanese territory. Indeed despite, and perhaps partially because of, Satō's efforts to raise the Japanese people's "defense consciousness," the arrival in 1968 of the nuclear powered US aircraft carrier *Enterprise* in the Japanese port of Sasebo was greeted by large crowds of protesters.[46] The visit seemed to solidify Japanese opposition to nuclear weapons, the US–Japanese alliance, and the Vietnam war, since the *Enterprise* was totemic of all three. Indeed Satō was astonished by the levels of violence caused by the protests and saw this as dashing his hopes to change Japanese attitude towards defense issues.[47]

168 *F. Hoey*

The Japanese public was also reported to be overwhelmingly opposed to Japan developing its own nuclear weapons. However, this attitude was apparently not as strongly held as it may have appeared, since an astonishing 75 percent of Japanese felt at the same time that it was inevitable that Japan would arm itself with nuclear weapons in the near future.[48] Furthermore, recent research has demonstrated that the Japanese public was not opposed to Japan possessing the capacity to defend itself, but feared the US–Japanese alliance could lead to entrapment in a conflict and that the Japanese government could abuse its military power for domestic political ends.[49] While the Japanese public held a deep mistrust of *US* nuclear power, opinions regarding Japanese nuclear power were more flexible and unpredictable.

As negotiations towards an international nonproliferation regime progressed in the mid-1960s, various strands of opinion emerged within the Japanese elite. Of particular concern (in common with other developed non-nuclear states) were issues of security, access to civilian nuclear technology and, perhaps most importantly, the loss of a free hand on achieving the status and prestige of a nuclear-weapon power in the future. For instance, in December 1967, as he was taking up his position as Japanese ambassador in Washington, Shimoda Takezo noted that any decision on foreswearing nuclear weapons was for future generations to make.[50] In this vein one of the main, and successful, Japanese demands regarding the NPT text was that the treaty be put under regular five-year reviews.[51] Other than such limited interventions, Japanese diplomats and leaders did not contribute to the evolving NPT as might have been expected given its great power inclinations and the fact that the treaty regime sought to contain, in part, Japan's future capabilities.[52]

One of the main reasons for Japan's approach to the NPT negotiations is that the Japanese people and Japanese decision makers had not yet decided on what Japan's nuclear future would look like. Was Japan to pursue an idealistic and purely pacifistic international policy and thus foreswear nuclear weapons on moral grounds? Such views were more likely to be held by opposition politicians and their supporters but also included members of the ruling and traditionally conservative Liberal Democratic Party. Others viewed the prospect of Japan being permanently relegated to second-class status in world affairs as anathema and argued that Japan needed to keep a "free hand." Such free-handers within the Liberal Democratic Party later coalesced into the so-called *Seirankai* (the Blue Storm Society), and were able to somewhat delay but not prevent Japan's ratification of the Non-Proliferation Treaty.[53]

The debate was joined by a new school of international relations scholars. These scholars eschewed both pacifism and great power pretensions and argued against an independent nuclear deterrent on the basis of (what they felt) were realist evaluations of Japan's position within the world. Such lines of argument were strongly articulated in a top secret expert report commissioned by Satō's Cabinet Office. The so-called *1968/70 report* (because the technical and political aspects were made available at different times) – which was leaked to the press in the mid-1990s – recommended that, while Japan had the ability to develop a

Japan 169

small number of nuclear weapons and could direct its missile technology towards the creation of a delivery system, Japan should forego acquiring an independent nuclear deterrent for a number of reasons.[54]

The authors of the report argued that Japan's large population and series of huge cities stretched along a narrow volcanic archipelago left no space for an appropriate test site. These geographical conditions also made mutually assured destruction, the necessary condition of deterrence, unworkable. China and the Soviet Union are large continental powers whose leaders could have conceivably concluded that a massive first strike directed against Japan would make a retaliatory strike nearly impossible. The report also concluded that a nuclear weapons program would cause such opposition and unrest that a regime similar to the wartime autocracy would be required in order to maintain public order. On balance the report deemed an independent nuclear deterrent both impracticable on military and dangerous on domestic political grounds and therefore concluded that Japan should not opt for an independent deterrent.

Given the archival situation, it is difficult to fully assess the impact that this report had on Satō and on other policy-makers. Nevertheless, it is significant that the report came at Satō's request at a time when he was attempting to come to a decision on nuclear issues. Suggestively, after the report's completion, Satō moved further away from toying with the idea of an independent deterrent and closer towards accepting the Non-Proliferation Treaty. But at the same time, he still cherished hopes of leveraging Japan's nuclear renunciation to the benefit of the reversion of Okinawa.

Bartering over the reversion of Okinawa

By the time Nixon entered office in January 1969, attitudes across Japan on the question of Okinawa reversion had grown intense. American diplomats in Japan signaled Washington that agreement on reversion would have to take place in the short term to avoid long-term damage to bilateral relations.[55] The public mood was also decidedly against waiving the non-introduction principle in order to allow the United States to retain its nuclear arsenal in Okinawa in the aftermath of reversion to Japan.[56] Satō had tried to maintain a "blank slate" and retain some measure of flexibility on the issue of US nuclear presence before entering into negotiations. However, he came to realize that this was politically unfeasible and, in March 1969, he publicly declared his intention to seek the withdrawal of US nuclear weapons from Okinawa in addition to the island's reversion to Japan.[57] Satō had been encouraged to pursue these aims by an internal Japanese report which indicated that the United States could maintain its nuclear deterrent over Japan by relying on submarine launched ballistic missiles, and thereby foregoing the need for land bases.[58]

Fortunately for Satō, Nixon was prepared to agree to the reversion of the islands to Japanese control. The US President was constrained by his need to satisfy the Pentagon that an agreement with Japan would not hinder US military capabilities in East Asia.[59] Accordingly, Nixon signed National Security Decision Memorandum

170   *F. Hoey*

May 13 on 28, 1969, which provided for reversion under the condition that "essential elements governing U.S. military use" were respected. The memo also afforded Nixon broad and personal discretion over the removal of nuclear weapons on the understanding that the US would retain "emergency storage and transit rights."[60] The removal of nuclear weapons followed by an agreement on emergency storage rights had been the solution to the question of US nuclear bases on Iwo Jima and Chichi Jima when they were returned to Japanese administration in 1968 and served as a template for Okinawa.[61]

However, Nixon had a separate personal and political concern. His election victory was helped, in part, by support from Southern states, whose textile industries were declining in the face of foreign competition from Japan and other East Asian countries. Nixon had promised Southern political leaders that he would solve this problem when in office. His upcoming meeting with the Japanese prime minister, who was seeking a major concession with regard to Okinawa, presented a seemingly perfect opportunity. Nixon intended to exchange a "voluntary" Japanese export restraint agreement in return for the reversion of Okinawa and the removal of US nuclear weapons.[62]

Satō was made aware of these preconditions by his private envoy to the White House, Professor Wakaizumi Kei.[63] Nonetheless, Satō seems to have ignored these reports and sought to link Japan's accession to the Non-Proliferation Treaty (which was then entering its final phase of negotiations) with the denuclearization of Okinawa. In his mind, joining the NPT would have made Japan a non-nuclear-weapon state with the obligation to avoid being host to any other nation's nuclear bases. Satō most likely concluded that since the US had been pushing for the global nonproliferation regime and had specifically targeted Japan, Washington would welcome Tokyo's policy proposal. In return, the US would grant the reversion of Okinawa and remove US nuclear weapons from military bases on the island. In this way, Satō would pull off a diplomatic triumph in return for a policy that already had support in Japan. Therefore, Satō stressed this line when he met with Nixon's Secretary of State William Rogers in July 1969.[64] Apparently satisfied with this meeting, Satō noted in his diary that "I wanted to entangle the Okinawa problem and the nonproliferation treaty, I am sure I was able to deepen [Rogers'] understanding."[65] He expanded on this theme at a press conference a few days later, stating that "the bottom line is that the existence of a nuclear capability within Japanese territory would mean that Japan could not be described as a non-nuclear nation."[66]

Unfortunately, this gambit of linking the nonproliferation treaty with Okinawa did not produce the desired reaction, since the Nixon administration was not willing to sacrifice US deterrent capabilities for the sake of furthering the nonproliferation treaty. In addition, neither Nixon nor his national security advisor Henry Kissinger were as concerned with nonproliferation as the preceding Democratic administrations had been.[67] When Satō met Nixon in November 1969 to finalize an agreement on Okinawa reversion, the US president seems to have given Satō a strong hint that Japan ought to develop an independent deterrent. While the official memorandum of the conversation noted that the US

Japan 171

president had meant only to encourage Japan's *conventional* and not nuclear capabilities, Nixon apparently left Satō confused.[68] Yet whatever ultimately happened, it was enough to alarm the State Department translator, who alerted his colleagues. Thus, US diplomats worked to "quietly sabotage the whole thing."[69]

On the issue of textiles, however, Nixon effectively ambushed Satō into accepting a comprehensive export limitation agreement in return for non-nuclear reversion. Satō, for his part, promised more than he could deliver on domestically. Thus, instead of being solved in a neat package, the textile saga lingered on for another two years.[70] Nor was the Okinawa question without complications. Nixon demanded a secret agreement, a so-called Agreed Minute to the Joint Communiqué, which granted the US the right to reintroduce its nuclear weapons to Okinawa in an emergency situation.[71] Yet Satō was uncomfortable signing such an agreement since, had it become publicly known, it would have placed him and his party in jeopardy. However, Satō had no choice but to comply. Tellingly, he kept his copy of the secret agreement in his personal papers, and did not deposit it in an official file, reasoning that in a perilous situation any future Japanese prime minister would respond positively to a US request to deploy nuclear weapons.[72]

As their diplomatic opening to Communist China developed, Nixon and Kissinger saw potential in using the prospect of a re-armed and/or nuclear-armed Japan to draw Beijing closer to the United States.[73] Following Japan's signature of the NPT in February 1970, Nixon indicated to Satō "Japan might take its time [on ratification] and thus keep any potential enemy concerned." Satō responded by re-affirming Japan's intention not to pursue an independent deterrent, going so far as to say that "all Japanese abhor nuclear weapons."[74] Some months later Nixon and Kissinger returned to this theme in a private conversation caught on the secret White House taping system. They dismissed the NPT as an achievement of the Democrats and the State Department, and noted the benefit of Japan developing nuclear weapons since this would, as Kissinger stated, "scare the living bejeezus out of the Chinese and force them towards us."[75]

Satō has been criticized for his attempt to link Japan's signature of the NPT with the reversion of Okinawa. Many have argued that Satō was the only senior policy-maker to attempt this linkage, and that he misread the mood in the LDP.[76] However, the failure of this initiative lies with Nixon not Satō, who should not be blamed for the fact that the Nixon administration seemed to outwardly favor the NPT, while keeping the actual policy private. Given these circumstances, with State Department envoys pushing for Japan's accession, it was reasonable for Satō to conclude that the US government was a supporter of the treaty. Had Satō a partner in seeking nonproliferation in the White House – which he clearly thought he had – then it is conceivable that Satō could have struck a grand bargain on Japan's nuclear posture and on the reversion of Okinawa. Such an agreement would have attracted overwhelming public support, which could well have overcome the opposition of "free-handers" within the LDP.

Satō's failure to link the NPT with Okinawa reversion should not undermine his success in leading Japan away from an independent nuclear arsenal and towards reliance on the US extended deterrent. Satō's policy line ultimately paved the way

172 *F. Hoey*

for Japan's eventual accession to the NPT. This was by no means automatic and involved patient diplomacy and domestic political maneuverings on the parts of his successors. It primarily involved negotiating a nuclear safeguards agreement with the International Atomic Energy Agency (IAEA) similar to the self-certification regime afforded to the members of the European Atomic Energy Community (EURATOM). This approach satisfied the representatives of the nuclear power industry, who were concerned that a more invasive inspections regime would leave Japanese companies vulnerable to industrial espionage.[77] The other opponents of NPT ratification were those LDP politicians in favor of Japan maintaining a free hand on the question of an independent deterrent, i.e., the Blue Storm society. They were never able to muster the strength to defeat ratification, but they were able to delay it. Ultimately, in the charged international atmosphere following India's nuclear test, and following the strong endorsement from the by then retired Satō, the Japanese government was able to secure Diet ratification in 1976.[78]

Conclusion

These developments did not quite put the question of an independent Japanese deterrent to rest. Unlike the representatives of the nuclear power industry the "free-handers" were not satisfied with the acquisition of technological prowess. Indicative of such sentiment was an episode in 1969 (prior to Japan's signature on the NPT) when Japanese diplomats greatly alarmed their West German counterparts at a policy planning retreat during which the joint development of an independent deterrent was broached. However their concerns related to the permanent loss of the right to a weapon rather than its actual creation.[79] These sentiments are shared by a body of elite opinion which remains committed to such a hedging strategy. From time to time leading conservative political figures will assert Japan's right to embark on a weapons program.[80] However these should also be understood in the context of a *tacit* or *latent* deterrent rather than an active desire to leave the NPT framework.[81] Moreover Japan remains reliant on and committed to US extended nuclear deterrence for its security, something that would be put in severe jeopardy were it to decide to go it alone.

Japan's acceptance of the NPT was quite a long and difficult journey. Crucial to this story was Satō Eisaku, the Prime Minister who helped define Japan's acceptance of non-nuclear status in return for the protection afforded by the US extended deterrent. His decisions and the changes in his thinking were the result of numerous factors. These included the international context, not least US non-proliferation policy, as well as domestic public opinion and the widespread discomfort regarding nuclear weapons whether Japanese or American. The most important factor was the reversion of Okinawa from US to Japanese control which cast a long shadow. In addition to these external factors Satō's own cautious and deliberate decision-making process should not be discounted. Though Satō found no partner in nonproliferation in Richard Nixon (whose priorities lay elsewhere), he was able to successfully guide his country towards adherence to the nonproliferation treaty regime.

Japan 173

Notes

1 See especially the sterling work of the National Security Archive, especially the "Nuclear Noh Drama" collection in its online "Nuclear Vault," www2.gwu.edu/~nsarchiv/nukevault/ebb291 (accessed October 6, 2014); in December 2015 researchers from the National Security Archive discovered photos of US nuclear bombs present on Okinawa in the US National Archives. See "Nuclear Weapons on Okinawa Declassified December 2015," http://nsarchive.gwu.edu/nukevault/ebb541-Nukes-on-Okinawa-Declassified-2016/#p-3 (accessed July 8, 2016); for an overview of releases by the Japanese Diplomatic Archive, see Kitaoka Shinichi *et al.*, "Iwayuru 'Mitsuyaku' Mondai Ni Kansuru Yūshikisha Iinkai Chōsa Hōkokusho" [Report of the Expert Committee into the Problem of the So-called 'Secret Agreements'], Ministry of Foreign Affairs, Japan, March 9, 2010, www.mofa.go.jp/mofaj/gaiko/mitsuyaku/pdfs/hokoku_yushiki.pdf (accessed October 8, 2014).

2 John Swenson-Wright, *Unequal Allies? United States Security and Alliance Policy toward Japan, 1945–1960* (Stanford CA: Stanford University Press, 2005), 150–159.

3 Ibid., 141, 150–186.

4 Satō, Lower House Budget Committee, December 11, 1967, Kokkai Kiroku [Record of the National Diet], http://kokkai.ndl.go.jp (accessed February 15, 2014).

5 Ariel Levite, "Never Say Never Again: Nuclear Reversal Revisited," *International Security* 27, no. 3 (2003): 71.

6 For example, the award of the Nobel Peace Prize to Satō was due, in part, to his Three Non-nuclear Principles. Following revelations that his private views on nuclear weapons were more pragmatic and less utopian the official history of the prize denounced Satō's prize as its greatest mistake. See Gavan McCormack, *Client State: Japan in the American Embrace* (Verso: London, 2007), 157; crying foul on Satō remains popular. See Steve Rabson, review of Yukinori Komine, "Okinawa Confidential, 1969: Exploring the Linkage between the Nuclear Issue and the Base Issue," *Diplomatic History* 37, no. 4 (2013): 807–840, www.h-net.org/~diplo/reviews/PDF/AR444.pdf (accessed February 9, 2014).

7 See especially Kurosaki Akira, *Kakuheiki to Nichibeikankei – Amerika no kakufu-kakusan gaikō to Nihon no sentaku, 1960–1976* [Nuclear Weapons and US–Japanese Relations: America's Nuclear Non-proliferation Diplomacy and Japan's Choice, 1960–1976] (Tokyo: Yushisha, 2006); and Ayako Kusunoki, "The Sato Cabinet and the Making of Japan's Non-Nuclear Policy," *The Journal of American-East Asian Relations* 15 (2008): 38f.; on reassessing Japanese opinion on security matters, see Paul Midford, *Rethinking Japanese Public Opinion and Security: From Pacifism to Realism?* (Stanford, CA: Stanford University Press, 2011).

8 Kusunoki, "The Sato Cabinet and the Making of Japan's Non-Nuclear Policy."

9 Kurosaki, *Kakuheiki to Nichibeikankei*.

10 See also Fintan Hoey, *Satō, America and the Cold War: US-Japanese Relations, 1964–1972* (Basingstoke; New York: Palgrave Macmillan, 2015).

11 "Japan Came Close to a Wartime A-bomb," *New Scientist* 147, no. 1988 (1995): 4; Glenn Davis, "Japan Scientist Breaks Silence on Bomb," *United Press International,* July 19, 1995; Kurosaki, *Kakuheiki to Nichibeikankei*, 5.

12 Ibid.

13 Nicholas Evans Sarantakes, *Keystone: The American Occupation of Okinawa and US–Japanese Relations* (College Station, TX: Texas A&M University Press, 2000), 40–59; Michael Schaller, *Altered States: The United States and Japan since the Occupation* (New York: Oxford University Press, 1997), 59–61; see also the Treaty of Peace with Japan, September 8, 1951, The World and Japan Database Project, University of Tokyo, www.ioc.u-tokyo.ac.jp/~worldjpn/documents/texts/docs/19510908.T1E.html (accessed February 15, 2014); see also MemCon (Dulles, Shigemitsu),

174 *F. Hoey*

August 19, 1956, *Foreign Relations of the United States* (FRUS), 1955–1957, XXIII, 1: Japan (Washington, DC: US GPO, 1991), 202ff.

14 Swenson-Wright, *Unequal Allies,* 133.

15 Robert S. Norris, William M. Arkin, and William Burr, "Where They Were: How Much did Japan Know?" *The Bulletin of the Atomic Scientists* 56, no. 1 (2000): 12.

16 Swenson-Wright, *Unequal Allies,* 137.

17 Office of the Assistant Secretary of Defense (Atomic Energy), "History of the Custody and Deployment of Nuclear Weapons (U), July 1945 through September 1977," February 1978, Office of the Secretary of Defense and Joint Staff, FOIA Requester Service Center, www.dod.mil/pubs/foi/operation_and_plans/Nuclear ChemicalBiologicalMatters/306.pdf (accessed October 6, 2014).

18 Norris *et al.*, "How Much did Japan Know?" 12.

19 Swenson-Wright, *Unequal Allies*, 138f.

20 Kurosaki, *Kakuheiki to Nichibeikankei*, 6.

21 Swenson-Wright, *Unequal Allies*, 143.

22 "Description of Consultation Arrangements under the Treaty of Mutual Cooperation and Security with Japan," and "Summary of Unpublished Agreements Reached in Connection with the Treaty of Mutual Cooperation and Security with Japan," June 1960, National Security Archive, Nuclear Vault, Nuclear Noh Drama, docs. 1 and 2, www2.gwu.edu/~nsarchiv/nukevault/ebb291 (accessed October 6, 2014).

23 Telegram from the Embassy in Tokyo to the Secretary of State, April 4, 1963, ibid.

24 Schaller, *Altered States,* 160f., 188; Nakashima Takuma, "Satō Eisaku: Okinawa Henkan Mondai He No Torikumi," [Satō Eisaku: Grappling with the Problem of Okinawa Reversion], in *Jinbutsu De Yomu Gendai Nihon Gaikō Shi: Konoe Fumimaro kara Koizumi Junichirō made*, eds. Sadō Akihiro, Komiya Kazuo, and Hattori Ryūji (Tokyo: Yoshikawa Kōbunkan, 2008), 190f.

25 Shane J. Maddock, *Nuclear Apartheid: The Quest for American Atomic Supremacy from World War II to the Present* (Chapel Hill, NC: University of North Carolina Press, 2010).

26 Report by the Committee on Nuclear Proliferation, January 21, 1965, FRUS, 1964–1968, XI, 174.

27 Maddock, *Nuclear Apartheid*, 181–216.

28 MemCon, November 23, 1964, FRUS, 1964–1968, XI, 122–125.

29 National Archives and Records Administration, College Park, MD, USA (NACP), Record Group 59 (RG 59) General Records of the Department of State, Records of the Ambassador at Large, Llewellyn E. Thompson, 1961–1970, Thompson Committee, 1964, Lot 67 D 2, Box 25; McNaughton to Thompson, November 20, 1964; Note this memo is heavily redacted. The names of the two countries in question are redacted. However, the descriptions of the two countries fit with India and Japan, given their location in Asia, their technological capacities for producing nuclear weapons, their vulnerability to a Chinese bomb, etc. Furthermore, these descriptions are repeated in other non-sanitized documents.

30 Telegram from the Embassy in Japan to the Department of Defense, December 29, 1964, FRUS, 1964–1968, XXIX, 2, 55ff.

31 Airgram from the Embassy in Japan to the Department of State, December 4, 1964, ibid., 48.

32 MemCon, January 12, 1965, ibid., 70; when this assurance recently came to light it drew press condemnation and was presented in the Japanese press as an attempt by the United States to nuclearize Japan. In response Robert McNamara defended the policy as a means of preventing Japan from developing its own nuclear weapons. "'Nichū sensō nara kaku hōfuku o' Satō shushō, 65 nen hōbei tokini" [Prime Minister Satō, on US trip in 1965 asked for US nuclear retaliation against China in the event of a Sino-Japanese war], *Asahi Shinbun*, December 12, 2008.

33 MemCon, January 12, 1965, FRUS, 1964–1968, XXIX, 2, 77.

Japan 175

34 Royama Michio and Kase Miki argue that Satō was bluffing. "Former PM Bluffed on Japanese Nukes," *Mainichi Daily News*, August 6, 1999.

35 Takashi Oka, "As the Japanese Say: Premier Sato would Tap his Way across a Stone Bridge to be Sure it was Safe," *New York Times*, November 16, 1969.

36 Progress on the MLF proposal was undermined by a combination of internal divisions in the Johnson administration, disquiet among members of Congress, French objections, and, the opposition of the Soviet Union and its Eastern European satellites. By early 1967 the US and Soviet policy had moved towards a global nonproliferation regime which killed off the proposal; cf. Maddock, *Nuclear Apartheid*, 251–284.

37 See Treaty of Peace with Japan. See also Memorandum of a Conversation between Secretary of State Dulles and Foreign Minister Shigemitsu, August 19, 1956, FRUS, 1955–1957, XXIII, 1, 202ff.

38 Nakashima, "Satō Eisaku: Okinawa Henkan Mondai He No Torikumi," 193f.

39 Satō to Lower House Budget Committee, December 11, 1967, Kokkai Kiroku [Record of the National Diet], http://kokkai.ndl.go.jp (accessed February 15, 2014).

40 Glenn Hook, "The Nuclearisation of Language: Nuclear Allergy as Political Metaphor," *Journal of Peace Research* 21, no. 3 (1984): 259–275; Kusunoki, "The Sato Cabinet and the Making of Japan's Non-Nuclear Policy," 25–50.

41 Wakaizumi Kei, *Tasaku Nakarishi Wo Shinzemuto Hossu* [I Should Like to Think this was the Best Course Available] (Tokyo: Bungei Shunjū, 1994), 140f.; Satō to Lower House, January 27, 1968, *Kokkai Kiroku* [Record of the National Diet], http://kokkai. ndl.go.jp (accessed February 15, 2014).

42 Entry of January 26, 1968, Kusuda Minoru, Kusuda Minoru Nikki, 159; Kusunoki, "The Sato Cabinet and the Making of Japan's Non-Nuclear Policy," 38f.; existing evidence does not confirm the view expressed by Kusonoki Ayako that Satō may have favored the retention of the non-introduction principle as a way of signaling his opposition to the retention by the US of its nuclear bases on Okinawa after reversion.

43 U.A. Johnson to Department of State, January 11, 1968, FRUS, 1964–1968, XXIX, 2, doc. 140, *n2*.

44 Entry of September 16, 1967, Kusuda Minoru, *Kusuda Minoru Nikki*, 260.

45 Kurosaki, *Kakuheiki to Nichibeikankei*, 186–224.

46 Hoey, *Satō, America and the Cold War*, 38ff. See also Thomas Havens, *Fire across the Sea: The Vietnam War and Japan, 1965–1975* (Princeton, NJ: Princeton University Press, 1987), 145–151; Schaller, *Altered States*, 207.

47 See Satō's diary entries for January 16–23, 1968, Satō Eisaku, *Satō Eisaku Nikki* [Diary of Satō Eisaku], ed. Itō Takeshi, vol. 3 (Tokyo: Asahi Shinbun Sha, 1998), 216–221.

48 Yasumasa Tanaka, "Japanese Attitudes toward Nuclear Arms," *The Public Opinion Quarterly* 34, no. 1 (1970): 34f.

49 Midford, *Rethinking Japanese Public Opinion and Security*, 36f.; Midford also warns against assuming the pacifist stance of the Socialist Party was held by its supporters.

50 Kurosaki, *Kakuheiki to Nichibeikankei*, 229.

51 MemCon, October 4, 1967, FRUS, 1964–1968, XI, 516ff.

52 Mohamed I. Shaker, *The Nuclear Non-proliferation Treaty: Volume 1 of 3. Origins and Implementation, 1959–1979*, 3 volumes (London: Oceana Publications, 1980).

53 Frank C. Langdon, "Japan's Reaction to India's Nuclear Explosion," *Pacific Affairs* 48, no. 2 (1975): 176; James Babb, "The Seirankai and the Fate of its Members: The Rise and Fall of the New Right Politicians in Japan," *Japan Forum* 24, no. 1 (2012): 83f.

54 This report came to light when a leaked copy was made public by the *Asahi Shinbun* newspaper, "Kaku kaihatsu Kanō da ga mottenu" [Able to develop nuclear weapons but will not], *Asahi Shinbun* 13 (November 1994); see also Yuri Kase, "The Costs and Benefits of Japan's Nuclearization: An Insight into the 1968/70 Internal Report," *The Nonproliferation Review* 8, no. 2 (2001): 55–68.

176   *F. Hoey*

55 Memo from the Country Director for Japan (Sneider) to the Assistant Secretary of State for East Asian and Pacific Affairs (W. Bundy), December 24, 1968, FRUS, 1964–1968, XXIX, 2, 310–313.

56 "Shasetsu: Sakadachi Shita 'Okinawa' Gaikō" [Editorial: Topsy-turvy 'Okinawa' Diplomacy], *Asahi Shinbun*, January 9, 1969; Wakaizumi Kei, "Japanese–American Relations after the Reversion of Okinawa," paper presented at Japan–US Kyoto Conference, January 1969, Copy in NACP, RG 59, Central Files, Subject Numeric File 1967–1969, POL 1 JAPAN-US; although the US adopted the "neither confirm nor deny" line it was as Satō himself told the Diet, "international common knowledge" that Okinawa was home to nuclear weapons; Satō to Upper House, March 17, 1969, Kokai Kaigi Roku [Record of the National Diet]; see also Takashi Oka, "US Officers Cling to Okinawa Bases: Fear Japan will Limit their Use after Reversion," *New York Times,* April 7, 1969.

57 Satō to Upper House Budget Committee, March 10, 1969, Kokai Kaigi Roku [Record of the National Diet]; it is difficult to state with confidence when the naturally cautious and taciturn Satō opted to pursue non-nuclear reversion, but he seems to have come to this conclusion between January and March 1969; cf. *Satō and America*, 87–90.

58 The committee which produced the report was chaired by Kusumi Tadao, formerly a captain in the Imperial Japanese Navy; cf. Sarantakes, *Keystone*, 169.

59 Nixon's Defense Secretary Melvin Laird told the author that the Pentagon had a "veto over the whole thing"; interview with Melvin R. Laird, August 7, 2007.

60 Richard M. Nixon Library, Yorba Linda, CA, USA [RNL], National Security Council (NSC) Files, VIP Visits, Box 925, National Security Decision Memorandum 13, Policy Toward Japan, May 28, 1969.

61 Information Memo from the Assistant Secretary of State for East Asian and Pacific Affairs (W. Bundy) to Secretary of State Rusk, March 23, 1968, FRUS, 1964–1968, XXIX, 2, 268ff.

62 I.M. Destler, Haruhiro Fukui, and Hideo Satō, *The Textile Wrangle: Conflict in Japanese–American Relations, 1969–1971* (Ithaca, NY: Cornell University Press, 1979). Schaller, *Altered States*, 215–225.

63 Wakaizumi and Swenson-Wright, *The Best Course Available*, 121.

64 Diplomatic Archive, Tokyo, Rekishi Shiryō Toshiteno Kachi ga Mitomereraru Kaiji [Disclosure of High Value Historical Materials], CD 1, 01–529; Satō sōri to Rogers kokumuchōkan tono kaidan yōshi [Summary of Conversation between PM Satō and Secretary of State Rogers), July 31, 1969; Secretary of State, Washington to American Embassy Bucharest, "Secretary's Call on PriMin Sato," August 2, 1969, in National Security Archive, *Japan and the United States*, doc. 1108.

65 Entry of July 31, 1969, Satō Eisaku, *Satō Eisaku Nikki*, 481; "Okinawa mondai to kaku fukakusan jōyaku to o karamasete hanashiatta tsumoride, rikai o fukumeru koto ga dekita to kakushinsuru."

66 Quoted in Wakaizumi and Swenson-Wright, *The Best Course Available*, 130.

67 Francis Gavin, *Nuclear Statecraft: History and Strategy in American's Atomic Age* (Ithaca, NY: Cornell University Press, 2012), 104–119, or Maddock, *Nuclear Apartheid*, 283f.

68 RNL, NSC Files, VIP Visits, Box 924; MemCon (Nixon, Satō), November 19, 1969.

69 Quoted in Seymour M. Hersh, *The Price of Power: Kissinger in the Nixon White House* (New York: Simon and Schuster, 1983), 381; see also Schaller, *Altered States*, 218f.

70 Wakaizumi and Swenson-Wright, *The Best Course Available*; or Destler *et al.*, *The Textile Wrangle*.

71 RNL, NSC Files, VIP Visits, Box 924. Memo for the President from Kissinger, "Meeting with Prime Minister Sato," November 18, 1969.

72 Wakaizumi and Swenson-Wright, *The Best Course Available*. Kitaoka Shinichi *et al.* "Iwayuru 'Mitsuyaku' Mondai Ni Kansuru Yūshikisha Iinkai Chōsa Hōkokusho"

Japan 177

[Report of the Expert Committee into the Problem of the So-called "Secret Agreements"], Ministry of Foreign Affairs, Japan, March 9, 2010, www.mofa.go.jp/mofaj/gaiko/mitsuyaku/pdfs/hokoku_yushiki.pdf (accessed October 8, 2014).

73 See Yukinori Komine, "The 'Japan Card' in the United States Rapprochement with China, 1969–1972," *Diplomacy and Statecraft* 20, no. 3 (2009): 494–514.

74 MemCon, January 7, 1972, in Digital National Security Archive, *Japan and the United States: Diplomatic, Security and Economic Relations, 1960–1976*, doc. 1500, http://nsarchive.chadwyck.com (accessed October 8, 2014).

75 A transcription of the conversation is in FRUS, 1969–1976, E-2, doc. 58; curiously, Kissinger's "bejeezus" comment is redacted from the printed transcript but can be heard on the audio copy. See RNL, White House Tapes, Conversation No. 732–11; available from www.nixontapes.org (accessed January 9, 2014).

76 Kurosaki, *Kakuheiki to Nichibeikankei*, 232.

77 B. Goldschmidt, "The Negotiation of the Non-Proliferation Treaty (NPT)," *IAEA Bulletin* 22, no. 3/4 (1980): 78ff.; Daniel I. Okimoto, "Japan's Non-Nuclear Policy: The Problem of the NPT," *Asian Survey* 15, no. 4 (1975): 317.

78 John E. Endicott, "The 1975–76 Debate over Ratification of the NPT in Japan," *Asian Survey* 17, no. 3 (1977): 275–292.

79 See, "'Kaku' o motometa Nihon" hōdō ni oite toriage rareta bunshonado ni kansuru Gaimushō chōsa hōkoku-sho [Ministry of Foreign Affairs archival investigation regarding "The Japan that possesses "Nuclears'" broadcast], Ministry of Foreign Affairs of Japan, www.mofa.go.jp/mofaj/gaiko/kaku_hokoku (accessed January 8, 2015); these revelations arose from a Japanese television investigation of German sources which led to a release of much pertinent information by the Diplomatic Archive in Tokyo. Unfortunately it is a rare example to date of archival openness on the subject.

80 See for example the comments made by former Defense Minister Ishiba Shigeru regarding Japan's "tacit" nuclear deterrent. Quoted in Chester Dawson, "In Japan, Provocative Case for Staying Nuclear: Some Say Bombs' Potential as Deterrent Argues for Keeping Power Plants Online," *Wall Street Journal*, October 28, 2011.

81 See Levite, "Never Say Never Again."

10 Mexican nuclear diplomacy, the Latin American nuclear-weapon-free zone, and the NPT grand bargain, 1962–1968

Jonathan Hunt

Mexican *Subsecretaría de Relaciones Exteriores* (Undersecretary of Foreign Affairs) Alfonso García Robles addressed the First Committee of the United Nations General Assembly (UNGA) on May 16, 1968 about the draft nuclear nonproliferation treaty that the Eighteen-Nation Committee on Disarmament (ENDC) had referred to two months earlier. He contrasted that treaty with the 1968 Treaty of Tlatelolco, which prohibited the introduction of nuclear weapons in Latin America, a region whose "special conditions" permitted "a multilateral instrument which, from the standpoint of disarmament and treaty law is undeniably far superior to the draft before us."[1] García Robles had guided the nuclear-weapon-free zone (NWFZ) treaty through a chain of shoals arising from Latin America's Cold War: US hegemony and anticommunism, Cuba's revolutionary isolation, and growing militarism in Argentina and Brazil.

With a General Assembly vote looming, García Robles insisted that two elements of the Treaty on the Non-Proliferation of Nuclear Weapons (NPT) would need to be bolstered if it was to achieve a commanding majority: nuclear-weapon states (NWS) would have to accept "first steps" towards disarmament and help with access to the peaceful uses of nuclear energy.[2] His intervention that day would yield a final handful of revisions in a long line of Mexican amendments whose collective addition helped level the playing field in the ensuing global nuclear order. The significance of Mexican nuclear arms control diplomacy in the 1960s lay in the relationship between concurrent efforts to prohibit nuclear weapons in Latin America and halt their spread elsewhere. The two negotiations were always seen as bearing upon one another. UN Secretary General U Thant expressed his hope in 1965 that the Latin American talks would have a "catalytic effect on other initiatives for denuclearization, for nonproliferation, and for other measures of disarmament," a view shared by US arms controllers.[3]

The Treaty of Tlatelolco opened for signature on February 14, 1967, seventeen months before the NPT was finalized. García Robles served as chair of the treaty's negotiating commission, where he helped orchestrate a low barrier to entry into force, language that effectively disallowed "peaceful" nuclear explosives, and a strong inspection regime managed by the International Atomic Energy Agency (IAEA) – the first time that the agency had been tapped to impose multilateral safeguards. Mexico thereafter stood in the vanguard of efforts to draft a nonproliferation treaty that better embodied a postcolonial conception of nuclear rights and responsibilities rather than a superpower-led effort to freeze the status quo. Its contributions to the final NPT text included four new articles and various preambular statements either inspired by the Treaty of Tlatelolco or formulated by Mexican officials to add technical assistance and arms control pledges to nonproliferation as legal pillars of the treaty's "grand bargain."

For García Robles, regional identity, economic interests, and antinuclear norms dictated how he set the course of Mexican nuclear diplomacy. On the one hand, Latin American solidarity was seen as crucial. On the other hand, Mexico's status as a non-nuclear-weapon state hungry for socio-economic development through nuclear technology was also determinative.[4] Finally, García Robles commitment to nuclear arms control and disarmament throughout his career reflected a sense of "duty" to avert nuclear war, which he portrayed as a threat to "the survival of the human race" and "the whole Earth."[5] Mexican nuclear diplomacy was thus shaped by Latin American traditions of anticolonialism and cooperation, politico-economic affinities with other postcolonial nation states, and an ethical inclination toward nuclear disarmament.

Connecting the histories of the Treaty of Tlatelolco and the NPT makes clear how regional powers such as Mexico availed themselves of multilateral tools to ensure that a global nuclear order accorded with their identities and interests. From this vantage point, more than US hegemony or Cold War politics drove the NPT; regional actors, including those from Latin America and the Global South more generally, had a hand in its construction.[6] Scholars have usually portrayed the NPT as a Cold War production meant to soothe European insecurity on account of Germany's division after the Second World War and the flux of US–Soviet relations.[7] Yet, nation-states in the Middle East, Africa, Asia, and Latin America were centrally involved, judging the value of nuclear prohibitions according to their own geopolitical circumstances, international reputations, societal priorities, and judgments about the international system's efficacy, equality, and justness.[8]

Mexico's role in the making of the NPT helps reframe our narratives about global nuclear diplomacy and Latin America's Cold War. Inter-American nuclear diplomacy in the 1960s exemplified the interactive relationship between the making of regional and global nuclear regimes. Correspondingly, it illustrated the active role that Latin American states could play in world affairs. The entangled negotiations showed that regional nuclear regimes did not simply compete with those of global purview; they also altered their constitutions by virtue of setting precedents, sharing actors, and setting up quid pro quo's.[9] As the hemisphere's hegemon, the United States could at times dictate terms to its southern neighbors.[10] Yet, Latin American actors could also exploit superpower interest in the region's ideological struggles to solicit financial assistance, military arms sales, and counterinsurgency training to fight those battles.[11] Latin Americans were savvy operators in multilateral forums and international

180 *J. Hunt*

organizations as well. In the case of the NWFZ, the United States made numerous concessions to Latin American diplomatic realities.

Thanks to the success of the Treaty of Tlatelolco and a tilt from the Industrial North to the Global South in the UNGA, where Latin American delegations had become a crucial voting bloc by 1965, Mexico also left a lasting imprint on global nuclear governance as a regime builder. At least in reference to nuclear war and peace, Latin America was not merely a "workshop of empire" during the Cold War. At critical junctures, it served as an architect of world order, helping transform the NPT from a superpower entente into a global settlement by informing how it would accommodate the interests of non-nuclear-weapon states, especially those dreaming of sovereign equality in the Global South.[12]

The origins of a Latin American nuclear-weapon-free zone

Various proposals for restricting the presence of nuclear weapons emanated from Latin America from 1958 to 1962. It was Brazil's representative to the UNGA, however, who first articulated the idea of a Latin America free of nuclear weapons on September 20, 1962, weeks before President John F. Kennedy announced the presence of Soviet missiles in Cuba.[13] Deliberations on the resolution set the tone for future debates about regional denuclearization. The original draft called for limits on the transit of "nuclear weapons or carrying devices" through the zone before even trivial limits on US military prerogatives were dropped "as a result of strong US objections."[14] Meanwhile, Argentina's envoy "strongly cautioned that a nuclear weapon-free zone could freeze Latin American states into a permanent state of nuclear inferiority."[15]

The Cuban Missile Crisis galvanized efforts to manage nuclear technology at the regional and global levels.[16] At the United States' urging, the Organization of American States (OAS) passed a resolution authorizing individual or collective action against Cuba. Denuclearization held out another potential solution to the standoff as well as a prophylactic against future crises. Washington gave a positive, if cautious, reply to Brasília's proposal as reward for the OAS resolution. Officials in the US Department of State deemed it a potential "face-saver." As a "bona fide Latin American initiative," it might permit Cuba's revolutionary Prime Minister, Fidel Castro, to concede without embarrassment.[17] The US Arms Control and Disarmament Agency (ACDA) endorsed the idea of NWFZs in Latin America and Africa given regional consensus, robust verification, other nuclear powers' acquiescence, and "freedom for US nuclear weapons to transit the zone." The agency concluded that denuclearization "would go a long way toward preventing similar problems from arising in that area in the future."[18] However, the Joint Chiefs of Staff (JCS) cautioned that denuclearization talks would not ensure the removal of Soviet missiles and might instead narrow options.[19] The White House took the middle course, insisting that Cuban "participation was essential" while presenting US views as favorable.[20]

Brazil tabled the motion at the UNGA the day after Khrushchev announced the withdrawal of Soviet missiles from Cuba. Bolivia and Chile co-sponsored free of nuclear weapons "to strive to make this situation a permanent and immutable one through a multilateral treaty [...] universally respected."[27] He was also haunted by the specter of the Second World War, in whose bloody course of mass violence he claimed his lifelong commitment to nuclear arms control had had its "gradual genesis."[28]

García Robles thus typified a generation of thinkers and politicians whose ethics were forged in the furnace of what Albert Camus called "more than twenty years of insane history" culminating in "a world threatened by nuclear destruction."[29] These searing experiences impelled him to work toward international solutions in an age of nuclear vulnerability.[30] After taking over as Undersecretary of External Affairs following the military coup in Brazil, he presented Brazilian Chancellor Hermes Lima with the idea of regional powers committing not to "manufacture, receive, store, or test nuclear weapons or devices for launching such weapons." Ultimately, five countries – Mexico, Brazil, Bolivia, Chile and Ecuador – issued a declaration along these lines in April 1963. On the occasion, Bolivian President Victor Paz Estenssoro praised the joint action as proof of "the peace-loving tradition of the peoples of the hemisphere."[31]

After Mexico and Brazil circulated the declaration at the ENDC – where the NPT was being negotiated – the five Latin American states convened informally to discuss the next steps. Six more regional partners joined them in petitioning the UN for technical assistance. Many of the core issues mirrored those raised by a global nonproliferation treaty: security assurances, economic development, and peaceful nuclear explosives. Others were unique to Latin America, namely the Cuban question and whether to include dependent territories, foreign military bases, and global shipping lanes. In a speech to the UNGA in November 1963, García Robles drew attention to the benefits of a nuclear-free zone, the "astronomical sums" that would be saved for development and the "incalculable benefit" of peaceful nuclear technology. He listed unsettled questions: the geographical extent; nuclear powers' compliance; how to distinguished peaceful from military activities; the relationship between the zone and decolonization; and methods of control.[32] Differences of opinion on these issues would eventually give rise to a diplomatic triangle between the United States, treaty promoters, and treaty spoilers.

The zone

That November, Mexico also invited the states of Latin America – with the exceptions of Cuba and Venezuela – to Mexico City for consultations. There, García Robles declared that a NWFZ would avert another hemispheric nuclear showdown and attest to Latin American solidarity and self-determination.[33] American support was "at best lukewarm," for various reasons. First, the Joint Chiefs of Staff cautioned that a regional pact might constrain military options by affecting their ability to move nuclear weapons through the Caribbean and the Panama Canal.[34] Revolutionary Cuba was also a vital concern for Washington

Latin American nuclear-weapon-free zone 181

the resolution, which was framed as offering a means by which to prevent such a crisis from recurring in the region. In a White House meeting with various Latin American ambassadors, a high US official stated that the United Nations should take charge of verifying the absence of nuclear weapons from Cuba "and that perhaps the draft [...] for denuclearization is indicating the path towards a solution." Many Latin American governments were more worried about communist subversion from Havana than in nuclear weapons, however.[21]

The issue of Cuban participation and its part in the region's ideological struggles would continue to bedevil talks. At the same time, Brazilian support for the scheme ebbed as the country drifted rightward after a US-backed military coup in 1964. Against this backdrop, leadership of the denuclearization campaign fell to Mexico, whose *Partido Revolucionario Institucional* (Institutional Revolutionary Party, PRI) was trying to steer between leftist and reactionary forces in the region and whose ambassador in Brasília – Alfonso García Robles – would assume the task of creating a firewall against nuclear weapons around a landmass stretching from the Caribbean Sea to Cape Horn.

The architect

With his European legal education, internationalist outlook, and Mexican identity, García Robles embodied the middle ground on which international nuclear diplomacy increasingly occurred as decolonization transformed the global community.[22] Born in Zamora, Michoacán in 1911, García Robles obtained a law degree at the Universidad Nacional Autónoma de México in 1934 and then postgraduate degrees from the University of Paris and the Academy of International Law in The Hague.[23] His first publication, *Pan-Americanism and the Good Neighbor Policy*, displayed the trademarks of his life's work – hemispheric solidarity, resource nationalism, the rule of law, and anticolonialism.[24]

García Robles joined the Mexican *Secretaría de Relaciones Exteriores* (Ministry of Foreign Affairs, SRE) after witnessing the outbreak of the Second World War in Sweden. Once in the Foreign Service, he defended the expropriation of Mexican oil from foreign (mostly US-based) firms, which soured opinion toward him in Washington for decades.[25] He attended the conferences at which the United Nations was founded and then worked for its Secretariat as Director of the Division of Political Affairs until 1957, when he returned to the SRE. He first heard of the nuclear-weapon-free zone initiative after becoming ambassador to Brazil in 1961. The scheme accorded with his background and worldview in three ways. First, it fitted his years of experience at the crossroads of multilateral and United Nations diplomacy. Second, it harmonized with his legal training and internationalist worldview that had at its heart the Bolivarian myth of Latin America as a laboratory for social democracy, constitutional republicanism, pan-Americanism, and anti-imperialism.[26] A constellation of universal values also inspired his actions – the survival of future generations, the preservation of the planetary environment, and his patriarchal sense of responsibility for both. He believed it was the "duty" of Latin Americans living

Latin American nuclear-weapon-free zone   183

and its anticommunist allies in the region. Washington was adamant that nuclear weapons stay out of Havana's hands, whether it participated or not in a NWFZ.[35] To worsen matters, embassy officials in Mexico City warned superiors about García Robles' "long record critical of US motives," including his defense of oil expropriations and his support for a UN resolution affirming non-intervention as a cardinal tenet of international affairs, with its implicit criticism of recent US covert operations.[36]

Other US officials were more supportive. Those at ACDA hoped that Latin American efforts might bail out nonproliferation proceedings, which were floundering in 1965.[37] Mexico was also seen as a key US ally in Latin America because the PRI represented a successful counterexample to the more radical Cuban revolution and Mexican diplomats and intelligence operatives maintained official and clandestine contacts with Castro's island that American intelligence officers found indispensable.[38] Top policy-makers appreciated Mexican military restraint as well. Secretary of State Dean Rusk judged the Mexican government "sincere [...] about disarmament" because it was the only ENDC member then cutting its military budget.[39] Washington therefore lent public support to the enterprise. UN Ambassador Adlai Stevenson commended it at the UNGA as a "constructive contribution," while stressing that leadership would have to come from "Latin American states themselves."[40] The UNGA endorsed the initiative with Resolution 1911 (XVIII) on November 27, 1963, which passed without a single "nay." The United States and ninety others voted "yes," while Cuba and its Warsaw Pact allies abstained.[41]

After the endorsement, a preliminary session of Latin American delegates established the *Comisión Preparatoria para la Desnuclearización de América Latina* (COPREDAL) to begin drafting the treaty.[42] The COPREDAL met in Mexico City four times between March 1965 and February 1967. Latin America's tradition of peaceful cooperation and common desire for economic independence and societal development were repeatedly invoked.[43] Three political circumstances meanwhile shaped the proceedings: the gravitational pull of the United States despite its absence; territorial disputes with extra-territorial nations; and the emergence of rival conservative and revolutionary powers in Latin America. Mexico's ambivalence to the regional hegemon was illustrative. García Robles was chosen as the committee's chair in part because of that proximity; even so, he would insist that the treaty regime have minimal formal ties to the OAS so as neither to ostracize Cuba, which had been expelled from the organization, nor advantage the United States.[44] Regional disagreements played out through committee procedures. Argentina proposed to split activities among three working groups that a coordinating committee would oversee. After Brazil seconded the motion, the commission adopted it. Group A would chart the zone's geographical scope. Group B would draft the verification, inspection, and control articles. And Group C would determine how to induce the nuclear powers to comply "in all aspects and consequences."[45] There was an ulterior motive to this distribution of labor. Mexico was assigned to Group B, whose purview was limited to matters in which Washington had less interest. Mexican

184   *J. Hunt*

Foreign Minister Carrillo Flores subsequently informed Fulton Freeman, the US ambassador in Mexico City, that Argentina and Brazil had conspired to weaken Mexican and hence North American influence.[46]

García Robles regained the initiative when the COPREDAL reconvened in August 1965. Since the verification, inspection, and control articles were comparatively uncontroversial, Group B could submit a preliminary draft with fourteen articles, including a recommendation that the IAEA provide inspection and oversight as an "unbiased" external authority. The US welcomed the agency's inclusion as a useful precedent for nonproliferation talks. However, fears that García Robles would promote non-intervention to the detriment of US interests proved well-founded.[47] The commission adopted a declaration of preambular principles that condemned outside interference, marginalized the US by rejecting formal ties to the OAS, and then organized a negotiating committee consisting of García Robles and two other chairmen. The delegates resolved knotty questions related to scope. In place of a subjective definition based on geography, language, or history, the zone would "equal the sum of the territories in which the treaty applies by virtue of the will of the governments ratifying the treaty."[48] This legal sleight-of-hand would simplify the zone's entry into force by depriving individual states of de facto vetoes.

The Chinese Communist nuclear test in October 1964 had crystallized Washington's interest in nuclear prohibitions.[49] At first, the Latin America initiative was seen as ancillary. But with talks at the ENDC faltering, ACDA officials hoped that it would lend a "new impetus" for the UNGA to call for continuing NPT negotiations. Even so, US ambassadors in Latin America were told to emphasize that "an international non-proliferation agreement would attain the essential objective of a nuclear-free zone."[50] Washington gradually moderated its demands, however, on account of its growing investment in nuclear nonproliferation, most notably when Rusk walked away from Cuban participation as a "*sine qua non* condition" for US support.[51]

After Mexican Foreign Minister Carrillo Flores dispatched a mission to Havana in hopes of persuading Castro to participate, he "confessed" his action to Rusk in October 1965.[52] The secretary of state was receptive, suggesting that the United States might even offer to include the Panama Canal Zone and Guantánamo if its nuclear transit rights were preserved – US forces and nuclear warheads traversed the canal when moving between the Atlantic and the Pacific.[53] This new flexibility became possible as opposition from the Pentagon waned; the previous April the Joint Chiefs of Staff had deemed NWFZs in the "overall security interest of the United States."[54] Rusk followed up by declaring to the Second Special Inter-American Conference in Rio de Janeiro on November 22 that the Latin American talks represented "constructive statesmanship in the best tradition of the hemisphere."[55]

Despite the US turnaround, the talks stalled because of Brazilian and Argentinian obstruction. Rusk inquired about Brazil and Argentina in his meeting with Flores, who characterized them as "unfriendly" and ascribed their hostility to the growing influence of the military in both countries.[56] Flores elaborated on this

Latin American nuclear-weapon-free zone   185

thesis to Freeman two months later based on a conversation with an Argentinian diplomat from which

> he [had] received [the] clear impression [that] Argentina expected [to] acquire its own nuclear capability within [a] "few years," and thus purchase its way into [the] nuclear club as [the] only way to exert its influence internationally on major discussion[s] [of] world affairs.[57]

Washington refused to press allies in Brasília or Buenos Aires, however, in the belief that any persuasion would "backfire," stoking resentment and anti-Americanism as well as "injecting matters in dispute among nuclear powers" into the regional proceedings. A Soviet diplomat would complain that the United States had "lost control" of its Brazilian ally. The State Department nevertheless opted to limit itself to "private and even discreet public support to Latin American efforts," so as "to avoid the impression of US interference or pressure."[58]

This policy left the United States with scant leverage in Mexico City. Delegates finished a draft treaty at the third session, which ran from April 19 to May 4, 1966. With 26 articles and two protocols, the text emphasized sovereign equality, economic development, and non-intervention. Protocol I mandated that nations with dependencies in the region adhere, while Protocol II called on nuclear-weapon states not to defy the zone, abet violators, or "use or threaten to use nuclear weapons" against states parties. Brazil and Colombia submitted an alternative draft as a Trojan horse which put forth a raft of conditions before the treaty would enter into force: ratification by all Latin American states plus extraterritorial powers, security assurances from all nuclear powers, and full-scope IAEA safeguards for all parties. Washington was caught flat-footed. A senior White House official complained that "the Brazilians are pulling the rug out of the LA NF[W]Z and it looks to me as if ACDA is just sitting there."[59] The crisis was averted when García Robles devised an ingenious workaround that took advantage of the zone's legal scope. The zone would enter into force in a piecemeal fashion. After each state party signed and ratified, it could waive the above conditions, after which the denuclearization zone would cover their territories. If they forwent the waiver, their territories would remain outside the zone until the conditions were met. The treaty thus covered willing parties regardless of whether others joined, while permitting other states wide latitude to participate or adhere on their terms.

The final session opened on January 31, 1967, when the definition of nuclear weapons and the legality of peaceful nuclear explosions (PNE) came to the fore. Argentina, Brazil, Colombia, and Venezuela pushed for a definition of nuclear weapons based on intent while Chile, Ecuador, Mexico, and most Central American states insisted that PNEs were intrinsically equivalent to those designed for war. Negotiators debated a final text over the course of two "frenetic" weeks. The US circulated an aide-mémoire characterizing a treaty that would sanction PNEs as "illusory" and reaffirmed its right to ship nuclear weapons through the future zone. Washington also discounted the value of nuclear powers signing

186 *J. Hunt*

Protocol II.[60] While the US position on nuclear transit carried the day, there were still misgivings about PNEs after an explicit reference to an international service was rejected whereby nuclear-weapon states would cheaply provide the explosives for development projects. The majority in Mexico City refused "to be dependent on the grace and favor of nuclear states." The PNE issue afforded countries such as Argentina and Brazil alibis for resisting a treaty that would force them to "forswear nuclear weapons capability on a hemispheric basis alone."[61] Brazil was especially intransigent after the arrival of General Artur da Costa e Silva further "hardened Brazil's position," as his administration touted nuclear energy and PNEs in "an attempt to appeal to a broad nationalist sentiment," harness anti-American opinion, and thereby solidify "considerable moderate and leftist support."[62]

Concerned with the allowance of PNEs, the US Department of State sent an urgent telegram to Ambassador Freeman in Mexico City. He was instructed to inform the COPREDAL that permissive language would prejudice Washington's views on the treaty. Freeman issued a strong dissent, arguing that the best possible compromise had already been reached and that "an additional demarche [...] would not only be totally unproductive but deeply resented."[63] Freeman's successful intervention avoided a rupture with those Latin American governments that generally supported international nuclear diplomacy. The tortured definition of peaceful versus military explosives in the treaty would cause trouble in Geneva and New York, but the United States could ill afford to anger Brazil or Mexico – which served on the ENDC – or the 24 Latin American delegations to the UNGA.

The United States accordingly endorsed the Treaty for the Prohibition of Nuclear Weapons in Latin America on February 14, 1967, when 21 Latin American nations, including Argentina and Brazil, signed it. Cuban officials were conspicuously absent. The final text featured numerous preambular declarations, 36 articles, and the two protocols for foreign powers. With talks at the ENDC set to resume, the US Department of State and ACDA were keen to link the Latin American settlement to their own arms control agenda. Rusk praised the treaty as "a milestone on the road to general and complete disarmament and [...] the conclusion of a worldwide treaty prohibiting the proliferation of nuclear weapons."[64] Officials in ACDA worried, however, that the refusal of the United States to sign Protocol II might prevent Mexican and, in turn, Latin American support from materializing in Geneva and New York.

Of quid pro quos

The successful conclusion of negotiations for a Latin American nuclear-weapon-free zone had a substantial impact on nuclear diplomacy elsewhere. Mexico used its seat on the ENDC as a platform from which to advocate for new preambular and operative language in a nonproliferation treaty that would better serve the interests of non-nuclear-weapon states in the Global South. Mexico also leaned on the nuclear-weapon states to sign Protocol II of the Treaty of Tlatelolco in

Latin American nuclear-weapon-free zone 187

exchange for its support – along with that of its Latin American allies. Argentinian and Brazilian spokesmen availed themselves of the ambiguous language covering PNEs in the Treaty of Tlatelolco to make a case for similarly permissive language in the NPT. Given that the Latin American vote in the UNGA was crucial lest the parliamentary body reject the treaty, the United States and the Soviet Union had to listen to these voices.

The clash of restrictive versus permissive definitions of nuclear explosives exemplified a larger dispute about where to draw the line on the dissemination and development of dual-use nuclear technology. Articles 1, 3, 8, and 13 of the Treaty of Tlatelolco outlawed "nuclear weapons" rather than "nuclear explosives," opening a potential loophole for a nuclear-weapon program.[65] In Geneva, Brazilian, and US representatives clashed over whether the treaty would prohibit "nuclear devices of any kind."[66] The US had promoted the economic benefits of PNEs since President Dwight Eisenhower's Atoms for Peace speech, when the Atomic Energy Commission established Project Plowshare to explore their use for blasting harbors, liberating shale gas, and carving a new pan-isthmian canal through Central America, among other applications.[67] Many observers suspected that Brasília and others backed the peaceful/military distinction to keep their options open.[68] Meanwhile, US and Mexican officials competed to use a US signature on Protocol II for diplomatic leverage. On their end, ACDA tried to trade America's signature for Mexico's endorsement of a restrictive definition of nuclear weapons and the nonproliferation enterprise more generally.[69] For his part, García Robles countered that nuclear-weapon states needed to sign before Latin American states contemplated adhering to another nuclear treaty whose features were less in line with their interests.[70]

In late 1967, ACDA ran an inter-agency review of the implications of signing Protocol II. Transit rights and PNEs remained the paramount concerns. The result was a list of five interpretive statements that would accompany a signature: (1) transit rights unchanged; (2) no effects on territorial claims; (3) non-use provision voided if a Latin American state (e.g., Cuba) backed by a nuclear-armed ally initiated hostilities; (4) territories of Protocol I signatories treated equivalently; (5) and a reissuing of US views that Articles 1 and 5 of the Treaty of Tlatelolco effectively ruled out PNEs.[71] In preparation for Mexican President Gustavo Díaz Ordaz's scheduled visit in October, Rusk advised US President Lyndon Johnson to sign Protocol II (though not Protocol I) without fanfare in concert with the interpretive statement. Johnson duly notified Díaz Ordaz that a signature was forthcoming after congressional consultations. National Security Adviser Walt Rostow brought the US Senate into the loop two weeks later, but the assurances were kept under wraps. Foster counseled waiting until more Latin American states had signed and ratified the Treaty of Tlatelolco, "unless other circumstances arise, such as the necessity of obtaining support for the NPT."[72]

The treaty's conclusion strengthened Mexico's hand in global nuclear diplomacy; it also prefigured forthcoming debates in Geneva and New York. Brazil and Argentina waited until May and September 1967, respectively, to sign the Treaty of Tlatelolco in an implicit complaint against the view of most Latin American

188   *J. Hunt*

states that the treaty ruled out explosives suitable for civil-engineering purposes because they were technically equivalent to advanced "clean" thermonuclear weapons.[73] Brazil then ratified in January 1968, while Argentina and Chile would defer until 1994. The UNGA commended the treaty in June 1968 with eighty-two votes for and zero against, with the sole Latin American holdout, Cuba, its Communist patrons, and France abstaining. García Robles had submitted the Treaty of Tlatelolco to the ENDC for consideration and commendation one week after it opened for signature. Even though he acknowledged then that the treaty lent "necessary stimulus" to a nonproliferation pact, he underscored that its provisions were "even more ambitious than those of a non-proliferation treaty."[74]

Non-nuclear-weapon states were increasingly vocal about what kind of nonproliferation treaty they would support. When the United States and the Soviet Union had tabled identical draft treaties in Geneva that August, Rusk notified Johnson that "the game" had "move[d] to the non-nuclear powers," who served in the ENDC as "first responders" for the broader international community: Brazil, Burma, Ethiopia, India, Mexico, Nigeria, Sweden, and the United Arab Republic.[75] A process that had heretofore survived attacks by the "Germans and the Italians," ACDA officials observed, now faced a "free-for-all" from non-aligned nations.[76]

The Treaty of Tlatelolco served as a touchstone as nuclear haves and have-nots debated the treaty at the ENDC. Because nonproliferation was an intrinsically unequal approach, states outside the superpower blocs called for compensatory articles that would, among other prerogatives, preserve rights to the peaceful uses of nuclear technology. In response, the United States put forward a new article that spelled out an "inalienable right" to exchanges of information as well as research and development "alone or in cooperation with other States" toward the "use of nuclear energy for peaceful purposes." "The idea for such an article," according to the US Department of State, "was originally derived from the Treaty of Tlatelolco," specifically Article 17, which Peru had suggested and Mexico seconded.[77] Then, in the fall of 1967, non-aligned delegates made speeches requesting various changes related to safeguards, technical assistance, peaceful explosives, treaty loopholes, security assurances, and disarmament progress.

Mexican diplomat Jorge Castañeda's presentation on September 19 was the most consequential. What became known as the Mexican amendments would lead to major revisions to the peaceful uses of atomic energy language in Article IV together with three new articles. Castañeda advanced two revisions to Article IV. First, the language should mandate that advanced nuclear powers had a "duty" to supply those states denied nuclear weapons with technical assistance rather than merely reserving a right to it. If some states were to renounce certain scientific and technological activities, it was incumbent upon privileged states to make up the difference. His admonition extended to PNEs. Though "nothing other than nuclear bombs," these devices held "enormous economic potential ... for instance in the execution of vast engineering projects." A new Article V would call for the expeditious establishment of an international service that would provide them cheaply and reliably.[78] Second, he called for a statement in the preamble that the treaty would not hinder the formation of NWFZs to be moved to the body, where it would become Article VII.

Castañeda sought a stronger disarmament mandate as well. While he admitted "it would be an imperfect obligation, since it would not be accompanied by sanctions," he noted that "it would be more than a statement of intention." He accordingly suggested that the committee revise the existing preambular language and insert the resulting language into the body: "Each nuclear-weapon State Party to this treaty undertakes to pursue negotiations in good faith for nuclear arms control and disarmament as well as general and complete disarmament."[79] His inclusion of the phrase "with all speed and perseverance," which was not included in the final treaty, elaborated upon the meaning of "good faith."[80] Alva Myrdal, the head of the Swedish delegation, likened what would become Article VI to a "promissory note."[81] It was significant that a Latin American state proposed these changes. US policy-makers had come to view the regional bloc as a vital ally in the United Nations, where one month earlier Latin American delegations helped moderate a resolution bearing on the aftermath of the June 1967 Arab–Israeli war in the Middle East. In August, the US Ambassador to the UN, Arthur Goldberg, had advised Johnson and his cabinet that "Latin American solidarity was important: [...] the more Latin Americans countries can be involved in world affairs, the better."[82]

Latin American support in the UNGA was indeed crucial. States in the Global South were now in the majority with a host of new member states arising through decolonization. The additional protocols to the Treaty of Tlatelolco were seen as bellwethers. Latin American states "will be observing US action on these protocols closely," Rusk advised Johnson once again, "as an indication of support for the [...] L[atin] A[merican] N[W]FZ and arms control measures generally."[83] The Mexican government was sensitive to American reservations about Protocol I, which would affect US territories, but Protocol II was another matter, particularly since the Soviet Union and France maintained that "they [would] adhere only if the US takes such action." Rusk warned Johnson that Mexico would "have serious problems in signing an NPT until [such] action is taken by the nuclear powers."[84] After the United Kingdom signed in 1967, Mexico doubled its efforts, informing ACDA that a US signature would have a "salutary effect in Latin America" in relation to a nonproliferation treaty. He relayed that Soviet officials had also assured him that they would follow the American lead and even intimated that a late Cuban entry into the zone was possible.[85]

American policy-makers knew that all of Latin America could withhold support from the Treaty of Tlatelolco, "and possibly on other arms control measures such as the NPT," if the US failed to sign.[86] Rusk summarized the state of play in February 1968: "An early public announcement, prior to signature of the Protocol, would be highly desirable in order to encourage ratification of the Treaty by additional Latin American nations and to obtain their support in the NPT negotiations."[87] When Díaz Ordaz visited the White House two days later, Rusk counseled Johnson to inform the Mexican president "that the United States intend[ed] to sign Protocol II," through the five-part interpretive statement.

190   *J. Hunt*

It would be the first time that the United States would voluntarily limit its "freedom of response with nuclear weapons." Rusk concluded "that the circumstances present in Latin America [were] such as to justify a departure from our past policy."[88]

Johnson announced the signature on the first anniversary of the Treaty of Tlatelolco's finalization, describing it as fitting that "this giant step forward should have had its genesis in Latin America, an area which has come to be identified with regional cooperation."[89] García Robles pressed France and the Soviet Union to follow the American example, reminding a Soviet diplomat that Mexico's support for the NPT was conditional on Moscow's signature. García Robles complained that the Soviets were walking away from their prior assurances.[90] Moscow disliked elements of the NWFZ treaty, however, most notably the freedom of nuclear transit and the permissive definition of nuclear explosives. Moreover, the Soviet foreign ministry remained supportive of Cuba's non-involvement on grounds that the treaty had not sufficiently addressed US bases and dependencies in the region.[91] US officials nonetheless urged their Soviet counterparts to sign lest allegations of the "unwillingness [of] nuclear powers themselves to undertake arms control measures" undermine negotiations for a nonproliferation treaty.[92]

When US Vice President Hubert Humphrey visited Mexico City to sign Protocol II in April 1968, he applauded "the inter-American system" for proving again "its capacity to advance the peace and security of the peoples of this hemisphere."[93] He neglected to mention that Latin America had also shown an ability to re-route the course of global nuclear diplomacy, as it transformed the draft nonproliferation from a product of superpower détente into a negotiated settlement that reflected the interests of the wider international community.

Winning over Latin America

Discord was rife in Geneva when the ENDC assembled in February 1968. The UNGA had instructed the committee to submit a draft treaty to it by a deadline of March 15. An Ethiopian delegate remarked that there were "as many ways of looking at this treaty as there were member nations."[94] Brazil still complained about the language outlawing PNEs and joined Romania, Sweden, and others in criticizing the lack of concrete disarmament requirements or security guarantees. Foster nevertheless "felt somewhat better about the reaction of our Southern hemispheric colleague," which had held itself back from outright opposition.[95] Washington's signature on Protocol II had meanwhile softened Mexico's attitude. The addition of three new articles and a stronger Article IV thanks to the Mexican amendments helped as well. García Robles concluded that the revisions had brought "substantial progress in relation to ... the peaceful use of nuclear energy and also an advance, albeit much smaller, in regard to the future adoption of measures of nuclear disarmament."[96]

The Soviet and US co-chairmen inserted some other provisions that neutral delegations wanted. Among these were quinquennial review conferences, fortified references in the preamble to security assurances, the long-stalled Comprehensive Nuclear Test Ban Treaty (CTBT) and peaceful nuclear rights; and a proposed UN Security Council resolution that would offer non-binding security assurances to states parties.[97] These modifications failed to achieve consensus in Geneva, however, as eleven states voted against endorsing the draft treaty. The Brazilians, Indians, and Italians even abstained on whether to submit the new draft to the UNGA. Even so, their decision not to vote against the measure was significant given that the committee's unanimity rule meant that a single rejection would have caused the ENDC to miss the UN-mandated deadline.

The Latin American bloc had considerable parliamentary leverage in the General Assembly even with its membership divided on the virtues of a global nonproliferation treaty. Brazil's UN ambassador and ex-foreign minister inveighed against it for conferring the "lion's share" of benefits on nuclear-weapon states, calling it an "instrument of North American imperialism in the nuclear domain."[98] The Chilean Foreign Minister criticized the United States and the Soviet Union for attempting "what represented for non-nuclear-weapon states the institutionalization of an even crueler form of imperialism, that of technological imperialism."[99] Peaceful nuclear explosives symbolized this perception of a form of technological discrimination that was at best arbitrary and at worst neocolonial.[100]

The General Assembly began discussing the draft treaty in April. It was far from a given that the organization would give the NPT its imprimatur, which was crucial lest the settlement suffer from an absence of political legitimacy. The 124-nation gathering's cosmopolitan make-up and cacophonous atmosphere posed new challenges. The ENDC's small size had moderated differences; the UNGA's larger membership meant greater representativeness, but it also erected more obstacles, namely the possibility that member states with marginal interests in arms control might demand unrelated or untenable concessions in exchange for their votes. According to the French ambassador, non-nuclear-weapon states would find it hard "to repudiate the approval they had always given in principle to the quest."[101] After all, the idea of nonproliferation had been repeatedly endorsed at the UN beginning with the Irish Resolution of 1961. Yet with nuclear-weapon states now decidedly in the minority, the possibility of inconclusive or adverse outcomes was all too real.

Brazil focused its energy on preserving a right to peaceful nuclear explosions. Members of the country's foreign ministry requested a permissive definition of nuclear weapons akin to that in the Treaty of Tlatelolco and consonant with the Costa e Silva administration's promotion of PNEs on developmental and geopolitical grounds. As US diplomats leaned on Latin American officials in the region's capitals, Brazil's attitude further hardened. In April, Foreign Minister Magalhães Pinto informed the US ambassador in Brasília that his government had no intention of signing a treaty that the masses considered "an affront to Brazilian sovereignty." Magalhães Pinto reportedly believed that there were enough like-minded governments in the General Assembly to thwart the treaty or, at minimum, narrow the margin of victory to the point of illegitimacy.[102]

Washington and Moscow maintained a common front as the treaty faced criticism from many quarters. The United States singled out Canada, Japan, Ethiopia, the UAR, and Mexico as the keys to isolating the "few near-nuclears from [the] overwhelming majority [of] countries having no prospect of developing nuclear weapons."[103] Washington also urged Moscow to sign Protocol II, while Soviet emissaries made inroads with their friends in the Third World. The superpowers wagered that the importance ascribed to US–Soviet détente by the international community would discourage a coordinated opposition campaign.

US and Soviet hopes were buoyed by India and Brazil's failure to rally others against the treaty. The Indians canvassed delegations about postponing a vote until after a Conference of Non-Nuclear-Weapon States met in August. Argentina, Brazil, and Chile were receptive, but when Magalhães Pinto met with Rusk, Foster, and others on May 6, he confessed that they did not have the numbers. The rest of Latin America had chosen to follow Mexico's lead. The Brazilians nevertheless suggested that the resolution "commend" rather than "endorse" the NPT.[104] Thus unsuccessful, India formally rejected the treaty on May 14 on grounds that it would "fossilize and legitimate the status quo."[105]

The Latin American and African blocs were the largest in the General Assembly, accounting for nearly half of delegations between them and, with the Western and Eastern delegations, more than two-thirds – a commanding majority. Mexico was now the key to Latin America. This presented García Robles with wide latitude to write into the NPT "greater facilities for the peaceful use of nuclear energy and stronger commitments of the nuclear powers for the adoption of practical disarmament measures." He was careful to avoid an open split with those Latin American states less enamored of nuclear prohibitions while still advocating on behalf of Mexico's interests as a non-nuclear-weapon state with an eye toward developing its nuclear-energy sector.[106]

These considerations favored a moderate approach. In a plenary speech to the First Committee, García Robles called for a reference in the preamble to the UN Charter's principles of non-intervention and non-interference and another to the Treaty of Tlatelolco in either the preamble, or the resolution, or both. He propounded an expansion of rights set forth in Article IV to include "equipment" and "materials," a new clause in Article V to set up an international PNE service "as soon as possible," and a broadening of Article VI to cover the "manufacture and perfection" of nuclear weapons.[107] References to non-intervention and non-interference chimed with long-standing postcolonial defenses of state sovereignty and self-determination. The proposed changes to Articles IV and VI, however, would authorize concrete new entitlements and obligations, unlocking the door for fissile materials and advanced machinery to flow into the developing world and putting a tighter lid on the US–Soviet arms race, respectively.

Washington decided to "hold [the] common front" with the Soviets lest García Robles "open the floodgates" to a cascade of new amendments. Rusk and Kuznetsov agreed to brook changes that would secure "significantly wider adherence" without dramatically altering the treaty's "basic substance." Kuznetsov identified Mexico as "the leader of the Latin American group" and requested

Latin American nuclear-weapon-free zone   193

help to "bring the Latin Americans into line." Rusk warned that bilateral pressure might not work given that García Robles acted "more Mexican than the Mexicans."[108] The Soviets had qualms with referencing the Treaty of Tlatelolco in the resolution, let alone the treaty itself, because they did not want to endorse the permissive definition of PNEs or the zone's large scope, the latter likely at Cuba's behest.[109]

The superpowers eventually accepted that revisions were necessary, however. They altered the draft resolution to commend rather than endorse the treaty and to note appreciation for the ENDC's work, rather than promoting it unconditionally, which cleared the way for amendments.[110] A new joint draft treaty incorporated most of García Robles' suggestions. The preamble affirmed the UN Charter's injunction against "the threat or use of force against the territorial integrity or political independence of any nation." Article IV outlined rights to "equipment" and "materials" in addition to information and Article V specified that signatories speedily negotiate the supply of PNEs through "an appropriate international body." Foster and Roshchin changed the preambular reference to arms control and disarmament so that it called for effective measures "as soon as possible," but held the line against barring "manufacture and perfection" of nuclear weapons, which would make the treaty contingent on a superpower agreement not to increase or modernize their nuclear forces.

The French ambassador observed that the modifications were meant to "dispel the reservations of the majority and, at least, those of the Latin American countries."[111] Twelve of them subsequently co-sponsored the resolution. As for African concerns, US officials reassured South Africa that IAEA oversight would not impair its uranium-mining industry. Pretoria's announcement that it supported the resolution but reserved a decision on signing seemed to placate its neighbors.[112] The First Committee approved the resolution on June 10, by a vote of 92 in favor to four against. The ensuing plenary of the UNGA confirmed the majority, with 95 countries voting "yes" against four "noes" and 21 abstentions.

Mexico was one of the first states to sign the NPT on July 26, 1968, ratifying early the next year. Because the Treaty of Tlatelolco was intended to help solve the security dilemma in Latin America, Mexico primarily judged the NPT according to how it would affect nuclear imports and global arms control. Given the country's immature nuclear infrastructure, the *Comisión Nacional de Energía Nuclear* (Mexican Nuclear Energy Commission) counseled an immediate signature because "international collaboration" and "the equipment and materials" were vital for harnessing the potential of nuclear energy, "one of the most important factors in the development of our country" as the natural successor to non-renewable fuels.[113] The commission listed various conditions that would accompany the signature, for example, an insistence on rights to breeder reactors that relied on enriched uranium that could be diverted to bomb-making purposes.[114] Mexico would allow international safeguards on its nuclear activities, but it refused to limit its ability to pursue energy technologies of its choosing.

All told, six Latin American states had ratified the treaty by the time it entered into force on March 5, 1970 following the ratification of 40 signatories. When

194   *J. Hunt*

the first NPT review conference met in 1975, that number was 14, including the newly independent nation of Grenada – the Bahamas joined in 1976.[115] In contrast, Argentina and Brazil remained outside of the global nuclear regime until 1995 and 1998, respectively, even after both entered the Latin American NWFZ unconditionally in 1994.[116] Cuba brought up the rear, consenting to both agreements in 2002. Patterns of receptivity or resistance to nuclear prohibitions among Latin American states were consistent whether the scope was regional or global, persisting throughout the Cold War and for more than a decade after the Soviet Union disintegrated.

"Among nations, respect for the rights of others is peace"

Between September 1962 and July 1968, Latin American and especially Mexican officials devised technopolitical systems to regulate nuclear power in the region and around the world. Regional compacts to forgo nuclear weapons had joined nonproliferation and comprehensive nuclear test ban treaties as the most promising avenues by which to curtail the risks associated with nuclear globalization.

Brazil's proposal of a Latin American NWFZ to the United Nations launched the initiative. The Cuban Missile Crisis then illustrated the virtues of firewalls against the introduction of nuclear arms into the region as well as the diplomatic hurdles erected by the Cold War. With new military governments in Argentina and Brazil increasingly at odds with Mexico's pursuit of regional denuclearization, Washington made a series of compromises with the aim of preventing neighbors from bringing weapons of mass destruction into its backyard once again and of easing its pursuit of a nonproliferation treaty. The treaty's ambiguities, openness, and Bolivarian themes let Mexico and its Latin American partners conclude the first NWFZ treaty that covered an inhabited region.

The Treaty of Tlatelolco was a major part of the context in which the NPT was negotiated. Brazil and Mexico's seats on the ENDC and Latin American numbers in the UNGA provided leverage with which to extract two kinds of concessions from nuclear-weapon states. First, the superpowers were asked to ratify Protocol II of the Treaty of Tlatelolco, which would bind them to respect its terms – the United States and the United Kingdom signed the protocol in 1967 and 1968, France in 1973, and the Soviet Union in 1978. Following the establishment of the Brazilian–Argentine Agency for Accounting and Control of Nuclear Materials in 1991, Argentina and Chile finally ratified the Treaty of Tlatelolco in January 1994, which occasioned Brazil's unconditional adherence months after. When Cuba then signed and ratified in 2002, the denuclearized zone came into full legal force.

Second, the superpowers acquiesced to new articles and preambular statements in the NPT that would help offset the costs borne by non-nuclear-weapon states with compensatory rights and obligations. Nuclear-weapon states would: endeavor to facilitate transfers of peaceful nuclear information, materials, and equipment; make speedy provisions for the supply of "peaceful" nuclear explosives; embrace

Latin American nuclear-weapon-free zone 195

the free creation of NWFZs; and pledge to curb the arms race and make progress toward disarmament. These concessions paved the way for the UNGA to commend the NPT in June 1968, authorizing a global regime with powers of inspection and enforcement over sovereign states' nuclear activities in accordance with the UN Charter.

The original understandings arrived at when that era's international community finalized the NPT remain subjects of vigorous debate.[117] Situating the nonproliferation campaign in the annals of multilateral nuclear diplomacy in the 1960s helps take stock of the treaty's contested origins.[118] The critical role played by Mexico undermines arguments that the NPT reflected only superpower interests by those who liken the treaty regime to neocolonialism as well as those who discount the importance of technical assistance and disarmament pledges to the treaty's "grand bargain."[119]

While Soviet–American collusion was necessary for the NPT to open for signature, it was far from sufficient. Creating a global nuclear regime capable of slowing the spread of nuclear weapons necessitated broad-based political legitimacy that only the UN system could bestow. Mexico's interventions in Geneva and New York amid its own campaign to create a nuclear-weapon-free zone in Latin America were critical contributions to the balance struck between nuclear nonproliferation, peaceful assistance, and arms control in the NPT.

Notes

1 The literature on the Treaty of Tlatelolco is slight. See Mónica Serrano, *Common Security in Latin America: The 1967 Treaty of Tlatelolco* (London: Institute of Latin American Studies, 1992); John R. Redick, *Nuclear Illusions: Argentina and Brazil*, Occasional Paper (Washington, D.C.: Henry L. Stimson Center, 1995), based on his doctoral dissertation, *The Politics of Denuclearization: A Study of the Treaty for the Prohibition of Nuclear Weapons in Latin America* (Dissertation, University of Virginia, 1970); Elias David Morales Martínez, "A Experiéncia de Tlatelolco: Um Estudo do Regime Latino-Americano e Caribenho de Proscrição de Armas Nucleares, 1963–2008" (Dissertation, Universidade de São Paulo, 2008); for Spanish- and English-language collections of contemporaneous speeches and draft treaties, respectively, see Alfonso García Robles, *El Tratado de Tlatelolco: Génesis, Alcance y Propósition de la Proscripción de las Armas Nucleares en la América Latina* (México: El Colegio de México, 1967); and *The Denuclearization of Latin America*, trans. Marjorie Urquidi (Carnegie Endowment for International Peace, 1967).
2 Verbatim Record, United Nations General Assembly (UNGA), 22nd Session, First Committee, 1569th Meeting, May 16, 1968 (A/C.1/PV.1569), 11, United Nations Audiovisual Library of International Law, http://legal.un.org/avl/ha/tnpt/tnpt.html (accessed March 15, 2014).
3 Statement, Sergio Duarte, UN High Representative for Disarmament Affairs, "Commemoration of the 45th Anniversary of the Signing of the Treaty of Tlatelolco," Mexico City, Mexico, February 14, 2012, www.un.org/disarmament/ HomePage/HR/docs/2012/2012–02–14-Opanal-Mexico.pdf (accessed March 17, 2014).
4 Memo Alfonso García Robles to President Gustavo Díaz Ordaz, "Mexico's Position with Respect to the Draft Treaty on the Non-Proliferation of Nuclear Weapons," February 13, 1968, folder B-278–12, 12, *Archivo Histórico Diplomático Genaro*

196　*J. Hunt*

Estrada de la Secretaría de Relaciones Exteriores de México, Mexico City, Mexico (SRE).

5　García Robles, *El Tratado de Tlatelolco*, 13, and *The Denuclearization of Latin America*, xx–xxi.

6　Tony Smith and Max Paul Friedman sound two calls to arms for taking the agency of political elites and public opinion in regional, middle, and smaller powers more seriously in our efforts to apprehend patterns of influence and consequence in the Cold War and in US–Latin American relations. See Tony Smith, "New Bottles for New Wine: A Pericentric Framework for the Study of the Cold War," *Diplomatic History* 24, no. 4 (2000): 567–551; Max Paul Friedman, "Retiring the Puppets, Bringing Latin America back in: Recent Scholarship on United States–Latin American Relations," *Diplomatic History* 27, no. 5 (2003): 621–636; a pericentric approach is evident as well in Odd Arne Westad's synthetic reappraisal of Cold War history, and other interpretations of its kind: *The Global Cold War: Third World Interventions and the Making of Our Times* (New York: Cambridge University Press, 2005).

7　Matthew Connelly, "Taking off the Cold War Lens: Visions of North–South Conflict during the Algerian War for Independence," *The American Historical Review* 105, no. 3 (2000): 739–769; a group of authors, most notably Marc Trachtenberg, regard the NPT as having aimed primarily at the tacit maintenance of a European political settlement among whose features the prevention of a nuclear-armed West Germany was prominent, Marc Trachtenberg, *A Constructed Peace: The Making of the European Settlement, 1945–1963* (Princeton, NJ: Princeton University Press, 1999); John Lewis Gaddis, *The Long Peace: Inquiries into the History of the Cold War* (New York: Oxford University Press, 1987); Susanna Schrafstetter and Stephen Twigge, *Avoiding Armageddon: Europe, the United States, and the Struggle for Nuclear Nonproliferation, 1945–1970* (Westport, CT: Praeger, 2004).

8　Taking off the "Cold War lens" demands more than refocusing on the inclination of the United States to maintain or reclaim its postwar nuclear monopoly, or on how Soviet–American efforts to draft a mutually acceptable nonproliferation treaty often came at allies' expense. Shane J. Maddock, *Nuclear Apartheid: The Quest for American Atomic Supremacy from World War II to the Present* (Chapel Hill: University of North Carolina Press, 2010); for works that underscore how nonproliferation diplomacy turned conventional Cold War alliance relationships on their heads, see Hal Brands, "Progress Unseen: US Arms Control Policy and the Origins of Detente, 1963–1968," *Diplomatic History* 30, no. 2 (2006): 253–285 and "Non-Proliferation and the Dynamics of the Middle Cold War: The Superpowers, the MLF, and the NPT," *Cold War History* 7, no. 3 (August 2007): 389–423; Roland Popp, "Introduction: Global Order, Cooperation between the Superpowers, and Alliance Politics in the Making of the Nuclear Non-Proliferation Regime," *The International History Review* 36, no. 2 (2014): 195–209.

9　Francesca Giovannini underscores how regional institutions built to manage nuclear technology resulted from states' efforts to band together to resist the hegemonic influence of global regimes that reflected American power: *Cooperating to Compete: The Role of Regional Powers in Global Nuclear Governance* (Dissertation, University of Oxford, October 2012), 134; she also emphasizes the importance of Brazil rather than Mexico in the region's denuclearization:

> [T]he regional nuclear regime of Latin America that has slowly emerged since the Cuban Missile Crisis in 1962 is the byproduct of two distinct yet concurrent processes: firstly, a process of resistance carried out by some Latin American countries – but by Brazil in particular – to [the] U.S. nuclear agenda internationally and within Latin America itself; secondly, a process of improbable and not always successful accommodation of diverging interests among Brazil, Argentina and Mexico, the three nuclear countries of Latin America.

Latin American nuclear-weapon-free zone 197

10 Two representative syntheses are Stephen G. Rabe, *The Killing Zone: The United States Wages Cold War in Latin America* (New York: Oxford University Press, 2012); and Lars Schoultz, *Beneath the United States: A History of U.S. Policy toward Latin America* (Cambridge, MA: Harvard University Press, 1998).

11 A recent example of this historiographical trend is Hal Brands, *Latin America's Cold War* (Cambridge, MA: Harvard University Press, 2010).

12 Greg Grandin, *Empire's Workshop: Latin America, the United States, and the Rise of the New Imperialism* (New York: Metropolitan Books, 2006).

13 Serrano, *Common Security in Latin America*, 11–18; or Redick, "The Politics of Denuclearization," 92f.

14 Report, Arms Control and Disarmament Agency (ACDA), "Latin American Nuclear-Free Zone," *Declassified Documents Reference Service* (*DDRS*): CK3100019048, 12.

15 Verbatim Transcript, UN General Assembly, 1335th Meeting, November 13, 1963, 122.

16 Graham T. Allison, *Essence of Decision: Explaining the Cuban Missile Crisis* (New York: HarperCollins, 1971); Renata Keller argues that the Cuban Missile Crisis was perceived in Latin America according to the region's political polarization, "The Latin American Missile Crisis," *Diplomatic History* 39, no. 2 (2015); this bottom-up approach overlooks the crisis's impetus for Latin American nuclear diplomacy. For an invaluable collection of primary documents bearing on the crisis, read James Hershberg and Christian F. Ostermann, eds., "The Global Cuban Missile Crisis: New Evidence from behind the Iron, Bamboo, and Sugarcane Curtains, and beyond," *Cold War International History Project Bulletin* 17/18 (2012): 135–298.

17 Cable, Harlan Cleveland, "Operation Raincoat," October 26, 1962 and Memorandum, US Department of State, "Evaluation of Brazilian Denuclearization Proposal," October 26, 1962, The Cuban Missile Crisis Revisited, *Digital National Security Archive* (DNSA).

18 ACDA, "Latin America Nuclear-Free Zone," 2–3.

19 Memoranda, Roger Hilsman, "Probable Soviet Attitude toward Regional Denuclearization Proposals" and US Joint Chiefs of Staff (US JCS), "Nuclear-Free or Missile-Free Zones," October 26, 1962, Cuban Missile Crisis Revisited, DNSA.

20 ACDA, "Latin American Nuclear-Free Zone," 4–5.

21 Letter, Vincente Sáncez Gavito to Manuel Tello, "White House Meeting re Cuba," November 14, 1962, SRE in Hershberg and Ostermann, "The Global Cuban Missile Crisis," 210ff.

22 Miguel Marín Bosch (ed.), "Alfonso García Robles: Una Entrevista," in *Armas Nucleares, Desarme y Carrera Armamentista* (México, D.F.: Ediciones Gernika, 1985), 25; for how international organizations altered the course of world politics, the essential book is Akira Iriye, *Global Community: The Role of International Organizations in the Making of the Contemporary World* (Berkeley: University of California Press, 2002).

23 Biographical information about García Robles from Alfonso García Robles and Miguel Marín Bosch, *Armas Nucleares, Desarme y Carrera Armamentista: Homenaje a Alfonso García Robles* (México, D.F.: Ediciones Gernika, 1985), 15–32; Fernando Solana, *Alfonso García Robles, Diplomático Ejemplar* (México, D.F: Secretaría de Relaciones Exteriores, 1990). Translations from Spanish by the author.

24 García Robles, *Le panaméricanisme et la politique de bon voisinage* (Paris: Les Éditions Internationales, 1938).

25 García Robles, *La Question du Pétrole au Mexique et le Droit International* (Paris: Les Éditions Internationales, 1939).

26 A thoroughgoing commentary on Bolivar's political philosophy is Simon Collier, "Simón Bolivar as Political Thinker," in *Simón Bolivar: Essays on the Life and Legacy of the Liberator*, eds. David Bushnell and Lester D. Langley (Lanham, MD:

198 *J. Hunt*

Rowman & Littlefield Publishers, 2008), 13–35; the second chapter of John Lynch's biography is enlightening, *Simón Bolivar: A Life* (New Haven, CT: Yale University Press, 2006), 22–39; for how the Bolivarian myth has been interpreted and co-opted in Latin American political thought and propaganda, see Michael Zeuske, *Simón Bolivar: History and Myth* (Princeton, NJ: Markus Wiener Publishers, 2013).

27 García Robles, *The Denuclearization of Latin America*, xxi.

28 Bosch, "Alfonso García Robles: Una Entrevista," 28.

29 Albert Camus, "Speech of Acceptance upon the Award of the Nobel Prize for Literature, Delivered in Stockholm on the Tenth of December, 1957," in *Fifty Years*, ed. Clifton Fadiman (New York: Alfred A. Knopf, 1965), 723.

30 Solana, *Alfonso García Robles*, 3.

31 Serrano, *Common Security in Latin America*, 23; "Speech Delivered at the 1333rd Meeting of the First Committee of the General Assembly of the United Nations on November 11, 1963," García Robles, *The Denuclearization of Latin America*, 4.

32 Speech Delivered at the 1333rd Meeting of the First Committee of the General Assembly of the United Nations on November 11, 1963," García Robles, *The Denuclearization of Latin America*, 4.

33 Serrano, *Common Security in Latin America*, 26.

34 Memorandum, US JCS, 849–63, "Latin American Nuclear Free Zone," November 1, 1963, cited in ACDA, "Latin American Nuclear-Free Zone," 5–6.

35 Memorandum, Adrian Fisher to Committee of Principals, "Position Paper on Nuclear Free Zones," July 30, 1965, quoted in ACDA, "Latin American Nuclear-Free Zone," 22–23.

36 Bosch, "Alfonso García Robles," 24–25; Telegram, Fulton Freeman to Dean Rusk, "Embassy Comments and Recommendations," May 21, 1964, Box 58, Cables, Country Files (CF)–Mexico, National Security Files (NSF), Lyndon Baines Johnson Library, Austin, TX (LBJL).

37 Circular, US State Department, CA-5598, November 29, 1963, quoted in ACDA, "Latin American Nuclear-Free Zone," 8.

38 Renata Keller, *Mexico's Cold War* (New York: Cambridge University Press, 2015).

39 MemCon, August 12, 1964, *Foreign Relations of the United States* (FRUS), 1964–1968, XI, 93–96.

40 ACDA, *Documents on Disarmament, 1963* (Washington, D.C.: ACDA, 1964), 582f.

41 García Robles, "Nobel Lecture: The Latin American Nuclear-Weapon Free Zone," December 11, 1982, www.nobelprize.org/nobel_prizes/peace/laureates/1982/robles-lecture.html (accessed April 20, 2015).

42 Preparatory Commission for the Denuclearization of Latin America.

43 Quoted from Letter, López Mateos' "Joint Declaration," March 21, 1963 in "Speech Delivered at the Opening Meeting of the Preliminary Meeting on the Denuclearization of Latin American," November 23, 1964, in García Robles, *The Denuclearization of Latin America*, 21.

44 Redick, "The Politics of Denuclearization," 32, 98, 106, 111–121, 193–196, 204–207, 219.

45 Cable, Fulton Freeman to Dean Rusk, "Preparatory Commission on Latin American Denuclearization," March 23, 1965, Box 58, CF–Mexico, NSF, LBJL, 1–2.

46 Ibid., 2–3.

47 "Speech Delivered at the Opening Meeting of the Second Session," August 23, 1965, in García Robles, *The Denuclearization of Latin America*, 36.

48 "Resolution 8" cited by García Robles in "Speech Delivered at the Closing Meeting of the Second Session of the Preparatory Commission, "September 2, 1965," ibid., 43.

49 Francis J. Gavin, "Blasts from the Past: Proliferation Lessons from the 1960s," *International Security* 29, no. 3 (2004): 100–135.

50 Circular, ACDA, "Meeting Proposed by Mexico to Discuss Denuclearization of Latin America," November 17, 1964, Box 58, CF–Mexico, NSF, LBJL.

Latin American nuclear-weapon-free zone 199

51 MemCon (Rusk, Carrillo Flores), October 7, 1965, Box 58, CF–Mexico, NSF, LBJL.
52 This was not the first time that a Mexican official contacted Havana about partaking in the talks. García Robles had sent a telegram to the Cuban foreign minister, Raul Roa, ahead of the first COPREDAL meeting the previous year. Redick, "The Politics of Denuclearization," 135f.
53 Ibid.
54 Memorandum, US JCS, 263–65, "Possible US Public Statements on Denuclearization of Certain Areas," April 9, 1965, quoted in ACDA, "Latin American Nuclear-Free Zone," 21.
55 *Documents on Disarmament, 1965*, 535–536, quoted in ACDA, "Latin American Nuclear-Free Zone," 27.
56 MemCon (Rusk, Carrillo Flores), October 7, 1965.
57 Cable, Fulton Freeman to Dean Rusk, "Brazilian and Argentinian Reluctance to Move Forward with LANFZ," December 9, 1965, Box 59, CF–Mexico, NSF, LBJL.
58 ACDA, "Latin American Nuclear-Free Zone," 24; Circular, ACDA, "Meeting Proposed by Mexico to Discuss Denuclearization of Latin America," November 17, 1964, Box 58, CF–Mexico, NSF, LBJL.
59 MemCon, "LA NWFZ," April 25–28, 1966, Box 4, Spurgeon Keeny Papers, NSF, LBJL, 1–2.
60 ACDA, "Latin American Nuclear-Free Zone," 34–38.
61 Memorandum, Leonard Meeker to Dean Rusk, February 10, 1967, quoted in ibid., 37.
62 Redick, "The Politics of Denuclearization," 227–233.
63 Cable, Fulton Freeman to Dean Rusk, tel. 4484 (1), February 13, 1967, quoted in ibid., 38.
64 *Documents on Disarmament, 1967*, 65.
65 Cable, Fulton Freeman to Dean Rusk *et al.*, August 28, 1966, Box 58, CF–Mexico, NSF, LBJL.
66 *Documents on Disarmament, 1967*, 126–128, 140–143.
67 Scott Kaufman, *Project Plowshare: The Peaceful Use of Nuclear Explosives in Cold War America* (Ithaca: Cornell University Press, 2013).
68 Trevor Findlay, *Nuclear Dynamite: The Peaceful Nuclear Explosions Fiasco* (Sydney: Pergamon Press Australia, 1990).
69 Memo Fisher to Dean Rusk, "Adherence of the US to the Protocols of the Treaty of Tlatelolco," June 1, 1967, in ACDA, "Latin American Nuclear-Free Zone," 43.
70 Letter, Mexican Secretariat of Foreign Affairs to William Foster, September 11, 1967, quoted in ibid., 44.
71 Memo Rusk to Lyndon Johnson, "Latin American Nuclear Free Zone Treaty," October 26, 1967, Confidential, quoted in ibid., 47.
72 Quoted in ibid., 50.
73 Cable, Freeman to Rusk, Box 58, CF–Mexico, NSF, LBJL.
74 Final Verbatim Record of the 287th Meeting of the ENDC, February 21, 1967, ENDC/PV.287, http://quod.lib.umich.edu/e/endc (accessed April 20, 2015).
75 Memo Rostow to Lyndon Johnson, August 10, 1967, FRUS, 1964–1968, XI, 494f.; Note, "Les non alignés de Genève et la non proliferation," October 20, 1967, Box 769, Cote 517INVA, *Archives diplomatique du ministère des affaires étrangères de la France*, Paris, France (AMAEF), 6–7.
76 MemCon (Tomkins, Fisher *et al.*), August 23, 1967, the Nuclear Nonproliferation Treaty (NPT), DNSA, www2.gwu.edu/~nsarchiv/nukevault/ebb253/doc05a.pdf (accessed April 20, 2015).
77 Circular, US Department of State," August 24, 1967, NPT, DNSA, 6–7, www2.gwu.edu/~nsarchiv/nukevault/ebb253/doc05b.pdf (accessed April 20, 2015); the article read:

200 *J. Hunt*

> Nothing in this Treaty shall be interpreted as affecting the inalienable right of all the Parties to the Treaty to develop research, production and use of nuclear energy for peaceful purposes without discrimination and in conformity with Articles I and II of this Treaty, as well as the right of the Parties to participate in the fullest possible exchange of information for, and to contribute, alone or in cooperation with other States to, the further development of the applications of nuclear energy for peaceful purposes.

78 Final Verbatim Record of the 331st Meeting of the ENDC, September 19, 1967, ENDC/PV.331, 4–11.
79 Ibid., 9f.; the operative paragraph ultimately read:

> Each nuclear-weapon State Party to this Treaty undertakes to pursue negotiations in good faith, with all speed and perseverance, to arrive at further agreements regarding the prohibition of nuclear weapon tests, the cessation of the manufacture of nuclear weapons, the liquidation of their existing stockpiles, the elimination of nuclear arsenals, of nuclear weapons and the means of their delivery, as well as to reach agreement on a treaty on general and complete disarmament under strict and effective international control.
>
> (Documents on Disarmament, 1967, 394f.)

80 For detailed analysis of the drafting and implementation of Article VI, see Mohamed Ibrahim Shaker, *The Nuclear Non-Proliferation Treaty: Origin and Implementation, 1959–1979*, vol. 2 (London; New York: Oceana Publications, 1980), 555–648; and George Bunn, R.M. Timerbaev, and James F. Leonard, *Nuclear Disarmament: How Much Have the Five Nuclear Powers Promised in the Non-Proliferation Treaty?* (Washington, D.C.: Lawyers Alliance for World Security, Committee for National Security, and Washington Council on Non-Proliferation, 1994).
81 Memo Keeny to Rusk, April 1, 1969, Box 5, Files of Spurgeon Keeny, NSF, LBJL.
82 Notes Tom Johnson, "Cabinet Meeting on August 2, 1967, 12:09 p.m. to 1:50 p.m.," August 2, 1967, Box 1, Tom Johnson's Notes of Meetings, LBJL, 7–8.
83 Memo Rusk to Lyndon Johnson, October 27, 1967, *DDRS*: CK3100170489.
84 Ibid.
85 MemCon (Mexican Ambassador, Fisher), February 10, 1968, *DDRS*: CK3100079612.
86 Rusk, "Background on Treaty of Tlatelolco."
87 Memorandum, Dean Rusk to Lyndon Johnson, "US Adherence to Protocol to Treaty Creating Latin American Nuclear Free Zone," February 12, 1968, *DDRS*: CK3100146716.
88 Editorial Note, FRUS, 1964–1968, XXXI, 762; Memo Rusk to Johnson, October 26, 1967, *DDRS*: CK3100446623.
89 Bulletin, US Department of State, March 14, 1968, 313–314, quoted in ACDA, "Latin American Nuclear-Free Zone," 52.
90 Cable, French Embassy in Mexico City to Paris, April 18, 1968, Box 769, Cote 517INVA, AMAEF.
91 Memo Latin American Department, Soviet Foreign Ministry, "Latin American Nuclear-Free Zone," May 15, 1967, Opis 27, Papka 55a, Delo 12, Listy 2–3, Fond 110, Foreign Policy Archive of the Russian Federation (AVPRF).
92 Cable 142418, US Department of State to New York, April 5, 1968, doc. 15, NPT, DNSA, www2.gwu.edu/~nsarchiv/nukevault/ebb253/doc15.pdf (accessed April 20, 2015).
93 ACDA, "Latin American Nuclear Free Zone," 53f.
94 Final Verbatim Record of the 364th Meeting of the ENDC, February 13, 1968, ENDC/PV.371.
95 Letter, Foster to Fisher, March 1, 1968, Folder 1, Box 13, William Foster Papers, George C. Marshall Library, Lexington, USA, 1.

Latin American nuclear-weapon-free zone 201

96 Ibid., 6.

97 MemCon, February 15, 1968, NPT, DNSA, www2.gwu.edu/~nsarchiv/nukevault/ebb253/doc13.pdf (accessed April 20, 2015).

98 Cable, French Embassy in Lima to Paris, April 19, 1968, Box 769, Cote 517INVA, AMAEF, 2.

99 Memo, García Robles to Ordaz, "Mexico's Position with Respect to the Draft Treaty on the Non-Proliferation of Nuclear Weapons," op. cit., February 13, 1968.

100 French Embassy in Lima to Paris, op. cit., April 19, 1968.

101 Note, Direction des Affaires Politiques for Maurice Couve de Murville, "Le traité de non proliferation des armes nucléaire – état de la negotiation," March 19, 1968, Box 768, Cote 517INVA, AMAEF, 5.

102 Intelligence Note-290, US Department of State, Bureau of Intelligence and Research, April 19, 1968, NPT, DNSA, 1–2, www2.gwu.edu/~nsarchiv/nukevault/ebb253/doc20a.pdf (accessed April 20, 2015).

103 Cable, 142418, US Department of State to New York, April 5, 1968, NPT, DNSA, 1–8.

104 MemCon, May 6, 1968, NPT, DNSA, 2, www2.gwu.edu/~nsarchiv/nukevault/ebb253/doc20b.pdf (accessed April 20, 2015).

105 Cable, Charles Lucet to Couve de Murville, May 16, 1968, Box 769, Cote 517INVA, AMAEF.

106 García Robles to Díaz Ordaz, "Mexico's Position," op. cit., 12ff.

107 Official Records, UNGA, 22nd session, First Committee, 1569th meeting, "Non-proliferation of nuclear weapons," May 16, 1968, United Nations Audiovisual Library of International Law, http://legal.un.org/avl/ha/tnpt/tnpt.html (accessed April 15, 2015), 4–11.

108 Cable 161473, US Department of State to New York, May 10, 1968, NPT, DNSA, www2.gwu.edu/~nsarchiv/nukevault/ebb253/doc23a.pdf (accessed April 20, 2015).

109 MemCon (Rusk, Kuznetsov *et al.*), May 17, 1968, FRUS, 1964–1968, XI, 598ff.

110 Cable, Berard to Couve de Murville, May 9, 1968, Box 769, Cote 517INVA, AMAEF, 1.

111 Ibid., 3.

112 Cable, Berard to Couve de Murville, June 3, 1968, Box 769, Cote 517INVA, AMAEF, 2.

113 Memorandum, Comision Nacional de Energia Nuclear, José Gorostiza to Díaz Ordaz and García Robles, "NPT," July 22, 1968," B-278–12, SRE, 2.

114 Ibid., 5–6.

115 United Nations Office for Disarmament Affairs, "Status of the Treaty on the Non-Proliferation of Nuclear Weapons," http://disarmament.un.org/treaties/t/npt (accessed April 15, 2015).

116 Organization for the Prohibition of Nuclear Armaments in Latin America, "Status of Signatures and Ratifications of the Treaty of Tlatelolco," www.opanal.org/opanal/Tlatelolco/P-Tlatelolco-i.htm (accessed March 22, 2014).

117 For the various debates relating to the NPT's core functions, see Steven E. Miller, *Nuclear Collisions: Discord, Reform and the Nuclear Nonproliferation Regime* (Cambridge, MA: American Academy of Arts and Sciences, 2012); and Bunn *et al.*, *How Much.*

118 Realists and liberal internationalism alike assume that nuclear prohibitions are driven by predetermined variables, either the distribution of material capabilities constitutive of state "power" or the self-evident rationality of enlightened self-interest that ultimately leads to collective action. For a liberal internationalist explanation of legal nuclear prohibitions, William Walker, "Nuclear Enlightenment and Counter-Enlightenment," *International Affairs* 83, no. 3 (2007): 431–453 and *A Perpetual Menace: Nuclear Weapons and International Order* (New York: Routledge, 2012); for the liberal-realist debate among IR-theorists and a sophisticated explanation of the

202   *J. Hunt*

effects of treaties from a realist perspective read, respectively, Beth A. Simmons, "Compliance with International Agreements," *Annual Review of Political Science* 1, no. 1 (1998): 75–93; and Dane E. Swango, *The Nuclear Nonproliferation Treaty: Constrainer, Screen, or Enabler?* (Dissertation, University of California, Los Angeles, 2009).

119 For an argument that the NPT regime was the product of superpower collusion, read Andrew Coe and Jane Vaynman, "Collusion and the Nuclear Nonproliferation Regime," *Journal of Politics* 77, no. 4 (2015): 983–997; Dane Swango has downplayed the importance of peaceful nuclear assistance in the eyes of US policymakers at the time, "The United States and the Role of Nuclear Co-Operation and Assistance in the Design of the Non-Proliferation Treaty," *The International History Review* 36, no. 2 (2014): 210–229.

11 "A glaring defect in the system"

Nuclear safeguards and the invisibility of technology

Jacob Darwin Hamblin[1]

Since the 1960s, nuclear-armed states have struggled, along with the International Atomic Energy Agency (IAEA), to manage the fate of technologies related to budding nuclear programs around the world. As diplomats and scientific experts considered handing over to the IAEA the responsibilities for ensuring civilian nuclear technologies were not diverted towards nuclear weapons programs, their arguments opened painful sores in international relations. Most famously, Indian and Brazilian diplomats characterized the dogged insistence by nuclear-weapon states on rigorous safeguards as an attempt to put the divide between "haves" and "have-nots" on a permanent basis. This so-called "nuclear apartheid," with its potent anti-colonial rhetoric, stood as a justification for these countries' nonparticipation in the Treaty on the Non-Proliferation of Nuclear Weapons (NPT) for decades.[2]

It is true that by suggesting strict standards for exports of nuclear materials and equipment and linking such exports to the acceptance of invasive verification mechanisms Western diplomats risked alienating the countries of the so-called developing world. Protecting sovereignty and economic development is a familiar theme, debated within various global regulatory regimes, from the NPT to environmental accords. However, the narrative of strict "haves" and loose "have-nots" sidesteps the fact that the strongest efforts to maintain a lax interpretation of what constituted nuclear equipment came just as often from the exporting states, as these actors were hoping to ensure markets for a range of technologies. This development can best be gleaned from examining episodes from the history of negotiating and implementing "safeguards" provisions, the rules by which nuclear transactions between states have been monitored by governments or by international organizations.

Establishing the provisions governing the implementation of international nuclear safeguards has never been a mere technical issue, but instead has been a smorgasbord of technical, political, commercial, national security, and social factors. Even its most basic challenge was hotly contested, namely identifying "triggers" – the kinds of transactions that would necessitate some kind of procedure to ensure that materials intended for peaceful use were not diverted to military ends. In the 1960s, discussions were entwined with other sources of tension: the credibility of the brand-new IAEA and its role vis-à-vis the European

204   *J.D. Hamblin*

Atomic Energy Community (Euratom); the French nuclear weapons program; American hopes for a multilateral nuclear force in Europe; commercial tenders for reactors in India; and the Chinese Communist bomb test, to name just a few. In those years, the nations of the world invested considerable energy into the question of what counted as worthy of safeguards. At the IAEA, the safeguards agreements negotiated in 1961 and 1965 became the foundation of interpreting nuclear proliferation under the NPT in subsequent years.

This chapter highlights how easily national imperatives, especially commercial pressures and security concerns in supplier states, dictated loose interpretations of what should "trigger" safeguards. My analysis is inspired by scholarship showing how the ambiguous notion of what it means to be a "nuclear thing" led to interpretive disparities about how to apply safeguards, to report transactions, or even to require health protection for workers.[3] It is also informed by scholarship emphasizing how commercial pressures and bureaucratic decisions rendered humans, material, and even entire countries invisible to would-be regulators.[4] Here I focus not on what equipment ended up in international accords, but rather on the ways the United States and other Western powers encouraged technological invisibility, relaxing restrictions rather than tightening them. Documents from safeguards negotiations reveal considerable anxiety about the invisibility of certain nuclear transactions. At a meeting of the IAEA Board of Governors, for example, British delegate M.I. Michaels made an economic analogy, pointing to Gresham's Law – the economic notion that "bad money" pushes "good money" out of circulation. In the nuclear realm, he said, lax interpretations of what constituted a nuclear technology would drive out stringent ones. In what he called a "glaring defect in the system," he argued that the IAEA safeguards agreements would allow a huge amount of nuclear-related technologies to pass from one country to another without being noticed by the IAEA.[5] What Michaels feared was precisely what ended up happening, as fewer aspects of global trade were ultimately identified as "nuclear" than might have been.

Nuclear supplier states not only tolerated technological invisibility, but also actively exploited loopholes within their own nonproliferation policies. In part this was due to lack of firm will on the part of the United States' government in the early 1960s about nonproliferation, providing ample opportunities for European nuclear suppliers to find ways to avoid scrutiny. Europeans (especially Britain, France, and West Germany) routinely pushed for exceptions to US nonproliferation strategies: Britain hoped to avoid inspections in its dual-use military facility; France struck deals with American companies despite the US knowing the equipment would be used in weapons research; and the FRG clamored not only for a multilateral nuclear force but also a Europe-only inspections program. By the time of negotiating the NPT, most of the supplier states were only grudging partners in strict nonproliferation, with only tepid commitment to restrictions on trade.[6] The result was an ongoing tolerance of *technological invisibility*, in which supplier states, despite being aware of the connection between specific equipment and possible weapon programs, sought to loosen rather than constrain nuclear trade.

Nuclear safeguards 205

Indecision on safeguards and nonproliferation

Policy indecision and lack of coordination about nonproliferation, particularly in the United States, encouraged loose interpretations of safeguards well into the 1960s. Although the United States had, since 1945, nominally opposed the proliferation of nuclear weapons, and restricted nuclear technology exports through the 1946 McMahon Act, Washington had made no coordinated attempt to promote such a restrictive approach internationally after the Baruch Plan to eliminate atomic weapons fizzled out in 1947. In fact US officials had quite different views of how the nation should be involved in international nuclear affairs. As historian John Krige has pointed out, the US State Department favored the 1957 creation of the European Atomic Energy Community (Euratom) as a way of fostering Europeans' political unity and keeping them in line with US security interests. By contrast, the US Atomic Energy Commission struck bilateral deals with various countries, included obligations to accept bilateral safeguards provisions into these transactions as required by US legislation, and hoped to ultimately hand over the responsibility for these safeguards agreements to an international agency. Meanwhile President Eisenhower in 1953 committed to the creation of an international agency (the IAEA, born in 1957) to promote nuclear solutions in non-military realms, in part as a propaganda exercise to show the world that the United States had more to offer than the destructive power of the Bomb. Having two new agencies in Europe – one regional and the other international – would prove to be an enormous headache throughout the later safeguards negotiations. American policy-makers often worked at cross-purposes with one another, with no unity on the purpose of the new international organizations.[7]

The IAEA provided the United States with the opportunity to disseminate its existing bilateral safeguards standards internationally, but the entire process was subject to international negotiation. As scholar Astrid Forland put it, "the technically ideal had to give way to the politically possible."[8] The Americans were not only keen to export their standards; they also wanted a non-US body to have responsibility for administering them. For instance, US diplomats repeatedly insisted that its nuclear deals with its recent enemy, Japan, included sufficient safeguard procedures. But Japan disliked the notion of foreign inspections by the United States. For its part, the US Atomic Energy Commission (AEC) did not want the responsibility of enforcing or monitoring safeguards for each bilateral agreement. From the Americans' perspective, assigning that responsibility to the IAEA would remove some pressure from the AEC while strengthening the IAEA by giving it a substantial role in international affairs. In the late 1950s, the United States, Japan, and others volunteered to hand over the task of overseeing their bilaterally agreed safeguards to the IAEA. Their efforts compelled quick international negotiations. By 1961 the IAEA had established the principles of a safeguard system covering research facilities and smaller (100 megawatt or less) reactors, but the debates were far from over. The Americans saw the system as "workable" rather than "foolproof," and perceived it as an exercise in "buying

206   *J.D. Hamblin*

time" and "stabilizing matters" for a few years. Trying to extend the safeguards to larger reactor systems, the IAEA reopened discussion in 1963.[9]

Despite encouraging the transfer of safeguards administration to the IAEA, as late as 1964, when the People's Republic of China conducted its first nuclear weapons test, the United States government did not have unified ideas about nonproliferation. For the Americans, the Chinese test sharpened the significance of safeguards discussions and nonproliferation in general. Aside from limiting access to nuclear fuel, were there particular kinds of equipment to keep away from the PRC? The cost of acquiring an atomic bomb no longer seemed to be a major barrier in itself. Just days after the Chinese test, US Secretary of Defense Robert McNamara reminded members of Congress that there were several countries which could similarly develop a bomb, and that the cost of doing so was now on the order of $120 million, well within the reach of governments.[10]

Only after the PRC's nuclear test did the US government take significant steps toward what became the NPT a few years later.[11] Despite Nationalist China's immediate panic ("We are the target!" Chiang Kai-Shek stated to American officials in Taipei),[12] most key American advisors cast the problem not as proliferation per se, but in terms of deterrence strategies. Should Japan or India now be encouraged to build bombs of their own? Military advisors in the Joint Chiefs of Staff began advising the Secretary of Defense that nuclear sharing among Asian allies might become necessary to deter China.[13]

The notion of sharing nuclear weapons materials or technology with Asian allies illustrated just how disparate strategic ideas had become on the subject of nuclear proliferation, and it put the US government at a policy crossroads. Two weeks after the Chinese test, President Johnson announced the creation of a special committee – the Task Force on Nuclear Proliferation, chaired by former Deputy Secretary of Defense Roswell Gilpatric. At that time, it was by no means obvious that strict nonproliferation should be the US policy. Secretary of State Rusk, for example, posed the question baldly to his colleagues: Should it always be the United States that would have to deter China? Would it not be preferable for India or Japan to act as a deterrent?[14] In meetings between President Johnson and Soviet Foreign Minister Andrei Gromyko, it seemed clear that the Soviets wondered if the Chinese situation would lead the Americans to allow West Germany to develop its own nuclear deterrent.[15]

Other Americans, notably those in the AEC, saw the answer not in furthering proliferation, but in putting teeth into the ongoing safeguards discussions at the IAEA in order to restrain the further spread of nuclear weapons. AEC Chairman Glenn Seaborg argued that any policy different from strict nonproliferation would mean a loss of US control in international affairs. For Seaborg, the real negotiations, on safeguards, were already taking place at the IAEA. The question was not whether to support nonproliferation, but rather how to best press other countries to place their reactors under safeguards, and to ensure that suppliers – such as the UK and Canada – demanded safeguard agreements in every commercial deal.[16]

The Gilpatric committee's work showcased the disunity of nonproliferation policy up to that point, and also highlighted renewed focus on safeguards

Nuclear safeguards 207

negotiations as a nonproliferation tool. The group ultimately had to choose between two worlds. One, which McNamara called "Model A," was for the United States to push for a world with no additional nuclear weapons states. The other, "Model B," would have the United States accept a limited amount of further nuclear powers. Several of the task force participants began with Model B – accepting that it was in US interest to have a few more nuclear powers – but by the end they came around to a new conviction that American policy should follow Model A. Chemist George Kistiakowsky, former science advisor to Eisenhower, noted that in his own lifetime, he might be content with Model B, but as his thoughts turned to his grandchildren, he renewed his commitment to Model A. We must "be prepared to lose individual battles," he observed, "but not the overall war."[17] Both Arthur H. Dean (the influential attorney who had helped to draft the Limited Test Ban Treaty) and retired general Alfred M. Gruenther, both of whom had favored allowing some proliferation to occur, now changed their minds, too. Cornell University President James A. Perkins argued that in order to ensure that Model A happened, even in advance of an international agreement – and possibly even without one – "we should beef up the IAEA to make it the inspectorial system around the world."[18] Although the IAEA was not designed to be a policing agency, or a "watchdog," Americans would increasingly see it in that light.

This apparent policy consensus within the US government came rather late, after most of the safeguards decisions had been made at the IAEA. In contrast to the new US view, the safeguards agreements negotiated in the first half of the 1960s were premised on facilitating the commercial expansion of nuclear power under reasonable verification mechanisms. These agreements were not focused on ensuring nonproliferation of nuclear weapons at any price. Yet the Gilpatric report provided the US President with a strongly worded plea for more concerted international action on stopping proliferation through nuclear commerce. Setting aside the typical rhetoric of "Atoms for Peace," the committee recognized explicitly that the promotion of peaceful nuclear power was actually part of the problem, not the solution. "The world is fast approaching a point of no return in the prospects of controlling the spread of nuclear weapons," the committee stated. "Nuclear power programs are placing within the hands of many nations much of the knowledge, equipment and materials for making nuclear weapons." The report recommended only helping friendly countries in developing nuclear power, but not promoting even these friendly countries' programs with special subsidies.[19]

Only after the Gilpatric committee made its recommendations did the United States government commit itself to nonproliferation.[20] The report itself was made available (or as the British characterized it, leaked) to ensure support of its most important ally. However, even this commitment came with reservations, and US actions made the Johnson administration seem as indecisive as ever.[21] The US continued to pursue a plan for a multilateral nuclear force in Europe, despite routine reminders by the Soviet Union and some allies that this contradicted nonproliferation goals. Toward the end of 1964, British Prime Minister Harold

208 J.D. Hamblin

Wilson stated forcefully that there should be no new fingers on the nuclear trigger, a remark aimed as much at the Federal Republic of Germany as any. Like the Soviets, the British were not pleased with the possibility of Germans playing a role in a European nuclear force. That potential rift in the Atlantic alliance, combined with the blasé attitude of the French about proliferation, and the anxiety of Germans hoping for nuclear sharing in NATO, pulled the United States in several directions as it imagined what nonproliferation might actually look like.[22] In the meantime, this indecision allowed for considerable latitude of interpretation in regard to the implementation of nuclear safeguards, the subject of the next section.

Loopholes and glaring defects

Nonproliferation concerns went hand in hand with worries about putting one's country at a commercial disadvantage. The Americans' renewed 1964 commitment to nonproliferation translated into some interesting turnarounds in safeguard negotiations, both bilaterally and through the IAEA, but ultimately the US would bow to the commercial interests favored by its allies. Although loose restrictions on nuclear trade are typically associated with the "have nots" in the so-called developing world, Europeans used commercial arguments to keep certain kinds of transactions invisible to would-be regulators.

When the US in 1964 tried to strengthen safeguards to close loopholes, key allies balked. For example, in one IAEA Board of Governors meeting, US Governor Henry DeWolf Smyth said that the safeguards system had one "great big hole in it."[23] He was referring to the "substitution" clause in drafts of the IAEA safeguards agreement. This was a loophole that allowed IAEA-safeguarded nuclear fuel to be returned to suppliers such as the US or UK after having been used in a reactor in a different country. Then it would be reprocessed in dual civilian-military facilities *without letting IAEA inspectors into such facilities*. The returned fuel would simply be temporarily replaced by similar material during reprocessing. The substitute material would act as a stand-in, for the purpose of implementing safeguards. The reason behind this practice was that both the US and the UK reprocessed fuel rods in their highly classified military sites, not yet having built separate ones for civilian use. But they also did not want to allow foreign inspectors inside such military facilities.

Until around 1964, the Americans had supported the idea of substitution, but they began to waffle with renewed interest in using safeguards standards to enforce nonproliferation goals. Now they implied that British practices could be a route of nuclear proliferation.[24] They did not, however, seriously debate the principle of substitution per se; instead the negotiators clashed over a specific phrase, "at a specified time." The British hoped to interpret this liberally, giving them months to make the substitution, to avoid paying interest on substitute material borrowed from other projects while it sat unused. Smyth (the American) claimed that suspending safeguards, even for a specified time, might provide opportunities to divert fuel for military purposes. Although the British were

Nuclear safeguards 209

irritated with the Americans' change of heart, they did not interpret it as Washington's genuine concern for nonproliferation. The British knew that the US had begun plans to construct a new reprocessing facility, not linked to military operations, to come online in just a few years.[25] That civilian-only facility would, the British imagined, be able to admit inspectors. To the British, it seemed self-serving for the Americans to condemn the UK approach only now.[26]

While many contested the timing of substitution, including the United States, no serious discussion of entirely closing the "substitution" loophole occurred. Britain's military plutonium production facility would continue participating in the global nuclear trade. Moreover, the Americans appeared satisfied simply raising the issue rather than insisting on getting their way. The final agreement (in 1965) conceded the whole point to the UK, giving it up to six months to reprocess nuclear material in its military facility without substituting it. Despite making claims of safeguards norms providing a "great big hole" in nonproliferation, the United States bowed to the wishes of its ally.[27]

This particular issue highlighted how some felt that proliferation risks could be overstated, with powerful effect, to secure advantageous conditions for business. To the British, it was a reminder of American commitment to maintaining its technological edge over its closest ally.[28] The Americans had been able to abuse their ally on "substitution," while highlighting their commitment to nonproliferation. Others joined in, "only too willing to put us in the pillory," British Governor M.I. Michaels complained, and he scoffed at such political opportunism, not just from the Americans but also the Canadians. Canada also criticized Britain's stand on the "substitution" clause, despite having what many Europeans believed were very lax arrangements helping India to build reactors. The Canadians joined the Americans' sanctimonious critique, Michaels said, only because they "want to appear *whiter than white*."[29]

Concerns about commercial disadvantage set the tone of international discussion at the IAEA's Board of Governors, and encouraged lax interpretations of what counted as nuclear-related equipment. In safeguards discussions, delegates routinely doubted the effectiveness of agreeing upon some kind of genuine technological barrier in formal agreements. The parties in a nuclear deal would find ways to work around the rules, as Oscar Quihillalt, the head of Argentina's National Atomic Energy Commission, observed. It was necessary for the parties not simply to be willing to sign an agreement. Deception was easy to accomplish, he noted. He argued that there needed to be a sense of moral obligation, not simply a legal one, to adhere to the safeguards system. The development of new techniques over time would make it a simple matter, he stated, to deceive inspectors.[30]

That sense of moral urgency was not achieved during the early 1960s safeguard negotiations at the IAEA; instead, most countries were eager to protect their commercial interests. Quihillalt knew quite well how toothless safeguards could be, when applying a legalistic framework. The previous year he had been questioned by US diplomats about Argentina's secret sale of 80 tons of uranium oxide to Israel. This was eight times more than the maximum sale permitted under the IAEA, and had the IAEA arranged the deal, there would have been specific safeguards agreements that included on-site inspections. Argentina had signed a sales contract with Israel in early 1963, with nothing more specific than an assurance by the government of Israel that the material would not be used for military purposes. After learning of the sale, the US government had "expressed its serious concern," stating that it believed the Argentines supported a common position not to sell uranium without some kinds of safeguards equivalent to what the IAEA would insist upon in its sales. Quihillalt's attitude was that his country was not obligated by international agreements – formal or otherwise – and there had been nothing to stop Argentina from making the sale. After all, major uranium suppliers like South Africa did this all the time, he noted. Quihillalt expressed deep skepticism about US attempts to monitor sales between other countries. Even if Argentina were to agree to apply safeguards because the Americans wanted them to do so, a buyer would simply shop elsewhere.[31]

What India, Argentina, Brazil, and Egypt expressed most concern about in safeguards discussions were constraints upon their sovereignty and economic development. The IAEA safeguards, as they developed in the mid-1960s, were drafted to accommodate their increasing demands for assurances that the international system would not be used to hamper a nation's economic interest. As Indian atomic energy chief Homi Bhabha put it to the IAEA Board of Governors in 1965, such agreements should be "implemented in a spirit of reason and common sense."[32] India's complaint about nuclear safeguards, voiced routinely by Bhabha, was that safeguards primarily targeted developing countries, and that they did not actually prevent countries wishing to pursue military applications from doing so. From a technological point of view, he noted, it was easier to use atomic energy for military purposes than economic ones. Bhabha preferred a control system that was confined to chemical processing and isotope separation plants. Controlling those would make other kinds of control unnecessary.[33]

Similarly, Hassan M. Tohamy of the United Arab Republic (Egypt) asserted that diplomats ought to focus their attention only on those facilities capable of producing material to be used in weapons. Trying to apply safeguards to other sites, technologies, or services, he declared, undermined the spirit of collaboration under the IAEA. Such intrusive verification would naturally lead to procedures "which would to a large extent mean the unnecessary domination of foreign powers in the scientific and economic fields." Should the Agency be the instrument of reinforcing existing international relationships? Extending safeguards to many kinds of equipment in the nuclear realm could disturb a country's economic plans, an effect which ran counter to the Agency's stated aim.[34] Like India, Egypt implied that identifying a broad range of equipment as worthy of safeguards would be quasi-colonial, mimicking North–South disparities. And yet plenty of Europeans were wary of including more equipment in safeguard agreements too, fearing restrictions on exports.

Supplier states had just as much interest in liberalizing the nuclear trade, hoping that nonproliferation concerns would focus on aspects of the nuclear production cycle outside their own economic interests. For example, it shocked no-one that South Africa objected to uranium itself being controlled at all. As a major supplier of uranium to the world's nuclear programs, South Africa had a vested interest in keeping uranium oxide away from confining agreements. To start with natural uranium as the object of control was "really to start off at the wrong end of the production cycle," foreign ministry official D.B. Sole argued. Similary, France – with its extensive sources of uranium from its colonial holdings in Africa – backed up South Africa's position.[35]

The safeguards system could not stop the spread of nuclear weapons, such arguments went, yet it could easily present a serious obstacle for using atomic energy for peaceful purposes. Soviet representative V.S. Emelyanov compared fissionable materials to Janus, the two-faced god. The doors to the shrine of Janus were open during wartime, but closed to mark times of peace. Unfortunately, in the case of the nuclear trade, the doors were never truly closed – no matter how peaceful the intent, there was always a chance that materials would be utilized for nuclear weapons.[36] It was true that participants in IAEA-supervised agreements were "morally obliged" not to use material for military purposes. "But that was, alas, not enough," said Swiss representative Urs Hochstrasser. The agreements would be impotent without inspections or other means of enforcing the safeguard provisions.[37]

If so few wanted stiff restrictions, yet were aware of the proliferation risks, what kinds of nuclear transactions would indeed be visible to the IAEA? Many objected to a framing of safeguards that would alert the IAEA to a broad range of equipment being sold by one country to another for use in nuclear facilities. Some negotiators hoped to deconstruct a phrase in the safeguards draft referring to "substantial assistance," and interpret it in a way that would leave room for as many un-safeguarded transactions as possible. As Congo's Governor Félix Malu put it,

> Clearly it was essential to avoid the ridiculous situation whereby a country receiving a reactor as a whole could add three screws to it and so claim exemption from safeguards, or, conversely, that whereby a country which had constructed a reactor itself but received assistance in obtaining minor items of equipment found that it was subjected to safeguards as a result.

Although recognizing that whole reactors might remain under safeguards, Malu hoped to limit what qualified as nuclear assistance. A reactor should only be subject to IAEA safeguards "if supplied entirely or very extensively assisted."[38]

Efforts to identify a broad range of equipment as subject to safeguards failed, not because of obstructionism from countries such as India, Egypt, or Congo, but because few anywhere genuinely wanted to implement constraints. Despite pointing out the proliferation risks, as the Americans and Canadians did when criticizing Britain on "substitution," in practice virtually no one insisted on wide-ranging restrictions. British Governor M.I. Michaels marveled at how so few were willing to take a serious stand – including in his own government – on putting major constraints into safeguards agreements. He felt that the 1965 IAEA

212   *J.D. Hamblin*

safeguards agreement might ultimately leave open significant proliferation pathways.[39] He had hoped that the negotiators would define, in specific terms, which items were significant enough to require reporting to the IAEA and possibly subject to safeguards. But negotiators failed to accomplish this, as Michaels put it, "for one reason or another, perhaps more political than technical." Almost no one wanted a detailed list of equipment to be reported to the IAEA. Instead negotiators agreed on an obligation to report "substantial assistance," a term defined so vaguely that it could be interpreted in widely divergent ways. While some might see a particular piece of technology as crucial to the reactor, potentially usable in a military application – and worth safeguarding – others might deem it to be peripheral, a thing to leave to conventional agreements between commercial firms.

Dismayed, Michaels saw a future with growing numbers of countries taking an interest in nuclear power, and the only formal guidelines from the IAEA would allow for a range of interpretations. Most of the trade in reactors and their component parts would be along commercial lines, covered by unreported bilateral agreements and thereby reduced and obscured from international oversight. The IAEA Board of Governors would never be in a position to agree or disagree, because it simply would not be made aware of the trade deal at all. The commercial firms and national governments would already have decided, in their interest, what was really worth subjecting to safeguards, long before inviting the IAEA to look into their arrangements. Some equipment might be invisible to the IAEA completely. "This seems to me a glaring defect in the system," Michaels argued, "and one it will be difficult to overcome."[40] Over time, he predicted, reactors would not be supplied in whole, or in major part, by supplier states (and thus visible to safeguards). Instead, suppliers would produce the larger part of the "bits and pieces" on the territory of the recipient state, in cooperation with local manufacturers.[41] What could be done about the bits and pieces?

No specific criteria ended up in the guidelines, and the IAEA Board of Governors congratulated itself on a successful negotiation on safeguards. Michaels worried that approving the safeguards system in 1965 would provide a "false sense of satisfaction," or a "false sense that the problem of safeguards has been solved."[42] He had favored bringing the matter into the open and inviting supplier states to develop a list of key items of equipment that should be subject to safeguards. "I recognize that such action would arouse intense Indian anger and accusation of the 'haves' ganging up against the 'have-nots'."[43] But in truth, extending safeguards to a broad range of equipment had few genuine advocates on either side of the North–South divide.

Grudging partners

Safeguards principles, within bilateral agreements and under the IAEA, were negotiated with no direct link to a future nonproliferation agreement. Not only did they pre-date the 1968 Treaty on the Non-Proliferation of Nuclear Weapons (NPT), they were set forth in a time when nuclear suppliers had ambiguous and conflicting views about nuclear nonproliferation. When it came to negotiating the NPT, negotiators not only failed to secure the adherence of key countries such as India and France, but could also not achieve a political willingness to prioritize the NPT over the commercial interests that nations had been at pains to protect during the previous safeguards discussions. The US was willing to make exceptions to its principles, and Europeans bent the rules as far as they could. In the case of some NATO allies, the eventual NPT arguably ran counter to their perceived security interests, leaving them with little desire to provide the NPT with genuine teeth. Because of that, trade in many nuclear-related technologies was loosely restricted or completely invisible to regulators.

The most prominent case of a grudging American partner in nonproliferation was the Federal Republic of Germany. Prior to its effort to create a nonproliferation treaty, the United States had planned to create a NATO nuclear force (the multilateral force, or MLF), which Bonn favored. This complicated the NPT negotiations tremendously. US diplomats failed to follow through on their commitment to the West Germans, contaminating relations within NATO. The Soviet Union balked at the idea of concluding any treaty that allowed the US to hand over control of nuclear weapons to Germans. In the NPT negotiations, not only was the United States in the invidious position of backtracking on its military plans with one ally, it also alienated the rest of them by negotiating primarily with the Soviet Union on treaty language. Toward the end of 1967, US national security advisor Walt Rostow remarked on the treaty, "Attitudes among top German politicians and officials range from total hostility [...] to grudging acceptance."[44]

Although the United States wore the leadership mantle in the quest for a nonproliferation treaty, in reality it applied its principles asymmetrically, applying lax interpretations of "nuclear" transaction when it suited commercial and security aims. Franco-American commerce is perhaps the most illustrative example of how loose interpretations of a technology's "nuclear" status drove out more strict ones. France by 1960 was a nuclear-armed power and subsequently was skeptical about trying to achieve nonproliferation globally. American officials in the early 1960s debated whether it was appropriate to share nuclear-related technology with the French, if US policy was to avoid nuclear proliferation. One such technology was the computer. A computer is not as obvious a route to proliferation as, say, a nuclear reactor, yet in 1964 the State Department was disturbed to see the pending transfer to France of two computers, one made by Control Data Corporation and the other by IBM. The first was to be used in a French weapons laboratory and the other in the French *Commissariat à l'Énergie Atomique* for general research. Were these "nuclear" technologies to be constrained by safeguards agreements?[45]

In the case of these computers, the Americans were confronted with a clear example of a technology that would be incorporated into France's nuclear weapons program. As part of the Gilpatric committee, American physicist Herbert York pointed out that weapons scientists without access to appropriate computers were severely handicapped. There were fewer obvious ways to slow

214   *J.D. Hamblin*

down progress on a nuclear weapon than to constrain access to computers. And yet, despite clear French intentions with regard to these machines, the task force had to consider the broader ramifications – perhaps some kind of commercial retaliation against US corporations operating in France. Given that the French would likely be able to get these computers elsewhere, was it fair to limit American sales to France?[46] Reasoning based on market competition, which was precisely how Argentina had justified uranium sales to Israel, led the US to allow computers to remain invisible as a proliferation-sensitive technology.

What seemed clear was that "the French are now subtly trying to probe the inadequately coordinated US control mechanism to achieve maximum advantage."[47] Given French views – expressed openly in various speeches and shared in bilateral conversations – that further proliferation was inevitable, these machinations troubled American officials, yet they did little to address them. De Gaulle had stated to Secretary Rusk, for example, that unless the nuclear powers physically suppressed it, proliferation would be impossible to avoid.[48]

The only major step the Americans took to address this kind of nuclear-related trade with France was to ask for formal assurances. In what became known as the Fowler–Debré agreement, the United States required assurances from the French government that any particular transaction would not be diverted for military use. This was identical to what Argentina had asked of Israel in its controversial uranium deal. Initially, Secretary of Treasury Henry H. Fowler wrote to his French counterpart, Minister of Economy and Finance Michel Debré, stating that the United States would not export computers to France "for use in devising, carrying out, or evaluating nuclear explosions, or in nuclear weapons development work."[49] Debré's response provided these assurances, but specifically mentioned the Saclay Center (a nuclear research site) as the recipient, and also used the words "intended use" rather than simply "use." Debré wrote:

> For my part, I confirm that it is not the present intention of the French Government to place any order for advanced computers which would be intended for the preparation or the carrying out of nuclear explosions or the development of nuclear weapons.

Debré made no mention of evaluating nuclear explosions, and the repeated focus on present intent, along with requirement of "no other formality than a written declaration" about their intended use, left considerable latitude for interpretation.[50]

Computers were rarely "visible" in nuclear-related transactions. They were not subject to IAEA safeguards, and in subsequent years commercial pressures thwarted American efforts to keep computers out of other nations' hands even on a bilateral basis. Again the French played a role, exploiting US export standards. For example, in 1979 the French wanted to sell a computer to TASS, the Soviet news agency. State Department officials were outraged, noting that the computer in question was capable of being used for "cryptologic operations, submarine design and nuclear weapons development." The Americans had already denied the sale of a Sperry Univac computer to TASS, and now the French seemed willing to exploit the situation, providing the Soviets with a much more robust computer than the Americans were willing to export.[51] In this case, the French could only assure the Americans that they themselves also had been assured by the Soviets that the computer would not be used for military purposes.

The commercial disadvantage of one nation (the US) seeing computers as militarily sensitive, but another (France) not feeling a need to limit trade was obvious. Lax interpretations of "nuclear" were driving out the strict interpretations and increasingly rendering critical technologies imperceptible. American computer manufacturers leaned heavily on US government agencies to be more permissive, so that they could export computers. In response, the agencies conceded, noting that the export restrictions had become "unnecessarily burdensome on both the government and on US industry." Delays in the approval process alone often led American firms to lose contracts to competitors, by some estimates curtailing export earnings by more than a billion dollars, "thus adversely affecting our balance of payments."[52]

To US government agencies, maintaining their own technology thresholds for proliferation had become too costly by 1979, and they agreed to apply scrutiny asymmetrically, only to cases where proliferation concerns were readily apparent, rather than the US's most important trading partners (including France). Thus, US officials agreed to change the definition for several countries (NATO military allies, Japan, Australia, New Zealand, and France) of what constituted an "advanced" computer, capable of contributing to nuclear weapons programs. In this case the new classification more than doubled the permissible bus rate of the central processing unit and increased the permissible processing data rate by five times. Conversely, the US kept a stricter limitation on exports to other countries, many of whom (unlike France) had signed the NPT.[53]

The above situation applied not only to whole computers but also their peripheral parts. For example, one agency to complain about this liberalization was the Department of Defense, which feared selling American-made hard disk drives that could be used in communist-made computer systems. How could a Western exporter be sure that the disk drive itself would be used in a computer used only for peaceful purposes? This was an echo of what the UK had early on seen as a "glaring defect," in which the bits and pieces of nuclear infrastructure fell out of view. The Department of Defense argued that neither the exporter nor any US licensing authority would have a way of monitoring that. The Department of Defense did not like the idea of "undue strengthening of a communist country's overall computing capacity," given that computing skills and resources passed so easily between civilian and military sectors. The counter-argument was that the US government was now putting itself in the position of blocking companies producing computer peripherals from establishing and maintaining customers. To continue to deny these disk drives to communist computer systems would be to cost peripheral exporters that market completely.[54]

Publicly, the US government claimed it was attempting to tighten exports, particularly those of sensitive technologies. During the presidential election

216   *J.D. Hamblin*

season, in September 1980, President Carter publicly directed his Secretary of Commerce and Attorney General to take steps to investigate and clamp down on such sensitive exports.[55] In reality, rules for some key nuclear-related technologies were being loosened.

Conclusions

Retelling the story of breakdowns in regulating trade in nuclear-related technology does not necessarily belittle the aims of bilateral or multilateral safeguards agreements, inside or outside the purview of the NPT – or the achievements of policy-makers who were sailing unknown waters in pursuit of their governments' interests. Instead, my aim is to highlight the ways in which technologies crucial for nuclear weapons programs have been rendered invisible to those attempting to monitor the nuclear trade. Inspired by the notion that in an open market, lax restrictions will drive out strict ones, this chapter has highlighted some of the ways in which early safeguards priorities, designed to protect commercial interests, pointed the way to a permissive trade in technologies employable within nuclear weapons programs. The responsibility for that situation lays as much in the supplier states as in recipient ones, and as much in the global North as the global South. Although anti-colonial discourse typically pointed to the suppliers as attempting to impose restrictions on non-nuclear-weapon states, creating a kind of "nuclear apartheid," the actions of the nuclear-weapon states suggest that they, as much as anyone, acted to prevent definitions of "nuclear" that might have led to more strict restrictions on nuclear trade.

The 1960s invocation of Gresham's Law – that bad money drives out the good – was a prescient prediction of governments' unwillingness to adopt strict safeguard rules and, after the NPT was in place, to adopt rigorous controls on equipment exports. Even a country openly committed to the NPT and to safeguards, such as the United States, ultimately (and sometimes quietly) simply gave up. In early 1981, for example, the State Department observed how the French were incredibly adept at manipulating the bilateral Fowler–Debré agreement to favor French manufacturers. IBM, an American firm, complained that it had lost six contracts, valued at $18 million, because of long delays in getting approval. The French government delayed providing the US with the required assurances about the computers' end-use for so long that exasperated French buyers decided to go with French suppliers instead. In an effort to finally resolve that particular problem, the United States government bowed to the pressures of US commercial firms, seeing it as impossible to maintain even the semblance of strict policies when others were not doing the same. Through interagency correspondence, a new policy emerged: nothing in the Fowler–Debré agreement required automatic assurances for each sale of advanced computing equipment. The procedure of insisting upon them could simply be discontinued, and any concerns about controls could be done on a case-by-case basis. In the final days of Jimmy Carter's presidency, the State Department recommended that the practice "be quietly discontinued," with no communication to the public or even to

Nuclear safeguards 217

the French government.[56] The US government would just let the commercial firms know that no-one was paying attention anymore. Like so many other bits and pieces of nuclear programs, that particular technology – widely applicable in many domains, but absolutely necessary for making nuclear weapons – became invisible.

Notes

1 The author wishes to thank Roland Popp, Liviu Horovitz, and Christopher McKnight Nichols for valuable feedback on this chapter.

2 Shane J. Maddock, *Nuclear Apartheid: The Quest for American Atomic Supremacy from World War II to the Present* (Chapel Hill, NC: University of North Carolina Press, 2014).

3 Gabrielle Hecht, *Being Nuclear: Africans and the Global Uranium Trade* (Cambridge, MA: MIT Press, 2012); Linda Marie Richards, "Rocks and Reactors: An Atomic Interpretation of Human Rights, 1941–1979," PhD dissertation, Oregon State University, 2014; on the shortfalls among scholars who insist on stark technical definitions, and the importance of recognizing the ambiguity of purpose in nuclear programs, see Itty Abraham, "The Ambivalence of Nuclear Histories," *Osiris* 21, no. 1 (2006): 49–65.

4 On bureaucratic context, i.e., political "pulling and hauling," rather than fixed technological definitions, see Graham Spinardi, "Aldermaston and British Nuclear Weapons Development: Testing the 'Zuckerman Thesis'," *Social Studies of Science* 27 (1997): 547–582; on the role of commercial advocacy in shaping constraints on technology, see Ted Greenwood, "Why Military Technology is Difficult to Restrain," *Science, Technology, and Human Values* 15, no. 4 (1990): 412–429; and Matthew Evangelista, *Innovation and the Arms Race: How the United States and the Soviet Union Develop New Military Technologies* (Ithaca, NY: Cornell University Press, 1988).

5 M.I. Michaels to R.C. Hope-Jones (British Embassy, Vienna), February 1, 1965, *UK National Archives*, Kew, UK, folder EG 8/2 "Nuclear Safeguard System."

6 Discrepancies among Europeans for observing nonproliferation rules are detailed in Grégoire Mallard, *Fallout: Nuclear Diplomacy in an Age of Global Fracture* (Chicago, IL: University of Chicago Press, 2014).

7 John Krige, "The Peaceful Atom as a Political Weapon: Euratom and American Foreign Policy in the Late 1950s," *Historical Studies in the Natural Sciences* 38, no. 1 (2008): 5–44.

8 Astrid Forland, "Negotiating Supranational Rules: The Genesis of International Atomic Energy Agency Safeguards System," PhD dissertation, University of Bergen, 1997, 12.

9 Forland, "Negotiating Supranational Rules," 84f.; on the IAEA's struggles to get nations to "take seriously" its role in establishing safeguards guidelines, even prior to the NPT, see David Fischer, *History of the International Atomic Energy Agency: The First Forty Years* (Vienna: IAEA, 1997), 245–252; and Paul C. Szasz, "IAEA Safeguards for NPT," *Review of European Community and International Environmental Law* 5, no. 3 (1996): 239–245.

10 McGeorge Bundy, Memorandum for the Record, October 19, 1964, *Foreign Relations of the United States* (FRUS), 1964–1968, XXX, doc. 60.

11 On US inaction prior to 1964, see William Burr and Jeffrey T. Richelson, "Whether to 'Strangle the Baby in the Cradle': The United States and the Chinese Nuclear Program, 1960–64," *International Security* 25, no. 3 (2000/01): 54–99.

12 Report of Meetings, Tapei, October 23–24, 1964, FRUS, 1964–1968, XXX, doc. 62.

13 Memo from the Joint Chiefs of Staff to McNamara, January 16, 1965, ibid., doc. 76.

14 MemCon, November 23, 1964, FRUS, 1964–1968, XI, doc. 50.

218   *J.D. Hamblin*

15 MemCon, December 9, 1964, ibid., doc. 54.
16 MemCon, November 23, 1964, ibid., doc. 50.
17 The quote is from Minutes of Discussion, Committee on Nuclear Proliferation, January 7–8, 1965, ibid., doc. 60.
18 Ibid.
19 Report by the Committee on Nuclear Proliferation, January 21, 1965, ibid., doc. 64.
20 The role of the report in helping the Johnson administration focus its priorities is emphasized in Hal Brands, "Rethinking Nonproliferation: LBJ, the Gilpatric Committee, and US National Security Policy," *Journal of Cold War Studies* 8, no. 2 (2006): 83–113; Brands explicitly contrasts his view with previous scholarship downplaying the committee's significance, especially George Perkovich, *India's Nuclear Bomb: The Impact on Global Proliferation* (Berkeley: University of California Press, 1999); and Shane Maddock, "The Nth Country Conundrum: The American and Soviet Quest for Non-Proliferation, 1945–1970," PhD dissertation, University of Connecticut, 1997.
21 The controversial aspects of the Gilpatric report, though it would "pave the way" for the Nuclear Nonproliferation Treaty, are highlighted in Francis J. Gavin, "Blasts from the Past: Proliferation Lessons from the 1960s," *International Security* 29, no. 3 (2004/2005): 100–135.
22 MemCon (William C. Foster and Lord Chalfont), August 1, 1965, FRUS, 1964–1968, XI, doc. 91.
23 R.C. Hope-Jones to M.I. Michaels, January 22, 1965, UK National Archives, EG 8/2.
24 On substitution, see Forland, "Negotiating Supranational Rules," 201–204.
25 In addition to the military reprocessing facilities, three commercial reprocessing facilities were built in the United States. These were General Electric's Midwest Fuel Recovery Plant in Morris, Illinois (completed but never fully in operation); Allied General Nuclear Services's plant in Barnwell, South Carolina (never went into operation); and Nuclear Fuel Service's facility in West Valley, New York (begun reprocessing in 1966). See "Plutonium Recovery from Spent Fuel Reprocessing by Nuclear Fuel Services at West Valley, New York from 1966 to 1972," prepared by US Department of Energy, February 1996, www.osti.gov/opennet/document/purecov/nfsrepo.html (accessed January 17, 2014).
26 M.I. Michaels to R.C. Hope-Jones, January 29, 1965, UK National Archives, EG 8/2.
27 See International Atomic Energy Agency, INFCIRC/66/Rev.1, September 12, 1967, www.iaea.org/Publications/Documents/Infcircs/Others/infcirc66r1.pdf (accessed January 23, 2014).
28 The point about nuclear technological supremacy is made well in John Krige, "US Technological Superiority and the Special Nuclear Relationship: Contrasting British and US Policies for Controlling the Proliferation of Gas-Centrifuge Enrichment," *The International History Review* 36, no. 2 (2014): 230–251.
29 M.I. Michaels to R.C. Hope-Jones, January 29, 1965, UK National Archives, EG 8/2.
30 IAEA Board of Governors, Official Record of the Three Hundred and Fifty-Sixth Meeting, February 25, 1965 (dated May 13, 1965), UK National Archives, EG 8/2.
31 American Embassy, Buenos Aires, to U.S. Department of State, February 3, 1965 (and enclosures), NARA 59, 1964–1966 Inco-Uranium, from http://digitalarchive.wilsoncenter.org/document/117168 (accessed January 7, 2014).
32 IAEA Board of Governors, Official Record of the Three Hundred and Fifty-Sixth Meeting, February 25, 1965 (dated May 13, 1965), UK National Archives, EG 8/2.
33 Ibid.
34 Ibid.
35 Ibid.
36 Ibid.
37 Ibid.
38 Ibid.

Nuclear safeguards 219

39 Report of the Working Group to review the Agency's Safeguards System, n. d., and C.E. Coffin, Submission to the Minister, February 19, 1965, UK National Archives, EG 8/2.
40 M.I. Michaels to R.C. Hope-Jones (British Embassy, Vienna), February 1, 1965, UK National Archives, folder EG 8/2 "Nuclear Safeguard System."
41 Ibid.
42 Ibid.
43 Ibid.
44 Memo from Rostow to President Johnson, November 7, 1967, FRUS, 1964–1968, XI, doc. 215.
45 Draft Minutes of Discussion of the Second Meeting of Committee on Nuclear Proliferation, December 13–14, 1964, ibid., doc. 56.
46 Ibid.
47 Ibid.
48 MemCon (Secretary's Meeting with the Gilpatric Committee on Non-Proliferation), January 7, 1965, FRUS, 1964–1968, XI, doc. 59.
49 Henry Fowler to Michel Debré, September 24, 1966, Jimmy Carter Presidential Library, Atlanta, GA (JCL), Remote Archives Capture Program (RAC), NLC-12–17-4-25–9.
50 Michel Debré to Henry Fowler, September 24, 1966, JCL, RAC, NLC-12–17–4-25–9.
51 Ernest B. Johnston, Jr., to Secretary, Department of State, briefing memo on "French Computer Export to TASS," December 8, 1979, JCL, RAC, NLC-12–17–6-16–7.
52 The agencies in agreement were: State, Energy, Defense, Treasury, Commerce, and the Arms Control and Disarmament Agency. See Thomas W. Hoya (Commerce) to Benjamin Huberman (National Security Council), April 10, 1979, JCL, RAC, NLC-12–41–2-6–5.
53 Ibid.
54 Summary of the SubACEP Meeting at the Commerce Department, June 21, 1978, JCL, RAC, NLC-12–24–9-4–9.
55 US Department of Commerce press release, "President Directs Tighter Controls to Prevent Illegal Exports," September 8, 1980, JCL, RAC, NLC-12–41–5-16–1.
56 Peter Tarnoff, Memo for Zbigniew Brzezinkski, January 7, 1981, JCL, RAC, NLC-12–17–4-25–9.

Part III
Conclusion

12 Nuclear technology and political power in the making of the nuclear order

Andreas Wenger and Liviu Horovitz[1]

At the core of the Treaty on the Non-Proliferation of Nuclear Weapons (NPT) lays the fundamental asymmetry between the unequal rights and obligations of the five recognized nuclear-weapon states (NWS) – the United States, Russia, China, the United Kingdom, and France – and all other adherents to the treaty, the non-nuclear-weapon states (NNWS).[2] Given this unique arrangement, it comes as no surprise that the same questions of balance, justice, and fairness that already dominated the public utterances during the treaty's negotiation resurface persistently, both during the NPT's periodic diplomatic meetings and within the accompanying policy publications.[3]

Within this context, the perennial question surrounding this treaty has been why an overwhelming majority of states was sooner or later willing to join such a discriminatory arrangement, even though India, Pakistan, Israel, and North Korea substantiated their nuclear ambitions outside the treaty's framework.[4] We build upon both the arguments presented in this volume, the debates within the international relations literature, and the broader historical scholarship on the Cold War to contend that the answer to this enduring puzzle reflects the fundamental relationship between nuclear technology and political power. Many states, we conclude, saw the NPT's emergence (1) as an encroachment upon their freedom of movement, but also (2) as an opportunity to pursue broader foreign policy interests, while (3) not necessarily representing a definitive nuclear choice.

To explain NPT adherence by NNWS, three theories can be discerned from the available literature. First, the "grand bargain theory" posits a link between the NNWS renunciation and a NWS promise of nuclear assistance for peaceful purposes and a pledge of eventual nuclear disarmament.[5] Second, the "cartel theory" emphasizes the role of coercion and bribery by the NWS.[6] Third, the "collusion theory" merges superpower pressure with a NNWS interest in coordinated restraint.[7] The empirical evidence presented within the chapters of this volume offers only partial support for any of these theoretical models. In relation to superpower behavior, "collusion theory" appears to be the most promising point of departure for future theorizing. However, the findings within this book and broader Cold War scholarship suggest NPT research within political science would benefit from less parsimonious explanatory frameworks to explain the behavior of NNWS.

224   *A. Wenger and L. Horovitz*

In this conclusion, we distill three central insights that might help towards better understanding the making of the nuclear order. First, as most states had a strong preference towards keeping all options open en route to an unpredictable future, numerous governments saw the NPT as limiting their autonomy. The treaty's emergence forced almost all into costly choices for both the present and – more important – the future, thereby causing noteworthy protestation from various states. Second, in addition to its constraints, the NPT also provided a forum for political bargaining about the future regional and global order, and the role of small, middle, and great powers in international politics. Thus, different elites – within diverse political, economic, and social contexts – perceived varying material and ideational benefits from actively participating in the establishment of the treaty. Finally, the ambivalence of both the legal agreement and its underlying technology alleviated strategic, status, and industrial concerns: where some could intertwine deterrence discussions with bargaining for political influence and prestige, others could hedge their nuclear bets under the treaty's cover, and again others saw their commercial ambitions unscathed.

This conclusion proceeds as follows: the first section details the three core insights we identify and systematize from the various chapters of this volume. The second delves deeper towards explaining what role these factors played within the negotiations on the political order in Europe. The third section outlines the implications of these chances and constraints for the establishment of the global regime. We end this conclusion with a brief discussion of avenues for further research.

Resenting potential costs, bargaining over benefits, and gauging ambiguity

Most contributions on the NPT and a majority of the broader analyses on states' rationale for joining international treaties tend to see decisions as immediate trade-offs: countries adhere or abstain subsequent to an assessment of costs and benefits in light of their current interests.[8] Following this logic, states with extant nuclear ambitions are screened by the treaty and self-select among abstainers. Conversely, all others have little to lose from ratifying a treaty that prohibits nothing they desire.[9] However, the contributions within this book reveal a much more complex decision-making mechanism, oriented towards the future and dominated by uncertainty. Faced with the emergence of a treaty likely to structure interstate relations far into the future, policy-makers assessed the various costs, benefits, and ambiguities the NPT encompassed, and bargained for the best possible outcome for themselves and their country.

A disagreeable choice, whatever you do

As both this book's chapters and other case-studies illustrate, countries keen to acquire their own nuclear weapons capability saw the NPT as imposing significant costs upon them.[10] While the five proliferators who had managed to

Conclusion 225

explode a nuclear device before January 1967 were recognized as legitimate owners of atomic arms, subsequent proliferators received no other option than to remain outside a treaty that eventually became nearly universal. In addition, abstaining from the treaty suggested one's proliferation ambitions before a nuclear detonation could display one's definitive capability, thereby pushing neighbors, rivals, and superpowers to rethink bilateral relations. Finally, the international pressure resulting from the refusal to ratify the NPT strengthened the hand of domestic pro-bomb lobbies, thereby limiting decision-makers' freedom of movement at home.

Emerging as a compromise between the United States and the Soviet Union, the NPT eliminated the Multilateral Force (MLF), an option long-considered within the Western coalition. Thus, it appeared to restrict, for instance, Italian, West German, or Dutch options to exercise influence within NATO, and therefore initially generated significant backlash, as the specific chapters reveal. On the one hand, strategists within Western European establishments worried about the credibility of US extended deterrence. On the other hand – and much more apparent within the findings offered within this volume – political leaders in Rome, The Hague, or Bonn worried about status questions, fearing nuclear inequality would place their country at a disadvantage within the broader European context.

Aside from immediate nuclearization pressures, various states preferred to keep their options open into an uncertain future. For various reasons, such governments did not consider nuclear acquisition momentarily auspicious. Nevertheless, policy-makers resented the additional costs the NPT was likely to add to a future nuclear reversal. For instance, verification mechanisms could potentially hamper covert acquisition. Additionally, both being caught red-handed and withdrawing from the agreement were likely to come at a price – suspicions that were confirmed by later proliferation instances. Moreover, becoming party to an international agreement would weaken the hand of bomb proponents in any future internal debate.[11]

Even decision-makers believing their state was unlikely to ever cross the nuclear Rubicon valued the benefits of uncertainty. Political leverage was available for as long as neighbors, rivals, or protectors believed nuclearization was a possibility. For instance, the chapter on the FRG argues that numerous policy-makers in Bonn thought uncertainty about their country's nuclear status provided them with clout in both Washington and Moscow. In contrast, the additional costs imposed by the NPT upon a country deciding to either build nuclear weapons covertly or withdraw from the treaty reduced this uncertainty, thereby diminishing diplomatic leverage.

Finally, many states were concerned with the treaty's impact upon their commercial interests. As nuclear technology is inherently dual-use, government officials worried that strengthened nonproliferation efforts would obstruct the development and trading of knowledge and machinery.[12] As the chapters on Mexico or Australia illustrate, where developing nations dreaded about their ability to import nuclear goods, technology owners were anxious about

226   A. Wenger and L. Horovitz

industrial espionage through international inspections, and exporters feared for their ability to sell their merchandise. Ultimately, as Leopoldo Nuti argues in the chapter on Italy, the treaty represented "an unpleasant choice" for many.[13]

Bargaining on the future global and regional order

Notwithstanding these costs, the emergence of the NPT also epitomized a unique opportunity for many states to pursue their particular interests. The treaty's negotiations advanced in the context of the broader geopolitical transformation from the so-called bilateral superpower détente of the early 1960s to the multilateral and global détente of the 1970s.[14] Within this setting, bilateral bargaining between allies and their protectors in both Europe and Asia, multidimensional consultations at the regional level within NATO or the Warsaw Pact, and multilateral negotiations within the Eighteen-Nation Committee on Disarmament (ENDC) and the UN General Assembly (UNGA) allowed committed participants to shape the redistribution of increasingly multidimensional political power.

These secondary actors employed the NPT to leverage a multitude of specific interests, such as instituting regional frameworks of mutual restraint, pursuing a rival's nuclear abstinence, tying in security guarantees and expanding influence within an alliance, increasing their foreign policy leeway, establishing themselves as an important diplomatic player, or expressing domestic political changes. Thus, what emerges from the chapters of this book is that the treaty's provisions were jointly produced by top-down superpower collusion on nonproliferation – as detailed in Roland Popp's chapter – and a bottom-up buy-in by small and medium powers, which saw at least some of their interests heeded. Ultimately, being directly dependent upon majority consent of multilateral UN bodies, an effective and legitimate agreement could only be obtained as a result of such bargaining – a reality both superpowers fully recognized, the chapters in this volume suggest.

For instance – and supporting a long-held institutionalist conceptual argument – the chapters on Australia or Japan exemplify how many states perceived the NPT as establishing a regional framework for mutual restraint, helping governments to credibly signal their commitment to desist from acquiring a nuclear arsenal.[15] Nevertheless, it is interesting to note that states with limited nuclear ambitions of their own also saw the treaty as an opportunity to lobby their protectors and pressure their neighbors to secure the latter's non-nuclear status. For instance, Bonn's adherence to the NPT in the absence of a multilateral nuclear force seems to have been pursued not only from Washington and Moscow, but considerably also from Rome, The Hague, East Berlin, or Warsaw.

In addition, both within NATO and the Warsaw Pact, smaller allies used the nonproliferation issue to expand the range and substance of multilateral political consultations. Unlike discussions on nuclear deterrence, which were largely carried among superpowers, the nonproliferation negotiations (somewhat) leveled the playing field. Thus, the erosion of the superpowers' ability to single-handedly determine the pace of political détente surfaced within both alliances,

Conclusion 227

albeit to different degrees.[16] After France's departure from the military structures of NATO, the Harmel reforms led to a less hierarchical and more political alliance.[17] Conversely, Soviet allies expanded political consultations, albeit within narrower limits, as the chapter on the Warsaw Pact indicates. However, the same chapter shows how Romania held much more parochial intentions, mainly attempting to misuse the nonproliferation talks to signal its increased independence from Moscow.

Furthermore, the NPT negotiations were linked to broader social changes.[18] The nuclear choices of small and great powers alike – as many chapters in this volume also illustrate – were influenced and constrained by a combination of international and domestic developments. First, electoral changes brought into office a new generation of political leaders who were interested in going beyond established nuclear policies. Second, distinct institutional fractions with a different vision of a more institutionalized global order emerged within various bureaucracies. Finally, a normative change took place within several countries, establishing increased support within broader segments of the population for anti-nuclear ideas. Thus, the NPT also provided an opportunity to align foreign policy with changing domestic values and perspectives.

A vague treaty on an ambivalent technology

In addition to costs and opportunities, both the legal ambiguity and the technological ambivalence of the regime contributed to the ultimate settlement. Insights from science and technology studies can help us better understand the link between nuclear knowledge and machinery on the one hand, and international politics on the other.[19] The almost unimaginable destructive power of nuclear technology, together with its great promise of progress and wealth, corroborated with its scarcity and durability renders it a perfect symbol of political status and influence as well as technological mastery and development.[20] Yet the link between nuclear technology and political order goes beyond symbolism. Within the context of NPT negotiations, the interaction between the highly technical and the eminently political had very practical meaning, creating and limiting the negotiating space, and distributing potential costs and benefits in various domains.

In Europe – as the next section will discuss in more detail and many chapters in this book reveal – policy-makers attempted to circumscribe the future regional and global order by means of a debate about nuclear ownership schemes. Allies debated endless versions of a multilateral nuclear force, both within NATO and with the members of the Warsaw Pact. Yet within all these discussions, the physical formula and the political formula of such a force were inextricably linked, and the uncertainty surrounding the utility of nuclear weaponry allowed for broad compromises: while questions of operational efficiency and effective deterrence were of secondary interests, the focus rested upon the consequences of such formulas for the distribution of political power and influence, not only in the short-term, but far into the future.

228 *A. Wenger and L. Horovitz*

Conversely, a technology that is inherently dual-use unavoidably creates opportunities for nuclear latency and hedging, key characteristics that can be manipulated politically.[21] In adversarial relationships, latency offers an opportunity to leverage the deterrence effects of a virtual capability, while at the same time avoiding the costs of overt proliferation. Within relations of extended deterrence, suspicion about allied intent can be leveraged for political influence, as the chapter on West Germany shows. Yet the shadow of the nuclear future can also serve as a fall-back option, in case the credibility of security guarantees erodes, as leaders in Tokyo appear to have assessed. Conversely, nuclear latency allows for ripping the domestic and international benefits of good citizenship, while essentially postponing a nuclear decision, as the chapter on Italy suggests.[22]

Lastly, the inability and unwillingness to define a "nuclear thing" in a narrow manner permitted both buyers and vendors of nuclear technology to support a treaty that threatened to curtail their economic interests. Questions related to the relative efficiency of mechanisms designed to expose covert proliferation were often outweighed by the implications of these verification procedures for the distribution of commercial opportunity, as the chapter on safeguards shows. It took decades for a majority of states to roughly accept a subordination of industrial interest to nonproliferation aims. Yet during the NPT negotiations, the inherent ambivalence of both nuclear technology and the emergent treaty allowed for flexible trade-offs among antithetic interests and values, ultimately enabling a compromise.

Nuclear negotiations and long-term political order in Europe

Nuclear policy on extended deterrence had been tightly linked with political dynamics since the establishment of the Western alliance.[23] Nevertheless, towards the end of the 1950s, the rapid nuclearization of NATO, coupled with a growing Soviet potential to damage the US homeland, linked discussions over Washington's technical ability and political willingness to extend a nuclear umbrella over its European allies to a decade-long debate on hierarchy, autonomy, and the future of political order on the continent. Limited nuclear sharing was established as a tool to reassure allies and prevent political decoupling, but a general expectation that the spread of nuclear weapons was unstoppable generated substantial doubts among European states. At the same time, the incipient détente between Washington and Moscow raised status anxiety and fears of superpower collusion among US allies.[24] It is within this context that various arguments made within this book – West Germany's limited nuclear revisionism, Italy's attempt to leverage the MLF to uphold parity among continental powers, the Dutch efforts to keep Washington engaged in European affairs, or the Warsaw Pact members' struggle to gain more leverage – should be seen.

Conclusion   229

Nuclear conundrums and the limits of the "constructed peace"[25]

Many within the incoming Kennedy administration (1961) believed that the Soviets doubted the US commitment to use nuclear weapons to defend West Berlin. Kennedy officials thought a credible deterrent could not rely upon an incredible threat of massive retaliation. Thus, the new administration shifted towards the concept of flexible response, stressing the broader spectrum of warfare. The unintended consequence, however, was that lifting the nuclear threshold demanded the ability to control escalation. Washington began to emphasize the integrated nature of the alliance's nuclear defense and the necessity of strict centralization. Allies' de facto physical control over warheads and the spread of independent nuclear deterrents had become a burden. Thus, not only did allied fears that the two superpowers would bilaterally decide the future of political order in Europe increase dramatically in the aftermath of the Berlin and Cuban crises in 1961–1962, but the emphasis on central control was perceived as undermining allies' political influence even further.[26]

Washington and Moscow finding a *modus vivendi* by linking the nuclear and the German questions was anathema to the superpowers' protégés, as it did not accommodate their key interests centered around political equality and autonomy. As a consequence, France, under de Gaulle's presidency, started a step-by-step withdrawal of military forces from NATO's command.[27] When, in June 1966, Paris embarked on a bilateral rapprochement with Moscow in an attempt to take the lead on political détente on the continent, what had been an ominous writing on the wall since 1963 seemed likely to become reality: the alliance might wither away by the end of the decade, letting West Germany conduct its affairs integrated within a European political union, or – under the even less appealing scenario – within a Soviet dominated security order.[28]

Within this broader political context, the concept of a multilateral nuclear force rapidly developed into the key policy tool to defuse growing European doubts about the credibility of the US nuclear guarantees, and thereby ensure the political integration of the FRG into the multilateral structures of NATO. Policymakers on both sides of the Atlantic believed only a hardware solution would give Bonn an appropriate role within the alliance, while permanent nuclear discrimination would force it to move closer to Paris. Attachment to this view seemed widely shared within the alliance's pecking order, as, for instance, the chapter on Italy shows, with diplomats in Rome believing that only a hardware solution would preserve Italy's equal status with regard to other European powers. Thus, nuclear sharing had become both a reassurance and a nonproliferation tool, a balance that ultimately resembled an attempt to square the circle. Yet the arduous debates within and between NATO and the Warsaw Pact on the link between sharing and nonproliferation created the space for a gradual convergence on the contours of the future European political order.[29]

Ultimately, for superpower détente to advance, the linkage between the nuclear and the German question had to be substantiated, and for that a nonproliferation treaty needed to be concluded. Here was the chance of smaller allies,

230   A. Wenger and L. Horovitz

not only within NATO but also within the Warsaw Pact, to expand their political role by forcing the two superpowers into lengthy consultations. As Laurien Crump-Gabreëls makes clear in the chapter on the Warsaw Pact, worried that the MLF was only a first step towards a West German nuclear force, East Berlin and Warsaw pressured Moscow to oppose an NPT that did not exclude an MLF option. In contrast, senior US officials tried to persuade their Soviet counterparts that an MLF would not grant the West Germans full control over nuclear weapons. Conversely, Moscow sent ambiguous signals as to the conditions under which it would accept a nonproliferation treaty that would not completely ban nuclear sharing. With no coherent policy on nonproliferation and nuclear sharing in either Washington or Moscow, a solution remained out of sight.[30]

Nonproliferation as a global issue and NATO's shift to a software solution

In 1964, however, the People's Republic of China's (PRC) nuclear test set in motion a number of developments that decisively impacted these European equations.[31] Most important, Beijing's nuclearization refocused US and Soviet policy-makers' attention onto the consequences of nuclear proliferation for the overall strategic environment.[32] Thus, even if the hardware solution specified in the British proposal for an Atlantic Nuclear Force (ANF) was kept nominally on the table for diplomatic reasons, Washington's diplomats proposed an ad hoc body within NATO to examine the means of improving the allies' participation in nuclear planning – a Select Committee, a software solution which would later become the Nuclear Planning Group.[33] Given the Johnson administration's relative reluctance to impose a specific nuclear sharing alternative upon its protégés, an intriguing question remains why Washington's allies ultimately accepted a software option. What surfaces from the chapters of this volume – and strengthens the findings of previous scholarship – is that European powers grudgingly realized that it was neither possible nor desirable to solve their differences over continental political order though the technical and legal parameters of a hardware formula.

The various physical formulas for a hardware solution that were circulated over time mirrored fundamentally different visions of political order in Europe. The core questions were how transatlantic, European, or pan-European various arrangements would and could be, and what consequences would they imply for the role and influence of particular countries. As Elmar Hellendoorn writes, the Dutch feared a French–German condominium, and therefore opposed any European nuclear option and wanted national control over US, British, and French nuclear forces. In contrast, Nuti notes, the Italians were concerned that a formula which did not allow for a European nuclear force would hand over continental leadership to France. The British, fearing a selective détente between Bonn and Moscow, opposed a European option based on majority voting but thought it unwise to exclude a future European force. Finally, as Andreas Lutsch outlines, the West Germans seemed willing to accept a non-production, but rejected a

Conclusion 231

non-transfer clause and lobbied for keeping the option of a European force open. Yet, to close this circle of complex interrelations, both the Soviets and the French opposed a significant nuclear role for the FRG.

Given these antithetic preferences, the European states realized that a software option constituted a compromise solution, both domestically and within the alliance. Where a hardware solution inherently created winners and losers, a software solution de-emphasized questions of political status and prestige, and provided the allies with a flexible tool to fine-tune the transformation of NATO towards an increasingly political – and somewhat less hierarchical – military alliance. While France left the alliance's military structures, Washington and Paris ultimately compromised through the Harmel process on a limited expansion of NATO's political machinery. The FRG's position was strengthened considerably by the US and UK willingness to involve Bonn in the establishment of a new consensus on military strategy and burden sharing within the trilateral talks. In addition, the FRG's demand for greater participation in NATO's nuclear weapons planning was heeded and Bonn could take the lead on the development of *Ostpolitik*. To accommodate the status anxieties of countries like Italy, the Nuclear Planning Group was expanded.[34]

In addition to these strategic considerations, the shift from a hardware to a software solution was eased by domestic political developments. Nuclear policy-making had been dominated in the 1950s by a small strategic elite, largely shielded from broader public debates. In contrast, in the 1960s, significant social forces became increasingly critical of the geopolitical status quo generated by the nuclear stalemate. Under these circumstances, politicians quickly realized that a hardware solution would establish winners and losers within and across political groupings and could become a rallying symbol for both anti-nuclear protesters and nationalist forces. In contrast, a software solution could deliver important benefits – a right to be consulted – while at the same time deflect public criticism of nuclear dependence from the United States. Consultations within NATO also provided elites with a forum to discuss nuclear policy that was sheltered from public scrutiny. Finally, electoral change in key capitals – from Washington to Bonn, The Hague, or Rome – eased the transition to new policies.[35]

On the other side of the Iron Curtain, as Crump-Gabreëls persuasively argues, Soviet diplomats also saw themselves drawn into multiple consultations with the other members of the Warsaw Pact. On the one hand, the PRC test had galvanized Soviet interests in concluding an NPT. On the other hand, the Soviet–Chinese split had offered Romania an opportunity to assert its political autonomy. Bucharest played the devil's advocate for Beijing and, at least for some time, successfully prevented a common position of the Warsaw Pact that would have been detrimental to Chinese interests. Nevertheless, while Romania's dissent forced the Soviets into complex diplomatic concoctions, Bucharest ultimately could not prevent Moscow from pushing ahead with its desired policy. Once it had achieved the abandonment of an MLF-type sharing scheme, the Soviet Union gradually shifted towards a compromise,

232 A. Wenger and L. Horovitz

accepting an increased German voice within NATO's nuclear planning and a number of other concessions. Thus, the two superpowers were now in agreement on the fundamentals of the future treaty.

The NPT and the future of the global order

This monumental bilateral agreement between Washington and Moscow was an indispensable condition for the NPT's emergence. However, the two superpowers recognized that broad global support was needed for a legitimate and effective treaty to emerge. On the one hand, both Americans and Soviets focused on bringing their own allies onboard. Many continued to oppose the agreement due to the remaining uncertainty about the eventual adherence of their neighbors and rivals, the enduring doubts about the treaty's consequences for commercial interests, and the political consequences of joining such an unequal treaty. As the relevant chapters show, countries like Italy and West Germany played a stalling game before ultimately acceding to the treaty. On the other hand, both superpowers began to jointly lobby for support within the Global South, where many perceived the NPT's asymmetry as a reflection of a global order that favored the developed North.[36] Thus, in addition to a yes/no decision about nuclear weapons, many within the South saw the NPT as a platform to advance sovereign equality and economic development. However, to the superpower's benefit, the Non-Aligned Movement (NAM) was far from coherent, its members split on what should be demanded for their support for the treaty.

Superpower incentives and constraints were a necessary but not sufficient condition to ensure wide-ranging adherence to the treaty. Overarching trends towards an increasingly multilateral and diffused global order facilitated numerous actors' decision-making. Nonetheless, multilateral NPT negotiations provided active participants with an opportunity to carve out a larger role for themselves in international affairs, a chance states seized to leverage their specific foreign policy interests. Three dynamics jointly help explain the eventual widespread backing for the NPT. First, norm entrepreneurs were essential in delivering regional legitimacy for a highly unequal treaty. Such states were prepared to accept the noncommittal disarmament pledges of the superpowers in exchange for solidifying their regional role and receiving assurances regarding access to nuclear technologies. Second, the inherent dualism of nuclear technology, coupled with relatively weak verification mechanisms, allowed for nuclear latency, thus rendering hedging compatible with support for the NPT. Finally, developing regional dynamics influenced states' diplomatic choices. Thus, neighbors' decisions, protectors' interventions, and domestic perceptions both constrained and facilitated calculations in nuclear diplomacy.

Regional norm entrepreneurs, compromises on disarmament, and political inequality

Mexico's diplomats – as Jonathan Hunt's chapter remarkably illustrates – skillfully employed the multilateral platform offered by NPT negotiations to establish

Conclusion 233

their country as an important regional actor and ensure a postcolonial conception of nuclear rights was anchored within the treaty. Already before the NPT's arrival on the international stage, the country had positioned itself as a driving force behind regional efforts to prohibit nuclear weapons. Establishing a nuclear-weapons free zone in Latin America and the Caribbean, the Mexico-driven Treaty of Tlatelolco emphasized regional self-determination and solidarity, thereby attempting to diminish Washington's regional clout. In short, Mexico employed the voting leverage of the Latin American delegations within the UN to transform the NPT from a collusion of superpower interests into a more global settlement that accounted for its own interests.

Once the NPT reached the ENDC in Geneva, numerous NNWS became increasingly vocal with respect to the kind of treaty they were willing to accept. Nevertheless, the NAM was split over many elements of the future treaty, and especially in regard to the NWS disarmament obligations, the right to peaceful nuclear explosions, and the inclusion of superpowers security guarantees. Countries like India, Brazil, or Argentina demanded, inter alia, more binding disarmament requirements. Delhi's diplomats even insisted that the treaty should be rejected on the grounds that it was a not a credible instrument towards the elimination of nuclear weapons. Overall, the discriminatory nature of the NPT was the key argument for these actors toward inducing other states to abstain from the treaty.

Nevertheless, the treaty's opponents ultimately failed to rally others against the NPT because norm entrepreneurs like Mexico (or Sweden) were prepared to accept the vague commitments on disarmament in exchange for satisfying some of their own interests. Thus, Mexico insisted upon obtaining NWS – and especially US – ratification of the Protocol II to the Tlatelolco treaty, a provision limiting NWS freedom of choice regarding nuclear use. In addition, Mexico argued the NPT would better preserve the interests of the NNWS in the global South if the economic goals of developing countries in regard to peaceful uses of nuclear technology were taken into account. Therefore, Mexican amendments to the draft focused on technical assistance and civilian benefits. Conversely, for both US and Soviet diplomats, a significantly widened adherence could be exchanged for provisions that did not dramatically alter the treaty's basic substance.[37]

Peaceful uses, technological invisibility, and economic development

Yet broad adherence was not only facilitated by superpower collusion, intra-alliance negotiations, and secondary provisions assuaging regional concerns. Both the inherent ambivalence of nuclear technology and the purposeful legal vagueness of the treaty's text allowed various actors to join the NPT without having made definitive choices. In addition – as Jacob Hamblin's chapter ably narrates – commercial ambitions caused policy indecision and a lack of coordination, ultimately resulting in lax control mechanisms. Before the NPT's arrival, both vendors and buyers had been reluctant to accept even modest commercial losses in exchange for strengthened verification mechanisms. When the Johnson administration decided to make nonproliferation a priority, a loose interpretation of safeguards was already in place. Thus, Washington's push for stricter control provisions turned into a losing battle. Ultimately, pressure from various corners thwarted US efforts to keep sensitive materials out of other nations' hands during the NPT's first years.

Concern about commercial disadvantage was the key reason why almost all countries opted for a lax interpretation of what counted as nuclear materials. While a majority of states eventually accepted the political asymmetry enshrined in the NPT, no coalition emerged in support of stricter safeguards. To the contrary, where countries with decipherable nuclear ambitions – like, for instance, India – brandished strict safeguards as incompatible with their sovereignty, numerous developing countries had honest concerns about their future access to the nuclear technologies they believed key to development and prosperity. In contrast, suppliers like France or South Africa had an interest in liberalizing nuclear trade. Even close American allies like the FRG were willing to actively exploit loopholes, and numerous entities within the United States lobbied for fewer restrictions upon their business interests.

Three factors emerge from Hamblin's contribution as having rendered coordination on strengthening nonproliferation particularly difficult. First, when one state insisted that another implement a certain export control or safeguards measure, it was quickly accused of shielding own economic interest behind the security reasoning. Second, numerous developing nations pointed out that – given the expected benefits – potential proliferators would actually bear the costs and substitute denied technology, but the burden imposed by export controls and safeguards upon the civilian side of the equation was unacceptable. Finally, states were rightly concerned that even if they were to deny an export, other suppliers would be easily found, thus doing nonproliferation no service while incurring important commercial losses. Technologies crucial for nuclear weapons programs were thus rendered temporarily "invisible" – as Hamblin argues – and weakened the treaty's constraints, but, at the same time, made NPT accession a less burdensome affair.

Regional security environments, alliance patterns, and decisions to abstain

In Europe, NPT negotiations linked military power to political détente and were intimately connected to considerations about the future of regional order. In contrast, other regions exhibited different political dynamics, shaped by their own geography, history, and culture – dynamics nowhere better exemplified than in the Asian context. When confronted with the NPT's emergence, policy-makers within this region had to consider significant interstate rivalry, weak security multilateralism, and a system of exclusive bilateral alliances between the United States and its most important regional partners. Early Sino-Soviet cooperation was stopped abruptly when the split between Beijing and Moscow developed

Conclusion 235

into an irreparable antagonism in the early 1960s. The PRC's nuclearization sent tremors throughout the region, prompting assessments that it would unleash a proliferation chain reaction. However, the Chinese Communist test both galvanized pressures towards national nuclear capabilities and spurred a growing desire to curb regional proliferation. Thus, superpower efforts to obtain support for the nascent NPT yielded a mixed outcome in Asia, as the chapters on India, Japan, and Australia in this volume show.

Deeply disturbed by the Chinese test – and assessing its reverberations upon the regional security in general and its rivalry with Beijing more specifically – Delhi's discourse on nuclear weapons shifted. Where it had emphasized nuclear disarmament as the ultimate goal of multilateral negotiations, India started underlining the discriminatory nature of superpower-designed frameworks of abstention and the need to build a sustainable nuclear infrastructure and an independent nuclear energy program. Given that the NPT did not provide a solution for dealing with Beijing's newfound strength, India's first and foremost interest was not letting the budding nonproliferation treaty constrain its own nuclear aspirations. As Vinod Kumar perceptively observes, the NPT's weak disarmament commitments were ultimately a saving grace for Delhi, enabling it to reject the agreement while keeping the moral high ground.

In Japan, the PRC's test had also triggered both strategic and status concerns. However, as Fintan Hoey shows, Tokyo's nuclear abstinence was the result of conflicting priorities that included the necessity to account for public perceptions, the constraints of the alliance with the United States, and an assessment of security needs. Japan remains the only country to have been attacked with nuclear weapons. As a consequence, public opposition against the presence of US nuclear weapons on Japanese territory had always been strong. Political elites gauged that the population would largely be opposed to national acquisition. Conversely, Washington's efforts to both reassure and constrain Tokyo and the realization among Japanese decision-makers that the reversion of Okinawa required a credible commitment towards nuclear abstention pushed Japan towards accepting the NPT. Finally, reliance upon US extended deterrence and a parallel policy of nuclear hedging rendered Tokyo's decision less costly.

Australia, as Christine Leah argues, can best be viewed as an Anglo-Saxon outpost in a precarious security environment that had moved towards nuclear latency already in the 1950s. Communist China's test triggered in Australia a fierce domestic debate, a struggle concluded in 1973 by the decision to ratify the NPT. While US security guarantees appear to have played some role in buying time, Canberra's ultimate decision to support the NPT seems to have been based on a number of converging factors. First, by 1973 the regional security environment had become more benign. Second, Australian policy-makers seem to have believed that accession to the treaty would better their overall relations to Washington. Third, some argued Australia's decision could contribute to bringing other regional actors within the treaty. Fourth, electoral change had weakened the pro-bomb lobby and brought to power decision-makers more supportive of the nonproliferation norm. Finally, Australian policy-makers had concluded that hedging under the NPT was perfectly possible, and aimed throughout the negotiations to enable a short lead time to be congruent with the treaty's provisions.

Future research on the making of the nuclear order

What emerges from the empirical chapters in this volume is that the making of the nuclear order reflected the ambiguous and often contingent character of individual states' nuclear decisions. At the macro-level, the NPT was produced by the convergences of superpower interests in preserving the nuclear status quo with the political interests of small and middle powers in carving out a bigger role for themselves in international politics. At the micro-level, however, the decision of individual countries to join the treaty was the product of complex and contradictory domestic, regional, and global forces, an interaction that often generated indefinite decisions.

Nevertheless, the inherently ambivalent nature of nuclear technology, the lax legal provisions of the treaty, and a general unwillingness to sacrifice commercial benefits for nonproliferation allowed – in most cases – for these unsettled national debates to be accommodated within the confines of the NPT. While the treaty's emergence through superpower collusion was seen by many governments as generating significant costs, the NPT did also offer remarkable opportunities for expanding secondary actors' influence, and nuclear latency accommodated ambiguous nuclear choices.

These empirical findings raise a number of questions for future research in both political science and international history. Numerous theoretical puzzles remain open for future scholars. For example, the arguments presented in this volume provide a few valuable hints about states' short- and long-term preferences, but much still needs to be done to explore the persistence of such an unequal multilateral regime and inquire into its value as a nonproliferation tool.[38] In addition, the contemporary debate would greatly benefit from better theories on the interaction between regional and global nonproliferation dynamics. Both the reactions to the 1964 PRC test in Asia and the European concerns in both West and East regarding Bonn's nuclear intentions provide good starting points for further analysis in this direction. Also, further grand theorizing on why states go nuclear or abstain does not seem likely to yield many insights – the ambiguity of nuclear choices, corroborated with the complex and contingent interaction between domestic and international influences do not allow simple models much explanatory power. Thus, future scholars might want to trade parsimony for increasingly complex but somewhat more elucidating theories.

For international historians, the NPT fits into the current global focus on contemporary Cold War history, while at the same time going beyond the established reading of the relationships between the superpowers and between them and their allies. More empirical work on non-Western states – both those which decided to acquire nuclear weapons and those which chose nuclear abstinence – will not only deepen our understanding of these complex interactions, but also provide a more solid base for further theory building.

Conclusion 237

Notes

1 The authors wish to thank Jonas Schneider, Roland Popp, and three anonymous reviewers for their insightful comments on previous versions of this chapter.
2 For an overview on the treaty's provisions, see Norman Dombey, "The Nuclear Non-Proliferation Treaty: Aims, Limitations and Achievements," *New Left Review* 52, no. 4 (2008): 39–66.
3 For a broad assessment of the multilateral negotiations record, see Mohamed Ibrahim Shaker, *The Nuclear Non-Proliferation Treaty: Origin and Implementation, 1959–1979*, vol. 2 (New York: Oceana, 1980). For questions of fairness and justice within the NPT, see Nina Tannenwald, "Justice and Fairness in the Nuclear Nonproliferation Regime," *Ethics and International Affairs* 27, no. 3 (2013): 299–317; Harald Müller, "Between Power and Justice: Current Problems and Perspectives of the NPT Regime," *Strategic Analysis* 34, no. 2 (2010): 189–201; or Nina Srinivasan Rathbun, "The Role of Legitimacy in Strengthening the Nuclear Nonproliferation Regime," *The Nonproliferation Review* 13, no. 2 (2006): 227–252.
4 "How exactly does the NPT work?" asked Scott D. Sagan in a much cited review. See "The Causes of Nuclear Weapons Proliferation," *Annual Review of Political Science* 14 (2011): 225–244.
5 Jed C. Snyder, "The Nonproliferation Regime: Managing the Impending Crisis," *Journal of Strategic Studies* 8, no. 4 (December 1985): 7–27; George Bunn, *Arms Control by Committee: Managing Negotiations with the Russians* (Palo Alto, CA: Stanford University Press, 1992); Leonard Weiss, "Nuclear-Weapon States and the Grand Bargain," *Arms Control Today* 33, no. 10 (December 2003).
6 Daniel Verdier, "Multilateralism, Bilateralism, and Exclusion in the Nuclear Proliferation Regime," *International Organization* 62, no. 3 (2008): 439–476.
7 Andrew J. Coe and Jane Vaynman, "Collusion and the Nuclear Nonproliferation Regime," *Journal of Politics* 77, no. 4 (2015): 983–997.
8 Jana von Stein, "Do Treaties Constrain or Screen? Selection Bias and Treaty Compliance," *American Political Science Review* 99, no. 4 (2005): 611–622; or Christopher Way and Karthika Sasikumar, "Leaders and Laggards: When and Why do Countries Sign the NPT?" Working Paper, Research Group in International Security (Montreal, 2005).
9 See the conclusions of Jacques E.C. Hymans, *The Psychology of Nuclear Proliferation: Identity, Emotions and Foreign Policy* (Cambridge, MA: Cambridge University Press, 2006); or Etel Solingen, *Nuclear Logics: Contrasting Paths in East Asia and the Middle East* (Princeton, NJ: Princeton University Press, 2007).
10 For instance, in relation to India, see also Leonard Weiss, "India and the NPT," *Strategic Analysis* 34, no. 2 (2010): 255–271; George Perkovich, *India's Nuclear Bomb: The Impact on Global Proliferation* (Berkeley, CA: University of California Press, 1999); or T.V. Paul, "The Systemic Bases of India's Challenge to the Global Nuclear Order," *The Nonproliferation Review* 6, no. 1 (1998): 1–11.
11 Jim Walsh, "Learning from Past Success: The NPT and the Future of Non-Proliferation," Weapons of Mass Destruction Commission (Stockholm, 2005).
12 John Krige, *American Hegemony and the Postwar Reconstruction of Science in Europe* (Cambridge, MA: MIT Press, 2006).
13 For a similar assessment of the German debate, see Jonas Schneider, "Beyond Assurance and Coercion: U.S. Alliances and the Psychology of Nuclear Reversal" (manuscript, Center for Security Studies, ETH Zurich, August 2015).
14 On the evolution of détente in the 1960s, see Andreas Wenger, Vojtech Mastny, and Christian Nuenlist (eds.), *Origins of the European Security System: The Helsinki Process Revisited, 1965–75* (London: Routledge, 2008); and especially Andreas Wenger and Vojtech Mastny, "New Perspectives on the Origins of the CSSCE Process," in *Origins of the European Security System: The Helsinki Process Revisited,*

238   *A. Wenger and L. Horovitz*

1965–75, eds. Andreas Wenger, Vojtech Mastny, and Christian Nuenlist (London: Routledge, 2008), 3–22.

15 See Arthur A. Stein, *Why Nations Cooperate: Circumstance and Choice in International Relations* (Ithaca, NY: Cornell University Press, 1993); for a more restricted recent perspective, Wilfred Wan, "Firewalling Nuclear Diffusion," *International Studies Review* 16, no. 2 (2014): 217–228.

16 Douglas Selvage, "The Warsaw Pact and Nuclear Nonproliferation 1963–1965," Working Paper, Cold War International History Project (Washington, D.C.: Woodrow Wilson International Center for Scholars, April 2001); Douglas Selvage, "The Warsaw Pact and the German Question, 1955–1970: Conflict and Consensus," in *NATO and the Warsaw Pact: Intrabloc Conflicts*, eds. Mary Ann Heiss and S. Victor Papacosma (Kent, Ohio: Kent State University Press, 2008), 179–180; Vojtech Mastny and Malcolm Byrne (eds.), *A Cardboard Castle? An Inside History of the Warsaw Pact, 1955–1991* (New York: Central European University Press, 2006); Andreas Wenger, Christian Nuenlist, and Anna Locher (eds.), *Transforming NATO in the Cold War: Challenges beyond Deterrence in the 1960s* (London: Routledge, 2006).

17 Helga Haftendorn, "Entstehung und Bedeutung des Harmel-Berichtes der NATO von 1967," *Vierteljahrshefte für Zeitgeschichte* 40, no. 2 (1992): 169–221; Andreas Wenger, "Crisis and Opportunity: NATO's Transformation and the Multilateralization of Détente, 1966–1968," *Journal of Cold War Studies* 6, no. 1 (2004): 22–74.

18 Jeremi Suri, *Power and Protest: Global Revolution and the Rise of Detente* (Cambridge, MA: Harvard University Press, 2005).

19 Itty Abraham, *The Making of the Indian Atomic Bomb: Science, Secrecy and the Postcolonial State* (London: Zed Books, 1998).

20 Anne Harrington and Matthias Englert, "How Much Is Enough? The Politics of Technology and Weaponless Nuclear Deterrence," in *The Global Politics of Science and Technology*, eds. Maximilian Mayer, Mariana Carpes, and Ruth Knoblich, vol. 2 (Berlin: Springer, 2014), 287–302.

21 Ariel E. Levite, "Never Say Never Again: Nuclear Reversal Revisited," *International Security* 27, no. 3 (2003): 59–88; or, more recently, Scott D. Sagan, "Nuclear Latency and Nuclear Proliferation," in *Forecasting Nuclear Proliferation in the 21st Century: A Comparative Perspective*, eds. William C. Potter and Gaukhar Mukhatzhanova, vol. 1 (Palo Alto, CA: Stanford University Press, 2010), 80–101.

22 In other words, whatever policy-makers valued and desired the ambivalent nature of nuclear technology and the vague treaty allowed all of them to accept the compromise.

23 Helga Haftendorn, *NATO and the Nuclear Revolution: A Crisis of Credibility, 1966–1967* (Oxford: Clarendon Press/Oxford University Press, 1996); Beatrice Heuser, *NATO, Britain, France, and the FRG: Nuclear Strategies and Forces for Europe, 1949–2000* (New York: St. Martin's Press, 1997).

24 Wenger *et al.*, *Transforming NATO in the Cold War.*

25 Marc Trachtenberg, *A Constructed Peace: The Making of the European Settlement 1945–1963* (Princeton, NJ: Princeton University Press, 1999).

26 On the shift in strategy from massive retaliation to flexible response, see Jane E. Stromseth, *The Origins of Flexible Response: NATO's Debate over Strategy in the 1960s* (Basingstoke: Palgrave Macmillan, 1988); McGeorge Bundy, *Danger and Survival: Choices about the Bomb in the First Fifty Years* (New York: Random House, 1988); or Andreas Wenger, *Living with Peril: Eisenhower, Kennedy, and Nuclear Weapons* (Lanham: Rowman & Littlefield, 1997).

27 On US–Soviet negotiations and the emergence of a modus vivendi, see Christof Münger, *Die Berliner Mauer, Kennedy und die Kubakrise: Die westliche Allianz in der Zerreißprobe 1961–1963* (Paderborn: Schöningh, 2003); or Andreas Wenger, "Der lange Weg zur Stabilität. Kennedy, Chruschtschow und das gemeinsame

Conclusion 239

Interesse der Supermächte am Status Quo in Europa," *Vierteljahrshefte für Zeitge-schichte* 46, no. 1 (1998): 69–99.

28 On de Gaulle's challenge and NATO's crisis, Frédéric Bozo, "Deux Stratégies pour l'Europe : De Gaulle, les Etats-Unis et l'Alliance Atlantique, 1958–1969," *Politique Etrangere* 61, no. 1 (1996): 215–219; and Thomas Alan Schwartz, *Lyndon Johnson and Europe: In the Shadow of Vietnam* (Cambridge, MA: Harvard University Press, 2003).

29 Wenger, "Crisis and Opportunity."

30 Hal Brands, "Non-Proliferation and the Dynamics of the Middle Cold War: The Superpowers, the MLF, and the NPT," *Cold War History* 7, no. 3 (2007): 389–423.

31 John Lewis and Litai Xue, *China Builds the Bomb* (Palo Alto, CA: Stanford University Press, 1991).

32 Roland Popp, "Introduction: Global Order, Cooperation between the Superpowers, and Alliance Politics in the Making of the Nuclear Non-Proliferation Regime," *The International History Review* 36, no. 2 (2014): 195–209; or Francis J. Gavin, "Blasts from the Past: Proliferation Lessons from the 1960s," *International Security* 29, no. 3 (2005): 100–135.

33 Andrew Priest, "From Hardware to Software: The End of the MLF and the Rise of the Nuclear Planning Group," in *Transforming NATO in the Cold War: Challenges beyond Deterrence in the 1960s*, eds. Andreas Wenger, Christian Nuenlist, and Anna Locher (London: Routledge, 2007), 148–161.

34 Wenger, "Crisis and Opportunity"; Oliver Bange, "Ostpolitik and Détente in Europa, Die Anfänge, 1966–1669" (Habilitation, University of Mannheim, 2004).

35 Holger Nehring, "Diverging Perceptions of Security: NATO, Nuclear Weapons, and Social Protest," in *Transforming NATO in the Cold War: Challenges beyond Deterrence in the 1960s*, eds. Andreas Wenger, Christian Nuenlist, and Anna Locher (London: Routledge, 2006), 131–147; A. Wenger and J. Suri, "At the Crossroads of Diplomatic and Social History: The Nuclear Revolution, Dissent and Détente," *Cold War History* 1, no. 3 (2001): 1–42.

36 Odd Arne Westad, *The Global Cold War: Third World Interventions and the Making of Our Times* (Cambridge: Cambridge University Press, 2007); Natasa Miskovic, Harald Fischer-Tine, and Nada Boskovska, *The Non-Aligned Movement and the Cold War* (London: Routledge, 2014).

37 Dane Swango, "The United States and the Role of Nuclear Cooperation and Assistance in the Design of the NPT," *The International History Review* 36, no. 2 (2014): 210–229.

38 For the first, Cecilia Albin, *Justice and Fairness in International Negotiation* (Cambridge: Cambridge University Press, 2001). For the second, Matthew Fuhrmann, *Atomic Assistance: How "Atoms for Peace" Programs Cause Nuclear Insecurity* (Ithaca, NY: Cornell University Press, 2012); and Dong-Joon Jo and Erik Gartzke, "Determinants of Nuclear Weapons Proliferation," *Journal of Conflict Resolution* 51, no. 1 (2007): 167–194.

Index

1955 Paris Accords 36
1967 Arab–Israeli war 189

Adenauer, Konrad 23, 34n80, 37–8, 45, 50n5, 51n6, 52n15, 53n28, 54n46, 54n57, 55n67; funeral 85; government 36, 40–2
Africa 179–80, 211
African bloc in UN 192; concerns 193; Organization of African Unity 16
Aiken, Frank, Irish Foreign Minister 19, 29n12, 32n55
Albania 99, 101
Anglo-American relations 87; nuclear alliance 11, 32n61
anti-Americanism 88, 91, 185–6
Argentina 27, 178, 180, 183–8, 192, 194, 195n1, 196n9, 199n57; demanding disarmament 233; National Atomic Energy Commission 209; sale of uranium to Israel 209–10, 214
arms control 5, 10, 16, 18, 20–1, 44, 46, 61, 64, 102, 126, 148, 178–9, 182, 189, 190, 191, 193, 195; activists 12; supporters 11, 17
Asia 33n69, 119–20, 131, 165, 174n29, 226, 234–6; allies 127, 206; Asia-Pacific 130; nations 145; Northeast 13; powers 89, 119; South 4; Southeast 121, 125
Asian MLF 164
Atlantic Nuclear Force (ANF) 42, 62–8, 66, 68, 70, 74n30; British proposal 45, 80, 230; negotiations 67; non-proliferation clause 65; nuclear force 69; Treaty 62–4; nuclear sharing element 62
Atlanticism 3, 48, 58, 61–2, 65, 71; and Dutch nuclear security policy 64; and Dutch preferences 58–9; and German leadership 43; and German orientation 42

Australia 91, 119–20, 132n4, 132n7, 133n31, 215, 225–6, 235; cooperation with UK 122, 132n15; defense policy 125, 135n78; nuclear agreement with France 123; uranium sales 131, 136n86
Australia NPT negotiations 127–9; decision on 119, 128–9, 235; ratification 130–1
Australia, nuclear 120; deterrent 124–5, 130; military ambitions 132n4; research 126; weapons 127
Australia–New Zealand–United States (ANZUS) Treaty 121, 124, 127
Australian National Archives 120, 130
Australian Atomic Energy Commission (AAEC) 121, 123–6, 129

ballistic missiles 123, 131; intercontinental (ICBMs) 11; Intermediate Range (IRBM) project/India 159n92; Intermediate Range/Medium Range (IR/MRBM)/Soviet Union 38; submarine launched 169
Berlin Crisis, second 99, 101, 113n12, 229
Bhabha, Homi 141, 147–8, 150–3, 156n29, 159n90, 160n106, 210
Blue Storm Society (Seirankai) 168, 172
Bodnaras, E. 103–5, 113n21, 113n33, 114n34, 114n35, 114n37
Bowles, Chester 146–7, 159n89
Brazil 22, 25, 27, 91, 143, 180–7, 190, 192, 194, 195n1, 196n9, 203; alternative draft 185; demanding disarmament 233; growing militarism 178; joint memorandum on non-proliferation 156n35; military coup 182; obstruction 184; PNE issue 186, 191; proliferation threat 161; safeguards discussions 210;

Index   241

signed Treaty of Tlatelolco 187–8; sovereignty 191

Brazilian–Argentine Agency for Accounting and Control of Nuclear Materials 194

Brezhnev, Leonid 102–6, 108, 111, 115n56

Britain (Great) 3, 11–12, 18, 25, 40, 42, 48, 86, 122, 204, 208–9; ANF proposal 61–2, 80, 230; bilateral cooperation with Australia 133n20; excluded from European Community 82; government 87–8; military plutonium production facility 209; NPT draft 43, 55n75; nuclear acquisition efforts 38; nuclear tests 122; nuclear weapons 120; nuclear weapons development 217n4; Prime Minister 42, 45; security guarantees 124; substitution clause 211; support for Dutch 68–9

British National Archives 77

Bulgaria 99

Canada 18, 35n96, 70, 123, 149, 153, 158n78, 192, 206, 209, 211

Ceaușescu, Nicolae 105–9, 114n43, 115n56, 115n61

Central America 187; states 185

China, People's Republic of (PRC) 4, 15, 22, 91, 98, 103–4, 113n12, 119, 121, 129, 138, 145, 149–50, 153, 159n84, 161, 169, 171, 206, 235; influence on Romanian leadership 98; military capabilities 128, 144; NPT 126, 138, 144, 157, 223; nuclear capability 17, 102, 124, 158n79, 159n91, 164–5; nuclear test (1964) 4–5, 17, 19, 125, 140–2, 147, 149, 152, 158n56, 159n82, 159n84, 184, 204, 206, 230, 235; preventive strile against nuclear program 30n26, 217n11; nuclear threat from 129, 131, 139, 146, 157n55, 158n56, 174n29; proposal for disarmament 103; satellite test 160n104; Soviet–Chinese split 11, 98–103, 106, 110, 113n12, 231, 234

Comitato Nazionale Energia Nucleare (CNEN) 86–8, 91

Commissariat à l'Energie Atomique (CEA) 86–8, 213

Comprehensive Nuclear Test Ban Treaty (CTBT) 63–4, 190–1

Council for Mutual Economic Assistance (COMECON) 100–1

Cuba 180, 182–3, 187–8, 194; entry into NWFZ 189; nuclear weapons in 181; revolution 183; Soviet missiles 180

Cuban Missile Crisis 14, 101, 194, 196n9, 197n16, 229

Czechoslovakia 99, 110; First Secretary 104; Polish–Czechoslovak proposal 23; Soviet invasion of 91

de Gaulle, President Charles 82, 214, 229, 239n28

de Ranitz, Jan 60–1, 63, 76n62

Democratic Party of Japan 161

Directorate General Political Affairs (DGPZ) 60–1, 63, 67, 74n27, 76n62

Directorate International Organizations (DIO) 58, 60–3, 66, 68–70, 72n4, 73n21, 76n62

Directorate NATO and WEU Affairs (DNW) 58–60, 63, 67–70, 73n27, 75n45, 76n62; Atlantic agenda 61; director 62

disarmament 1, 5, 10, 18, 20, 106; general and complete 17, 111, 140, 142, 186, 189, 200n79; nuclear 61, 64, 107, 138, 167, 179, 190, 223, 235

DNW–DIO relations 64–5

East Asia 4, 165, 169–70

East Germany *see* German Democratic Republic (GDR)

Egypt 22, 69, 83, 164, 210–11

Eight Nation Joint Memo 18, 33n65, 34n81, 143

Eighteen-Nation Disarmament Committee (ENDC) 16–19, 20, 33n65, 43, 47, 59, 65, 90, 100, 111, 143, 145–6, 157n40, 183–4, 186, 190–1, 193–4, 233; debates 138, 150, 155n14, 156n19, 226; draft treaty 22–5, 44, 84, 89, 106–7, 141; joint memorandum on non-proliferation 156n35; Mexico–Brazil declaration 182; Treaty of Tlatelolco 188

Eisenhower, US President Dwight D. 10–11, 28n5, 28n7, 29n10, 163, 205, 207, 238n26; Atoms for Peace speech 187

Erhard, Ludwig 42, 48, 55n78, 55n84, 56n100, 56n111, 57n137; government 42–7

Euro-American ties 60; decoupling in security affairs 66; split 58, 65

242 *Index*

EURODIF (European Gaseous Diffusion Uranium Enrichment Consortium) 86, 88

European Atomic Energy Community (EURATOM) 90, 172, 204–5; Commission 85; members 23–5; safeguards 22–3, 33n63, 81, 84; self-inspection 20

European nuclear force 19, 45, 48, 59, 65–6, 68–9, 230; creation of 62–3, 67, 73n21, 81; German role within 208; independent 29n10; internationalists opposed 71

export controls 214–16

extended deterrence 2, 228; credibility 4, 130; US 38, 165, 167, 225, 235

extended deterrence for Japan 162–3, 165, 167, 172

Federal Republic of Germany (FRG) 1, 3, 14–15, 19, 28n2, 36–50, 51n11, 56n110, 69, 80, 82, 97–8, 108, 127, 164, 172, 206, 208, 213, 225, 229, 232, 234; acceded to the NPT 38; anti-NPT movement 23; British–Dutch–West German project 86; Chancellor 23, 89; denied nuclear equality 33n67; diplomatic relations with Romania 106; economic prowess 39; fuel cycle technologies 38; German Permanent Representative to NATO 44; government 37, 41–2, 45, 47; in NATO 36, 49, 225, 229; NATO consultations 75n47; interest in European nuclear force 68; militarists 104; NPT negotiations 57n126; nuclear ambitions 16, 20–1, 36–7, 41–2, 49, 50n3, 51n6, 51n9, 66, 100–1, 103, 108, 110, 127, 204, 230–1; nuclear status 21, 37, 50, 91; nuclear threshold status 25, 40; proliferation threat 161; uranium enrichment 95n35; waiver of 1954 17, 37, 54n46

Fenoaltea, Ambassador Sergio 80–1, 83, 93n7, 94n13

Fissile Material Cut-Off Treaty (FMCT) 10, 64

France 3, 11–12, 15, 22, 25, 27, 40–1, 42, 45, 48, 68, 79, 82, 86, 88, 111, 191, 193, 208, 213, 217, 230; bilateral Fowler–Debré agreement 216; *Commissariat à l'Energie Atomique* (CEA) 86–7; computers 214–5; disagreed with NPT 106; exceptions to US non-proliferation 204; independent deterrent 164; liberalizing nuclear trade 234; military nuclear assistance 120; NPT 223; nuclear acquisition 38; nuclear enrichment 92, 123; nuclear power 83; nuclear weapons program 204, 213; opposition to MLF 42, 175n36; opposition to nuclear FRG 231; proliferation 124; sources of uranium 211; testing in the Pacific 128; Treaty of Tlatelolco 188–90, 194; US corporations in 214; withdrawal from NATO 46, 227, 229, 231

Freund, Richard 65, 74n34

Gaullists 42, 45, 48

Geneva Committee on Disarmament 16

German Democratic Republic (GDR) 16, 46, 98–102, 103, 106, 108, 110; PCC meeting in Warsaw 101; proposal on nonproliferation 103–5; use of WP 112

German question 41, 44, 75n47, 98, 100, 229

Germany, division 179; reunification 38–9, 44; US High Commissioner in 43; *see also* German Democratic Republic (GDR); Federal Republic of Germany (FRG)

Gheorghiu-Dej, Gheorghe 100, 103–5, 113n22

Gilpatric Committee 17, 22, 31n42, 43, 206–7, 213, 218n20

Giovannini, Francesca 196n9

Global South 4, 179–80, 186, 189, 216, 232–3

Great Proletarian Cultural Revolution 106, 109

Grewe, Wilhelm G. 44, 48, 53n28, 53n40, 55n86

Gromyko, Andrei (Soviet Foreign Minister) 14, 31n39, 32n59, 32n61, 141, 157n54, 206

Hamblin, J.D. 5, 233–4

Hellendoorn, E. 3, 230

Hoey, F. 5, 235

Horovitz, L. 5

Hungary 99; premier 109

Hunt, J. 5, 232

India 2, 4–5, 17–19, 21, 23, 25, 27, 34n88, 35n96, 69, 89, 91, 127, 130–1, 138–51, 154, 157n52, 165, 188, 191–2, 212, 233, 235; AEC 141; atomic energy chief 210;

diplomatic activism 4, 152; draft resolution (1954) 155n11; government 137, 142, 153, 157n55; non-alignment 143, 146, 158n56; nuclear ambitions 139, 147, 151, 153, 155n12, 155n14, 159n89, 164, 223–4; nuclear capabilities 174n29, 206; nuclear energy 142; nuclear testing 138, 158n78, 172; obstructionism 211; opposing the NPT 137–9, 147, 154, 156n38, 157n40, 192; PNEs 148, 158n78; possible Chinese attack 159n84; proliferation threat 161, 164; reactors 204, 209; safeguards 210; space program 160n106; uranium 136n86

Indian Ocean 127

Indonesia 4, 22, 119–20, 121, 123, 125, 127, 132n11; military capabilities 125, 128; nuclear ambitions 123

Inter-American 190; nuclear diplomacy 179; Second Special Conference in Rio de Janeiro 184

International Atomic Energy Agency (IAEA) 5, 10, 126, 203, 207, 217n9; Board of Governors 91, 204, 209–10, 212, 218n30, 218n32; inspection regime 178, 184; oversight 193; safeguard agreements 26, 172, 204–5, 208; safeguards 18–19, 23–4, 64, 84, 90, 185, 206, 210–12, 214, 217n9; supervised agreements 211; supervision of PNEs 148; verification 23

Ireland 12–13, 141, 155n15

Irish Resolution 12–14, 29n12, 41, 59, 62, 191

Israel 21, 27, 83, 91, 161, 164; Arab–Israeli war 189; nuclear ambitions 223; uranium from Argentina 209–10, 214

Italy 3, 12, 22–32, 46, 68, 77–81, 82–5, 87–92, 127, 188, 191, 225; Ambassador to NATO 94n26; civilian program 95n37; centrifuge organization 95n41; ENDC delegation 93n9; EURODIF 88; FIG nuclear agreements 93n4; foreign minister 18, 143, Foreign Ministry 77, 81, 90, 96n75; foreign policy goals 78, 80–1, 92, 93n3; MLF 93n9, 228; navy 87–8; nonproliferation 91–2, 96n66; NPT 22–3, 85, 93, 94n20, 226; participation in Urenco 86; plutonium 88; postwar foreign policy 77–8; support for new draft 83; three principles 81; UNGA resolution 90; uranium enrichment 86

Italy, nuclear 77; activities 86; aspirations 12, 80, 85; fuel supply 87; decision postponed 228; proliferation 83

Jain, J.P. 139

Japan 4–5, 17, 21, 26, 69, 91, 119, 121, 123, 126–7, 130, 161–2, 166–8, 170–2, 215; Atomic Energy 89; Blue Storm Society 168, 172; Diplomatic Archive 173n1; Liberal Democratic Party 161; near-nuclear 192; non-nuclear policy 175n42; Okinawa reversion 169; press and nuclear revelations 174n32; Prime Minister 165–6; proliferation 164; public opinion 173n7, 175n49; security 167; television investigation 177n79; territory 235; Three Non-Nuclear Principles 5, 173n6; Treaty of Mutual Cooperation and Security 174n22; Treaty of Peace 175n37; US nuclear deterrent 169; US occupation 163

Japan NPT 168–9, 226, 235; accession to 163, 170–2

Japan nuclear 166; ambitions 161–4, 168, 174n29, 174n32, 175n54, 177n79, 177n80, 206; deals 205; deterrence 162, 165, 167, 169

Johnson, US President Lyndon B. 19, 32n59, 32n62, 33n69, 33n74, 34n80, 34n81, 43, 45, 47, 53n31, 56n101, 68, 73n21, 85, 100, 145–6, 157n53, 164–5, 187–90, 199n71, 199n75, 200n83, 200n87, 206; administration 15, 17, 19–20, 61, 84, 87, 90, 103, 146, 175n36, 207, 218n20, 230, 234

Kapur, Ashok 139, 142

Kennedy, President John F. 15, 29n21, 30n27, 53n41, 180; administration 30n24, 30n34, 40, 42, 79, 164, 229

Khrushchev, Nikita 10–11, 16, 28n7, 29n18, 29n2, 99–100, 102, 110, 113n12, 180

Kiesinger, Kurt-Georg (West German Chancellor) 23, 48, 53n28, 53n31, 89

Korea 125; North 223; South 130

Korean War 121

Kosygin, Soviet Premier A. 19, 115n56, 146, 157n52, 157n55

Kremlin, the 74n34, 98–103, 105–6, 109, 111–12

Kumar, A. Vinod 4, 235

Latin America 5, 16, 178–83, 185–90, 192–4, 196n6, 196n9; bloc 191–2; Cold

244 *Index*

Latin America *continued*
War 178–9, 197n10, 197n11, 233;
initiative 184; Missile Crisis 197n16;
nuclear-weapon-free zone 195, 233;
nuclear weapons 180, 196n9; political
thought 198n26; tradition of peaceful
cooperation 183; Treaty for the
Prohibition of Nuclear Weapons 186;
Treaty of Tlatelolco 193, 195n1;
US–Latin American relations 196n6
Leah, C.M. 4, 235
Limited Nuclear-Test-Ban Treaty (LTBT)
15–16, 20, 111, 140–1
Liu Fan 103–5, 113n21, 113n33, 114n34,
114n35, 114n37
Lok Sabha 149, 151, 155n11, 157n42;
Debate on Foreign Affairs 158n60,
160n101, 160n103
Lucky Dragon incident 161, 163
Lutsch, A. 3, 28n2, 230

Maurer, Ion Gheorghe 106, 113n22,
114n35, 115n56
Medium Range Ballistic Missiles
(MRBM) 40, 42; collective force 44;
Dutch considerations 72n7; problem 46,
48–9; Soviet 38
Middle East 124, 179, 189
military alliances 14, 19, 32n61, 56n110,
231
Mirchandani, G.G. 139
missiles 10, 79, 152; Cuban Crisis 101,
180, 194, 196n9, 197n16; delivery
systems 128; dual-use 163; intercontinental 125; long-range 45, 131;
multilateral nuclear fleet 73n21; Polaris
15; technology 169; UK program 122;
see also ballistic missiles
Morgenthau Plan 23
Multilateral Force (MLF) 16, 18, 21,
28n2, 29n10, 30n24, 30n27, 31n44,
33n74, 40, 42–4, 48, 55n87, 61–3,
69–70, 72n4, 73n20, 73n21, 75n45,
75n47, 83, 92, 101–3, 104, 106, 108,
175n36, 196n8, 230–1, 239n30,
239n33; concept 14–15, 19; continued
official support 17; East German and
Polish stance 98, 30n24, 64; leverage
228; NATO 11–12, 59–60, 79, 97, 100,
164, 213, 225; negotiations 80, 93n9;
opposition 65–6; prevention 110;
problems 30n25; Soviet objections 67,
105, 112

near-nuclear countries 6n3, 25, 27, 192
Netherlands 3, 59–71, 86, 120–1, 224;
European clause 75n47; feared French–
German condominium 230; influence
within NATO 225; Ministry of Foreign
Affairs organization 73n13; records on
the NPT 72n4; support for Bonn 23
Nixon, President Richard M. 169–71, 173
non-aligned 12, 19, 30n35, 74n34, 188;
audiences 89; countries 63, 67, 141,
143; eight members of ENDC 18, 20,
23; leadership 4; Movement (NAM)
232–3; position on MLF 17, Second
Summit Conference 16
non-nuclear 50, 62, 126, 143, 146; states
2–5, 13, 18–19, 31n49, 38, 41, 43, 45–6,
56n110, 63, 68, 81–3, 89, 91–2, 106,
109, 127, 142, 145, 168, 170, 188; status
15, 37, 162, 172, 226
non-nuclear-weapon states (NNWS) 1–2,
4, 9, 13, 17–18, 23, 32n58, 32n61, 41,
143, 147, 170, 179, 188, 191, 194, 223;
assistance from nuclear powers 145;
concessions to 24; Conference of 192;
group 68–9; interests 180, 186, 233;
intrusive verification measures 26;
responsibilities 137; restrictions 216;
role model 44; security guarantees 25,
107–8, 146; status 37–9, 48
non-Soviet Warsaw Pact (NSWP) 110;
members 97, 101–2, 107, 109, 111–12
Norstad, Lauris 40, 53n41, 54n46, 60,
72n6
North Atlantic Council 22, 53n28, 54n42,
84
North Atlantic Treaty Organization
(NATO) 10, 12, 15, 50n4, 53n28, 66,
68, 70–1, 72n4, 74n27, 76n62, 78, 80,
89, 91, 97, 107–9, 112n11, 121, 124,
127, 225–7, 229–31; allies 42–3, 59,
164, 213, 215; Archives 52n19;
concessions to USSR 69; Council
53n41, 54n42, 54n51, 55n76, 55n86, 64,
70; crisis 239n28; Directorate 58;
erosion 44; French military withdrawal
from 229; FRG status within 46, 48–9;
Ministerial Council 81; non-nuclear
states 56n110; nuclearization 228;
Russian opposition 64; Secretary
General 82; Select Committee 79;
Special Committee of Defense Ministers
31n44; Supreme Allied Commander
Europe (SACEUR) 40, 54n46, 60;
stockpile agreements 14; transformation

238n17, 239n33, 239n35; Trilateral Negotiations 57n137; West German accession 36, 38, 99

North Atlantic Treaty Organization (NATO) Ambassador, to 62, 67, 69, 75n47; Italian 94n26; US 84

North Atlantic Treaty Organization (NATO) nuclear 48, 59–60, 66, 72n6, 213; alliance 41; arrangements 13, 21, 46, 65, 67, 69; collective nuclear 11, 43, 45, 48; debate 98; defense posture 42; force 60, 66, 72n6, 213; Multilateral (MLF) 17, 79, 97, 100; sharing 12, 30n25, 53n37, 62, 100, 102, 208; structures 49

North Atlantic Treaty Organization (NATO) Nuclear Planning 65; Group 31n44, 48–9, 57n139, 130, 230–1, 239n33

nuclear blackmail 19, 126, 129, 151

nuclear-free zones 13; benefits of 182; objectives 184; *see also* nuclear-weapon-free zone

nuclear sharing 4, 10–13, 18–19, 21, 41–2, 59, 60, 62, 71, 78, 100, 102, 110, 164, 208, 228–30; Allied 66; Asian allies 206; opposition to 17; US 79–81, 127; *see also* North Atlantic Treaty Organization (NATO) nuclear

nuclear technological supremacy 218n28

nuclear technology 1, 6, 35n105, 123, 130, 204, 223, 233; access to 234; ambivalence 236, 238n22; buyers and vendors 228; civilian 129, 168, 203; destructive power 227; development 119; dissemination of 142; dual-use 187, 225, 232; field 88; global management 180; Indian 151; Japanese 161; peaceful 147, 182, 188; regional institutions 196n9; restricted exports 205; Romania negotiations 112n8; safeguards agreements 213; socio-economic development 179; transfers 5, 122

nuclear test ban 30n33, 74n34, 144; agreement 15–16; comprehensive 17, 138, 142; debate 14

nuclear test ban treaty 194; comprehensive (CTBT) 24, 64, 191; Limited (LTBT) 15, 30n33, 30n34, 111, 140, 207; partial 42

nuclear test(ing) 12, 35n96, 48, 122, 138–41, 153, 182, 206; environmental aspects 15; French 128; India's 148–51, 155n14, 159n89, 172

nuclear umbrella 141, 164, 167; US 38–9, 44, 48, 50, 119, 127–9, 158n56, 162, 167, 228

nuclear-weapon-free zone (NWFZ) 5, 29n18, 182–4, 189; Australian endorsed 128; initiative 181; Latin American 180, 195, 198n41; regional 13, 16, 25; treaty 178, 190, 194; *see also* nuclear-free zones

nuclear weapons 1, 12, 36, 60–1, 71, 125, 145, 155n12, 156n35, 161, 172, 176n56, 187, 190–1, 225, 232; abolition of 152; access to 17, 100; acquisition 40, 236; compacts to forgo 194; control over 3, 38, 46, 49, 59, 62–3, 101, 213, 230; decoupling 66, 100, 228; for defense 128–9; deployments 78–9, 171; development of 25, 66, 130, 147, 159n84, 165, 174n32, 175n54, 214; FRG 41–2, 45, 54n46, 231; in India 159n89, 235; in Latin America 178, 180–2; manufacture 2, 26, 37, 108, 127, 141, 146, 151, 155n15, 156n19, 192–3, 200n79; negative security guarantee 107, 142; options 121, 126, 139–40; possession of 138, 143, 162; preventing spread of 10, 13, 22, 137, 195, 211, 228; proliferation 119, 150, 153, 164, 186, 205; thermonuclear 124, 188; threat to use 39, 185; transfer of 14, 32n61, 67, 70, 156n32; use of 11, 18–19, 43, 68, 129; *see also* United States (US) nuclear weapons

nuclear weapons capability 119, 174n29, 224

nuclear weapons programs 203; Chinese 161, 165; contribution of computers 215; French 204, 213; German 40, 50n3; Indian 138, 150–1; Japanese 169; relevant technologies 216, 234

nuclear weapon states (NWS) 1, 20, 24–7, 48, 107, 137–8, 158n56, 159n84, 178, 185–7, 191, 203, 216; concessions from 194; disarmament obligations 233; European 63; participating 43, 69; recognized 223

Nuti, L. 3, 226, 230

Organization of American States (OAS) 180, 183–4

Ortona, Egidio (Secretary General of the Italian Foreign Ministry) 81–2, 89, 94n11, 96n62, 96n66

Pakistan 27, 69, 130, 139, 154, 164, 223; Pakistani initiative 25

246 *Index*

peaceful nuclear explosions (PNEs) 23–5, 89–90, 140, 144, 149, 152–3, 158n78, 187–8, 191, 193, 233; allowance of 186; legality 185; outlawing 190; right to 138, 147–8; services 26, 192

People's Republic of China (PRC) 27, 101; leadership 103, 106; nuclear ambitions 15; nuclear test 4–5, 17, 19, 43, 59, 102–4, 123, 164–5, 206, 230–1, 235–6; Romanian collusion 98–9

Perkovich, George 139

plutonium 26, 88, 148; for nuclear bombs 123, 159n94; production 152; production facility 209; reprocessing 87, 218n25; for research purposes 147; separation 151

Poland 16, 97, 99, 100, 102, 104, 106, 110; stance on MLF 98

Polish–Czechoslovak proposal 23

Political Consultative Committee (PCC) 99, 101, 107, 113n23, 113n32, 114n43, 114n45; meeting 97–8, 100, 102–7, 109–10, 113n27, 113n28, 113n30, 114n48, 114n50, 114n51, 114n52, 114n53, 115n57; Records 33n73

Popp, R. 2, 226

Poulose, T.T. 139

Quihillalt, Oscar 209–10

Rajiv Gandhi Action Plan 145, 157n45

Rajya Sabha 146, 151, 156n39, 157n41, 158n56, 158n75, 158n76, 158n79, 158n82, 159n84, 159n85, 160n102

ratification of NPT 24–5; Australian 119, 127–8, 130–1; Japanese 164, 168, 171–2, 177n78; Latin American 185, 189, 193

ratification of Treaty of Tlatelolco 201n116; Protocol II 233

Robles, Alfonso García 178–9, 181–5, 187–8, 190, 192–3, 195n1, 195n4, 197n22, 197n23, 198n36, 198n41, 198n43, 198n47, 198n48, 199n52, 201n99

Romania 4, 98–102, 103–11, 112n4, 113n15, 113n16, 113n21, 114n38, 190, 227, 231; attitude towards superpowers 112n4, 113n31; collusion with PRC 103–4; foreign minister 104; foreign policy 108; leadership 97, 99–102, 112; manifesto on equality 113n16; NPT negotiations NPT Draft 114n44

Rusk, US Secretary of State Dean 14, 24, 29n21, 29n22, 31n39, 31n41, 31n44,

31n45, 32n59, 32n61, 32n62, 33n63, 33n64, 33n74, 34n76, 34n80, 34n81, 34n91, 34n92, 35n100, 40, 43–4, 53n28, 53n31, 54n46, 54n48, 54n49, 54n50, 54n55, 54n57, 55n73, 55n87, 55n93, 56n104, 56n118, 76n67, 81–3, 85, 90, 93n7, 94n13, 94n31, 157n54, 164, 176n61, 183–4, 186–90, 192–3, 198n36, 198n45, 199n51, 199n56, 199n57, 199n61, 199n63, 199n65, 199n69, 199n71, 199n73, 200n81, 200n86, 200n87, 200n88, 201n109, 206, 214

Sarabhai, Vikram 147, 151–3, 158n69, 159n92, 160n106

Sato Eisaku, Prime Minister 162–73, 173n4, 173n6, 174n32, 175n34, 175n39, 175n42, 175n47, 176n56, 176n57, 176n64, 176n65, 176n71

Second World War 78, 163, 182; fighting in the Pacific 120

security guarantees 107, 138–9, 142, 145–6, 147, 150, 226; credibility 228; for Japan 165; lack of 190; non-nuclear states 19, 144; positive 25; superpowers 158n56, 233; threatened withdrawal 37; US 4, 11, 39, 124–7, 235

Shaker, M.I. 28n3, 29n12, 29n17, 34n77, 35n103

Sino-Soviet split 98–103, 106, 110, 113n12, 113n18, 129, 231, 234

South Africa 27, 161, 193, 210–11, 234

Soviet Bloc 98–9, 112, 113n16, 127; abstention 12; voting behaviour 13

Soviet draft 24, 31n44, 54n52, 56n96, 108, 114n44, 115n58, 115n59, 143, 156n32, 188

Soviet Intermediate Range/Medium Range Ballistic Missiles (IR/MRBM) 38, 40

Soviet Union (SU) 3, 10–11, 14–16, 17–18, 20–2, 28n3, 38–9, 41, 45, 48, 59, 61, 65, 67–71, 81, 97–9, 100–3, 106, 108–9, 111–12, 113n12, 121, 124, 142, 146, 169, 175n36, 179, 185, 187, 189–92, 194, 207, 211, 213, 217n4, 225, 227–8, 230–1, 233; alliance 99, 229; disarmament treaty 62, 141; Foreign Minister 14, 206; Foreign Ministry 106, 190, 200n91; invasion of Czechoslovakia 91; leadership 19, 105–6, 108–9; missiles in Cuba 180; nuclear warheads 98; objections to MLF 59; opposition to MLF proposal 175n36; safeguards issue 23

Soviet–American 196n8; collusion 195; negotiations on NPT 99
Soviet–Chinese *see* Sino-Soviet split
Special Sessions of Disarmament (SSODs) 145
Subrahmanyam, K. 139, 151–2, 154n8, 159n91, 159n93
Subterranean Nuclear Explosion Program (SNEP) 148, 150
superpowers 2, 4, 10, 12–13, 19, 20–1, 24, 37, 41, 98–9, 111, 126, 141, 143, 179, 192–5, 196n8, 225–6, 230, 232, 23–56; agreement 25, 42, 46, 48–9, 106, 193; arms race 140; assurances 151; blocs 188; collusion 11, 180, 202n119, 228; *détente* 190, 229; deterrence 152; negotiations 1, 9, 16–17, 18, 22, 26–7, 28n2, 97, 102, 145; NPT *fait accompli* 47; nuclear parity between 39, 44; Romanian attitude towards 112n4; security guarantees 146, 158n56, 233
Sweden 13, 18, 21, 25, 143, 156n35, 181, 188–90, 233; initiative 13; resolution 13, 29n17

thermonuclear weapons 124, 161, 188; test 161
Third World 192, 196n6
Three Non-Nuclear Principles 5, 162–3, 166–7, 173n6
treaty of Almelo 86
Treaty of Tlatelolco 178–80, 187–8, 191–3, 195n1; additional protocols 189; anniversary of finalization 190; Protocol II 186, 194, 233
Treaty of Tlatelolco Protocol II 185–7, 189–90, 192; ratification 194, 233
Treaty on the Non-Proliferation of Nuclear Weapons (NPT) 1, 9, 12, 16–20, 22, 25, 27, 28n3, 32n59, 35n99, 37, 39, 46–7, 49, 56n110, 58, 63–5, 67, 70, 83, 85–6, 88–9, 103–10, 119–20, 126, 131, 134n62, 134n64, 136n86, 138, 149, 152, 154, 161, 178–9, 191–2, 195, 196n7, 196n8, 204, 206, 212, 216, 217n9, 223–4, 235; accession to 2, 4–5, 48, 50, 163, 172; adhering to 151, 154n3; asymmetry 234; conclusion of 90, 97–8, 107, 111; emergence 3, 92, 142, 226; European clause 74n41; impact 88; inequality 237n3; main provisions 14; opposition 23, 93, 203, 230; rejection 41, 43, 137, 139, 144–5, 160n104, 233;

signing 36, 91, 99, 123, 125, 127, 140, 146, 148, 153, 157n52, 189, 193, 215, 237n8; Soviet interest 29n21, 33n71, 231; support for 187, 190, 232
Treaty on the Non-Proliferation of Nuclear Weapons (NPT) Articles 47; Article I 20, 81, 106; Article II 55n92; Article III 23–6, 34n81, 47, 81; Article IV 24, 35n105, 47, 127, 188, 190, 192–3; Article V 188, 192–3; Article VI 21, 35n93, 47, 138, 144, 189, 192, 200n80; Article VII 189; Article VIII 90
Treaty on the Non-Proliferation of Nuclear Weapons (NPT) First Review Conference (1975) 26, 194
Treaty on the Non-Proliferation of Nuclear Weapons (NPT) negotiations 2–5, 9, 20–1, 30n35, 31n46, 36, 61, 71, 85–7, 90, 93n9, 99, 109–10, 127–8, 138, 141, 143–5, 147–8, 153, 168, 182, 184, 189, 204, 213, 227–8, 232, 234
Treaty on the Non-Proliferation of Nuclear Weapons (NPT) ratification 24, 119–20, 128–31, 162, 172, 225, 235
Treaty on the Non-Proliferation of Nuclear Weapons (NPT) Review and Extension Conference 26, 35n104, 96n67
Treaty on the Non-Proliferation of Nuclear Weapons (NPT) text 148, 150, 153, 168; drafts 3, 19, 23, 43–5, 55n75, 60, 81, 87, 105, 142–3, 134n52, 135n65, 195n4, 201n99; final 20, 23, 25, 32n58, 149, 179; language 32n58, 47–8, 187
trilateral negotiations 80, 231
Trivedi, V.C. 23, 32n53, 34n82, 141–3, 146–8, 156n33, 156n34, 158n73

UK–Australia cooperation 122
Ulbricht, Walter 100–5, 110, 112, 113n20, 113n22, 114n47
UN Disarmament Commission 18, 142, 155n11, 156n35
UN General Assembly (UNGA) 12–13, 18, 25, 107, 141, 143, 155n15, 157n51, 178, 180, 182–3, 190, 195n2, 226; disarmament 157n47; draft submitted 191; draft treaty 90, 154n1; Jawaharlal Nehru's Speech 155n13; Latin American activities 186, 187, 189, 194; memorandum on non-proliferation 156n23, 156n35; NPT resolution 139, 144–5, 195

248 *Index*

UN Security Council (UNSC) 138, 146; guarantee 147; Resolutions 25, 145, 191

Undén, Östen 13; *see also* Sweden, resolution

United Arab Republic *see* Egypt

United Kingdom (UK) 24–5, 28n2, 32n61, 42, 68, 119–20, 123, 125, 132n15, 209, 231; ANZUS Treaty 121; Atomic Energy Agency (UKAEA) 86–7, 95n48; draft 43; Foreign Office 88; LTBT 15; missiles program 122; nuclear infrastructure 215; nuclear rapprochement with US 11; reprocessing 208; safeguard agreements 206; signed NPT 90; Treaty of Tlatelolco signed 189, 194

United Kingdom (UK) nuclear weapons 45, 124, 127, 223; thermo-nuclear weapons 124

United States (US) 3, 17, 24, 27n2, 34n77, 45–7, 60, 76n64, 77, 82, 85, 89, 101, 131, 146, 158n78, 176n56, 181, 185, 192, 208–9, 217n11, 228, 231, 234; alliances allies 18, 23, 27, 59, 108, 119, 130, 234; ANSUZ Treaty 121, 124; Atomic Energy Act 32n61; Atomic Energy Commission (AEC) 205; commercial firms 216; consultations with NATO partners 12; covert operations 183; disarmament proposals 29n21; extended deterrence for Japan 162–3, 165, 167, 172; guarantee for India 159n91; intelligence community 123; Irish Resolution 59; opening to China 129; participation in Europe's security 69; Plowshare program 148; rejection of package deal 31n49; technological superiority 218n28; Treaty of Tlatelolco protocols 199n69, 233; Vietnam War 103

United States (US) Arms Control and Disarmament Agency (ACDA) 32n59, 44, 94n13, 180, 183, 185–7, 189; Administrative History 31n40; Deputy Assistant Director 65; Deputy Director 69; Director Foster 21–2, 64, 84; Director's Office NPT files 77; United States (US) Atomic Energy Commission 87, 205–6; Chairman 33n63, 206

United States (US) draft treaty 19, 44, 68, 81–2, 84, 156; amendments 32n58; disarmament 141, 143; final 31n44; joint 144; new 77, 89; nonproliferation 18; Position Paper 31n41

United States (US) government 64, 81, 127, 165, 171, 206–7, 210, 215, 217; administration 64, 91, 102, 106; Congress 19, 122; Department of Defense 14; Department of Energy 218n25; Department of State 15, 19, 52n19, 64, 67, 73n27, 87–8, 90, 127, 133n27, 142, 147, 151, 171, 180, 186, 188, 191, 197n17, 198n37, 199n77, 200n89, 200n92, 205, 213; government officials 144; Secretary of Defense 43; Secretary of State 10, 13–14, 81, 156n38; Senate 90, 187

United States (US) nonproliferation 16, 31n42, 33n71, 37, 54n64, 64, 162, 172, 175n36, 204; draft treaty 18; export controls/computers 214–16

United States (US) nuclear 162, 167; armed warships 164; bases 170; bases on Okinawa 175n42; deterrent 61; deterrent power in East Asia 165; extended deterrence 38, 119, 128, 163, 165, 167, 172, 225, 235; guarantees 163, 166, 229; Nevada Test Site 122; planning with NATO 18; rapprochement with UK 11; retaliation 174n32; sharing 80; strategic forces 54n42; transit 186; umbrella 38, 44, 48, 50, 129

United States (US) nuclear weapons 42, 59, 78, 124, 161, 163, 167, 169–71, 229, 180, 235; commitment to use 229; prohibiting transfer of 156n32; sharing with Japan 165; threat to use 39; transport 161, 180, 182, 185; world without 154

United States (US) President 165, 207; Eisenhower 10; John F. Kennedy Presidential Library 53n41; Johnson 19, 47, 68, 85, 100, 145, 164, 187; Kennedy 164; Nixon 169–70; Presidential science adviser 147; Vice President 190

uranium 193, 218n31; Australian policy 135n76; developing 163; enrichment 3, 14, 26, 77, 85–6, 87–8, 95n35, 95n47, 95n48, 123; global trade 217n3; mining 122, 129, 152; sales 131, 136n86, 209–10, 214; suppliers 210–11; supplies 86

Urenco 86, 88, 95n36

US–Japanese alliance 166–8; relations 162, 173n7, 173n10, 173n13, 176n56, 176n62

USSR 14–16, 18, 25, 28n2, 64, 69, 83, 90, 114n40, 152

van der Stoel, M. 3, 58–9, 61, 65–71, 73n13, 74n37, 74n39, 75n42, 75n43, 75n44, 75n47, 75n48, 75n55, 76n62, 76n63

Varghese, B.G. 149–50, 154n3, 157n52, 159n89, 159n91, 159n92

Warsaw Pact (WP) 3, 30n36, 97–101, 104–6, 108–12, 112n2, 112n7, 113n16, 229–30, 238n16; allied countries 42, 103, 107, 183, 226; creation of new organ 102; decision making 4; leaders 113n20; members 46, 56n110, 227–8, 231; Political Consultative Committee 33n73; PRC observer status 113n12; threat 38–9

Wenger, A. 5

West Germany *see* Federal Republic of Germany (FRG)

Taylor & Francis eBooks

Helping you to choose the right eBooks for your Library

Add Routledge titles to your library's digital collection today. Taylor and Francis ebooks contains over 50,000 titles in the Humanities, Social Sciences, Behavioural Sciences, Built Environment and Law.

Choose from a range of subject packages or create your own!

Benefits for you
- Free MARC records
- COUNTER-compliant usage statistics
- Flexible purchase and pricing options
- All titles DRM-free.

Benefits for your user
- Off-site, anytime access via Athens or referring URL
- Print or copy pages or chapters
- Full content search
- Bookmark, highlight and annotate text
- Access to thousands of pages of quality research at the click of a button.

REQUEST YOUR FREE INSTITUTIONAL TRIAL TODAY

Free Trials Available
We offer free trials to qualifying academic, corporate and government customers.

eCollections – Choose from over 30 subject eCollections, including:

Archaeology	Language Learning
Architecture	Law
Asian Studies	Literature
Business & Management	Media & Communication
Classical Studies	Middle East Studies
Construction	Music
Creative & Media Arts	Philosophy
Criminology & Criminal Justice	Planning
Economics	Politics
Education	Psychology & Mental Health
Energy	Religion
Engineering	Security
English Language & Linguistics	Social Work
Environment & Sustainability	Sociology
Geography	Sport
Health Studies	Theatre & Performance
History	Tourism, Hospitality & Events

For more information, pricing enquiries or to order a free trial, please contact your local sales team:
www.tandfebooks.com/page/sales

 The home of Routledge books

www.tandfebooks.com